T0334189

ESSENTIAL CONCEPTS OF GLOBAL ENVIRONMENTAL GOVERNANCE

Aligning global governance to the challenges of sustainability is one of the most urgent international issues to be addressed. This book is a timely and up-to-date compilation of the main pieces of the global environmental governance puzzle.

Essential Concepts of Global Environmental Governance synthesizes writing from an internationally diverse range of well-known experts. Each entry defines a central concept in global environmental governance, presents its historical evolution and related debates, and includes key bibliographical references. This new edition takes stock of several recent developments in global environmental politics including the 2015 Paris Agreement on Climate Change, the UN Global Pact for the Environment attempt in 2017, and the 2018 Oceans Plastics Charter. More precisely, this book:

- offers cutting-edge analysis of the state of global environmental governance;
- presents an up-to-date debate on sustainable development at the global level;
- gives an in-depth exploration of the current architecture of global environmental governance;
- examines the interaction between environmental politics and other policy fields such as trade, development, and security;
- provides a critical review of the recent global environmental governance literature.

Innovative thinking and high-profile expertise come together to create a volume that is accessible to students, scholars, and practitioners alike.

Jean-Frédéric Morin is Full Professor at the Political Science Department of the Université Laval (Québec City, Canada) and chair holder of the Canada Research Chair in International Political Economy.

Amandine Orsini is Professor of International Relations at the Université Saint-Louis – Bruxelles, Belgium.

"*Essential Concepts of Global Environmental Governance* is an incredibly useful resource for students. It provides short introductory entries for students new to the field or from a related field. The authors compiled an impressive and cohesive list of entries that provides an excellent foundation for all students of global environmental governance."

— *Gabriela Kuetting, Professor of Global Politics,*
Rutgers University, USA

"This volume provides an essential glossary of critical terms and concepts in the field of international environmental politics for diplomats, analysts and students. The interdisciplinary array of expert authors provides [a] terse and authoritative overview of the key concepts and debates that have defined the field of international environmental governance over the years. The entries carefully survey the intellectual ecosystem of the concepts applied to understanding and managing our global environmental crisis."

— *Peter M. Haas, Professor of Political Science,*
University of Massachusetts Amherst, USA

"This volume is an indispensable resource for distilling what is most important for understanding the vast terrain of global environmental policy. Written by leading scholars, this book offers an authoritative lexicon to which one can turn for a quick, in-depth, and reliable reference. I wish this book was around when I was a student. I'm glad it is around now that I'm a professor."

— *Paul Wapner, Professor of Global Environmental Politics,*
American University, USA

ESSENTIAL CONCEPTS OF GLOBAL ENVIRONMENTAL GOVERNANCE

Second Edition

*Edited by Jean-Frédéric Morin
and Amandine Orsini*

Routledge
Taylor & Francis Group

LONDON AND NEW YORK

earthscan
from Routledge

Second edition published 2021
by Routledge
2 Park Square, Milton Park, Abingdon, Oxon OX14 4RN

and by Routledge
52 Vanderbilt Avenue, New York, NY 10017

Routledge is an imprint of the Taylor & Francis Group, an informa business

First edition published by Routledge 2015

British Library Cataloguing-in-Publication Data
A catalogue record for this book is available from the British Library

Library of Congress Cataloging-in-Publication Data
Names: Morin, Jean-Frédéric, editor. | Orsini, Amandine, editor.
Title: Essential concepts of global environmental governance /
Edited by Jean-Frédéric Morin and Amandine Orsini.
Description: Second edition. | Abingdon, Oxon; New York: Routledge, 2021. |
Includes bibliographical references and index.
Identifiers: LCCN 2020014270 (print) | LCCN 2020014271 (ebook) |
ISBN 9780367418700 (hardback) | ISBN 9780367418694 (paperback) |
ISBN 9780367816681 (ebook)
Subjects: LCSH: Environmental policy–International cooperation. |
Environmentalism–International cooperation. |
Environmental protection–International cooperation.
Classification: LCC GE170 .E77 2021 (print) |
LCC GE170 (ebook) | DDC 363.7/01561–dc23
LC record available at https://lccn.loc.gov/2020014270
LC ebook record available at https://lccn.loc.gov/2020014271

ISBN: 978-0-367-41870-0 (hbk)
ISBN: 978-0-367-41869-4 (pbk)
ISBN: 978-0-367-81668-1 (ebk)

Typeset in Baskerville
by Newgen Publishing UK

To Léa, Julie, Anaïs, Naomie, Adrien, and all other kids of their generation.

CONTENTS

CONTENTS

PREFACE
120 shades of green in a pink jacket

Pink is a rather surprising color for the cover of a book on global environmental governance. Of course, it is not an innocuous choice, but a deliberate editorial statement. It is meant to illustrate three key assumptions underlying this book. First, we perceive global environmental governance as a unique—and at times surprising—academic field, full of innovative concepts, out-of the-box ideas, and unexpected findings. Second, global environmental governance is not an exclusively "green" field populated by a homogeneous group of activists, but rather a diverse field fueled by several hot debates and heated controversies. Third, global environmental governance has broad impacts on our societies, going well beyond environmental concerns and covering issue-areas such as security, trade, agriculture, health, and gender relations.

Essential Concepts of Global Environmental Governance does not only have a unique cover, but a unique format as well. It is organized as an encyclopedia, with 120 independent and short entries presented in alphabetical order. Each entry defines a concept of global environmental governance, provides an original and critical review of the literature on it, and suggests key references for further reading.

We believe this non-linear format suits particularly well the readers' practices and needs. At times, they can use the table of contents or the index to quickly find the specific information they are looking for. At other times, they can navigate through the book following their mood and explore its content by jumping from one entry to the other with the help of the cross-referencing system. This flexibility favors a learning process by which the reader progressively connects the dots and expands their knowledge system according to their interests, starting with what they already know.

This flexibility is not achieved at the expense of quality. Entries are written by renowned scholars and comply with the most rigorous academic standards. In total, more than 129 academic experts from 91 different institutions and 22 different countries contributed to this volume. Beyond their geographical diversity, the contributors come from various academic disciplines, including sociology, law, economics, geography, philosophy, and political science, proposing different analytical lenses on global environmental governance.

Eclecticism is also reflected in the list of entries. While the encyclopedia covers the classical and well-established concepts of the field, it also discusses emerging and innovative ideas. The aim here is to celebrate the diversity and richness of global environmental governance.

Hoping that our aim is achieved, we warmly thank all our contributors for their enthusiasm in cooperating on this project, while accepting strict guidelines, short deadlines, and demanding suggestions for revisions. If editing the textbook was so pleasing, it was thanks to the contributors' professionalism. We also thank Simon Paquet for his careful and diligent assistance with this edition. Finally, we would like to thank our students. They were always in our mind and provided the purpose and the meaning for this book.

Jean-Frédéric Morin and Amandine Orsini

ABBREVIATIONS

ABS	Access and benefit sharing
AOSIS	Alliance of Small Island States
APEC	Asia-Pacific Economic Cooperation
ASEAN	Association of Southeast Asian Nations
ATS	Antarctic Treaty System
AU	African Union
BASIC	Brazil, South Africa, India, and China
BBNJ	Biodiversity beyond national jurisdiction
BINGO	Business initiated nongovernmental organization
BRICS	Brazil, Russia, India, China, and South Africa
CANZ	Canada, Australia, and New Zealand
CBD	Convention on Biological Diversity
CBDR	Common but differentiated responsibility
CCAMLR	Convention on the Conservation of Antarctic Marine Living Resources
CDM	Clean Development Mechanism
CDP	Carbon Disclosure Project
CETA	Comprehensive Economic and Trade Agreement
CFC	chlorofluorocarbons
CfRN	Coalition for Rainforest Nations
CHH	Common heritage of humanity
CITES	Convention on International Trade in Endangered Species of Wild Fauna and Flora
CLRTAP	Convention on Long-Range Transboundary Air Pollution
COMNAP	Council of Managers of National Antarctic Programs
COP	Conference of the Parties
CSR	Corporate social responsibility
DDT	dichloro-diphenyl-trichloroethane
ECHR	European Convention for the Protection of Human Rights
ECT	Environmental courts or tribunals
EIG	Environmental Integrity Group

EKC	Environmental Kuznets curve
EMS	Environmental management systems
EROI	Energy return on investment
ES	Ecosystem service
ESF	Environmental and Social Framework
ESG	Environmental, social, and governance
ETS	Emissions Trading System
EU	European Union
FAO	Food and Agriculture Organization
FCPF	Forest Carbon Partnership Facility
FSB	Financial Stability Board
FSC	Forest Stewardship Council
G7	Group of 7
G20	Group of 20
G77	Group of 77
GATT	General Agreement on Tariffs and Trade
GDP	Gross domestic product
GEF	Global Environment Facility
GEG	Global environmental governance
GEO	Global Environmental Outlook
GHG	Greenhouse gases
GMO	Genetically modified organism
GPE	Global Pact for the Environment
GPG	Global public good
GRI	Global Reporting Initiative
HCFC	hydrochlorofluorocarbon
HLPE	High Level Panel of Experts
HLPF	High-Level Political Forum on Sustainable Development
IAASTD	International Assessment of Agricultural Knowledge, Science and Technology for Development
IACHR	Inter-American Court on Human Rights
IATI	International Aid Transparency Initiative
IBRD	International Bank for Reconstruction and Development
IBSA	India, Brazil, and South Africa
ICC	Inuit Circumpolar Conference
ICJ	International Court of Justice
ICLEI	International Council for Local Environmental Initiatives

ICPDR	International Commission for the Protection of the Danube River
ICSID	International Centre for Settlement of Investment Disputes
IDMC	International Displacement Monitoring Center
IEA	International Energy Agency
IIRC	International Integrated Reporting Council
ILC	International Law Commission
ILO	International Labour Organization
IMF	International Monetary Fund
IMO	International Maritime Organization
INTERPOL	International Criminal Police Organization
IOM	International Organization for Migration
IOTC	Indian Ocean Tuna Commission
IPBES	Intergovernmental Science-Policy Platform on Biodiversity and Ecosystem Services
IPCC	Intergovernmental Panel on Climate Change
IPES-Food	International Panel of Experts on Sustainable Food Systems
IPR	Intellectual property rights
IPSO	International Programme on the State of Ocean
ISA	International Seabed Authority
ISO	International Organization for Standardization
ITLOS	International Tribunal for the Law of the Sea
ITPGRFA	International Treaty on Plant Genetic Resources for Food and Agriculture
IUCN	International Union for Conservation of Nature
IWC	International Whaling Commission
JUSCANZ	Japan, United States, Canada, Australia, and New Zealand
JUSSCANNZ	Japan, United States, Switzerland, Canada, Australia, Norway, and New Zealand
LDC	Least developed country
LDN	Land degradation neutrality
MDGs	Millennium Development Goals
MEA	Millennium Ecosystem Assessment
MOP	Meeting of the Parties
MSC	Marine Stewardship Council
NAAEC	North American Agreement on Environmental Cooperation
NAFTA	North American Free Trade Agreement

NATO	North Atlantic Treaty Organization
NDCs	Nationally determined contributions
NGO	Nongovernmental organization
ODA	Official development assistance
ODS	Ozone-depleting substances
OECD	Organisation for Economic Co-operation and Development
OPEC	Organization of Petroleum Exporting Countries
OWG	Open Working Group on Sustainable Development Goals
PAN	Pesticide Action Network
PDD	Platform on Disaster Displacement
PES	Payments for ecosystem services
PFOA	perfluorooctanoic acid
PIC	Prior informed consent
POP	Persistent organic pollutant
PPP	Polluter pays principle
RAINS	Regional Acidification Information System
REDD	Reducing emissions from deforestation and forest degradation
RFMO	Regional Fishery Management Organization
SALs	Structural adjustment loans
SDGs	Sustainable Development Goals
STS	Science and technology studies
TCFD	Taskforce on Climate-related Financial Disclosures
TEC	Transnational environmental crime
TFEC	Total final energy consumption
TGNs	Transgovernmental networks
TNC	Transnational corporation
TPP	Trans-Pacific Partnership
UN	United Nations
UNCCD	United Nations Convention to Combat Desertification
UNCED	United Nations Conference on Environment and Development
UNCLOS	United Nations Convention on the Law of the Sea
UNCOPUOS	United Nations Committee on the Peaceful Uses of Outer Space
UNDP	United Nations Development Programme
UNDRIP	United Nations Declaration on the Rights of Indigenous Peoples

UNECE	United Nations Economic Commissions for Europe
UNEP	United Nations Environment Programme
UNESCO	United Nations Educational, Scientific and Cultural Organization
UNFCCC	United Nations Framework Convention on Climate Change
UNGA	United Nations General Assembly
UNHCR	UN High Commissioner for Refugees
UNODC	United Nations Office on Drugs and Crime
US	United States of America
WBCSD	World Business Council for Sustainable Development
WCED	World Commission on Environment and Development
WCO	World Customs Organization
WHO	World Health Organization
WMO	World Meteorological Organization
WTO	World Trade Organization
WWF	World Wildlife Fund

TIMELINE OF THE MAIN TREATIES AND DECLARATIONS

Timeline of the main treaties and declarations

2018 Escazú Agreement on Access to Information, Public Participation and Justice in Environmental Matters in Latin America and the Caribbean

2017 Treaty on the Prohibition of Nuclear Weapons

2015 Paris Agreement under the United Nations Framework Convention on Climate Change General Assembly resolution on the Sustainable Development Goals

2013 Minamata Convention on Mercury

2012 The Future We Want, final document of the United Nations Conference on Sustainable Development Rio + 20

2010 Nagoya Protocol on access to genetic resources and the fair and equitable sharing of benefits arising from their utilization

2009 Agreement on Port State Measures to Prevent, Deter and Eliminate Illegal, Unreported and Unregulated Fishing

2007 International Convention on the Removal of Wrecks

2006 International Tropical Timber Agreement

2002 Johannesburg Declaration on Sustainable Development

2001 Stockholm Convention on Persistent Organic Pollutants International Treaty on plant genetic resources for food and agriculture

2000 Cartagena Protocol on Biosafety to the Convention on Biological Diversity

1999 Aarhus Convention on Access to Information, Public Participation in Decision-Making and Access to Justice in Environmental Matters

1998 Rotterdam Convention on the Prior Informed Consent Procedure for Certain Hazardous Chemicals and Pesticides in International Trade

1997 Kyoto Protocol to the United Nations Framework Convention on Climate Change Convention on the Law of the Non-Navigational Uses of International Watercourses

1996 Comprehensive Nuclear Test Ban Treaty

1994 Convention to Combat Desertification in those Countries Experiencing Serious Drought and Desertification, particularly in Africa Convention on Nuclear Safety Protocol on the Reduction of Sulfur Emissions to the Convention on Long-Range Transboundary Air Pollution International Tropical Timber Agreement

1992 Convention on Biological Diversity United Nations Framework Convention on Climate Change
Agenda 21
Rio Declaration on Environment and Development
Non-Legally Binding Authoritative Statement of Principles for a Global Consensus of the Management, Conservation and Sustainable Development of all Types of Forests
Convention on the Transboundary Effects of Industrial Accidents
Convention on the Protection and Use of Transboundary Watercourses and International Lakes

1991 Madrid Protocol on Environmental Protection to the Antarctic Treaty Bamako Convention on the Ban of the Import into Africa and the Control of Transboundary Movement and Management of Hazardous Wastes within Africa Espoo Convention on Environmental Impact Assessment in a Transboundary Context

1989 Basel Convention on the Control of Transboundary Movements of Hazardous Wastes of Pollution and their Disposal

1987 Montreal Protocol on Substances that Deplete the Ozone Layer

1986 Convention on early Notification of a Nuclear Accident

1985 Vienna Convention for the Protection of the Ozone Layer Helsinki Protocol on the Reduction of Sulfur Missions or their Transboundary Fluxes by at least 30percent to the Convention on Long-Range Transboundary Air Pollution

1983 International Tropical Timber Agreement

1982 United Nations Convention on the Law of the Sea Commercial Whaling Moratorium

1980 Convention on the Conservation of Antarctic Marine Living Resources

1979 Convention on the Conservation of Migratory Species of Wild Animals / Convention on Long-range Transboundary Air Pollution

1977 Convention on the Prohibition of Military or any other Hostile use of Environmental Modification Techniques

1976 Convention for the Protection of the Mediterranean Sea against Pollution

1973 Convention on International Trade in Endangered Species of Wild Fauna and Flora

1972 Declaration of the United Nations Conference on the Human Environment

1971 Ramsar Convention on Wetlands of International Importance especially as Waterfowl Habitat

1967 Treaty on Principles Governing the Activities of States in the Exploration and use of Outer Space, including the Moon and other Celestial Bodies

1963 Treaty Banning Nuclear Weapon Tests in the Atmosphere, in Outer Space and under Water

1962 General Assembly resolution 1803 (XVII) of 14 December 1962, Permanent Sovereignty over Natural Resources

ADAPTATION

Simon Paquet
Université Laval, Canada

The Intergovernmental Panel on Climate Change (IPCC) defines adaptation as an "adjustment in natural or human systems in response to actual or expected climatic stimuli or their effects, which moderates harm or exploits beneficial opportunities" (IPCC 2001: 982). Although adaptation is mainly discussed in reference to climate change, it can be used in reference to various environmental changes, including biodiversity loss, deforestation, water pollution, or desertification. Adaptation implies preparedness for immediate environmental changes, such as rising sea levels and more frequent extreme weather events (see **Disasters**). It also includes preparedness for direct and indirect consequences of environmental changes, such as reduced agricultural yields, population displacements, pandemics, and more generally greater uncertainty. It ranges from specific adjustments, such as seawalls to prevent flooding, to major structural political and economic reforms (see **Critical political economy** and **Degrowth**).

In the **climate change regime**, adaptation has not received as much attention as mitigation (Dzebo 2019). For long, it has been assumed that mitigation (addressing the causes of climate change) requires global coordinated efforts, while adaptation programs (addressing its consequences) should be primarily a national or a local responsibility, as vulnerability and capacity vary greatly across communities.

However, this assumption was progressively questioned and adaptation has come to be considered a global issue (Persson and Dzebo 2019: 357). First, out of normative concerns, communities' vulnerability to climate change and their capacity to adapt are not randomly distributed. Poor **indigenous and local communities** in developing countries are among the most vulnerable to climate change and they often have limited resources, inadequate infrastructures, and weaker governance systems. From an **environmental justice** perspective, countries that contributed the most to climate change should provide financial and technical assistance for adaptation of poor and vulnerable communities (Khan et al. 2019; see also **Common but differentiated responsibilities**). Second, under a consequential logic, adaptation also calls for a global response because, in a globalized and interdependent world, failure to adapt in one community can have transnational consequences, for example by affecting global value chains, migration flows, food systems, or water management.

Under pressure from developing countries and faced with the fact that climate change is already occurring, international institutions devote increasing attention to adaptation. The United Nations Framework Convention on Climate Change (UNFCCC) states that parties should "assist the developing countries [...] in meeting costs of adaptation" (Article 4). In order to do so, a multilateral Adaptation Fund was established in 2001 with the mandate to channel funds directly to recipient countries. In 2009, developed countries made their first major pledge to "support the implementation of adaptation action in developing countries." The following year, Parties to the UNFCCC established the Cancun Adaptation Framework with the objective of strengthening and establishing regional adaptation centers and networks. In 2015, the Paris Agreement established the "global goal on adaptation of enhancing adaptive capacity, strengthening resilience and reducing vulnerability to climate change," and recognized the "importance of support for and international cooperation on adaptation efforts and the importance of taking into account the needs of developing country Parties" (Article 7). Importantly, the Paris Agreement creates a **transparency** framework in which parties disclose their measures to implement the agreement, including their "adaptation actions."

Several other intergovernmental organizations are involved in financing climate adaptation in developing countries, including the **World Bank**, the International Organization for Migration, the United Nations Development Programme, and the Organisation for Economic Co-operation and Development. Another major source of adaptation **aid** is provided bilaterally by donor countries, although not necessarily to countries with the lowest adaptive capacity (Weiler et al. 2018: 65). Finally, beyond financing adaptation, various transnational initiatives aim to support adaptation to environmental changes. Transnational city networks are particularly active in shaping environmental resilience (Papin 2019).

References

Dzebo, Adis. 2019. "Effective Governance of Transnational Adaptation Initiatives." *International Environmental Agreements: Politics, Law and Economics* 19(4): 447–466.

Intergovernmental Panel on Climate Change (IPCC). 2001. *Climate Change 2001: Impact, Adaptation, and Vulnerability.* Cambridge, Cambridge University Press.

Khan, Mizan, Stacy-Ann Robinson, Romain Weikmans, David Ciplet, and J. Timmons Roberts. 2019. "Twenty-Five Years of Adaptation Finance through a Climate Justice Lens." *Climate Change.* Epub ahead of print October 29, 2019. https://doi.org/10.1007/s10584-019-02563-x

Papin, Marielle. 2019. "Transnational Municipal Networks: Harbingers of Innovation for Global Adaptation Governance?" *International Environmental Agreements: Politics, Law and Economics* 19(4–5): 467–483.

Persson, Åsa and Adis Dzebo. 2019. "Special Issue: Exploring Global and Transnational Governance of Climate Change Adaptation." *International Environmental Agreements: Politics, Law and Economics* 19(4–5): 357–367.

Weiler, Florian, Carola Klöck, and Matthew Dornan. 2018. "Vulnerability, Good Governance, or Donor Interests? The Allocation of Aid for Climate Change Adaptation." *World Development* 104: 65–77.

AGROECOLOGY

Olivier De Schutter
UCLouvain, Belgium

Agroecology has been defined as the "application of ecological **science** to the study, design and management of sustainable agroecosystems" (Altieri 1995: 6). It seeks to improve agricultural systems by mimicking or augmenting natural processes, thus enhancing beneficial biological interactions and synergies among the components of agrobiodiversity Agroecology is highly knowledge-intensive, based on techniques that are not delivered top-down but developed on the basis of farmers' knowledge and experimentation. Its practices require the diversification of the tasks on the farm, linking them to the diversity of species (including animals) that interact at field level.

A variety of techniques have been developed and successfully tested in a range of regions that are based on this approach (Pretty 2008), such as *integrated nutrient management, agroforestry, water harvesting,* and the *integration of livestock into farming systems.* A wide range of experts within the scientific community and international agencies (see **Epistemic communities**) view these techniques as a way to improve the resilience and sustainability of food systems (Wezel and Soldat 2009). In 2018 and 2019, a series of landmark international reports by international institutions and **boundary organizations** examined how agricultural development and food systems reform could contribute to the achievement of the **Sustainable Development Goals** (SDGs).

The growing global consensus on the importance of agroecology in meeting the SDGs can be explained by the many channels through which it can contribute not only to food security, but also to other development goals. First, agroecology can guarantee to the local communities (see **Indigenous peoples and local communities**) adequate nutrition through the provision of diversified, safe, and balanced diets. Whereas the "Green Revolution" implemented in the 1960s and 1970s contributed to micronutrient malnutrition in many developing countries (Demment et al. 2003), varied agroecosystems ensure a more diversified nutrient output from farming systems (Kennedy et al. 2017). Second, agroecology can also improve the incomes of small-scale farmers, particularly in developing countries, by lowering the costs of production and improving resilience of farming systems against weather-related events, including those linked to climate change. Resilience, indeed, is strengthened by the use and promotion of agricultural biodiversity at ecosystem, farm system, and field levels. Third, agroecology can also make a significant contribution to climate change mitigation both by reducing the use of external inputs that depend on fossil energy and emit nitrous oxide and by preserving and enhancing soil health and agrobiodiversity, allowing soils to function as carbon sinks and to maintain their function of regulating water cycles. Fourth, agroecology can significantly improve agricultural productivity where it has been lagging behind, and thus increase production where it needs most to be increased (i.e. primarily in poor, food-deficient countries), while at the same time improving the livelihoods of smallholder farmers and preserving ecosystems. Moreover, it would contribute to rural development and preserve the ability of succeeding generations to meet their own needs (see **Sustainable development**). In addition, the resulting higher incomes in the rural areas would contribute to the growth of other sectors of the economy by stimulating demand for non-agricultural products (Adelman 1984).

Four major lock-ins still form obstacles to the agroecological revolution (IPES-Food 2016). First, technologies and infrastructures are biased in favor of achieving economies of scale through the reliance on large monocultures that can be more easily mechanized. Second, dominant agribusiness (see Business and corporations) actors are better positioned to supply markets with low-priced foodstuffs, against which other actors, using other, more sustainable modes of production, are unable to compete.

Third, the lifestyles of the urban middle class have evolved and favor an industrial way of producing food with processed foods increasingly favored around the world. Fourth and finally, political obstacles remain: large agribusiness actors forcefully lobby against any significant change that would threaten their position in the food system, in favor of farmers.

References

Adelman, Irma. 1984. "Beyond Export-led Growth." *World Development* 12(9): 937–949.

Altieri, Miguel A. 1995. *The Science of Sustainable Agriculture*, second edition. Boulder, CO, Westview Press.

Declerck, Fabrice A.J., Jessica Fanzo, Cheryl Palm, and Roseline Remans. 2011. "Ecological Approaches to Human Nutrition." *Food and Nutrition Bulletin* 32(1): S41-S50.

Demment, Montague W., Michelle M. Young and Ryan L. Sensening. 2003. "Providing Micronutrients through Food Based Solutions: A Key to Human and National Development." Journal of Nutrition 133: 3879S–3885S.

IPES-Food. 2016. *From Uniformity to Diversity: A Paradigm Shift from Industrial Agriculture to Diversified Agroecological Systems.* International Panel of Experts on Sustainable Food Systems.

Kennedy, Gina, Danny Hunter, James Garrett, and Stefano Padulosi. 2017. "Leveraging Agrobiodiversity to Create Sustainable Food Systems for Healthier Diets." *UNSCN News* 42: 23–31.

Pretty, Jules. 2008. "Agricultural Sustainability: Concepts, Principles and Evidence." *Philosophical Transactions of the Royal Society of London. Series B, Biological Sciences* 363(1491): 447–465.

Wezel, Alexander and V. Soldat. 2009. "A Quantitative and Qualitative Historical Analysis of the Scientific Discipline of Agroecology." *International Journal of Agricultural Sustainability* 7(1): 3–18.

AID

Åsa Persson
Stockholm Environment Institute, Sweden

Whereas formal definitions of environmental aid based on activities (e.g. nature conservation measures, subsidies of cleaner cooking stoves) have been developed by organizations such as the Organisation for Economic Co-operation and Development (OECD) for statistical purposes, it can also be simply defined as bilateral or multilateral financial or technical assistance to developing countries which has a likely positive environmental impact (regardless of the objective of the aid activity) (see Hicks et al. 2008). Environmental aid from public sources is a core feature of contemporary global environmental governance, both for strategic reasons, in that it can act as a concession or side payment for getting recipient countries to participate in international cooperation, and **effectiveness** reasons, in that it can enhance the capacity of recipient countries to ensure the implementation of and compliance with international **regimes** and thus provide **global public goods**.

Environmental aid emerged as a topic in the 1980s when negative environmental impacts of aid projects, among others led by the **World Bank**, were first highlighted, and subsequently addressed through impact **assessments** procedures. In the 1990s, especially after the 1992 Rio Conference, a more proactive approach emerged where environmental protection became the principal or a significant objective of aid. According to official data from the OECD Development Assistance Committee, a third of all official development assistance (ODA) supported environment and climate in 2017 (US$40 billion) and this share has increased significantly over the last ten years, especially so the share focusing on climate change mitigation and adaptation (OECD 2019).

Some independent analyses have also estimated the magnitude of environmentally negative or "dirty" aid. Hicks et al. (2008) found that in the 1990s, aid with likely positive environmental impact was outweighed by aid with likely neutral or negative impact by a factor of seven and three, respectively. Using the same database, a later study showed that the ratio of "dirty" to "environmental" was still roughly three in 2008 (Marcoux et al. 2013). The trend is one of gradual improvement, but still poor overall performance.

Why do donors offer environmental aid? It has been found that donors' economic and political interests are the drivers of environmental aid rather than altruism (see example from the whaling issue in Miller and Dolšak 2007). National wealth, strong environmental advocacy groups, and post-materialist values appear to improve the environmental impact of a donor's aid. "Green and greedy" environmental technology lobbies also appear to have a greening effect on aid, in particular when it comes to addressing global environmental problems rather than local ones (Hicks et al. 2008). Mitigating global environmental problems directly benefits donor countries as well, which has sometimes raised concern among recipient countries that funds are diverted from urgent local environmental problems. Provision of environmental aid to address global environmental problems may also be perceived by donors as more cost-effective or politically more feasible than taking stronger domestic action. According to environmental aid statistics, the trend is increased aid for global problems.

There are two complementary strategies for environmental aid (Arndt and Tarp 2017): specialized environmental aid, disbursed through specific environment-related bilateral and multilateral funds and programs, some of which are operated by the **Global Environment Facility**; and the integration (or mainstreaming) of environmental concerns into all kinds of aid. For the latter purpose, donor agencies have developed various tools, ranging from project-level impact assessment to tools for more strategic decision-making (Persson 2009). While the advantages of effective integration of environmental concerns in mainstream aid are clear, there have also been concerns arising from the general proliferation of issues and objectives to be mainstreamed into aid (e.g. gender, human rights, HIV/AIDS) and that it means a de facto delegation of critical value judgments to implementing agencies as opposed to political decision-makers.

Starting in the 1980s, critique was voiced against the perceived use of "green" conditionality, i.e. that donors required environmental commitments on the part of recipients even though they were not necessarily the immediate priorities of the affected communities (Mori 2011). In 2005, the Paris Declaration on Aid Effectiveness was agreed, in an effort to reframe the relationship between donors and recipients, including sensitivities surrounding conditionality. Key principles included stronger recipient country ownership, donor harmonization, and results-based management—and a related trend is to use broader budget support programs rather than specific projects. It is difficult to assess whether these principles and trends will be largely positive or negative for the environmental impact of aid, as it depends to a large extent on detailed **compliance and implementation** arrangements.

A debate that has been reinvigorated by recent negotiations surrounding climate finance (see **Sustainable finance**) under the **climate change regime** is that of additionality of resources. The 1992 Rio Summit (see **Summit diplomacy**) served to put the spotlight on global environmental public goods, with the adoption of several international conventions. Financial assistance to help developing countries implement such conventions became a new focus of environmental aid. However, developing countries have questioned whether such assistance is indeed "new and additional" to existing ODA budgetary commitments, as stipulated in several key texts. It has been argued that such assistance should be considered as a form of restitution, reflecting the historical responsibility of developed countries and the **common but differentiated responsibilities** principle, rather than as aid. Concern surrounding additionality is one of the driving forces behind recent initiatives for increased transparency in aid allocation and aid results, such as the International Aid Transparency Initiative (IATI) and the database AidData.

The ultimate question is whether aid—in general and environmental aid in particular—is effective. This is an ongoing debate with strong divergence, including more pessimistic views expressed by scholars such as Dambisa Moyo and William Easterly and more optimistic ones by Paul Collier and Jeffrey Sachs. Part of the challenge is nuancing the question; what do we mean by **effectiveness** and success (e.g. GDP growth or other metrics) and under what particular conditions does aid work or not.

References

Arndt, Channing and Fin Tarp. 2017. "Aid, Environment and Climate Change." *Review of Development Economics* 21(2): 285–303.

Hicks, Robert, Bradley Parks, J. Timmons Roberts, and Michael Tierney. 2008. *Greening Aid? Understanding the Environmental Impact of Development Assistance.* Oxford, Oxford University Press.

Marcoux, Christopher, Bradley Parks, Christian Peratsakis, J. Timmons Roberts, and Michael Tierney. 2013. "Environmental Aid and Climate Finance in a New World: How Past Environmental Aid Allocation Impacts Future Climate Aid." *WIDER Working Paper.* Helsinki, UNU-WIDER.

Miller, Andrew R. and Nives Dolšak. 2007. "Issue Linkages in International Environmental Policy: The International Whaling Commission and Japanese Development Aid." *Global Environmental Politics* 7(1): 69–96.

Mori, Akihisa. 2011. "Overcoming Barriers to Effective Environmental Aid: A Comparison between Japan, Germany, Denmark, and the World Bank." *Journal of Environment and Development* 20(1): 3–26.

OECD (Organisation for Economic Co-operation and Development). 2019. *Development Co-operation Profiles.* Paris, OECD.

Persson, Åsa. 2009. "Environmental Policy Integration and Bilateral Development Assistance: Challenges and Opportunities with an Evolving Governance Framework." *International Environmental Agreements* 9(4): 409–429.

ANTARCTIC TREATY SYSTEM

Alan D. Hemmings

University of Canterbury, New Zealand

The Antarctic Treaty System (ATS) comprises the 1959 Antarctic Treaty, the 1972 Convention on the Conservation of Antarctic Seals, the 1980 Convention on the Conservation of Antarctic Marine Living Resources (CCAMLR), the 1991 Protocol on Environmental Protection to the Antarctic Treaty (Madrid Protocol), and measures in force under these instruments. Three of these apply to the area south of 60° south. CCAMLR's northern boundary approximates the Antarctic convergence, a biologically rich zone where Antarctic waters meet the waters of the sub-Antarctic. The ATS is one of the longest established **regimes** (Rothwell and Hemmings 2018).

Its purpose is international governance of the region, since although seven states claim territorial **sovereignty** over parts of the continent, these claims are not generally recognized and many see Antarctica as **common heritage of humanity**.

Thirty states plus the European Union are decision-making parties, and thirty more are non-decision-making parties to one or more ATS instruments. A number of intergovernmental organizations (such as the Council of Managers of National Antarctic Programs (COMNAP), **United Nations Environment Programme** (UNEP), and Food and Agriculture Organization (FAO)), **nongovernmental organizations** (including environmental groups and tourism and fishing industry associations), and hybrid organizations such as International Union for Conservation of Nature (IUCN) have observer status. The three pillars of the ATS are peaceful purposes (avoiding militarization), environmental protection, and freedom of scientific enquiry. The latter two and operational management of human activities under way in the region are the subject of measures adopted within the ATS (Saul and Stephens 2015). Responsibility for whaling lies entirely outside the ATS, with the **International Whaling Commission** (IWC).

Current ATS foci include: the vexed issue of establishing large marine protected areas in Antarctic waters alongside commercial interests in fishing (see **Fisheries governance**); sustaining international Antarctic **science** and associated logistics collaboration, particularly around globally significant climate change research, although not yet climate policy (Leane and McGee 2019); and managing the regional consequences of the changing world order.

While the ATS historically claims **effectiveness**, in ensuring peaceful order and addressing management issues around the conduct of activities and the environment, it is long-lived in international relations terms and faces challenges if it is to continue to effectively manage the region (Dodds et al. 2017). Globalization challenges its Antarctic exceptionalism model of governance, wherein issues were addressed through specific instruments negotiated under the ATS. Increasingly, there are pressures to leave regulation to market forces or administrative action, or to global instruments. Increasing scale, pace, and complexity of technology-enabled Antarctic activities, less constrained by Antarctica's remoteness and harshness than in the past, require improved ATS institutional integration and instrumental coverage. Further, the architecture of the ATS has its foundations in the Cold War, and rising international powers such as Brazil, India, South Africa, and particularly China, plus the broader community of **emerging countries**, few of which are presently within the ATS, will need to be assured that it now serves their interests too (Hemmings 2014).

References

Dodds, Klaus, Alan D. Hemmings, and Peder Roberts (Eds.). 2017. *Handbook on the Politics of Antarctica*. Cheltenham and Northampton, Edward Elgar.

Hemmings, Alan D. 2014. "Re-justifying the Antarctic Treaty System for the 21st Century: Rights, Expectations and Global Equity." In *Polar Geopolitics: Knowledges, Resources and Legal Regimes*, Eds. Richard Powell and Klaus Dodds, 55–73. Cheltenham and Northampton, Edward Elgar.

Leane, Elizabeth and Jeffrey McGee (Eds.). 2019. *Anthropocene Antarctica: Perspectives from the Humanities, Law and Social Sciences*. London, Routledge.

Rothwell, Donald R. and Alan D. Hemmings. 2018. "Introduction: The Context of International Polar Law." In *International Polar Law*, Eds. Donald R. Rothwell and Alan D. Hemmings, xiii–xliv. Cheltenham and Northampton, Edward Elgar.

Saul, Ben, and Tim Stephens (Eds.) *Antarctica in International Law*. Oxford and Portland, Hart.

ANTHROPOCENE

Manuel Arias-Maldonado

University of Málaga, Spain

The Amsterdam Declaration on Global Change, adopted by a community of scientists in July 2001, stated that:

> human activities are significantly influencing Earth's environment in many ways in addition to greenhouse gas emissions and climate change. Anthropogenic changes to Earth's land surface, oceans, coasts and atmosphere and to biological diversity, the water cycle and biogeochemical cycles are clearly identifiable beyond natural variability. They are equal to some of the great forces of nature in their extent and impact
>
> (Moore et al. 2001)

This is an apt summary of what the Anthropocene, a concept introduced a year earlier by natural scientists Paul Crutzen and Eugene Stoermer (2000), tries to convey. The Anthropocene, or "Human Epoch," is a period whose defining feature is the massive anthropogenic disruption of natural systems at a planetary level. Due to the aggregation of human activities across time and space, social and natural systems have now become entangled and thus human beings must be reckoned as environmental forces in their own right. For a number of geologists, the anthropogenic impact has also been registered in the fossil record, so that the Earth would have abandoned the Holocene and entered into a new geological epoch— a significant transition that still awaits official recognition. However, geology is not indispensable for the Anthropocene to be accepted. Earth system science provides empirical observations that are robust enough to support the hypothesis of unprecedented global environmental change. It is because the anthropogenic disruption occurs at a planetary level that a "rupture" in Earth history has been suggested (Hamilton 2016).

The Anthropocene is not a "fact," but rather a scientific theory that encompasses a number of empirically observable "facts" (see **Science**). As much as global environmental change is real, the Anthropocene does not exist "out there" but "in here," namely as a conceptual proposition about the state of planetary systems and socionatural relations. In this regard, the role of computerized models and data-gathering satellites has been highlighted as the foundation of a "second Copernican revolution" that provides new ways for understanding Earth as an integrated system (Schellnhuber 1999). While seeing the Earth as a system involves a departure from the analytical habits of traditional earth and life sciences, it can provide a new phenomenological experience of the planet and thus reveal a shift in human subjectivity—moving from a Cartesian "I" to a planetary "We" (Hamilton 2019). The formulation of the Anthropocene is thus made synchronous with a moment of social self-reflexivity in which humans acknowledge their fragility in the face of global environmental threats (Steffen et al. 2007; see also **Risk society**). In the Anthropocene, it is often said, we must live and think differently.

This moral prescription shows how the Anthropocene hypothesis resonates well beyond the natural sciences. In fact, it has received an enthusiastic welcome on the part of social sciences and the humanities— a multidisciplinary response that deals with the meanings and normative implications of both the concept *and* the reality that the concept describes. Yet this response also entails the problematization of the Anthropocene. A recurrent critique concerns the identity of the *anthropos*, i.e. the humanity whose activity is said to have transformed natural systems. It has been pointed out that such universal, undifferentiated humanity does not exist—there are situated social groups, among which some have made greater contribution than others to the "production" of the Anthropocene (Malm and Hornborg 2014). The European elites that pushed industrialization forward, for instance, are more responsible than the working classes that filled the factories (see also **Common but differentiated responsibilities**). A universal view of the human species may also "naturalize" ecological destruction, eclipsing the key role of "fossil capitalism"—hence the alternative concept of the "Capitalocene" (Moore 2015). However, global environmental change is not inherent in economic inequality among social groups: a more equal planet would be more, not less, anthropogenic (Chakrabarty 2009). Moreover, the Anthropocene connects existing societies with the deep time of geology, which transcends that of modernity and capitalism. The relation between the latter and the Anthropocene is more ambiguous than it seems.

Actually, there should be room for a nuanced account of socionatural relations that combines two analytical perspectives: that of the human species whose aggregated impact on the environment causes significant transformations on the latter at a global level; and that which distinguishes the particular contributions of each social group. The same goes for individual actions, like driving a car or having a shower; they have an "episodic life" that only lead to "systemic" effects once they converge in global interconnected networks of causation (Jamieson and Di Paola 2016). This ambivalence shows how difficult it is to deal with the

Anthropocene, let alone advancing towards a "good Anthropocene" that is politically democratic, ecologically sustainable, and socially fair.

As for global governance, the Anthropocene has been presented as an inescapable condition that demands radical institutional change: given the inability of Holocene institutions to adapt to a more unstable Earth system, greater reflexivity in a polycentric framework is required (Dryzek and Pickering 2019) (see **Polycentricity**). For those who perceive decentralization as fragmented and ineffective, a more centralized approach built around multilateral institutions is preferable (Bierman 2014). There is no clear answer yet to the question of how the Anthropocene should be governed. Addressing the complex challenges that it poses will thus require a great deal of theoretical debate and institutional experimentation in the coming years.

References

Biermann, Frank. 2014. *Earth System Governance: World Politics in the Anthropocene.* Cambridge, MA, The MIT Press.

Chakrabarty, Dipesh. 2009. "The Climate of History: Four Theses." *Critical Inquiry* 35(2): 197–222.

Crutzen, Paul and Eugene Stoermer. 2000. "The 'Anthropocene'." *Global Change Newsletter* 41: 17.

Dryzek, John and Jonathan Pickering. 2019. *The Politics of the Anthropocene.* Oxford, Oxford University Press.

Hamilton, Clive. 2016. "The Anthropocene as Rupture." *The Anthropocene Review* 2(1): 59–72.

Hamilton, Scott. 2019. "I Am Uncertain, But We Are Not: A New Subjectivity of the Anthropocene." *Review of International Studies* 45(4): 607–662.

Jamieson, Dale and Marcello Di Paola. 2016. "Political Theory for the Anthropocene." In *Global Political Theory*, Eds. David Held and Pietro Maffetone, 254–280. Cambridge, Polity Press.

Malm, Andres and Alf Hornborg. 2014. "The Geology of Mankind? A Critique of the Anthropocene Narrative." *The Anthropocene Review* 1(1): 62–69.

Moore, Berrien, Arild Underdal, Peter Lemke, and Michel Loreau. 2001. "Challenges of a Changing Earth: Global Change Open Science Conference." Amsterdam, 10–13 July 2001.

Moore, Jason. 2015. *Capitalism in the Web of Life: Ecology and the Accumulation of Capital.* London, Verso.

Schellnhuber, Hans. 1999. "'Earth System' Analysis and the Second Copernican Revolution." *Nature* 402(6761): 19–23.

Steffen, Will, Paul Crutzen, and John McNeill. 2007. "The Anthropocene: Are Humans Now Overwhelming the Great Forces of Nature?" *Ambio* 36(8): 614–621.

ARCTIC COUNCIL

Olav Schram Stokke

University of Oslo and Fridtjof Nansen Institute, Norway

The Arctic Council is an international soft-law institution established in 1996 to address issues of environmental protection and **sustainable development** in the Arctic. Its membership comprises the eight states with **sovereignty** over territory north of the Arctic Circle: Canada, Denmark/Greenland, Finland, Iceland, Norway, Russia, Sweden, and the USA (see also **Regional governance**). Several transnational **indigenous and local communities** associations, including the Inuit Circumpolar Council and the Saami Council, have Permanent participant status, with full consultation in all Council meetings and activities, but decisions are taken by the member states. Such active **participation** by indigenous peoples' organizations features prominently in the Council's self-presentation. Numerous non-Arctic states, international bodies, and **nongovernmental organizations** participate as observers.

Biennial ministerial meetings adopt declarations directing Council activities, with implementation overseen by the members' Senior Arctic Officials. A permanent **secretariat** has been operational since 2013. Working groups in areas including environmental monitoring, biodiversity protection (see **Biodiversity regime**), and **sustainable development** prepare environmental **assessments** and other studies, often with non-binding recommendations, on matters such as environmental toxins, climate change, oil and gas activities, and Arctic shipping (Koivurova et al. 2015). Ad hoc task forces have dealt with, inter alia, the development of legally binding agreements (adopted by the member states, not the Council) on Search and Rescue (2011), Marine Oil Pollution Preparedness and Response (2013), and Cooperation in Arctic **Science** (2017).

The formation of the Arctic Council, enabled by the late-1980s thaw in East–West relations, and its subsequent institutional development reflect the importance of global processes for Arctic governance (Young 2016). Funds for program activities and cross-boundary capacity enhancement have been available partly because this well-functioning circumpolar body, which includes Russia and its Western neighbors under a common umbrella, is deemed conducive to regional security objectives. The notable continuity in activities through the Ukraine crisis (Byers 2017) indicates that the Council helps to shield Arctic cooperation from oscillations in global geopolitical tensions.

The Council's 2013 acceptance of several new observer applications, also from **emerging countries** like China and India, reflects acknowledgment that many activities that produce Arctic environmental challenges occur outside the region or fall under the full or partial jurisdiction of non-Arctic states. Examples include discharges of greenhouse gases, persistent organic pollutants, and heavy metals, as well as Arctic shipping. Handling such challenges requires regulatory action beyond the Arctic Eight, typically in global institutions such as the **Stockholm Convention on Persistent Organic Pollutants**, the **climate change regime**, and the International Maritime Organization. Involving non-regional states more deeply in knowledge- and capacity-building Council activities may promote efforts by Arctic states for regulatory advances in broader international institutions crucial to the **effectiveness** of Arctic governance (Stokke 2014).

The structure of the Arctic Council has grown firmer and its activities have expanded to cover knowledge building, capacity enhancement, and norm development. While the **Law of the Sea Convention** ensures that the Arctic five coastal states predominate in decisions on oil and gas as well as in **fisheries governance**, while **regimes** with broader membership are weightier for environmental and shipping regulation, the Council is well-placed to improve **institutional interactions** among these levels of governance.

References

Byers, Michael. 2017. "Crises and International Cooperation: An Arctic Case Study." *International Relations* 31(4): 1–28.

Koivurova, Timo, Paula Kankaanpaa, and Adam Stępień. 2015. "Innovative Environmental Protection: Lessons from the Arctic." *Journal of Environmental Law* 27(2): 285–311.

Stokke, Olav Schram. 2014. "Asian Stakes and Arctic Governance." *Strategic Analysis* 38(6): 770–783.

Young, Oran. 2016. "The Arctic Council at Twenty: How to Remain Effective in a Rapidly Changing Environment." *UC Irvine Law Review* 6(1): 99–119.

ASSESSMENTS

Joyeeta Gupta

University of Amsterdam, Netherlands

Environmental assessments have evolved from individual literature review papers, through single organization assessments (e.g. World Resource Institute reports), to structured and regular representative assessments (e.g. Intergovernmental Panel on Climate Change (IPCC)). These latter assessments are sometimes linked to international policy processes (see also **Reporting**). Environmental assessments are produced by joint expert **participation** and analysis of the existing issue-specific **science** (Clark et al. 2006) with policy implications (Mitchell et al. 2006). It may include collation and analysis of data and responses to specific questions. It can, but mostly does not, include original research. However, it triggers original research subsequently published in journals and referred to in the assessments.

These assessments can potentially bridge the science–policy gap between their respective communities (see also **Boundary organizations**) (Caplan 1979; Woodhouse and Nieusma 2001). This gap includes differing assumptions, goals, methods, and reward system. There is also uneven North–South coverage (Annan 2003). Assessments can be classified linearly in a science-policy interface ladder (Gupta 2014). The bottom rung is an informal science-policy interface as on biofuels (where there is neither systematic review of biofuel science nor a centralized governance process), moving up through structured, formalized, regular assessments provided to a formalized negotiating process as in climate change.

Assessments are very diverse. On forests, the Global Forest Resource Assessment of the Food and Agriculture Organization (FAO) uses completed questionnaires from member countries and expert consultations and feeds into the ongoing FAO work. In the **ozone regime**, there are Advisory Panels on Science, Environment, Technology, and Economics that also address specific questions. In 1988 the World Meteorological Organization and the **United Nations Environment Programme** (UNEP) established IPCC. This formal body assesses the scientific literature and derives policy relevant conclusions under a strictly organized regime of writing and responding to the scientific and government review processes. IPCC interacts closely with the UN **climate change regime** negotiations (see **Treaty negotiations**). Since 1995, UNEP has published six Global Environmental Outlooks (GEOs), which are becoming increasingly formalized and structured but aim also at being simpler and more communicative. Since 2003, tri-annual World Water Development Reports have been published by UN-Water and United Nations Educational, Scientific and Cultural Organization (UNESCO) to advise the water community. There are a few one-time assessments such as the 1995 Millennium Ecosystem Assessment, followed fifteen years later by the Intergovernmental Platform on Biodiversity and Ecosystem Services (Larigauderie and Mooney 2010). The **Desertification Convention** has no such international assessments that suggest policy options (Bauer and Stringer 2009; Grainger 2009).

After forty years of global environmental assessments there is increasing demand for a better understanding of the policy landscape in order to improve it more accurately; as well as growing complexity in the way assessments are conducted which requires greater management skills and larger resources (Jabbour and Flachsland 2017). At the same time, such assessments are progressively having greater impact on policy processes. They enhance the way these processes discuss risks, increase the scientific information for negotiating processes, enhance reflexive learning, continue to emphasize the need for action, and improve and enlarge the community of scholars who can work in the environmental field in different parts of the world and their ability to engage with their own policymakers (Riousseta et al. 2017). However, an enduring weakness of the assessment process is that it is mostly male scholars from the North that are engaged in writing processes (see **Ecofeminism**) (Timpte et al. 2018).

The more structured, formalized, regular assessments assess the available global knowledge, structure the information into usable knowledge, point to knowledge conflicts and gaps, and prepare simple summaries for policymakers. However, they cannot compensate for patchy global knowledge or cover all languages, and tend to focus on "peer reviewed" journals, thus excluding gray literature including indigenous and local communities knowledge, **nongovernmental organizations and business and corporations** assessments, and civic knowledge (Bäckstrand 2003) as well as court cases on relevant issues. Moreover, they may focus on best practices and panaceas as opposed to contextual knowledge. Finally, as these assessments become influential, they come under heavy scientific and journalistic scrutiny.

References

Annan, Kofi. 2003. "A Challenge to the World's Scientists." *Science* 299(5612): 1485–1485.

Bäckstrand, Karin. 2003. "Civic Science for Sustainability: Reframing the Role of Experts, Policy-Makers and Citizens in Environmental Governance." *Global Environmental Politics* 3(4): 24–41.

Bauer, Steffen and Lindsay C. Stringer. 2009. "The Role of Science in the Global Governance of Desertification." *The Journal of Environment and Development* 18(3): 248–267.

Caplan, Nathan. 1979. "The Two-Communities Theory and Knowledge Utilization." *American Behavioral Scientist* 22(3): 459–470.

Clark, William C., Ronald B. Mitchell, and David W. Cash. 2006. "Evaluating the Influence of Global Environmental Assessments." In *Global Environmental Assessments: Information and Influence*, Eds. Ronald B. Mitchell, William C. Clark, David W. Cash, and Nancy M. Dickson, 1–28. Cambridge, MA, MIT Press.

Grainger, Alan. 2009. "The Role of Science in Implementing International Environmental Agreements: The Case of Desertification." *Land Degradation and Development* 20(4): 410–430.

Gupta, Joyeeta. 2014. "Science and Governance: Climate Change, Forests, Environment and Water Governance." In *The Role of Experts in International Decision-Making: Irrelevant, Advisors or Decision-Makers*, Eds. Monika Ambrus, Karin Arts, Helena Raulus, and Ellen Hey, 148–170. Cambridge, Cambridge University Press.

Jabbour, Jason and Christian Flachsland. 2017. "40 Years of Global Environmental Assessments: A Retrospective Analysis." *Environmental Science and Policy* 77: 193–207.

Larigauderie, Anne and Harold A. Mooney. 2010. "The Intergovernmental Science-Policy Platform on Biodiversity and Ecosystem Services: Moving a Step Closer to an IPCC-like Mechanism for Biodiversity." *Current Opinion in Environmental Sustainability* 2(1–2): 9–14.

Malte Timpte, Jasper Montana, Katrin Reuter, Maud Borie, and Jascha Apkes. 2018. "Engaging Diverse Experts in a Global Environmental Assessment: Participation in the First Work Programme of IPBES and Opportunities for Improvement." *Innovation: The European Journal of Social Science Research* 31(S1): S15–S37.

Mitchell, Ronald B., William C. Clark, David W. Cash, and Nancy M. Dickson. 2006. *Global Environmental Assessments: Information and Influence*. Cambridge, MA, MIT Press.

Riousseta, Pauline, Christian Flachsland, and Martin Kowarsch. 2017. "Global Environmental Assessments: Impact Mechanisms." *Environmental Science and Policy* 77: 260–267.

Woodhouse, Edward J. and Dean A. Nieusma. 2001. "Democratic Expertise: Integrating Knowledge, Power, and Participation." In *Knowledge, Power and Participation*, Eds. Hisschemöller Matthijs, Jeery R. Ravetz, Rob Hoppe, and William N. Dunn, 73–95. New Brunswick, NJ, Transaction Publishers.

AUDITS

Olivier Boiral
Université Laval, Canada

Iñaki Heras-Saizarbitoria
University of the Basque Country, Spain

Environmental audits can be defined as systematic, documented, and, as far as possible, impartial evaluations of environmental practices and compliance with standards, regulations, specifications, or any other pre-established requirements related to environmental issues. As such they are tools for **compliance and implementation**. Environmental audits can focus on a large variety of issues such as sustainable forest management or environmental risks (Hillary 1998). Nevertheless, over the last decade, two forms of environmental audits have taken center stage: the external verification of environmental management systems (EMS) and the auditing of environmental or sustainability reports (Boiral and Gendron 2011).

First, the external audits of EMS generally focus on the conformance of **business and corporations** with an established standard, such as ISO 14001, which is the most widespread with more than 360,000 certified organizations in 2017. This standard is based on the implementation of management principles: structure, resources, and responsibilities of the EMS, policy and objectives, and so on. The certification process, which is sometimes considered as a self-regulation mechanism (Prakash and Potoski 2006), assumes that the conformance of the EMS with the ISO standard has been verified by external and supposedly independent auditors. Nevertheless, organizations can also conduct internal audits based on ISO 14001 to improve their internal practices.

Second, the verification of environmental or sustainability reports focuses on conformance with a **reporting** standard, notably the Global Reporting Initiative (GRI), which is the most widely used. The auditing process—often called assurance or external assurance process—is supposed to verify the application of various reporting principles and indicators that are generally not limited to environmental issues. This assurance process is often conducted by auditing firms also involved in financial audits, and it aims to ensure the accuracy, reliability, and **transparency** of the released information.

Although the focus and scope of environmental audits may be very different, the principles underlying the certification process are quite similar. Like **labeling and certification** in general, environmental audits are primarily intended to inspire trust among stakeholders and to reinforce organizations' social legitimacy. This quest for legitimacy through external audits reflects the emergence of an "audit society," which is characterized by common rituals of verification and an obsession with control (Power 1997). The use of environmental audits as trust-providing mechanisms also raises critical questions that remain largely underexplored (Boiral and Gendron 2011): to what extent can commercial issues underlying the auditing practice undermine the alleged independence of third-party auditors? What are the impacts of the current lack of regulatory and professional guidance on the quality of environmental audits? What are the real impacts of these external audits on organizations' internal practices?

References

Boiral, Olivier and Yves Gendron. 2011. "Sustainable Development and Certification Practices: Lessons Learned and Prospects." *Business Strategy and the Environment* 20(5): 331–347.

Hillary, Ruth. 1998. "Environmental Auditing: Concepts, Methods and Developments." *International Journal of Auditing* 2(1): 71–85.

Power, Michael. 1997. *The Audit Society: Rituals of Verification*. Oxford, Oxford University Press.

Prakash, Aseem and Matthew Potoski. 2006. *The Voluntary Environmentalists: Green Clubs, ISO 14001, and Voluntary Environmental Regulations*. Cambridge, Cambridge University Press.

BIODIVERSITY REGIME

G. Kristin Rosendal

Fridtjof Nansen Institute, Norway

The Convention on Biological Diversity (CBD) (1992) builds on a threefold, interacting objective: the conservation of biological diversity, the sustainable use of its components, and the fair and equitable sharing of the benefits arising from utilization of genetic resources (see **Conservation and preservation**). The CBD is comprehensive in scope, as biodiversity is defined as species and ecosystems worldwide, as well as the genetic diversity within species. With 196 parties, the CBD has almost universal ratification, except for the US. It is governed by a conference of the parties and supported by a **secretariat** and a Subsidiary Body on Scientific, Technical, and Technological Advice (see **Treaty design**). The CBD parties are obliged to develop national biodiversity strategies, integrate biodiversity conservation in all sectors, and establish systems of protected areas. The CBD is equipped with a monitoring mechanism—national **reporting**—and an incentive mechanism—the **Global Environment Facility**. Since 2012, biodiversity-related treaties are sought bolstered with stronger scientific pull through the Intergovernmental Panel on Biodiversity and Ecosystem Services (IPBES).

Spurring CBD negotiations were increased awareness and agreement that the rate of species extinction was extremely high compared with the natural average rate along with loss of genetic diversity in domesticated plants, with risks of reduced food security. A steady input of genetic material (seeds) is necessary for overcoming disease outbreaks or adjusting to climatic changes. This coincided with increased economic interests: The value of genetic resources was acknowledged as gene technology made patenting more feasible in the life sciences sectors (Kate and Laird 1999).

The bulk of terrestrial species diversity is found in tropical, mainly developing countries, and this gave them added pull in the CBD negotiations. Developing countries had a normative breakthrough for economic compensation: (1) for costly biodiversity conservation work and (2) for lack of revenues from technology-rich users, tending to patent genetic material that they access free of charge in the South (Rosendal 2000). CBD parties designed Access to Genetic Resources and Equitable Benefit Sharing (known as the ABS regime) to avoid misappropriation (biopiracy) of genetic resources (Shiva 1997). ABS was also seen as a prerequisite for conservation of biodiversity. The CBD reconfirmed national sovereign rights to genetic resources (see **Sovereignty**) and sought to balance intellectual property rights (IPRs) through the principles that access to genetic resources shall be on mutually agreed terms and be subject to prior informed consent (Swanson 1995). It has, however, proved difficult to transform the CBD principles into practical policies. While the bulk of developing (provider) countries have enacted ABS legislation, effective ABS implementation is unlikely without compatible legislation in user countries (Gehl Sampath 2005; Oberthür and Rosendal 2014). Implementation of the ABS regime is currently further complicated by technological developments in synthetic biology and digital genetic information (Lai 2019).

The CBD has developed two protocols. First, the Cartagena Protocol on **Biosafety** (2000) builds on a **precautionary principle** approach, establishing an advanced informed procedure to help countries in decisions on import of genetically modified organisms. Precaution potentially clashes with "sound science" principles of the **World Trade Organization** (WTO) (Falkner and Gupta 2009). Second, the Nagoya Protocol (2010) re-establishes the CBD objectives, aiming to remedy the lack of **implementation** of the ABS regime.

In addition to the direct economic values of genetic resources, biodiversity as a whole provides **ecosystem services**, such as local water and climate regulation, building materials, firewood, pollination, and soil fertility. There are also cultural, recreational, and intrinsic values of biodiversity (see **Ecocentrism**). The greatest threat to biodiversity lies in land use change, and the CBD ecosystem approach recommends reducing market distortions that undervalue natural systems and provide perverse incentives and subsidies (EC 2008). The CBD parties have repeatedly agreed on goals for halting and reversing the loss of biodiversity, last with the Aichi Targets (2010). Still, IPBES' Global Assessment Report (2019) concludes that biodiversity and ecosystem functions and services are rapidly deteriorating worldwide: Two-thirds of the world's oceans and three-quarters of terrestrial areas are significantly altered by human activities, with 85% of wetlands lost and 1 million of the world's species threatened by extinction. Failing to reverse the loss of biodiversity is expected to undermine 80% of the UN **Sustainable Development Goals** (SDGs), as biodiversity is key for agriculture, health and mitigating climate change (IPBES, 2019). With renewed aspirations, the Conference of the Parties aims to adopt a global biodiversity framework towards a 2050 Vision of "Living in Harmony with Nature." States are also currently negotiating a new international legally binding instrument under the United Nations Convention on the Law of the Sea on the conservation and sustainable use of marine biological diversity of areas beyond national jurisdiction (see **Ocean protection**).

The balance between ABS and IPRs remains contested. Also contested are safeguarding rights of **indigenous peoples and local communities**' traditional knowledge of biodiversity (Posey and Dutfield 1996). Increasingly studied are **institutional interactions**, including processes to enhance policy coherence between biodiversity-related conventions and the Food and Agriculture Organization (Chiarolla 2011), the WTO (Pavoni 2013) and the **climate change**

regime. IPCC (2019: 21) cautions (with *high confidence*) that climate measures such as bioenergy-plantations that greatly encourage demand for land conversion are unsustainable and increase the deterioration of ecosystems.

References

Chiarolla, Claudio. 2011. *Intellectual Property, Agriculture and Global Food Security—The Privatization of Crop Diversity*. Cheltenham and Northampton, Edward Elgar.

EC (European Communities). 2008. *The Economics of Ecosystems and Biodiversity*. Wesseling, Welzel and Hardt.

Falkner, Robert and Aarti Gupta. 2009. "The Limits of Regulatory Convergence: Globalization and GMO Politics in the South." *International Environmental Agreements* 9: 113–133.

Gehl Sampath, P. 2005. *Regulating Bioprospecting: Institutions for Drug Research, Access and Benefit Sharing*. New York, United Nations University.

IPBES. 2019. Global Assessment Report on Biodiversity and Ecosystem Services of the Intergovernmental Science-Policy Platform on Biodiversity and Ecosystem Services. Bonn, Germany, IPBES Secretariat.

IPCC. 2019. *Special Report on Climate Change and Land: Summary for Policymakers*. Draft, 7 August 2019.

Kate, Kary ten and Sarah Laird. 1999. *The Commercial Use of Biodiversity: Access to Genetic Resources and Benefit-Sharing*. London, Earthscan.

Lai, Hung-En, Caoimhe Canavan, Loren Cameron, Simon Moore, Monica Danchenko, Todd Kuiken, Suzana Sekeyová, and Paul S. Freemont. 2019. "Synthetic Biology and the United Nations." *Trends in Biotechnology* 37(11): 1146–1151. https://doi.org/10.1016/j.tibtech.2019.05.011

Oberthür, Sebastian and G. Kristin Rosendal (Eds.). 2014. *Global Governance of Genetic Resources: Access and Benefit Sharing after the Nagoya Protocol*. London, Routledge.

Pavoni, Riccardo. 2013. "The Nagoya Protocol and WTO Law." In *The 2010 Nagoya Protocol on Access and Benefit Sharing in Perspective*, Eds. Elisa Morgera, Matthias Buck, and Elsa Tsioumani, 185–213. Leiden, Martinus Nijhoff.

Posey, Darrel A. and Graham Dutfield. 1996. *Beyond Intellectual Property: Toward Traditional Resource Rights for Indigenous Peoples and Local Communities*. Ottawa, International Development Research Centre.

Rosendal, G. Kristin. 2000. *The Convention on Biological Diversity and Developing Countries*. Dordrecht, Kluwer Academic Publishers.

Shiva, Vandana. 1997. *Biopiracy: The Plunder of Nature and Knowledge*. Cambridge, MA, South End Press.

Swanson, Timothy (Ed.). 1995. *Intellectual Property Rights and Biodiversity Conservation*. Cambridge, Cambridge University Press.

BIOSAFETY

Robert Falkner

London School of Economics and Political Science, UK

Biosafety refers to the prevention of large-scale loss of biological integrity. In the context of agricultural biotechnology, it is more narrowly concerned with the potential threats to human health and the environment from genetically modified organisms (GMOs). Genetically modified (GM) crops were first introduced to commercial agriculture in 1996. In 2018, 26 countries grew 191.7 million hectares of GM crops (mainly maize, soybeans, cotton, and canola), of which over 90% were planted in just five countries (USA, Brazil, Argentina, Canada, India). GM crops have proved popular with some farmers and governments as they promise higher and more reliable agricultural yields. Critics point to several environmental risks, such as the reduction of biological diversity in GMO-growing areas and the potential to create new weeds through cross-pollination.

The United States and the European Union have adopted sharply divergent approaches to dealing with biosafety risks. While the EU requires comprehensive, technology-based regulation of GMO risks (see **Risk society**) based on the **precautionary principle**, the US relies on a product-based assessment of risks focused on scientifically proven harm (see **Science**). The transatlantic divide on biosafety reflects differences in regulatory institutions and styles and conflicting commercial interests, but also differences in cultural values (Stephan 2012). Despite losing a **World Trade Organization** (WTO) dispute over its precautionary GMO rules in 2006 (Punt and Wesseler 2016), the EU further strengthened its regulations by introducing a general labeling (see **Labeling and certification**) and traceability requirement for GMOs. Transatlantic regulatory polarization has had some influence on how developing countries regulate biosafety risks but has not prevented significant regulatory diversity to emerge in the Global South (Falkner and Gupta 2009).

At the international level, within the **biodiversity regime**, the Cartagena Protocol on Biosafety (CPB) to the Convention on Biological Diversity is the main regulatory regime for trade in GMOs. The CPB was adopted in 2000, after increasingly protracted negotiations between countries demanding strict rules on biosafety (EU and most developing countries) and a small US-led group of countries objecting to the trade-intrusive nature of the treaty (Falkner 2009). Supporters of the agreement welcome the fact that it strengthens a country's right to regulate, and potentially restrict, GMO imports based on the **precautionary principle**. In contrast, critics accuse the agreement of being in breach of WTO rules and undermining confidence in agricultural biotechnology (Wüger and Cottier 2008).

References

Falkner, Robert. 2009. "The Global Politics of Precaution: Explaining International Cooperation on Biosafety." In *Cooperating Without America: Theories and Case Studies of Non-Hegemonic Regimes*, Eds. Stefan Brem and Kendall Stiles, 105–122. London, Routledge.

Falkner, Robert and Aarti Gupta. 2009. "The Limits of Regulatory Convergence: Globalization and GMO Politics in the South." *International Environmental Agreements* 9(2): 113–133.

Punt, Maarten J. and Justus Wesseler. 2016. Legal But Costly: An Analysis of the EU GM Regulation in the Light of the WTO Trade Dispute Between the EU and the USA. *The World Economy* 39(1): 158–169.

Stephan, Hannes R. 2012. "Revisiting the Transatlantic Divergence over GMOs: Toward a Cultural-Political Analysis." *Global Environmental Politics* 12(4): 104–124.

Wüger, Daniel and Thomas Cottier (Eds.). 2008. *Genetic Engineering and the World Trade System*. Cambridge, Cambridge University Press.

BOUNDARY ORGANIZATIONS

Maria Carmen Lemos
University of Michigan, United States

Christine Kirchhoff
University of Connecticut, United States

The concept of a "boundary" for science emerged when scientists increasingly felt the need to demarcate scientific from other non-scientific activities. And while a hard boundary protected **science** from fraud or pseudo-science, it was less effective in areas where the production of science aimed to go beyond the identification and framing of a problem (i.e. basic science) to inform the design of solutions to address it (i.e. applied science). The existence and need for this boundary became increasingly contested as societies came to perceive the potential of science to solve humanities' super-wicked problems. The emphasis shifted from a total separation of science and decision-making towards a blurred boundary (Jasanoff 1990) that bridged science and decision-making while providing protection from both the undue influence of politics on science ("politicization of science") and the excessive domination of science in the design and implementation of policy ("scienticization of policy") (see **Treaty design** and **Compliance and implementation**).

Boundary organizations embody both a process and a structure whose primary purpose is to bridge and stabilize the gap between science and its practical application. As bridgers, boundary organizations facilitate the co-production of science and policy by sustaining collaboration between scientists and non-scientists and by brokering and tailoring scientific knowledge to different decision environments (Kirchhoff et al. 2013). For example, the Subsidiary Body on Scientific, Technical and Technological Advice to the Convention on Biological Diversity (CBD) (see **Biodiversity regime**) is a boundary organization aiming to bring science into the policy process to protect global biodiversity. As stabilizers, boundary organizations provide a forum that fosters the **participation** of multiple perspectives, the convergence of multiple knowledge systems, and the creation of peer communities around specific issues while allowing participants to remain within their professional boundaries and constituencies. Similarly, the Intergovernmental Panel on Climate Change (IPCC) plays this role in the **climate change regime** by helping to create a "fragile international knowledge order" including a broad range of scientific organizations and political and social actors from numerous countries and a variety of issue areas (Hoppe et al. 2013: 288). Both bridging and stabilizing are necessary for usability; without one or the other usability suffers. For example, as a stabilizer, the IPCC functions well; but, as a bridge to policy it is hamstrung by a variety of challenges in a highly politicized arena where climate is a super-wicked problem (Vardy et al. 2017).

Boundary organizations have at least three characteristics. First, they create a legitimizing space and sometimes incentivize the production and use of "boundary objects"—mechanisms, processes, material things, and even epistemologies that transcend the science/non-science divide and provide a means for producers and users of science to collaborate while maintaining their separate identities (Guston 2001; Star and Griesemer 1989). Second, boundary organizations involve information producers, users, and mediators in "boundary work"—efforts undertaken to protect science from political activities and pseudo-science

(Gieryn 1983). Third, boundary organizations reside between producer and user worlds, maintaining accountability to each while supporting a combined scientific and social order (Guston 2001).

References

Gieryn, Thomas F. 1983. "Boundary-work and the Demarcation of Science from Non-science: Strains and Interests in Professional Ideologies of Scientists." *American Sociological Review* 48(6): 781–795.

Guston, David H. 2001. "Boundary Organizations in Environmental Policy and Science: An Introduction." *Science, Technology, and Human Values* 26(4): 399–408.

Hoppe, Rob, Anna Wesselink, and Rose Cairns. 2013. "Lost in the Problem: The Role of Boundary Organizations in the Governance of Climate Change." *Wiley Interdisciplinary Reviews: Climate Change* 4(4): 283–300.

Jasanoff, Sheila. 1990. *The Fifth Branch: Science Advisers as Policymakers*. Cambridge, MA, Harvard University Press.

Kirchhoff, Christine J., Maria C. Lemos, and Suraje Dessai. 2013. "Actionable Knowledge for Environmental Decision Making: Broadening the Usability of Climate Science." *Annual Review of Environment and Natural Resources* 38(1): 393–414.

Star, Susan L. and James R. Griesemer. 1989. "Institutional Ecology, 'Translations' and Boundary Objects: Amateurs and Professionals in Berkeley's Museum of Vertebrate Zoology 1907–39." *Social Studies of Science* 19(3): 387–420.

Vardy, Mark, Michael Oppenheimer, Navroz K. Dubash, Jessica O'Reilly, and Dale Jamieson. 2017. "The Intergovernmental Panel on Climate Change: Challenges and Opportunities." *Annual Review of Environment and Resources* 42(1): 55–75.

BUSINESS AND CORPORATIONS

Doris Fuchs
University of Münster, Germany

Bastian Knebel
German-South African Youth Association, Germany

Business actors play a pivotal role in global environmental governance. They are active individually and via more or less formal roundtables, coalitions or associations, as well as through business initiated (and funded) **nongovernmental organizations** (BINGOs), at all levels of governance (see **Scale**). Formal business associations took a dominant role in the past, especially at the national and regional (European) levels (see **Regional governance**). Today, however, a substantial share of business influence generates from the activities of individual or small groups of transnational corporations (TNCs), which have realized that their interests frequently diverge from the interests of small and medium sized businesses and are able to invest enormous resources in political activities by themselves.

Research has shown that the power of (large) business actors in global governance in general, and in global environmental governance specifically, has dramatically increased over the last decades relative to the power of other players (civil society, states, but also small business actors) in the political arena (Fuchs 2005). In fact, one may argue that the only major remaining check on business power is provided by other businesses. In other words, business influence is relatively more limited in those instances in which corporations lobby on more than one side. However, on many of the major questions of (de-)regulation large business actors tend to agree.

An interesting question regarding business's role in global (environmental) governance, moreover, relates to the question of the intertwining of corporate power and state power (Nölke and May 2018) (see also **Critical political economy**). While a focus on the transnational nature of corporate activity has been dominant in research, for a long time, recent publications have argued that we also need to take into account the territorial dimension of corporate power (Mikler 2018). Such arguments are supported by the recent rise in international disputes, relating to tariffs, subsidies, **taxation** as well as other aspects of regulation (such as **transparency** or accounting).

From a theoretical standpoint, the power of business and corporations in global environmental governance can be differentiated on the basis of how this power is exercised. Fuchs (2005), for example, uses a three-dimensional framework to differentiate between business's instrumental, material-structural, and ideational-structural (discursive) power. In this conceptualization, instrumental power is the power business actors exercise on policy outputs via lobbying or campaign financing. The material structuralist perspective captures corporations' agenda-setting power, i.e. influence on the input side of the political process, deriving from their status in global political economy and control over investments, jobs, and market access. In turn, ideational (or discursive) power shapes societal perceptions and values through the promotion of certain ideas, such as **corporate social responsibility**, or the characterization of actors, for example.

Importantly, TNCs have increasingly become rule-setters in global governance themselves, via **private regimes**, for instance in terms of voluntary **labeling and certification** schemes, or public–private **partnerships**, in the last decades. This development indicates an enormous acquisition of political authority and legitimacy, while its implications are very controversial among scholars and practitioners. Some observers argue that private actors effectively and efficiently help overcome international problems of collective action, and contribute to the production of **global public goods**. Other observers, however, argue that private environmental governance often is limited to greenwashing activities. For instance, statistical analyses have failed to find evidence of a positive influence of the Responsible Care program and membership on the rate of environmental improvement among its members supporting such perspectives (King and Lenox 2000). Critical observers also point out that business investment in environmental governance is (only) likely in cases in which win–win situations exist, e.g. improvements in energy efficiency leading to a reduction of production costs. Numerous areas of environmental concern exist, however, in which the costs of addressing environmental problems outweigh the economic benefit to business actors.

Prominent examples of private rule-setting activities are the ISO 14000 series of environmental management standards and standards for "sustainable" forestry (see **Audits**). The ISO 14000 standard has been criticized for weak environmental prescriptions and yet was adopted by the International Organization for Standardization in 1996 and soon recognized by other international governmental organizations (Clapp 1998). Private forestry standards, in contrast, started in a promising way, when a coalition of business, trade unions, **indigenous peoples and local communities**, and environmental **nongovernmental organizations** developed the Forest Stewardship Council's (FSC) **labeling and certification** scheme. However, coalitions of business actors soon developed competing labels with weaker standards (e.g. the Sustainable Forestry Initiative of the American Pulp and Paper Association), which provide a source of confusion to consumers and serve to undermine the effectiveness of the FSC label (Gale 2002).

Most fundamentally, such labeling and certification schemes are of little help when it comes to sufficiency and **degrowth**, prerequisites for humanity to stay within planetary boundaries according to many scholars of global sustainability governance (Kalfagianni et al. 2019, see also **Critical political economy** and **Carrying capacities paradigm**). Indeed, the major challenge for business now and in the future is that much of the global economy is built on promoting mass production and consumption. Few if any successful business models exist to promote sufficient lifestyles. Thus, business opposition to effective global environmental governance that can be noted in practice cannot come as a surprise.

In sum, business actors in general and corporations in particular have become decisive actors in global environmental governance. Their power challenges not only national **sovereignty** but also international regulatory approaches and democracy in general. More fundamentally, their power poses a major challenge to the urgently needed sustainability transformation.

References

Clapp, Jennifer. 1998. "The Privatization of Global Environmental Governance." *Global Governance* 4(3): 295–316.

Fuchs, Doris. 2005. "Commanding Heights? The Strength and Fragility of Business Power in Global Politics." *Millennium – Journal of International Studies* 33(3): 771–801.

Gale, Fred. 2002. "Caveat Certificatium." In *Confronting Consumption*, Eds. Thomas Princen, Michael Maniates, and Ken Conca, 275–300. Cambridge, MA, MIT Press.

Kalfagianni, Agni, Lena Partzsch, and Miriam Beulting. 2019. "Governance for Global Stewardship: Can Private Certification Move Beyond Commodification in Fostering Sustainability Transformations?" *Agriculture and Human Values*. Epub ahead of print July 5, 2019. https://doi.org/10.1007/s10460-019-09971-w

King, Andrew and Michael Lenox. 2000. "Industry Self-Regulation without Sanctions." *Academy of Management Journal* 43(4): 698–716.

Mikler, John. 2018. *The Political Power of Corporations*. London, Polity.

Nölke, Andreas and Christian May (Eds.). 2018. *Handbook of the International Political Economy of the Corporation*. Cheltenham, Edward Elgar.

CARRYING CAPACITIES PARADIGM

Nathan F. Sayre

University of California at Berkeley, United States

Adam Romero

University of Washington Bothell, United States

Carrying capacity can be defined as *the quantity of some X that can or should be supported or conveyed by some Y*; in most of its many applications, exceeding a carrying capacity is considered damaging to X, Y, or both.

Scholars in many fields have discarded the concept of carrying capacity, but it persists and has in recent decades proliferated in debates about human populations and the environmental conditions on which they depend at the **scale** of Earth or significant subunits thereof. Although the term itself is not always used, carrying capacity is thus a pivotal idea for the **Anthropocene**, **population sustainability**, and **sustainable development**.

The carrying capacities paradigm can be defined as the suite of methods, concepts, and assumptions that inform and support the view that human–environment interactions can and should be understood in terms of the $X:Y$ ratios that carrying capacities describe or prescribe. Developing and improving methods to measure and communicate such ratios is central to debates about the limits to growth, **ecosystem services**, planetary boundaries, and natural capital. But the origins and implications of the paradigm's supporting concepts and assumptions frequently pass unexamined.

At its origins in the mid-twentieth century, the paradigm married the concerns of neo-Malthusians regarding world population with the methods of systems analysis and **scenarios**. The most influential example is *The Limits to Growth* (Meadows et al. 1972), the landmark report of the Club of Rome's Project on the Predicament of Mankind. After defining the Predicament as reconciling economic and population growth with the limits of a finite world, the Club—a think-tank of "world citizens" from business, politics, and academia—turned to Professor Jay Forrester (1971) of the Massachusetts Institute of Technology to develop "a formal, written model of the world" based on "the scientific method, systems analysis, and the modern computer" (Meadows et al. 1972: 21).

Although far more sophisticated than Malthus's principle of population, *The Limits to Growth* model relied, like Malthus, on the mathematical disparity between arithmetic and geometric (or exponential) growth. Exponential or "nonlinear" growth involves complicated positive feedbacks among subsystems; left unchecked, the authors warned, "the limits to growth on this planet will be reached sometime in the next one hundred years. The most probable result will be a rather sudden and uncontrollable decline in both population and industrial capacity" (Meadows et al. 1972: 23).

The Limits to Growth sparked raging debates in scholarly and policy realms, and its authors have twice published updates based on current data and model refinements (Meadows et al. 1992, 2004). But the basic conceptual framework has persisted while tools for quantifying the Xs and Ys of carrying capacity have proliferated. These include the "IPAT

31

formula" (Impact = Population × Affluence × Technology), and eco-logical footprint analysis, which measures humanity's impacts in terms of the number of planets identical to Earth needed to supply our demands and absorb our wastes indefinitely (Wackernagel and Rees 1996). Values over 1.0 indicate and quantify "overshoot," and were reached in the late twentieth century; online "calculators" now enable consumers, investors, firms, **cities**, and nations to measure their ecological footprints in units of land and water.

More recently, a team of prominent scholars has proposed "planetary boundaries," a suite of nine metrics that together define "the dynamic biophysical 'space' of the Earth System in which humanity has evolved and thrived." Three of the nine boundaries have already been surpassed (related to climate, biodiversity, and nitrogen), while two others remain unquantified because of insufficient scientific knowledge (atmospheric aerosols and chemical pollution). More precautionary than predictive, these scholars characterize "the human predicament in the Anthropocene" as a paradox of high system resilience coupled with the potential for abrupt catastrophic change (Rockström et al. 2009).

Criticisms of the carrying capacities paradigm have also persisted, mainly among economists and other proponents of **liberal environ-mentalism** and **ecological modernization**. Some have challenged the quality of the models used in *The Limits to Growth* and subsequent studies. Others have simply dismissed the paradigm's advocates as Cassandras whose predictions of collapse have failed the test of time. The recent world economic crisis and growing evidence of anthropo-genic climate change, on the other hand, have buttressed the paradigm's supporters, who point out that Cassandra was, in fact, correct.

Overlooked in the debates are the underlying concepts and assumptions of the carrying capacities paradigm itself. From systems analysis, it inherited a commitment to models that were necessarily bounded and closed, so that they could be constructed and run as com-plex programs of equations and algorithms (see **Thermoeconomics**). This was (and arguably still is) seen as the cutting edge of scientific and technological practice, but it can account neither for un-modeled exogenous factors, nor for endogenous qualitative change in the model components and variables themselves.

Even more serious are the conceptual difficulties internal to the concept of carrying capacity itself. It would seem impossible, by def-inition, that humanity's ecological footprint could exceed 1.0 Earths.

Proponents aver that lags in system response permit such a scenario. But this begs the question. Any $X:Y$ ratio derived from logic or models is an idealist postulate, empirical violations of which necessitate the invocation of some mediating factor or opposing force that simultaneously enforces the putative limits—if not immediately, then in some indefinite future—and explains (away) the disparity between the ideal and the real. Exploiting the combination of positive and normative in its very definition, carrying capacity becomes immune to empirical test (Sayre 2008).

Over-shoot, in systems analysis, refers not to the measured disparity between burden and capacity, but to the failure of effective feedback mechanisms to enforce the postulated limit. Proponents of the carrying capacities paradigm are, in effect, trying to function as such a mechanism by alerting society to the growing environmental and social ills of industrial capitalism. It is a salutary ambition, but the rhetorical power of quantitative science does not appear sufficient to the task.

References

Forrester, Jay W. 1971. *World Dynamics*. Cambridge, Wright-Allen Press Inc.

Meadows, Donella H., Dennis L. Meadows, Jorgen Randers, and William W. Behrens III. 1972. *The Limits to Growth*. New York, Universe Books.

Meadows, Donella H., Dennis L. Meadows, and Jorgen Randers. 1992. *Beyond the Limits*. Post Mills, VT, Chelsea Green Publishing.

Meadows, Donella H., Jorgen Randers, and Dennis L. Meadows. 2004. *Limits to Growth: The 30-Year Update*. White River Junction, VT, Chelsea Green Publishing.

Rockström, Johan, Will Steffen, Kevin Noone, Åsa Persson, F. Stuart Chapin III, Eric Lambin, Timothy M. Lenton, Marten Scheffer, Carl Folke, Hans Joachim Schellnhuber, Björn Nykvist, Cynthia A. de Wit, Terry Hughes, Sander van der Leeuw, Henning Rodhe, Sverker Sörlin, Peter K. Snyder, Robert Costanza, Uno Svedin, Malin Falkenmark, Louise Karlberg, Robert W. Corell, Victoria J. Fabry, James Hansen, Brian Walker, Diana Liverman, Katherine Richardson, Paul Crutzen, and Jonathan Foley. 2009. "Planetary Boundaries: Exploring the Safe Operating Space for Humanity." *Ecology and Society* 14(2): 32.

Sayre, Nathan F. 2008. "The Genesis, History, and Limits of Carrying Capacity." *Annals of the Association of American Geographers* 98(1): 120–134.

Wackernagel, Mathis and William E. Rees. 1996. *Our Ecological Footprint*. Philadelphia, PA, New Society Publishers.

CITES

Daniel Compagnon

Sciences Po Bordeaux, France

The Convention on International Trade in Endangered Species of Wild Fauna and Flora (CITES) addresses one of the sources of biodiversity depletion, the global trade in wildlife and wildlife products. Booming with globalization it is worth billions of dollars every year. Although not all animals and plants regulated under CITES are threatened with extinction, unlike the black rhino, the Asian tiger or the African elephant, the widely publicized Red List of Threatened Species released annually since 1963 by the International Union for Conservation of Nature (IUCN) vindicates the need for international cooperation to regulate trade in wildlife (see **Conservation and preservation**).

A draft text adopted by the IUCN congress in 1963 led to the agreement signed in Washington on March 3rd, 1973. The convention came into force on July 1st, 1975, and there are now 183 parties to it. Adopted in the wake of the 1972 Stockholm conference, it is one of the few multilateral environmental agreements (see **Regimes**) where the United States—on the basis of its robust domestic conservation legislation—still plays the role of a lead state, and one reflecting from the onset predominantly Western concerns about wildlife protection (Mofson 1997).

About 35,000 species are listed on Appendix 1 (banning trade), Appendix 2 (allowing limited trade with a quota system), or Appendix 3 (voluntary listing by at least one range state to monitor trade) with different sets of countries involved, and various political and economic implications. Therefore, it is more an aggregation of species-specific sub-regimes within a common framework. CITES has been shaped by norms and ideas as much as power relations or economic interests: the concept of "endangered species" for instance was constructed through intense debates over the case of the African elephant or big whales (Epstein 2006), in particular the debate between **conservation and preservation** (Mofson 1997: 168, 180).

Relying on a system of imports/exports permits enforced by the member states' customs and police, CITES is a relatively effective agreement in terms of outputs and outcomes (see **Effectiveness**), but its impact has remained limited if only because the causal relationship between trade and species extinction is problematic in most cases (Curlier and Andresen 2001) —as exemplified by the controversy over the polar bear at the 2013 Conference of the Parties (COP). There are also several loopholes in the treaty: as a two-thirds majority vote is required for (de) listing, a small number of range states and partners in trade can exert a veto power. In addition, a member state can enter reservations alleging vital national interests within 90 days of the decision's adoption, and is then considered a non-party for such listing.

In practice, few of the 30–50 listing decisions voted at an average COP session are really controversial and in most cases outvoted states— even powerful ones—tend to accept unpalatable decisions, to preserve the credibility of the institution. Even the most discontented parties— such as the Southern Africa states after the 1989 elephant ivory ban— tend to remain in the regime and attempt to change it from within (Mofson 1997).

Although a species listing allocates costs and benefits to different parties and, therefore, is opened to bargaining, coalition building, and veto power, CITES passed numerous decisions through logic or arguing rather than bargaining. CITES procedures tend to favor decisions based on reasoned arguments largely—if not unequivocally—science-based, as population **assessments** are usually disputed. The COP adopts or rejects proposals put forward by the Secretariat (see **Secretariats**), based on scientific information and a large deliberation process, in line with the reinforced listing criteria adopted in 1994 at COP 9 in Fort Lauderdale. When such consensus emerges stakeholders' bargaining power has limited impact even on reservations entered (Gehring and Ruffing 2008).

CITES' effectiveness relying on a capacity to enforce specific trade sanctions (Sand 2013) is limited, however, by **compliance and implementation** deficits in many range states, in particular in least developed countries (LDCs), where political commitment and state enforcement capacities are often very weak (Compagnon et al. 2012), but also **emerging countries** where demand is thriving for illegally traded wildlife products (Zimmerman 2003) (see **Transnational crime**).

References

Compagnon, Daniel, Sander Chan, and Ayçem Mert. 2012. "The Changing Role of the State." In *Global Environmental Governance Reconsidered*, Eds. Frank Biermann and Philipp Pattberg, 237–263. Cambridge, MA, MIT Press.

Curlier, Maaria and Steinar Andresen. 2001. "International Trade in Endangered Species: The CITES Regime." In *Environmental Regime Effectiveness: Confronting Theory with Evidence*, Eds. Edward L. Miles, Arild Underdal, Steinar Andresen, Jørgen Wettestad, Jon Birger Skjaerseth, and Elaine M. Carlin, 357–378. Cambridge, MA, MIT Press.

Epstein, Charlotte. 2006. "The Making of Global Environmental Norms: Endangered Species Protection." *Global Environmental Politics* 6(2): 32–54.

Gehring, Thomas and Eva Ruffing. 2008. "When Arguments Prevail Over Power: The CITES Procedure for the Listing of Endangered Species." *Global Environmental Politics* 8(2): 123–148.

Mofson, Phyllis. 1997. "Zimbabwe and CITES: Illustrating the Reciprocal Relationship between the State and the International Regime." In *The Internationalization of Environmental Protection*, Eds. Miranda A. Schreurs and Elisabeth C. Economy, 162–187. Cambridge, Cambridge University Press.

Sand, Peter H. 2013. "Enforcing CITES: The Rise and Fall of Trade Sanctions." *Review of European, Comparative and International Environmental Law* 22(3): 251–263.

Zimmerman, Mara E. 2003. "The Black Market for Wildlife: Combating Transnational Organized Crime in the Illegal Wildlife Trade." *Vanderbilt Journal of Transnational Law* 36: 1657–1689.

CITIES

Marielle Papin

Université Laval, Canada

Cities can be broadly viewed as spaces in which large numbers of people live and work, and which represent hubs for governments, commerce and services, and transportation. The proliferation and the expansion of cities represent major trends of the twenty-first century. Urban areas today gather 55% of the world's population. A crucial issue related to their spread is their environmental footprint. In addition to issues of soil erosion, biodiversity loss, and high water demand, urban areas produce around 70% of all greenhouse gas emissions. They are themselves vulnerable to environmental change.

Despite their growing environmental impacts, a paradigm shift has started to see cities as promising entities for climate and environmental governance (Elmqvist et al. 2018; Bulkeley 2013). Problems of coordination among states have indeed led observers to look for solutions to be developed by non-state actors, including cities. As local actors, cities generally manage water demand, waste, energy efficiency, and mobility. Direct access to various resources enables them to experiment and adopt innovative environmental policies. Cities have also progressively become global actors. Global cities, which attract vast amounts of financial and political resources, are prominent in globalization processes (Sassen 1991). Furthermore, the growing entanglement of sectors and levels of action of global governance facilitates the formal and informal participation of cities in decision-making processes. Cities further act in global environmental governance through **transgovernmental networks** of municipalities. These enable cities to exchange information and obtain technical, political, and financial tools to strengthen their actions and defend their interests in global environmental institutions.

The question of the **effectiveness** of cities is often raised, however. In the case of climate change, although numerous promising local policies have propagated, their mitigation effects appear insufficient. Since they remain constrained by a lack of resources needed to sustain their efforts, cities will unlikely lead to the rapid greenhouse gas emission decrease needed. Yet, the scope of the current environmental crisis requires looking beyond commonly used short-term quantitative metrics of effectiveness. It is necessary to question the possible contribution of cities to a transformative change that will radically alter the current production and consumption system. Doing so implies assessing qualitatively the capacity of cities to foster new path-dependent policies in line with decarbonization and sustainability examining, for instance, how these initiatives might affect other **scales** (van der Ven et al. 2017). Through this lens, cities' actions might have a catalytic effect, which, in the years to come, will prove crucial to global environmental governance.

References

Bulkeley, Harriet. 2013. *Cities and Climate Change*. New York, Routledge.

Elmqvist, Thomas, Xuemei Bai, Niki Frantzeskaki, Corrie Griffith, David Maddox, Timon McPhearson, Susan Parnell, Patricia Romero-Lankao, David Simon, and Mark Watkins. 2018. *Urban Planet*. Cambridge, Cambridge University Press.

Sassen, Saskia. 1991. *The Global City: New York, London, Tokyo*. Princeton, NJ, Princeton University Press.

van der Ven, Hamish, Steven Bernstein, and Matthew Hoffmann. 2017. "Valuing the Contributions of Nonstate and Subnational Actors to Climate Governance." *Global Environmental Politics* 17(1): 1–20.

CLIMATE CHANGE REGIME

Harro van Asselt

University of Eastern Finland, Finland

Climate change gained prominence on the international political agenda in the 1980s, due to an emerging scientific consensus about the anthropogenic causes of the problem and heightened public awareness. The commencement of **treaty negotiations** in 1990 exposed the diverging viewpoints of developed and developing countries on international climate policy (Bodansky 1993). The 1992 United Nations Framework Convention on Climate Change (UNFCCC) delivered a compromise through a framework agreement that postponed the more difficult questions related to its overall ambition and the distribution of efforts. All countries acknowledged that developed countries had emitted the bulk of greenhouse gases during their rapid industrialization processes and that these countries should lead by reducing their emissions and provide financial and technological assistance to developing countries. However, the Convention did not include legally binding emission reduction targets or specify how much assistance was needed.

The ultimate objective of the UNFCCC is to achieve "stabilization of greenhouse gas concentrations in the atmosphere at a level that would prevent dangerous anthropogenic interference with the climate system" (Article 2). In addition, the Convention lists several principles, most importantly that of **common but differentiated responsibilities** (CBDR). This principle was effectuated in the Convention by the introduction of a binary system of obligations for developed (Annex I) and for developing (non-Annex I) countries.

Following the framework-protocol example of the **ozone regime**, the 1997 Kyoto Protocol elaborated on the Convention's provisions by introducing legally binding emission targets for developed countries, which agreed to reduce their emissions by 5% compared with 1990 levels between 2008 and 2012. To assist developed countries in achieving these targets, it also introduced three **market**-based flexibility mechanisms: Joint Implementation, the Clean Development Mechanism (CDM), and international emissions trading. It further established a novel mechanism for promoting **compliance and implementation**. However, critics of the Protocol (e.g. Victor 2011) point to: the Kyoto targets' low ambition levels; the absence of targets for developing countries; the limited contribution of flexibility mechanisms to global greenhouse gas emission reductions; and weaknesses in the compliance mechanism (which did not prevent Canada from withdrawing from the Protocol in 2011).

In the mid-2000s, international climate talks began to focus on how to continue after the first commitment period of the Kyoto Protocol would end in 2012. These negotiations displayed fault lines among parties in particular with respect to the Annex I/non-Annex I "firewall." Concerned by the growing emissions of **emerging countries** such as China, developed countries such as the United States argued that developing countries should step up their mitigation efforts. Developing countries, however, were disappointed by the lack of progress of developed countries, in particular with respect to the provision of climate finance and the transfer of clean technologies.

In 2007, countries began to negotiate a new climate agreement, but two years later they notoriously failed to do so. The 2009 Copenhagen Accord—which was negotiated among a very small group of countries—nevertheless signaled how the regime was going to evolve (Bodansky 2016). The direction indicated by the Copenhagen Accord was one that shifts from the "targets-and-timetables" approach introduced by the Kyoto Protocol, toward a system of self-selected mitigation actions accompanied by international **reporting** and review procedures. Under this new approach, differentiation between developed and developing countries was becoming increasingly less important.

This shift was confirmed when countries commenced negotiations on a new international climate agreement for the post-2020 period in 2012. These negotiations resulted in the 2015 Paris Agreement, in which countries agreed to submit five-yearly national climate plans, known as "nationally determined contributions" (NDCs), with a view to achieving the long-term goal of keeping global warming well below 2 degrees Celsius (and make efforts to keep it below 1.5 degrees). The NDCs are not legally binding, but they need to conform to the **principle of non-regression**. Moreover, in addition to introducing new reporting and review procedures applying to all countries and a mechanism for compliance and implementation, the Paris Agreement established a five-yearly "global stocktake" to assess countries' collective ambitions. Although the Paris Agreement moved away from the bifurcation between developed and developing countries that characterized the UNFCCC and the Kyoto Protocol, it introduced new ways of differentiation tailored to specific issues, such as mitigation, **adaptation**, finance, and **transparency** (Rajamani 2016). Moreover, to appease concerns by developing countries, the Paris Agreement puts greater emphasis on issues that matter most to developing countries, such as the provision of climate finance, and loss and damage arising from climate change impacts.

The Paris Agreement thus heralds a new era of international cooperation on climate change. However, whether its ambitious goals will be achieved will much depend on domestic implementation (Keohane and Victor 2016). Although participation is near-universal, the announcement by the world's second-largest emitter, the United States, that it would withdraw at the earliest possible opportunity in 2020, is a sign of the challenges ahead. Nevertheless, in 2018 countries agreed on the main rules to put the Paris Agreement in practice, meaning that most of the attention is shifting toward the ambition levels of countries' NDCs.

While primarily directed at states, the Paris outcome also draws attention to climate actions taken by non-state actors such as **cities**, **business and corporations**, and **nongovernmental organizations** in areas such as carbon markets, promoting renewable energy (see **Energy transition**), reducing short-lived climate pollutants, and tackling deforestation (Hoffmann 2011; Hale 2016). It thereby seeks to advance the global response to climate change, reaping the benefits of its fragmented nature and **polycentricity** (Biermann et al. 2009; Jordan et al. 2018).

References

Biermann, Frank, Philipp Pattberg, Harro van Asselt, and Fariborz Zelli. 2009. "The Fragmentation of Global Governance Architectures: A Framework for Analysis." *Global Environmental Politics* 9(4): 14–40.

Bodansky, Daniel M. 1993. "The United Nations Framework Convention on Climate Change: A Commentary." *Yale Journal of International Law* 18(2): 451–558.

Bodansky, Daniel M. 2016. "The Paris Climate Change Agreement: A New Hope?" *American Journal of International Law* 110(2): 288–319.

Hale, Thomas. 2016. ""All Hands on Deck": The Paris Agreement and Nonstate Climate Action." *Global Environmental Politics* 16(3): 12–22.

Hoffmann, Matthew J. 2011. *Climate Governance at the Crossroads.* New York, Oxford University Press.

Jordan, Andrew, Dave Huitema, Harro van Asselt, and Johanna Forster (Eds.). 2018. *Governing Climate Change: Polycentricity in Action?* Cambridge, Cambridge University Press.

Keohane, Robert O., and David G. Victor. 2016. "Cooperation and Discord in Global Climate Policy." *Nature Climate Change* 6: 570–575.

Rajamani, Lavanya. 2016. "Ambition and Differentiation in the 2015 Paris Agreement: Interpretative Possibilities and Underlying Politics." *International & Comparative Law Quarterly* 65(2): 493–514.

Victor, David G. 2011. *Global Warming Gridlock*. Cambridge, Cambridge University Press.

COMMON BUT DIFFERENTIATED RESPONSIBILITIES

Steve Vanderheiden

University of Colorado Boulder, United States

The 1992 Rio Earth Summit yielded two influential formulations of this principle of international law and North–South equity in **sustainable development**. The first, from the Rio Declaration, states that:

> In view of the different contributions to global environmental degradation, states have common but differentiated responsibilities. The developed countries acknowledge the responsibility that they bear in the international pursuit of sustainable development in view of the pressures their societies place on the global environment and of the technologies and financial resources they command.
>
> (Principle 7)

In the second, 192 signatory nations adopted this "common but differentiated responsibilities" (or CBDR) framework for assigning national climate change burdens through the **climate change regime**. While the primary manifestation of CBDR in international climate policy development was in the division of parties into Annex I developed countries that were assigned greenhouse gas reduction targets under the 1997 Kyoto Protocol and non-Annex I developing country parties that were not, the principle suggests bases for further differentiation of climate change-related burdens. As a result, scholars look to this treaty language in an effort to apply CBDR principles to the design of fair or just burden-sharing arrangements, despite the shift away from prescribed national mitigation burdens under the 2015 Paris Agreement.

Scholars identify CBDR as a key burden-sharing principle, along with equity and capacity, which appear alongside it in the treaty, but interpret those principles differently and defend them in various combinations in articulating competing **environmental justice** frameworks. Equity has often been taken to entail equal per capita national emissions entitlements, while scholars typically rely upon gross domestic product (GDP) or renewable energy potential as measures of "respective capability," with more affluent states being assigned greater burdens and poorer ones lesser burdens or categorical exemptions from mandatory action. Some have suggested modifications that account for shares of GDP associated with development interests (Baer et al. 2009), and others use capacity as a proxy for beneficiary-pays principles on the assumption that states benefitting most from past emissions are more affluent as a result (Page 2012).

Neither equity nor capacity has received the attention paid by scholars to CBDR, which has been interpreted in two primary ways with several variants on each. Since it appeals to each party's "differentiated responsibility" for contributing to climate change, this responsibility is widely viewed as a function of national greenhouse gas emissions. However, different approaches focus upon different national emissions data, and propose different modifications to that data in order to arrive at distinct burden-sharing formulae. Historical responsibility approaches rely upon each nation's full historical emissions, going back to early industrialization, resulting in relatively greater responsibility assigned to early industrializers such as Europe and the United States and relatively lesser burdens for later-developing countries, for example **emerging countries** such as China and India (Shue 1999). Others propose baseline years before which national emissions are exempted from responsibility **assessments**, arguing that prior emissions resulted from excusable ignorance, thus constituting causal but not moral responsibility for climate change. 1990 is often proposed as a baseline year, since it marked the release of the first Intergovernmental Panel on Climate Change assessment report (see also **Boundary organizations**), clearly linking human activities with climate change and thus undermining subsequent claims that governments lacked adequate knowledge of such causes.

Apart from differences in national greenhouse gas emissions records used to assess differentiated responsibility, scholars have proposed other modifications to or exemptions from such emissions data. Drawing on analyses similar to those associated with excusable ignorance, in which parties are held liable for that share of their causal contributions to a problem for which they can be faulted or expected to act otherwise (see **Liability**), some have proposed distinctions between those emissions associated with meeting basic needs (or survival emissions) and those associated with further affluence (or luxury emissions), counting the latter but exempting the former from national responsibility assessments (Vanderheiden 2008). If accepted, this exemption would shift burdens away from developing countries with relatively low per capita emissions onto developed countries with relatively high luxury emissions. Similarly, scholars have proposed variations in calculation of survival emissions in order to account for geographical or other differences in the energy or land use budgets needed to satisfy basic needs.

All CBDR formulations share the normative foundation for assigning national burdens for climate change in some version of the **polluter pays principle**, but interpret the demands of that principle differently. Historical responsibility versions follow accounts based on strict liability, assigning national burdens in proportion to total historical national emissions, given the long atmospheric life of greenhouse gases and commitment to viewing causation as the basis for responsibility. Those proposing various exemptions to national emissions records invoke fault-based interpretations of the principle, appealing either to legal constructions of fault in liability or accounts of moral responsibility that distinguish between faultless and culpable causation. In addition to offering competing formulations of that principle, scholars defend competing burden-sharing formulae in which versions of CBDR are paired with equity or capacity principles (Caney 2005), combining multiple environmental justice principles.

Politically, CBDR remains a core ideal for burden-sharing arrangements associated with international climate policy, and of sustainable development more generally, but one around which agreement has been elusive. Since different formulations entail different assignments of national liability for climate change, national delegations to climate policy conferences tend to endorse formulations that reflect national interests, with India defending historical responsibility approaches combined with exemptions for survival emissions and developed countries generally seeking to avoid official adoption of responsibility-based liability criteria. The United States has expressly rejected any interpretation of CBDR in international law that implies acceptance of "any international obligations or liabilities, or any diminution in the responsibilities of developing countries" (French 2000). Nonetheless, considerations of environmental justice in international efforts to fairly allocate the burdens associated with climate change demand that attention be paid to the development of such principles, acceptable versions of which may be necessary for the world's nations to overcome the **tragedy of the commons** that frustrates cooperative international action on climate change and produce agreement upon effective remedial climate policy architecture.

References

Baer, Paul, Tom Athanasiou, Sivan Kartha, and Eric Kemp-Benedict. 2009. "Greenhouse Development Rights: A Proposal for a Fair Climate Treaty." *Ethics, Place and Environment* 12(3): 267–281.

Caney, Simon. 2005. "Cosmopolitan Justice, Responsibility, and Global Climate Change." *Leiden Journal of International Law* 18(4): 747–775.

French, Duncan. 2000. "Developing States and International Environmental Law: The Importance of Differentiated Responsibilities." *International and Comparative Law Quarterly* 49(1): 35–60.

Page, Edward. 2012. "Give it Up for Climate Change: A Defense of the Beneficiary Pays Principle." *International Theory* 4(2): 300–330.

Shue, Henry. 1999. "Global Environment and International Inequality." *International Affairs* 75(3): 531–545.

Vanderheiden, Steve. 2008. *Atmospheric Justice: A Political Theory of Climate Change.* New York, Oxford University Press.

COMMON HERITAGE OF HUMANITY

Scott J. Shackelford

Indiana University, United States

In 1968, during the 22nd session of the UN General Assembly, Arvid Pardo, the Maltese delegate, called for an international **regime** to "govern the deep seabed" under international waters (Viikari 2002: 33) (see also **Ocean protection**). He proposed that the seabed should be declared the common heritage of humanity (CHH), which it eventually became in 1970, leading to Pardo being called the "Father of the Law of the Sea conference." What made the CHH concept so revolutionary is that it was the first codification of a common property rights concept that transcended national **sovereignty**. Instead of countries, the CHH dealt directly with humanity as a whole in a way that "transcends national boundaries and unites all peoples under the flag of universalism," a form of cosmopolitan global governance (Baslar 1998: 25).

The CHH arose from two observations. First, some valuable natural resources, such as the ones managed under the **fisheries governance**, were close to exhaustion, and developing nations wanted to

44

ensure that they had some degree of access before they were depleted. Second, the technological divide between developing and developed nations prohibited developing states from reaping the rewards that the developed nations would enjoy as technological advances enabled access to valuable new resource domains, unless **technology transfer** was enforced. The notion was to create a level playing field or, short of that, to share benefits equitably (Baslar 1998: 301).

Neither scholars nor policymakers have agreed on a common understanding of the CHH, but a working definition would likely comprise five main elements (Frakes 2003: 411–413). First, there can be no appropriation of a common heritage space, though some scholars have argued that this prohibition should not necessarily be viewed as a significant impediment to regulation (Baslar 1998: 90, 235). Second, "it required a system of management in which all users have a right to share" (Goldie 1983: 87). As collective management is impractical, though, a specialized agency must be created to aid in coordination, such as the International Seabed Authority (ISA) that manages deep seabed mining. Third, all nations must share in the benefits derived from exploiting global common pool resources in common heritage regions. Fourth, these spaces should be used for peaceful purposes. But what constitutes "peaceful" differs depending on the common heritage region in question; the **Antarctic Treaty System**, for example, equates peaceful use with barring "any measures of a military nature" (Baslar 1998: 106), which differs from the more permissive definition in the 1967 Treaty on Principles Governing the Activities of States in the Exploration and Use of Outer Space, Including the Moon and Other Celestial Bodies. The latter accord, commonly known as the Outer Space Treaty, preserves space "exclusively for peaceful purposes" and even addresses the "harmful contamination" of outer space, but it has not directly led to the sustainable, peaceful use of space, in part because of ambiguity in the treaty language (see **Space debris**). Finally, common heritage regions must be protected for posterity, highlighting the intergenerational equity considerations at the heart of the CHH (see **Justice**).

The CHH concept has been the subject of debate in disciplines ranging from archaeology and economics to public international law, including space law and international environment law. It is now treaty law in the 1982 **Law of the Sea Convention** of the United Nations, the 1983 International Understanding on Plant Genetic Resources, and has found expression in the controversial 1979 Agreement Governing the Activities of States on the Moon and Other Celestial Bodies. However, the amorphous CHH concept that has in large part governed global commons areas since the 1960s is under stress (Baslar 1998: 372–373). For example, international environmental treaties have avoided CHH terminology to describe the atmosphere (Boyle 1991: 1–3).

What, then, is the future of the CHH concept and its ability to ward off a **tragedy of the commons**? Some legal scholars such as Professor Kemal Baslar have argued for a return to common property regulation through recognizing the CHH in environmental governance as a **human and environmental right** and general principle of international law, which could foster greater acceptance of the concept by the international community (1998: 368–369). Others prefer incorporating the core tenets of the CHH concept into the **sustainable development** movement and its pillars of economic and social development, as well as inter- and intra-generational equity and environmental **conservation and preservation** (Ellis 2008: 644). Although sustainable development suffers from some of the same ambiguities as the CHH concept, by avoiding the controversies surrounding the CHH concept, sustainable development may help carry the core CHH element of the equitable, sustainable use of global common pool resources into the twenty-first century.

References

Baslar, Kemal. 1998. *The Concept of the Common Heritage of Mankind in International Law*. The Hague, Martinus Nijhoff Publishers.

Boyle, Alan E. 1991. "International Law and the Protection of the Atmosphere: Concepts, Categories and Principles." In *International Law and Global Climate Change*, Eds. Robin R. Churchill and David Freestone, 7–19. London, Kluwer Law International.

Ellis, Jaye. 2008. "Sustainable Development as a Legal Principle: A Rhetorical Analysis". In *Select Proceedings of the European Society of International Law*, Eds. Hélène Ruiz Fabri, Rüdiger Wolfrum, and Jana Gogolin, 641–660. Oxford, Hart Publishing.

Frakes, Jennifer. 2003. "The Common Heritage of Mankind Principle and the Deep Seabed, Outer Space, and Antarctica: Will Developed and Developing Nations Reach a Compromise?" *Wisconsin International Law Journal* 21: 409–434.

Goldie, L.F.E. 1983. "A Note on Some Diverse Meanings of the 'Common Heritage of Mankind'." *Syracuse Journal of International Law and Commerce* 10(1): 69–112.

Viikari, Lotta. 2002. *From Manganese Nodules to Lunar Regolith: A Comparative Legal Study of the Utilization of Natural Resources in the Deep Seabed and Outer Space*. Lapland, Lapland University Press.

COMPLEX SYSTEMS

Rakhyun E. Kim

Utrecht University, The Netherlands

Complex systems are systems that display unique properties such as emergence and self-organization. Their behavior is inherently unpredictable due to nonlinear relationships between interdependent parts and processes. This makes complex systems different from systems that are just complicated by possessing many parts. Diverse types of complex systems exist, but global governance scholars have paid particular attention to complex adaptive systems. These systems operate at the edge of chaos (neither random nor uniform) and display seemingly coordinated and adaptive behavior in the absence of central control.

Two key rationales exist for looking through a complexity lens in **global environmental governance studies**. The first relates to the need to increase the **effectiveness** of governance in complex systems (Young 2017). As humanity is entering the **Anthropocene**, global (environmental) risks are becoming increasingly networked, creating super-wicked problems. The increasing complexity of problems at hand demands critical reflection on the form and function of global governance (Galaz 2019). Here, an emerging view in the literature is that governance needs to be modeled on systems-to-be-governed, which requires a complexity-informed approach to global governance (Kim and Mackey 2014).

The second relates to the idea that global governance systems themselves are complex (Orsini et al. 2019). The proliferation of **regimes**, often articulated in hundreds of multilateral environmental agreements (e.g. **Wetlands Convention**) and administered by treaty **secretariats**, has resulted in a complex web of **institutional interactions** (Oberthür and Stokke 2011). The resultant structures are sometimes described as "regime complexes" (Orsini et al. 2013) or governance "architectures" (Biermann and Kim 2020). These large web-like structures display properties of complex systems such as reflexivity and **adaptation**, and they evolve through a process akin to natural selection (Morin et al. 2017).

These two analytical dimensions—the "governance of complexity" and the "complexity of governance"—together comprise an emerging research agenda on institutional complexity. The two are interrelated: the effective governance of complexity is at least in part a function of certain characteristics of complex governance systems. Key research questions have therefore been both analytical and normative: What makes a global governance system more or less complex? What are the effects of institutional complexity? How should we govern complex systems and to what end?

A key variable here is the complexity of global governance systems, for which there are two notable approaches to operationalization. An agency-oriented approach, on the one hand, seeks to identify when the complexity of a governance system reaches beyond the cognitive capacity of agents operating therein. Here, perceived rather than objective complexity is what matters. This approach to detecting complexity has been adopted by social scientists interested in the ethical or political dimensions of complexity, for example, by examining who is empowered or disempowered by increasing institutional complexity.

A structure-oriented approach, on the other hand, seeks to measure complexity as a quality inherent in a governance system. So far institutional diversity and multiplicity have been employed as key measures, with recent attempts at detecting complexity using topological signatures such as small-world and scale-free properties (Kim 2019). The expectation is that, by using a quantifiable measure of complexity, we may compare various governance systems, and explain the relationship between institutional complexity and governance outcomes, such as effectiveness, **environmental justice**, and **participation**.

The complex systems approach is generating novel insights on the role of complexity in and for global governance. Paradoxically, however, the enhanced understanding has not and will not necessarily increase our predictive power. A theory of complexity is still far from our reach. What complexity thinking has allowed us, though, is to embrace the complex reality, rather than denying it and thereby coming to misleading conclusions.

References

Biermann, Frank and Rakhyun E. Kim (Eds.). 2020. *Architectures of Earth System Governance: Institutional Complexity and Structural Transformation*. Cambridge, Cambridge University Press.

Galaz, Victor (Ed.). 2019. *Global Challenges, Governance, and Complexity: Applications and Frontiers*. Cheltenham, Edward Elgar.

Kim, Rakhyun E. 2019. "Is Global Governance Fragmented, Polycentric, or Complex? The State of the Art of the Network Approach." *International Studies Review*: 1–29.

Kim, Rakhyun E. and Brendan Mackey. 2014. "International Environmental Law as a Complex Adaptive System." *International Environmental Agreements: Politics, Law and Economics* 14(1): 5–24.

Morin, Jean-Frédéric, Joost Pauwelyn, and James Hollway. 2017. "The Trade Regime as a Complex Adaptive System: Exploration and Exploitation of Environmental Norms in Trade Agreements." *Journal of International Economic Law* 20(2): 365–390.

Oberthür, Sebastian and Olav Schram Stokke (Eds.). 2011. *Managing Institutional Complexity: Regime Interplay and Global Environmental Change.* Cambridge, MA, MIT Press.

Orsini, Amandine, Jean-Frédéric Morin, and Oran Young. 2013. "Regime Complexes: A Buzz, a Boom, or a Boost for Global Governance?" *Global Governance* 19(1): 27–39.

Orsini, Amandine, Philippe Le Prestre, Peter M. Haas, Philipp Pattberg, Malte Brosig, Oscar Widerberg, Laura Gomez-Mera, Jean-Frédéric Morin, Neil E. Harrison, Robert Geyer, and David Chandler. 2019. "Complex Systems and International Governance." *International Studies Review* 70: 1–31.

Young, Oran R. 2017. *Governing Complex Systems: Social Capital for the Anthropocene.* Cambridge, MA, MIT Press.

COMPLIANCE AND IMPLEMENTATION

Sandrine Maljean-Dubois

CNRS and Aix-Marseille Université, France

Since the 1990s and after three decades of abundant law-making activities, scholars and practitioners are still searching for ways and means to improve the **effectiveness** of international environmental law, in particular that of treaty-based obligations. Indeed, the implementation of international law suffers from longstanding difficulties, implementation being understood as measures—legislative, administrative, or judicial—that parties take so as to make international agreements operative in international and domestic law (Young 1999).

The lack of implementation comes from various factors, including the softness of international obligations in this field (often vague, indeterminate, open-textured, non-quantified, and non-self-executing) or the specificities of environmental harm. It can also come from the fact that states have no or little available capacity to meet the various requirements imposed by international environmental law.

Traditional means of response to violations of international obligations do not fit the needs in the environmental field, and even though international **dispute resolution mechanisms** are developing, they are still exceptional and in several respects poorly tailored to control compliance to obligations arising from multilateral treaties. Similarly, countermeasures are not particularly suited for environmental protection because states' obligations are non-reciprocal and based on a collective and superior interest.

One of the ways to address these difficulties and enhance the protection of the environment is to improve the monitoring and response mechanisms to non-compliance (Sand 1992). Such monitoring has to be tailored to the numerous peculiarities of this specific field of international cooperation. In the eyes of the common interest pursued by all Contracting Parties, it is more appropriate to financially or technically assist the state in difficulties than to ask for state **liability** (Chayes and Chayes 1995). In most cases, cooperation and assistance will fruitfully replace sanction. With a view to promoting treaty implementation, some means for remedy are proposed to the states, along with possible legal, technical, and financial assistances if necessary. Some believe it is more important to promote compliance than to punish non-compliance, especially as the use of sanctions would discourage states' participation and thus encourage free-riding.

All these factors prompted efforts to find alternative ways of settling disputes with an essentially preventive vocation and to the introduction of innovative international monitoring procedures inspired in part by tried and tested methods in other legal fields (such as disarmament or human rights). Since the 1990s, several environmental agreements have succeeded in reinventing themselves, and completed **reporting** and other monitoring methods (monitoring networks, inquiries) with more specific, ambitious, global, and coherent mechanisms to institutionalize monitoring and response to non-compliance.

In most cases, a compliance committee is established by the Conference of Parties (COP), which specifies its composition, mandate, decision-making powers, rules of procedure, and its relationship to other bodies. Most of these committees are designed to prevent non-compliance and facilitate compliance. When non-compliance is found, they can help non-compliance states to return to compliance, for example using **technology transfer** or capacity building assistance. They can also sanction non-compliance and settle disputes. In such cases, monitoring and control are no longer bilateral and reciprocal but multilateral and centralized, placed in the hands of treaty bodies (COP, subsidiary organs, and **secretariats**) as a response to non-compliance, which includes assistance and incentives in addition to actual sanctions (carrots and sticks). Collective measures appear to be more readily adopted, better tolerated, and, in principle, less discretionary. Procedures are implemented with flexibility, using soft enforcement and generally a non-adversarial approach (Hedemann-Robinson 2018). Although in theory the different stages of the compliance-control cycle can be distinguished, in practice the boundaries between these stages are porous, and a situation can trigger the whole extent of compliance-control procedures and stages, from facilitation to enforcement. Non-compliance mechanisms are alternatives to traditional dispute resolution mechanisms but they leave them untouched. Consequently, dispute resolution mechanisms can—at least in theory—complement non-compliance ones in certain cases. Finally, these procedures are used for assessing the **effectiveness** of states' obligations as well as clarifying and developing these obligations. They also foster collective "learning by doing" and increase **transparency**, which in turn builds confidence and limits free-riding (Brown Weiss and Jacobson 1998; Maljean-Dubois and Rajamani 2011).

The first non-compliance procedure of an environmental treaty was drawn up in 1990 in the framework of the Montreal Protocol of the **ozone regime**. This pioneering procedure has already been taken up and adapted by fifteen other environmental conventions, becoming little by little a standard practice. Although inspired by the same model, all these procedures have peculiarities of their own.

The Kyoto Protocol of the **climate change regime** has for instance given rise to the most comprehensive non-compliance procedure to date. The monitoring and control procedure was very coherent and intrusive. Divided into two branches, a facilitative branch and an enforcement one, the Compliance Committee was quasi-judicial. Potential sanctions were essentially intended to be dissuasive. This procedure has been replaced by a more flexible one within the 2015 Paris Agreement, combining an individual monitoring (the "transparency framework"), a collective assessment (the "global stocktake"), and a soft compliance mechanism (the "mechanism to facilitate implementation of and promote compliance").

The non-compliance mechanism of the Aarhus Convention on Access to Information, Public Participation in Decision-Making and Access to Justice in Environmental Matters (1998) provides another remarkable example because of the powers the public is granted under the Compliance Committee's procedure. It may be triggered by a party making a submission on compliance by another party, a party making a submission concerning its own compliance, a referral by the **secretariat** and, something that remains most unusual in non-compliance mechanisms, by members of the public who can submit communications concerning a party's compliance with the Convention. In practice, this is by far the most used and it greatly improves **participation** (Treves 2009).

References

Brown Weiss, Edith and Harold K. Jacobson. 1998. *Engaging Countries: Strengthening Compliance with International Environmental Accords.* Cambridge, MA, MIT Press.

Chayes, Abram and Antonia H. Chayes. 1995. *The New Sovereignty: Compliance with Treaties in International Regulatory Regimes.* Cambridge, MA, Harvard University Press.

Hedemann-Robinson, Martin. 2018. *Enforcement of International Environmental Law: Challenges and Responses at the International Level.* London, Routledge.

Maljean-Dubois, Sandrine and Lavanya Rajamani (Eds.). 2011. *Implementation of International Environmental Law.* The Hague, The Hague Academy of International Law, Martinus Nijhoff.

Sand, Peter. 1992. *The Effectiveness of International Environmental Law: A Survey of Existing Legal Instruments.* Cambridge, Grotius Publications.

Treves, Tullio (Ed.). 2009. *Non-Compliance Procedures and Mechanisms and the Effectiveness of International Environmental Agreements.* The Hague, Asser Press.

Young, Oran. 1999. *The Effectiveness of International Environmental Regimes: Causal Connections and Behavioral Mechanisms.* Cambridge, MA, MIT Press.

CONSERVATION AND PRESERVATION

Jean-Frédéric Morin
Université Laval, Canada

Amandine Orsini
Université Saint-Louis – Bruxelles, Belgium

How should the environment be protected? Two opposite stances have addressed this question. Proponents of a conservationist approach argue that humans have to intervene on the environment to actively favor its sustainability. They believe for example that **ecosystem services** and goods provided by forests (timber, recreation, landscapes, etc.) can only be enjoyed by several generations over time if forestry techniques (species selection, logging methods, etc.) are used to ensure that cover and quality of forests remain constant over time. In contrast, advocates of a preservationist approach consider that humans should shy away as much as possible from nature. They claim that management techniques often have harmful unintended consequences, while natural processes, such as wildfires or species extinction, are necessary regenerative episodes that should be neither favored nor prevented by human intervention (Epstein 2006).

Among the first conservationist advocates were hunters, farmers, and fishermen who, at the end of the nineteenth century, called for international cooperation to ensure the sustainable exploitation of natural resources and secure their activity. As a result of their efforts, several agreements were concluded such as the 1881 International Phylloxera Convention, which aimed at protecting European wineries from American pests, or the 1902 Convention for the Protection of Birds Useful to Agriculture, protecting insectivorous birds. Since the 1980s, several developing countries have endorsed this conservationist approach as a way of protecting their economic interests. For example, they actively support the 1992 **biodiversity regime**, which aims at favoring the conservation of biodiversity, its sustainable use, and the sharing of benefits that arise from this use.

Preservationist arguments have also deeply influenced international environmental politics. **Nongovernmental organizations** such as the Sierra Club and the Royal Society for the Protection of Birds have pushed states to create protected areas to preserve wildlife. Several international treaties were concluded to promote the creation of natural parks, including the 1940 Convention on Nature Protection and Wildlife Preservation in the Western Hemisphere, the 1971 **Wetlands Convention** and the 1972 Convention Concerning the Protection of World Cultural and Natural Heritage. In some controversial cases, the creation of protected areas on preservationist grounds led to the eviction of **indigenous peoples and local communities** from their traditional land (Adams and Hutton 2007, Ybarra 2018). Other preservationist agreements aim at preserving specific species irrespective of their location, such as the 1973 **CITES** and the 1979 Bonn Convention on Migratory Species of Wild Animals. These treaties are based on scientific, recreational, esthetic grounds or on **ecocentrism**, not on the desire to conserve natural resources for future exploitation.

In some international **regimes**, conservationist and preservationist views openly clash. It is notoriously the case at the **International Whaling Commission**, where Japan advocates for sustainable hunting practices while the United States and other countries support preservation and are opposed to all whaling activity, even for species that are not endangered. There are also heated debates under the CITES, as some African countries, such as Kenya, favor a strict ban on the trade of ivory while others, including Zimbabwe, argue that an unmanaged elephant population can negatively impact the ecosystem while ivory sales can fund conservation (Stiles 2004).

References

Adams, William and Jon Hutton. 2007. "People, Parks and Poverty: Political Ecology and Biodiversity Conservation." *Conservation and Society* 5(2): 147–183.
Epstein, Charlotte. 2006. "The Making of Global Environmental Norms: Endangered Species Protection." *Global Environmental Politics* 6(2): 32–54.
Stiles, Daniel. 2004. "The Ivory Trade and Elephant Conservation." *Environmental Conservation* 31(4): 309–321.
Ybarra, Megan. 2018. *Green Wars: Colonization and Conservation in the Maya Forest.* Oakland, CA, University of California Press.

CORPORATE SOCIAL RESPONSIBILITY

Jennifer Clapp and Ian H. Rowlands
University of Waterloo, Canada

Corporate social responsibility (CSR) refers broadly to actions that **business and corporations** voluntarily undertake both to promote social and environmental goals and to minimize any potential social and environmental costs associated with their business activities. The rationale behind CSR is that firms themselves are best placed to ensure **compliance and implementation** and to monitor progress toward their own environmental and social performance targets and will do so because it makes good business sense.

The 1960–70s saw strengthening of environmental regulations in many states, and environmental agencies to uphold those rules were established in most countries by the early 1980s. With the rise of **liberal environmentalism** after the mid-1980s, however, state-driven "command-and-control" type environmental regulations began to lose favor with governments, opening space for more flexible voluntary corporate-driven approaches to governing the environmental impact of business and corporations. Initially there was some concern about whether firms that adopted CSR within their business model would be able to fulfill their fiduciary duty to shareholders to prioritize financial earnings. This concern followed Milton Friedman's belief that firms' primary responsibility is to generate profits and not take social issues into consideration (Fleming et al. 2013).

By the early 1990s, business leader Stephan Schmidheiny, then head of the Business Council for Sustainable Development, an organization established in 1990 to represent the voice of business leaders at the 1992 Rio Earth Summit (see **Summit diplomacy**), began to champion CSR. He argued that firms must "change course" to put social and environmental issues at the center of their decision-making because he believed it was in the firm's economic interest to do so. He termed this concept "eco-efficiency." The rationale was simple: CSR would help firms to cut costs through efficiency gains from fewer required inputs and reduced waste, while at the same time the green image of firms would help to create new **markets** (Schmidheiny 1992).

Most global business leaders embraced CSR by the early 2000s and it became widely accepted in corporate circles that business knows best how to design and implement environmental measures more efficiently than one-size-fits-all command-and-control regulations. Today, many see CSR as a de facto condition for business success. Most international firms, including a growing number of firms in developing countries, undertake some sort of CSR-type activities, such as **reporting, labeling, and certification**, demonstrating how entrenched CSR has become as a normative frame in global governance (Crane et al. 2019).

Individual CSR reporting by firms is perhaps the most widespread type of CSR activity. Most transnational corporations now produce regular CSR reports. Self-reported CSR activities typically range from broad statements about commitment to "doing right" for the environment to details on specific programs or initiatives. Such reporting might be defensive in the early stages, especially for firms that are in higher-risk industries, or proactive, as is often the case with firms with high public profiles (Shabana et al. 2017). One of the drawbacks of individual CSR reporting is that firms can be selective in what they choose to report, shaping their own environmental image without necessarily meeting any externally set standards. For example, in 2000 the transnational oil firm BP widely trumpeted its green energy activities in a major public relations campaign "Beyond Petroleum," while the vast majority of its investments remained in oil and gas exploration in subsequent years. This type of selective CSR approach led to claims by critics of greenwashing.

The vulnerability of firms to external critique for selective CSR reporting was one of the factors behind the rise of collective approaches to CSR. An early industry-established environmental code of conduct was Responsible Care, a chemical industry environmental and safety initiative that was a direct industry response to the chemical **disaster** in Bhopal, India, in 1984. Some corporate codes of conduct involve nonindustry stakeholders, such as **nongovernmental organizations** and/or international organizations. The Global Reporting Initiative, for example, is a multi-stakeholder initiative that establishes standards for CSR reporting (Vigneau et al. 2015).

Other multi-stakeholder initiatives involve standards to which firms could gain certification, such as the Forest Stewardship Council (FSC) standards for sustainable timber and the International Organization for Standardization's ISO 14000 series of environmental management standards (Auld 2014). ISO 26000 (launched in 2010), for example, guides businesses and organizations on best practices regarding social responsibility. While the growing participation of firms in collective CSR initiatives such as those outlined here does show firms' commitment to a higher level of scrutiny over their practices, they are still voluntary and typically do not apply sanctions for non-compliance. Moreover, they have been critiqued for lacking **transparency** and for being process rather than outcome focused.

Debates that define the literature on CSR today tend to fall into two broad categories. The first focuses on firm-level behavior and examines firms' motivations for undertaking CSR and whether activities are transformational, transitional, or marginal in terms of their impact (Crane et al. 2019). Detailed case studies on the impact of CSR and its variation across sectors and according to firm size and location have begun to shed light on these questions, but as yet the jury is still out on the broader questions of firm motivation and impact.

The second key area under debate with respect to CSR focuses on implications of industry self-regulation for governance more broadly. A key question is whether CSR activities are sufficient "replacements" for state-based regulation, such as performance standards or **taxation**. These debates also probe what kinds of influence corporations have in shaping global environmental governance and ask what the implications of their **participation** in multi-stakeholder initiatives are for broader goals such as legitimacy, accountability, transparency, and **effectiveness** (Scherer and Palazzo 2011). Broader conceptual work on these questions has pointed to a blurring of the public and private realms with respect to governance, but whether the firm level "eco-efficiency" (some business and corporations being "less bad") can lead to a more transformational "eco-effectiveness" (all businesses and corporations doing "good") (McDonough and Braungart 2010) remains to be seen.

References

Auld, Graeme. 2014. *Constructing Private Governance: The Rise and Evolution of Forest, Coffee, and Fisheries Certification.* New Haven, CT, Yale University Press.

Crane, Andrew, Dirk Matten, and Laura J. Spence (Eds.). 2019. *Corporate Social Responsibility: Readings and Cases in a Global Context.* London and New York, Routledge.

Fleming, Peter, John Roberts, and Christina Garsten. 2013. "In Search of Corporate Social Responsibility." *Organization* 20: 337–348.

McDonough, William and Michael Braungart. 2010. *Cradle to Cradle: Remaking the Way We Make Things.* New York, Macmillan.

Scherer, Andreas G. and Guido Palazzo. 2011. "The New Political Role of Business in a Globalized World: A Review of a New Perspective on CSR and its Implications for the Firm, Governance, and Democracy." *Journal of Management Studies* 48(4): 899–931.

Schmidheiny, Stephan. 1992. *Changing Course: A Global Business Perspective on Development and the Environment.* Cambridge, MA, MIT Press.

Shabana, Kareem M., Ann K. Buchholtz, and Archie B. Carroll. 2017. "The Institutionalization of Corporate Social Responsibility Reporting." *Business & Society* 56(8): 1107–1135.

Vigneau, Laurence, Michael Humphreys, and Jeremy Moon. 2015. "How Do Firms Comply with International Sustainability Standards? Processes and Consequences of Adopting the Global Reporting Initiative." *Journal of Business Ethics* 131(2): 469–486.

CRITICAL POLITICAL ECONOMY

Peter Newell

University of Sussex, United Kingdom

Critical political economy approaches to the study and practice of global environmental politics take a range of different forms, but often have as their starting point a set of questions about who governs and how, what is to be governed (and what is not) and on whose behalf (Newell 2008). Though these relate to the classic concerns of political economy: who wins, who loses, how and why, most critical accounts tend to situate global institutional arrangements established to manage the global environment within broader social relations (of class, race, and gender for example) and structures of power. This helps to clarify who is afforded environmental protection by global environmental governance, who is not, how and why. They also place relationships of power between states, **business and corporations** (capital), and international institutions at the heart of their analysis because these affect the nature of global action on the environment and what states are able to do (Paterson 2001). Thus, for many critical perspectives, capitalism and its inequities and the organization of the global economy along neoliberal lines offer more clues to the nature and extent of responses to the environment than a narrower focus on specific features of institutions charged with managing the environment and a primary focus on the state in isolation from these social relations.

Many critical accounts developed in the wake of the Earth Summit in 1992 from a political ecology tradition drew attention to the power and influence of businesses and corporations in undermining effective global responses to environmental threats such as climate change and biodiversity loss (Chatterjee and Finger 1994) and promoting a model of development that was at odds with the stated aim of protecting the environment. Academics then sought to develop theoretical approaches to explain the way in which challenges to capitalism were muted and managed by powerful actors and interests to protect the prevailing economic order. Some made use of Gramsci's understanding of hegemony to explore the ways in which state and corporate elites accommodate challenges to their power and profits while developing responses to environmental threats that enhance their power, through the creation of **markets** in carbon, water, and forests, for example, rather than altering patterns of production and consumption from which they benefit. They focused on the material, organizational, and discursive strategies employed by powerful corporate actors to secure policy responses that left their control over production, technology, and finance intact (Levy and Newell 2002), enabling incremental forms of transition (see **Energy transition**) but resisting broader transformations (Newell 2018).

Less concerned with governance per se, other critical political economy approaches from ecological Marxism questioned the premise of **ecological modernization** and other liberal approaches such as **liberal environmentalism**, which argued that capitalist growth could be compatible with responding to the ecological crisis (see **Degrowth**). They suggested instead that a second contradiction of capitalism (O'Connor 1994) was its tendency to destroy its own ability to reproduce the ecological conditions necessary for its own survival.

In sum, what unites an array of accounts that might be described by the label critical political economy is a concern with explaining the existing landscape of power in global environmental politics and identifying possibilities for change in the prevailing order of global (environmental) governance on the basis that the current system is incapable of delivering either **sustainable development** or social or **environmental justice**. Many such approaches either look to the possibility of strategic alliances among powerful actors that might break down opposition to environmental action, or to more bottom-up forms of resistance and alternatives that seek to construct **green economies** along non-capitalist lines (Scoones et al. 2015); Newell 2019.

References

Chatterjee, Pratap and Matthias Finger. 1994. *The Earth Brokers: Power, Politics and World Development*. London, Routledge.

Levy, David and Peter Newell. 2002. "Business Strategy and International Environmental Governance: Toward a Neo-Gramscian Synthesis." *Global Environmental Politics* 2(4): 84–101.

Newell, Peter. 2008. "The Political Economy of Global Environmental Governance." *Review of International Studies* 34(3): 507–529.

Newell, Peter. 2018. "Trasformismo or Transformation? The Global Political Economy of Energy Transitions." *Review of International Political Economy* 26(1): 25–48.

Newell, P. (2019) Global Green Politics. Cambridge, Cambridge University Press.

O'Connor, Martin (Ed.). 1994. *Is Capitalism Sustainable? Political Economy and the Politics of Ecology*. New York, Guilford Press.

Paterson, Matthew. 2001. *Understanding Global Environmental Politics: Domination, Accumulation, Resistance*. Basingstoke, Palgrave.

Scoones, Ian, Melissa Leach and Peter Newell (Ed.). 2015. *The Politics of Green Transformations* Abingdon, Routledge.

DEEP ECOLOGY

Kate Booth

University of Tasmania, Australia

Deep ecology was highly influential in environmental thought, politics, and spirituality during the late 1980s and early 1990s. It was a spiritual guide for those concerned about human ecological impacts, a touchstone for changing the relationship between humans and nature, a political rationale for defending wilderness values, and a significant influence in the governance of natural areas and species **conservation**.

The appeal of deep ecology pivoted upon the ideas of philosopher Arne Næss who described deep ecology as a movement characterized by a relational ontology, biospherical egalitarianism, principles of diversity and symbiosis, an anti-class posture, opposition to pollution and resource depletion, a focus on complexity not complication, and support for local autonomy and decentralization (Næss 1973). He distinguished this from the shallow ecology movement, the central objective of which is the well-being of affluent populations. This was later refined into the Deep Ecology Platform—a set of principles that described the aspirations shared by supporters of the deep ecology movement (Devall and Sessions 1985). However, tensions began to emerge as deep ecology took on a double meaning: on one hand was the plurality and activist-oriented deep ecology movement (Seed et al. 1988); and, on the other, a narrower philosophical expression.

The latter was heavily influenced by Næss's articulation of self-realization—the process of identifying with the interests of nonhuman beings, forming an expansive sense of self, and then naturally acting in the interests of nature. This focus brought about disagreements between deep ecology proponents. For example, Fox (1995) placed a heavy emphasis on self-realization, which was subsequently described as a misunderstanding of Næss, compounding existing confusion about the nature of the deep ecology movement, creating unnecessary friction that sidelines potential deep ecology supporters, and destroying deep ecology by undermining philosophical plurality.

Deep ecology also came under sustained external critique (Katz et al. 2000). This included ecofeminists who observed that deep ecology failed to recognize the historical linkages between anthropocentrism and androcentrism, and that deep ecology embodied a familiar masculine stance for control and dominance (e.g. Salleh 2018; see **Ecofeminism**). Another source of critique pertained to the possibility of some deep ecological ideas harboring fascist tendencies.

Since the 1990s there has been a dissipation of interest in deep ecology, in part due to a loss of interest in environmental philosophy and increasing pragmatic concerns (Hay 2002). However, both philosophical and practical ideas originating from deep ecology continue to resonate, for example, in branches of ecological justice, education, environmental management, psychology, and politics (e.g. de Jonge 2017). It remains to be seen if or how this interest intersects with contemporary issues such as climate change **adaptation** and resilience.

References

De Jonge, Eccy. 2017. *Spinoza and Deep Ecology: Challenging Traditional Approaches to Environmentalism*. London, Routledge.

Devall, Bill and George Sessions. 1985. *Deep Ecology: Living as if Nature Mattered*. Layton, UT, Gibbs Smith.

Fox, Warwick. 1995. *Toward a Transpersonal Ecology: Developing New Foundations for Environmentalism*. Totnes, UK, Green Books.

Hay, Peter. 2002. *Main Currents in Western Environmental Thought*. Sydney, University of New South Wales Press.

Katz, Eric, Andrew Light and David Rothenberg (Eds.). 2000. Beneath *the Surface: Critical Essays in the Philosophy of Deep Ecology*. Cambridge, MA, MIT Press.

Næss, Arne. 1973. "The Shallow and the Deep, Long-Range Ecology Movements: A Summary." *Inquiry* 16(1–4): 95–100.

Salleh, Ariel. 2018. "Deeper than Deep Ecology: The Eco-Feminist Connection." In *Feminist Ecologies: Changing Environments in the Anthropocene*, Eds. Lara Stevens, Peta Tait, and Denise Varney, 25–33. Cham, Switzerland, Palgrave Macmillan.

Seed, John, Joanna Macy, Pat Fleming and Arne Næss. 1988. *Thinking Like a Mountain: Toward a Council of All Beings*. Philadelphia, PA, New Society Publishers.

DEGROWTH

Barbara Muraca

University of Oregon, United States

Degrowth is a provocative, overarching idea that connects different social-ecological movements, research, and political projects working towards a radical transformation of growth-based societies through "a democratic and redistributive downscaling of the biophysical size of the global economy" (Asara et al. 2015: 375) (see **Carrying capacities paradigm**). However, the main goal of degrowth is not just to shrink the economy in its current form, but to radically transform the basic structure of society and to collectively explore alternative ways of living beyond the capitalistic growth imperative (see **Critical political economy**).

In addition to an extensive critique of the monetary and material dimension of economic growth, degrowth also challenges the pervasive logic of acceleration, competition, and expansion that guides neoliberal policies and informs social relations, practices, and institutions in late capitalistic societies (Muraca and Döring, 2018).

Rooted in the early waves of growth critique, which was triggered by the environmental crisis of the 1970s and embraced by anti-productivist and feminist intellectuals (see also **Post-environmentalism** and **Ecofeminism**), degrowth re-emerged in the late 1990s as radical alternative to **sustainable development** and as a project for the repoliticization of environmentalism against technocratic and eco-modernist solutions (D'Alisa et al. 2014).

On the one hand, degrowth is understood as an ethical and political imperative to implement true sustainability. Institutional-oriented approaches call for degrowth "by design" aimed at reforming basic institutions to guarantee well-being to all with a smaller "material flow" of the economy. Sufficiency-oriented approaches claim a necessary radical turn in individual and collective behavior towards voluntary simplicity.

On the other hand, degrowth is framed as an alternative, utopian scenario after the crisis of growth-based societies. Accordingly, the structural function that growth had for the social reproduction and political stabilization of industrial, capitalistic societies after World War II, by securing economic support for the welfare state, reducing inequalities, and legitimizing democracies, is plausibly coming to an end. Long-term economic shrinking under business-as-usual conditions brings about stagnation, poverty, increasing inequality, and a threat to democracy (Kallis et al. 2018). Against such a threat, degrowth embodies a radical, democratic (see also **Green democracy**), and equitable alternative to bleak post-growth scenarios. With the slogan "your recession is not our degrowth" activists claim that degrowth disentangles societies from their structural dependency on growth and creates spaces for "concrete utopias" that envision radical alternatives. Degrowth represents a liberation from alienation and oppression and a path towards a truly democratic self-determination of the basic conditions for common living.

Despite lacking the homogeneity of a social movement in the strict sense (see also **Grassroots movements**), degrowth successfully operates as a "provocative political slogan that questions the hegemony of the growth paradigm" and brings together "quite diverse and sometimes contradictory currents and positions," thus mobilizing a "mosaic of alternatives," through which diverse prefigurative social experiments assemble around the degrowth idea to build cross-cutting alliances (Burkhardt et al. 2020: 12ff).

References

Asara, Viviana, Iago Otero, Federico Demaria, and Esteve Corbera. 2015. Socially Sustainable Degrowth as a Social-ecological Transformation: Repoliticizing Sustainability. *Sustainability Science* 10(3): 375–384.

Burkhart, Corinna, Matthias Schmelzer, and Nina Treu (Eds.). 2020. *Degrowth in Movement(s): Exploring Pathways for Transformation.* Winchester, Zero Books.

D'Alisa, Giacomo, Federico Demaria, and Giorgios Kallis (Eds.). 2014. *Degrowth: A Vocabulary for a New Era.* New York, Routledge.

Kallis, Giorgos, Vasilis Kostakis, Steffen Lange, Barbara Muraca, Susan Paulson, and Matthias Schmelzer. 2018. "Research on Degrowth." *Annual Review of Environment and Resources* 43(1): 291–316.

Muraca, Barbara and Ralf Döring. 2018. "From (Strong) Sustainability to Degrowth: A Philosophical and Historical Reconstruction." In *Routledge Handbook of the History of Sustainability*, Ed. Jeremy L. Caradonna, 339–361. London, Routledge.

DESERTIFICATION CONVENTION

Steffen Bauer

German Development Institute, Germany

According to the Intergovernmental Panel on Climate Change (IPCC), in 2019, deserts and drylands currently cover 46.2% of the global land area, inhabited by roughly 3 billion people. The share of drylands that is subject to desertification remains hard to assess and is therefore contested. According to the Millennium Ecosystem Assessment, up to 70% of the world's drylands were considered to be degraded at the turn of the twenty-first century (MEA 2005).

International efforts to address dryland degradation and recurring droughts date back to the 1960s. Yet these remained largely ineffectual until **summit diplomacy** resolved to tackle "desertification" by means of an international convention during the 1992 United Nations Conference on Environment and Development (see **Treaty negotiations**). In 1994 the United Nations finally adopted the United Nations Convention to Combat Desertification in Those Countries Seriously Affected by Drought and/or Desertification, Particularly in Africa (UNCCD) to deal with this specific environmental problem and to facilitate **sustainable development** for the people affected by it.

In the convention text, desertification is defined as "land degradation in arid, semi-arid and dry sub-humid areas resulting from various factors, including climatic variations and human activities" (Article 1 (a)). The convention furthermore declares desertification to be of concern for all humankind as one specific aspect of global ecological interdependence. In this sense, the notion of desertification is itself a product of globalization as it bundles together localized biogeophysical phenomena that can be observed across the globe (Bauer 2007).

Yet, the concept of desertification is contested. Much like the term sustainability, it is employed to encapsulate a number of causes, effects, symptoms, and interactions that are attributed to a highly complex phenomenon. Consequently, the interpretation of the UNCCD, its specific scope, and its role and relevance in global environmental governance have been subject to much debate. The framing of desertification as both an environment and a development issue was key to conceptualize the UNCCD as a sustainable development convention rather than as yet another multilateral environmental agreement (Bruyninckx 2005). However, this overly ambitious stand-alone quality proved a major obstacle to the effective **compliance and implementation** of the convention.

While developing countries routinely emphasize poverty as both a cause and a consequence of desertification, developed countries remain reluctant to subscribe to the UNCCD as an additional instrument for development assistance. At the same time, the former are generally more concerned with development than environmental protection and the latter remain lukewarm in their acknowledgment of desertification as a global problem, even as dryland degradation dynamically progresses in many developed countries. Yet, the framing of desertification as a global issue has tangible implications for the interpretation and implementation of the convention. For instance, it was instrumental in establishing dryland degradation as eligible for funding through the **Global Environment Facility**. Ultimately, the strategic framing of desertification at the international level provides a strong case in point for the influence of non-state actors—in this case notably **nongovernmental organizations** and the UNCCD **Secretariat**—in the realm of intergovernmental politics (Corell and Betsill 2001; Bauer 2009).

This notwithstanding, the UNCCD struggles to mobilize adequate attention and, indeed, resources from member states (Akhtar-Schuster et al. 2011). Hence, the successful negotiation of the UNCCD on the one hand testifies to an increased bargaining power of developing countries in view of global ecological interdependence (Najam 2004). On the other hand, its advocates failed to capitalize on the evident importance of drylands and dryland-related **ecosystem services** for sustainable development (Stringer 2009). This weakness is compounded by the pre-eminence that is attributed to both the **climate change regime** and the **biodiversity regime**, especially in the global North.

To some extent, this may be explained by the UNCCD's failure to establish an effective **boundary organization** that could enhance well-informed decision-making at the global level (Bauer and Stringer 2009). More importantly, however, it can be argued that the UNCCD has come to represent an almost ideal typical showcase for a host of structural problems that permeate North–South politics and for that matter global environmental governance at the fault-line of socioeconomic needs and ecological concerns.

Having said that, recent issue linkages in the context of the United Nations' 2030 Agenda for Sustainable Development have helped to increase political attention for desertification and the value of dryland ecosystems. Indeed, the objective to achieve land degradation neutrality by 2030 has been anchored as target 15.3 under the **Sustainable Development Goals**, and the mandate to monitor its implementation has raised the UNCCD's profile. Moreover, interdependencies with global warming, and loss of biodiversity and ecosystems are increasingly recognized as they have been underpinned by major scientific **assessments**, including by the 2019 IPCC *Special Report on Climate Change and Land* and the 2018 Intergovernmental Science-Policy Platform on Biodiversity and Ecosystem Services *Assessment Report on Land Degradation and Restoration*.

References

Akhtar-Schuster, Mariam, Richard J. Thomas, Lindsay C. Stringer, Pamela Chasek, and Mary K. Seely. 2011. "Improving the Enabling Environment to Combat Land Degradation: Institutional, Financial, Legal and Science-Policy Challenges and Solutions." *Land Degradation and Development* 22(2): 299–312.

Bauer, Steffen. 2007. "Desertification." In *Encyclopedia of Globalization, Vol. I*, Eds. Roland Robertson and Jan Aart Scholte, 302–306. London, Routledge.

Bauer, Steffen. 2009. "The Desertification Secretariat: A Castle Made of Sand." In *Managers of Global Change: The Influence of International Environmental Bureaucracies*, Eds. Frank Biermann and Bernd Siebenhüner, 293–317. Cambridge, MA, MIT Press.

Bauer, Steffen and Lindsay C. Stringer. 2009. "The Role of Science in the Global Governance of Desertification." *Journal of Environment and Development* 18(3): 248–267.

Bruyninckx, Hans. 2005. "Sustainable Development: The Institutionalization of a Contested Concept." In *International Environmental Politics*, Eds. Michele M. Betsill, Kathryn Hochstetler, and Dimitris Stevis, 265–298. Basingstoke, UK, Palgrave Macmillan.

Corell, Elisabeth, and Michele M. Betsill. 2001. "A Comparative Look at NGO Influence in International Environmental Negotiations: Desertification and Climate Change." *Global Environmental Politics* 1(4): 86–107.

MEA (Millennium Ecosystem Assessment). 2005. "Ecosystems and Human Well-Being: Desertification Synthesis." Washington, DC, World Resources Institute.

Najam, Adil. 2004. "Dynamics of the Southern Collective: Developing Countries in Desertification Negotiations." *Global Environmental Politics* 4(3): 128–154.

Stringer, Lindsay C. 2009. "Reviewing the Links between Desertification and Food Insecurity: From Parallel Challenges to Synergetic Solutions." *Food Security* 1(2): 113–126.

UNEP (United Nations Environment Programme). 2019. "Land and Soil." In *Global Environment Outlook GEO-6: Healthy Planet, Healthy People*, Ed. UNEP, 201–232. Cambridge, Cambridge University Press.

DISASTERS

Raymond Murphy

University of Ottawa, Canada

In 2004, an earthquake followed by a tsunami struck Indonesia in one of the worse natural disasters in modern times. In 2010, BP's Deepwater Horizon failsafe valve failed to be safe on its oil drilling rig, resulting in the biggest technological disaster in American history. The sharp distinction between a natural disaster and a socio-technological one is an oversimplification. A natural disaster becomes devastating because of socially constructed vulnerabilities: the 2004 tsunami killed people and damaged property because there were no tsunami warning alarms and buildings were not robust in this poor region. A socio-technological disaster becomes ruinous because of imprudent human interactions with nature: BP's unsafe drilling under immense deepwater pressures. Disasters are best defined as interactions between socio-technological constructions and nature's constructions that result in harmful consequences, with two types of initiating processes: naturogenic and anthropogenic. This captures both the commonalities and differences of phenomena such as earthquakes and oil spills. Both types require pre-paredness, robustness, **adaptation**, and resilience to reduce harm, and mitigating socio-technological disasters requires prevention.

Human activities are now unleashing more intense cyclones, flooding, wildfires, invasive species, and so on, due to fossil-fueled global warming (see **Anthropocene**). Calamities are already being intensified by warming that has increased the ocean level by 66 mm since 1993 (IPCC 2019). **Science** predicts the increase will be five times more in best case **scenarios** by 2100 and probably twenty times more (IPCC 2019). Imagine the disasters children born today will experience when they are eighty years old in 2100 from storm surges, hurricanes, and so on, because of melting land-based glaciers and thermal expansion of water in this **risk society** and new **climate change regime**. The cost of disasters, both slow-onset and sudden, has increased exponentially as populations grow and place expensive constructions in harm's way. Fatalities are highest in poor countries, which raises issues of vulnerability and justice (Tierney 2019) (see **Environmental justice**). Reliance on tightly coupled technologies like electrical grids can propagate vulner-ability to extreme disturbances of nature far afield (Murphy 2009).

Governance of rapid-onset disasters is typically multi-**scale** from the bottom up: local communities deal with small calamities; when their capacities are exceeded, regions and provinces take charge; when their capacity is surpassed, national governments act, especially finan-cially; and when a particularly destructive catastrophe strikes poor countries lacking resilience, other nations **aid**. A panoply of **non-governmental organizations** (Hannigan 2012) are tasked with pro-viding disaster relief (e.g. Red Cross) or reducing social vulnerability to hazards by alleviating poverty. The United Nations Disaster Relief Office provides **aid** whereas its Development Programme and the **United Nations Environment Programme** attempt to reduce vul-nerability. **Boundary organizations**, such as the Intergovernmental Panel on Climate Change (IPCC), contribute understanding of dangers. Unless they practice **corporate social responsibility**, profit-seeking **corporations** like BP cause technological disasters, but others such as the re-insurance industry promote robustness, resilience, and **precau-tionary principles**. Moreover, the **World Bank** has a disaster risk reduction unit.

References

Hannigan, John. 2012. *Disasters without Borders*. Cambridge, Polity.

IPCC. 2019. The Ocean and Cryosphere in a Changing Planet: *Summary for Policymakers*. https://report.ipcc.ch/srocc/pdf/SROCC_SPM_Approved.pdf

Murphy, Raymond. 2009. *Leadership in Disaster*. Montreal, McGill-Queen's University Press.

Tierney, Kathleen. 2019. *Disasters: A Sociological Approach*. Cambridge, UK, Polity

DISPUTE RESOLUTION MECHANISMS

Carrie Menkel-Meadow

University of California, Irvine, United States

Perhaps the most important issue in international environmental governance is not the making of environmental rules and laws, but how such rules and standards can be enforced. Arguably, effective **compliance and implementation** require appropriate dispute resolution mechanisms from the onset.

The first international environmental dispute to have been legally settled at the international level occurred at the end of the 1930s. At that time, there was no formal international court to resolve the United States' claim that fumes discharged by a Canadian-owned mining and smelting company were causing environmental damage in the US state of Washington. This case, the Trail Smelter Case, was thus resolved by an international, voluntarily agreed to, arbitration panel. This famous case not only established the **preventive action principle**, but also that voluntarily constituted bodies, such as an *arbitration panel*, could order injunctions or desist orders.

This first form of dispute resolution set in motion the development of formal environmental **litigation**. Many formal dispute resolution mechanisms are now active in global environmental governance, including the International Court of Justice (ICJ) (a rare but important adjudicator of interstate environmental disputes), the International Tribunal of the Law of the Sea (ITLOS) (an adjudicative body that has decided very few cases since its inception in 1982), regional courts, such as the European or Inter-American Court of Human Rights (where claims are now made for **human and environmental rights**), even by individuals, the **World Trade Organization**'s arbitral panels and Appellate Body, the International Centre for Settlement of Investment Disputes (ICSID) (see **Investment protection**), national courts (which may resolve both intra- and interstate disputes), international environmental agreements or treaties (which use implementation and monitoring committees), and, more recently, a new breed of specialized environmental courts or tribunals (ECTs or "green courts") (Pring and Pring 2012) (see **Regional governance**).

It has long been argued that many environment disputes are non-zero-sum games and that they can be settled more effectively by dialogic, negotiated, and managerial, rather than adversarial, approaches. As a result, many multilateral environmental agreements (MEAs) provide for requirements for mediation, negotiation, and conciliation, before binding arbitration (which is called "tiered dispute resolution"). Other well-established alternative dispute resolution mechanisms include fact-finding bodies, such as the **World Bank**'s Independent Inspection Panel, which investigates and performs fact finding for environmental disputes for communities and World Bank-funded projects.

Other mechanisms are even less formal and more collaborative. They include consensus building and community planning processes, as well as more formal negotiated rule-making ("reg-neg") of pre-rule adoption negotiation by interested stakeholders (Susskind et al. 1999). For example, for the **transboundary water regime** and many land use and wild-life preservation disputes, newer forms of collaborative and consensus building processes attempt to bring all stakeholders together to share scientific information, legal claims, and expertise (Menkel-Meadow 2008). With the help of professional facilitators, they craft "community agreements" or draft rules and regulations that provide for more flexible standards and monitoring, with provisions for adaptive management, revisions, and contingency planning when conditions "on the ground" change (Camacho 2005). These processes assume more party input (with often hundreds of participants) and a growing group of experts, trained in environmental mediation and facilitation. This is often called the "New Governance" model (Karkkainenen 2004).

While consensus building and mediative processes are still mostly public processes, there is growing evidence that private environmental dispute resolution can bolster **effectiveness**. Private parties set up private regimes to use supply chain contracts, loan agreements, codes of conduct commitments (such as the **Global Pact for the Environment**), and tiered dispute resolution to demand environmental standards and enforcement.

Yet, these less formal and collaborative processes for resolution of environmental disputes raise a host of as yet unanswered questions: How can key environmental principle issues, such as the **precautionary**

principle, be dealt with in collaborative processes? Do powerful actors exercise stronger control in less formal settings? How can we assess the effectiveness of these processes? How can we ensure access for **participation** and appropriate representation for all interested parties? How much **transparency** should there be when **business and corporations** make deals with communities? How do we provide sufficient incentives for institutions to adapt to new information or changed conditions? How do we balance the need to resolve short-term disputes and episodic crises such as **disasters** against the need to focus on long-term and intergenerational issues such as climate change and environmental justice?

As many continue to deny climate change (the current United States administration) and withdraw from public commitments (such as the Paris Climate Accord) it remains to be seen how formal and informal processes can be used to effect environmental change. One substantially new form of dispute processing is social media in which new generations of activists, such as Greta Thunberg, dramatically bring to the attention of the public environmental crises and issues, which raise the stakes, provide important public information and continue to engage the world's population to mobilize political advocacy at both national and international (and also local) levels (see **Influential individuals**).

References

Camacho, Alejandro E. 2005. "Mustering the Missing Voices: A Collaborative Model for Fostering Equality, Community Involvement and Adaptive Planning in Land Use Decisions." *Stanford Environmental Law Review* 24(1): 3–69.

Karkkainen, Bradley C. 2004. " 'New Governance' in Legal Thought and in the World: Some Splitting as Antidote to Overzealous Lumping." *Minnesota Law Review* 89(2): 471–496.

Menkel-Meadow, Carrie. 2008. "Getting to Let's Talk: Comments on Collaborative Environmental Dispute Resolution Processes." *Nevada Law Journal* 8: 835–852.

Pring, George and Catherine Pring. 2012. "The Future of Environmental Dispute Resolution." *Denver Journal of International Law & Policy* 40: 482–491.

Susskind, Lawrence E., Sarah McKearnen, and Jennifer Thomas-Larmer. 1999. *The Consensus Building Handbook: A Comprehensive Guide to Reaching Agreement.* Thousand Oaks, CA, Sage Publications.

Weiss, Edith Brown and Harold K. Jacobson (Eds.). 2000. *Engaging Countries: Strengthening Compliance with International Environmental Accords.* Cambridge, MA, MIT Press.

DUMPING

Josué Mathieu
Université libre de Bruxelles, Belgium

Environmental dumping (or eco-dumping) is defined as the use of lax environmental standards or poorly enforced regulations to export goods at a cost advantage or to attract foreign investments (Rauscher 1994). Critics of the effects of trade liberalization use the concept to highlight that a comparative advantage generated by a low level of environmental protection is unfair, as industries located in "pollution havens" do not bear the cost of environmental externalities, contrary to high-standards abiding industries (Hamilton 2001). This definition of environmental dumping must be distinguished from dumping as merely price discrimination—selling "below cost"—and from dumping as the export of **hazardous wastes** (see also **Rotterdam Convention**).

Concerns over environmental dumping often lead to calls for imposing countervailing or antidumping duties (labeled "environmental tariffs," "green tariffs," or "eco-tariffs"). Proponents consider that environmental tariffs are necessary not only to offset unfair competitive advantages (Hudec 1996), but also to induce responsible behavior in countries with low environmental standards. Opponents argue that upward harmonization of environmental standards can happen without any external imposition of standards on foreign countries (see **Policy diffusion**).

Environmental dumping is increasingly discussed in relation to carbon leakage—where efforts to reduce emissions in one jurisdiction are offset by resulting increased emissions in another. In this context, environmental dumping is said to occur because some countries and their industries free-ride efforts to mitigate climate change in order to attract foreign direct investments, benefit from industry relocations, and gain market shares thanks to comparatively lower production costs (Janzen 2008). Environmental duties, as well as border tax adjustments measures (Pirlot 2017), have been proposed in order to equalize conditions of competition.

Some trade and investment agreements provide that parties may not use low environmental protection to gain a competitive edge in trade and investments, requiring **compliance and implementation** of existing standards (see for instance art. 18.3(2) of the Colombia-US (2006) Free Trade Agreement). However, international trade law does not recognize environmental dumping as a practice that may be subject, as such, to antidumping or countervailing duties. To this general rule, the law of the European Union (EU, see also **Regional governance**) contains an exception, as it takes into consideration the level of environmental protection in case of market distortions. Under certain circumstances, EU law therefore determines ETC the existence of dumping based on a benchmark country with an "adequate level of social and environmental protection" (art. 2 (6a) of Regulation (EU) 2017/2321).

References

Hamilton, Clive. 2001. "The Case for Fair Trade." *Journal of Australian Political Economy* 48: 60–72.

Hudec, Robert E. 1996. "Differences in National Environmental Standards: The Level-Playing-Field Dimension." *Minnesota Journal of Global Trade* 5(1): 1–28.

Janzen, Bernd. 2008. "International Trade Law and the 'Carbon Leakage' Problem: Are Unilateral U.S. Import Restrictions the Solution?" *Sustainable Development Law and Policy* 8(2): 22–26, 84–85.

Pirlot, Alice. 2017. *Environmental Border Tax Adjustments and International Trade Law.* Cheltenham, Edward Elgar.

Rauscher, Michael. 1994. "On Ecological Dumping." *Oxford Economic Papers* 46: 822–840.

Vogel, David. 1995. *Trading up: Consumer and Environmental Regulation in a Global Economy.* Cambridge, MA, Harvard University Press.

ECOCENTRISM

Sheryl D. Breen

University of Minnesota Morris, United States

Ecocentrism is an ethical worldview based on an interconnected web of dynamic relationships among living entities and systems that include land and climate as well as animate individuals, species, and the ecological processes that link them. By emphasizing the intrinsic worth of ecological systems, ecocentrism stands in particular opposition to an anthropocentric approach to environmental thought and governance, which calls for protection on the basis of instrumental value to human needs and interests. In contrast, ecocentrism is founded on the notion that all parts of nature—human and nonhuman, living and nonliving—have inherent value and are constituted by and dependent on the all-encompassing interrelatedness of ecological communities.

Ecocentrism is not unique to the contemporary environmental movement; ethical systems that see humanity as enmeshed within the multilayered realms of the natural world are contained within many indigenous worldviews (Selin 2003). Within industrialized nations, ecocentrism developed in response to **liberal environmentalism** and modern conservation management techniques (see **Conservation and preservation**). The approach has drawn particular philosophical inspiration from Aldo Leopold's holistic "land ethic," which argues that we must reposition humans' connection with their biotic world through a new ethic that "changes the role of *Homo sapiens* from conqueror of the land-community to plain member and citizen of it" (Leopold 1968 [1949]: 204). In this way, according to Leopold, we must learn to "think like a mountain" in our understanding of the interrelationships between species and their environments (Leopold 1968 [1949]: 129–133).

A second foundational theorist, Arne Næss, moved ecocentric thought toward an emphasis on cosmological consciousness with his separation between an ecocentric **deep ecology** and "shallow" anthropocentric forms of environmental thought (Næss 1973). With further development by George Sessions and Bill Devall, the eight-point deep ecology platform incorporates the principle of intrinsic value, rejects the pursuit of higher living standards in favor of life quality, and calls for a commitment to change, including reduced human interference with the nonhuman world and a decrease in human population (Devall and Sessions 1985: 69–73).

Early proponents and critics of ecocentric theory conversed primarily within the philosophical discipline of environmental ethics. Robyn Eckersley brought the discussion into the realm of politics with her examination of ecocentric thought as an "emancipatory" phase within the dialogue of environmental crisis (Eckersley 1992). She analyzed ecocentrism's enlarged notions of emancipation and autonomy and highlighted the diverging ecocentric components that can be found within intrinsic value theory, deep ecology, and **ecofeminism**. Eckersley described an ecocentric polity as one that incorporates greater economic and political equality with multilayered democratic decision-making structures and market controls, united by "the flowering of an ecocentric emancipatory culture" (Eckersley 1992: 85).

Current debates employ ecocentric frameworks on both moral issues and policy fronts. For example, Freya Mathews proposes an ethic of bio-proportionality, raising the threshold from species viability to a threshold of optimal populations for all species (Mathews 2016). In its policy-oriented campaign, the Nature Needs Half coalition of conservation scientists and environmental leaders uses ecocentric principles in its call to protect and interconnect 50% of the world's land and seascapes (Dinerstein et al. 2017).

Commentators have offered a range of criticisms. First, some charge that ecocentrism's holistic egalitarianism is misanthropic and that this worldview promotes eco-authoritarianism rather than **green democracy**. In response, ecocentric theorists argue that ecocentrism's emancipatory and egalitarian elements augment and extend rather than replace advances in **human and environmental rights** and **environmental justice**. Second, critics contend that ecocentrism relies on a false dichotomy based on an erroneously harsh definition of anthropocentrism. This concern has encouraged more complex analyses of anthropocentrism and inspired approaches that move further from deep ecology toward a value-pluralist ethic. Third, because nonhumans, species, and ecosystems are unable to represent their interests, critics charge that ecocentrism is neither philosophically coherent nor implementable. In response, ecocentrists are examining ways to incorporate nonhuman interests in political decision-making through designated representation in green state structures (Eckersley 2004).

References

Devall, Bill and George Sessions. 1985. *Deep Ecology: Living as if Nature Mattered.* Salt Lake City, UT, Gibbs Smith.

Dinerstein, Eric, David Olson, Anup Joshi, Carly Vynne, Neil D. Burgess, Eric Wikramanayake, Nathan Hahn, Suzanne Palminteri, Prashant Hedao, Reed Noss, Matt Hansen, Harvey Locke, Erle C. Ellis, Benjamin Jones, Charles Victor Barber, Randy Hayes, Cyril Kormos, Vance Martin, Eileen Crist, Wes Sechrest, Lori Price, Jonathan E. M. Baillie, Don Weeden, Kierán Suckling, Crystal Davis, Nigel Sizer, Rebecca Moore, David Thau, Tanya Birch, Peter Potapov, Svetlana Turubanova, Alexandra Tyukavina, Nadia de Souza, Lilian Pintea, José C. Brito, Othman A. Llewellyn, Anthony G. Miller, Annette Patzelt, Shahina A. Ghazanfar, Jonathan Timberlake, Heinz Klöser, Yara Shennan-Farpón, Roeland Kindt, Jens-Peter Barnekow Lillesø, Paulo van Breugel, Lars Graudal, Maianna Voge, Khalaf F. Al-Shammari, and Muhammad Saleem. 2017. "An Ecoregion-Based Approach to Protecting Half the Terrestrial Realm." *BioScience* 67(6): 534–545.

Eckersley, Robyn. 1992. *Environmentalism and Political Theory: Toward an Ecocentric Approach.* Albany, NJ, SUNY Press.

Eckersley, Robyn. 2004. *The Green State: Rethinking Democracy and Sovereignty.* Cambridge, MA, MIT Press.

Leopold, Aldo. 1968 [1949]. *A Sand County Almanac, and Sketches Here and There.* New York, Oxford University Press.

Mathews, Freya. 2016. "From Biodiversity-Based Conservation to an Ethic of Bio-Proportionality." *Biological Conservation* 200: 140–148.

Næss, Arne. 1973. "The Shallow and the Deep, Long-Range Ecology Movement: A Summary." *Inquiry* 16: 95–100.

Selin, Helaine (Ed.). 2003. *Nature across Cultures: Views of Nature and the Environment in Non-Western Cultures*. Boston, MA, Kluwer Academic Publishers.

ECOFEMINISM

Mary Phillips

University of Bristol, United Kingdom

Ecofeminism encompasses a range of views and has been described as a quilt "made up of different 'patches' constructed … in particular social, historical and materialist contexts" (Warren 2000: 66). It is therefore more accurate to talk about ecofeminisms rather than ecofeminism. Challenging the cross-cutting systems of domination that justify colonialism, racism, sexism, and the subordination of nature is common across ecofeminist philosophies. These share a commitment to overcome the oppression of women, nature, and other groups, not in an atomistic way, but through the radical restructuring of social and political institutions to obtain a more just world for all. The three pillars of ecofeminisms that underpin this are: the need to recognize humanity as part of a web of life (see **Gaia theory** and **Deep ecology**), the revaluation of epistemological frameworks to include what rationality currently denies (Glazebrook, 2005), and a focus on an ecocentric ethic of care as a moral imperative and call for action (Phillips 2019) (see **Ecocentrism**).

Some ecofeminisms stress historical, biological and experiential connections between women and nature, with their joint oppression being the result of male domination and control. They seek to create and celebrate women's cultures that would herald a new spiritual relationship to the planet (e.g. Starhawk 1988). This is critiqued as essentialist for its claims of women's special affinity with nature based in biologically determined and embodied experiences. Other ecofeminisms tend to focus on the social and political rather than personal and spiritual aspects of ecofeminisms, although they would reject a political/spiritual dualism. They point to dominant Western culture and its relationship to nature as the product of patriarchal logic expressed in the dualism of nature and reason (Plumwood 2002). MacGregor (2006) highlights approaches focusing on care as part of a feminist ecological citizenship. Ecofeminists have also drawn on the experiences of indigenous peoples, particularly women in the global South (e.g. Mies and Shiva 2014) and those of North American first nations. Some of this has been critiqued for lacking analysis of historical forms of power and violence built into "holistic," non-Western frameworks.

Despite the diversity of ecofeminisms, the main ecofeminist imperative can be summarized as the need to develop and practise different ways to live within the web of life built on foundations of respectful care that leave behind hyper-rational societies—or we will not survive.

Ecofeminisms led the way in areas such as current work on post-humanism and new materialism. Contemporary ecofeminisms draw on and develop a range of theories including poststructural feminism, postcolonial theory, and animal studies.

References

Glazebrook, Trish. 2005. "Gynocentric Eco-logics." *Ethics and the Environment* 10(2): 75–99.

MacGregor, Sherilyn. 2006. *Beyond Mothering Earth: Ecological Citizenship and the Politics of Care*. Vancouver, UBC Press.

Mies, Maria. and Vandana Shiva. 2014. *Ecofeminism*. London, Zed Books.

Phillips, Mary. 2019. "'Daring to Care': Challenging Corporate Environmentalism." *Journal of Business Ethics* 156(4): 1151–1164.

Plumwood, V. 2002. *Environmental Culture: The Ecological Crisis of Reason*. New York, Routledge.

Starhawk. 1988. *The Spiral Dance: A Rebirth of the Ancient Religion of the Great Goddess*. New York, HarperCollins.

Warren, Karen J. 2000. *Ecofeminist Philosophy: A Western Perspective on What It Is and Why It Matters*. Lanham, MD, Rowman and Littlefield.

ECOLOGICAL MODERNIZATION

Maarten Hajer
Utrecht University, Netherlands

Ecological modernization refers to the theory claiming that there are reformist solutions to the environmental problems facing society. With this pragmatist outlook, it distinguishes itself from **critical political economy** that suggests that the "ecological crisis" calls for a complete overhaul of Western (capitalist) societies or radical changes in consumer behavior.

The term "ecological modernization" is attributed to Martin Jänicke and Joseph Huber who started using and promoting it in the early 1980s in Germany. Important theorists of ecological modernization are the environmental scientist Ernst-Ulrich von Weiszäcker (Weiszäcker et al. 2009), sociologists Gert Spaargaren and Arthur Mol (Mol et al. 2009). Maarten Hajer provided a critical analysis (1995). Although "ecological modernization" is an academic term, it is important to keep in mind that many of its protagonists played a role in politics, either in the shadows or on the actual stage. Ecological modernization is, in that sense, transdisciplinary in its intent, creating a perspective for change. The 1987 Brundtland report, *Our Common Future*, can be seen as a hallmark policy document based on the principles of ecological modernization. It coins the phrase "**sustainable development**" but is silent on more critical issues such as the future of nuclear power or the need for shifts in (Western) patterns of consumption.

Ecological modernization has five core components: (1) it believes "decoupling" of economic growth from environmental degradation is possible; (2) it regards environmental degradation as a problem of collective action, to be overcome by coordination and better incentive setting; (3) it makes environmental damage calculable hence it seeks to allow for an analysis of costs and benefits of environmental pollution; (4) it seeks to internalize environmental costs into mainstream calculations, whether that is on the level of **business and corporations** or in terms of the analysis of macro-economic performance, thus "greening the economy" (see **Green economy**); and (5) it has a firm belief in the potential of technological and social innovation.

The Organisation for Economic Co-operation and Development (OECD) has been intellectually pushing eco-modernist thinking since the 1980s and reports from the International Monetary Fund (IMF) and **World Bank** have taken up eco-modernist thinking as well (IMF 2013; World Bank 2013) as has the World Business Council for Sustainable development (WBCSD). The eco-modernist discourse is broadly respected within international institutions yet it has not institutionalized into a coherent policy regime.

References

Hajer, Maarten A. 1995. *The Politics of Environmental Discourse—Ecological Modernization and the Policy Process*. Oxford, Oxford University Press.

International Monetary Fund. 2013. *Energy Subsidy Reform.* Washington, DC, IMF.

Mol, Arthur J.P., David A. Sonnenfeld, and Gert Spaargaren (Eds.). 2009. *The Ecological Modernization Reader—Environmental Reform in Theory and Practice.* London, Routledge.

Weiszäcker, Ernst Ulrich von, Karlson "Charlie" Hargroves, Michael H. Smith, Cheryl Desha, and Peter Stasinopoulos (Eds.) 2009. *Factor Five: Transforming the Global Economy through 80% Improvements in Resource Productivity.* London, Earthscan.

World Bank. 2013. *Turn Down the Heat.* Washington, DC, World Bank.

ECOSYSTEM SERVICES (PAYMENTS FOR)

Stefanie Engel

University of Osnabrueck, Germany

Payments for ecosystem services (PES) are a popular approach to promote the provision of ecosystem services (ES). The exact definition has been subject to debate, but most agree that PES are a positive economic incentive where ES providers can voluntarily apply for a payment conditional either on ES provision or on an activity clearly linked to ES provision (Engel 2016). Payments can be made for adopting an activity (e.g. afforestation) or refraining from a damaging activity (e.g. deforestation). Payment amounts may lie anywhere between the minimum payment required to compensate ES providers for their incremental cost of providing the service and the maximum payment represented by society's full valuation of the services. It is therefore misleading to interpret payments as "the" value of the ES, nor is economic valuation necessarily required to implement PES.

A first debate relates to the degree to which PES should rely on private sector involvement through **business and corporations**. PES examples range from decentralized, user-financed ("Coasean") to government-financed ("Pigouvian") schemes (Engel et al. 2008). The former result from a negotiation process between ES buyers and ES providers, while in the latter the government acts on behalf of ES buyers. The potential of pure Coasean PES is highly limited as many ES are local or **global public goods**, implying an important role for intermediaries. Many PES schemes, including Costa Rica's famous 1996 PES program, are hybrid **partnerships** involving some private sector

ES buyers, but also giving a substantial role for the government or other third parties.

A second debate relates to the degree to which PES can and should address environmental and social objectives at the same time. PES implement a "steward rewarded" rather than a **polluter pays principle**, providing an alternative income source to ES providers. Whether these providers are poor differs across contexts. Impacts depend on the poor's eligibility, willingness, and ability to participate in PES schemes and whether other groups (e.g. customary forest users) are affected (Pagiola et al. 2005). Recently, it has been argued that considering social equity in PES design may not only be relevant for social **justice** reasons, but that perceived inequity can undermine environmental outcomes of PES (Pascual et al. 2014).

A third debate centers on the actual performance of PES approaches. Empirical studies show that the environmental **effectiveness** of PES often falls behind expectations (Börner et al. 2017). It has been argued that this can be due to ignoring important PES design lessons (Wunder et al. 2018) and that effective PES design is a complex and context-dependent task (Engel 2016). Major design issues include, among others, assuring additionality, the degree of conditionality, differentiating payments, targeting payments in light of scarce budgets, paying for activities vs. outcomes, dealing with leakage and assuring permanence of ES provided (see **REDD+**), promoting spatial coordination, and avoiding reduction of intrinsic conservation motivations.

Ongoing research aims to assess the performance of PES via randomized controlled trials and to incorporate behavioral economic insights in PES design.

References

Börner, Jan, Kathy Baylis, Esteve Corbera, Driss Ezzine-de-Blas, Jordy Honey-Rosés, Martin U. Persson, and Sven Wunder. 2017. "The Effectiveness of Payments for Environmental Services." *World Development* 96: 359–374.

Engel, Stefanie. 2016. "The Devil in the Detail: A Practical Guide on Designing Payments for Environmental Services." *International Review of Environmental and Resource Economics* 9(1–2): 131–177.

Engel, Stefanie, Stefano Pagiola, and Sven Wunder. 2008. "Designing Payments for Environmental Services in Theory and Practice—An Overview of the Issues." *Ecological Economics* 65(4): 663–674.

Pagiola, Stefano, Agustin Arcenas, and Gunars Platais. 2005. "Can Payments for Environmental Services Help Reduce Poverty? An Exploration of the

Issue and the Evidence to Date from Latin America." *World Development* 33(2): 237–253.

Pascual, Unai, Jacob Phelps, Eneko Garmendia, Katrina Brown, Esteve Corbera, Adrian Martin, Eric Gomez-Baggethun, and Roldan Muradian. 2014. "Social Equity Matters in Payments for Ecosystem Services." *BioScience* 64(11): 1027–1036.

Wunder, Sven, Roy Brouwer, Stefanie Engel, Driss Ezzine-de-Blas, Roldan Muradian, Unai Pascual, and Rute Pinto. 2018. "From Principles to Practice in Paying for Nature's Services." *Nature Sustainability* 1(3): 145–150.

EFFECTIVENESS

Detlef F. Sprinz

Potsdam Institute for Climate Impact Research and University of Potsdam, Germany

Effectiveness is defined as the degree of improvement in environmental performance (impact) that can be causally attributed to governance, for example by way of international treaties, international **regimes**, domestic policies, or international **nonregimes**. While often confused with **compliance and implementation**, the various concepts point to different aspects. Compliance and implementation refer to obligations taken on by parties to a treaty or unilaterally in view of domestic audience costs—which may or may not have effects on environmental performance. Global environmental politics may even have effects in the absence of an international regime (e.g. if a nonregime induces domestic politics to undertake actions nationally that eschew international cooperation) or when international regimes may have effects on non-members. Effectiveness as the improvement of environmental quality or reduction in pollution loads may occur for reasons, inter alia, of international policies, uncoordinated national policies, the coordination of national and international policies, technological change, or lifestyle changes.

How can we measure effectiveness? In the absence of any policy, we can only take observations of the environment, using chemical, physical, social, political, or welfare measures to characterize the state of the environment and potential changes over time. Most common among social scientists is the interest in the ex post or ex ante *effects* of specific policies on environmental quality, such as specific pollution reduction policies at different **scales** (the domestic, regional (e.g. Asian or European) or international levels), changes in land use (e.g. designation of nature protection areas), or **adaptation** measures (e.g. building dams to prevent flooding in coastal areas due to the threat of sea-level rise). In the environmental field, policies often take a considerable amount of time to demonstrate an unequivocal break with the past, thereby demanding a sufficiently long time frame for **assessments**. In addition, the policy must be causally related to the effect to afford appropriate attribution. This is captured by the attention that needs to be placed on counterfactual reasoning, i.e. the environmental performance witnessed in the absence of a particular policy or a range of policies. Effectiveness can be measured at the output, outcome, or impact level. Measurement at the impact level best captures environmental effectiveness. As a second best solution, outcomes that are causally related to impacts should be considered, for example changes in pollution levels.

The Oslo-Potsdam Solution has served as a benchmark concept to measure the effectiveness of global, international, and EU policies. Building on Underdal (1992), Sprinz and Helm (1999) and Helm and Sprinz (2000) developed a synoptic approach (Hovi et al. 2003a). At the outset, a dimension (e.g. pollution levels or an environmental quality index) has to be chosen that is causally linked to environmental quality. Subsequently, three components have to be located on this dimension: (1) the non-policy counterfactual in the absence of the policy (lower bound); (2) the pollution level actually associated with a specific policy; and (3) the collective optimum of an ideal (counterfactual) policy performance (upper bound). If the distance traveled from the no-policy counterfactual to the actual policy (2–1) is divided by the potential for improvement of the environment (collective optimum minus non-regime counterfactual, 3–1), a simple effectiveness score can be computed, ranging from zero to one (Helm and Sprinz 2000). The Oslo-Potsdam Solution to measuring regime effectiveness has proven useful in a range of applications in research on environmental policy as well as in other fields of international studies (e.g. Grundig 2006) and has enjoyed a range of extensions.

To date, the Oslo-Potsdam Solution is the only numerical solution to measuring the effect of international treaty regimes and EU policies (both aggregate and country-specific effects), but could easily be used in the context of nonregimes (to elucidate whether these have effects), domestic policies, or multiple dimensions (necessitating a procedure of aggregation across dimensions). The Oslo-Potsdam Solution has received fruitful criticism by the scholarly community. A friendly exchange between the proponents of the Oslo-Potsdam Solution and Oran Young (Young 2001, 2003; Hovi et al. 2003a, 2003b) clarified a range of opportunities and shortcomings of the Oslo-Potsdam Solution.

Empirically, the early regulations under the **transboundary air pollution regime** have received the strongest attention in terms of effectiveness assessments. Depending on the method chosen, the early sulfur and nitrogen protocols have generated only mild to medium effects on environmental quality, thus leaving substantial scope for improved policy design (e.g. Helm and Sprinz 2000). Recent research showed benign effects of (1) the EU on member countries during the first compliance period under the Kyoto Protocol on climate change as well as (2) legally binding (compared with legally nonbinding) international agreements on European water quality (Avrami and Sprinz 2019; Köppel and Sprinz 2019).

Perhaps the most heralded global environmental agreement is the **ozone regime** (Montreal Protocol and amendments) on substances that deplete the stratospheric ozone layer. Since 1980, ozone-depleting substances have been reduced very substantially, yet recovery to 1980s levels is not foreseen before the 2060s.

The **climate change regime** on greenhouse gas mitigation and especially its 2015 Paris Agreement will hopefully witness a similar trajectory.

References

Avrami, Lydia and Detlef F. Sprinz. 2019. "Measuring and Explaining the EU's Effect on National Climate Performance." *Environmental Politics* 28(5): 822–846.

Grundig, Frank. 2006. "Patterns of International Cooperation and the Explanatory Power of Relative Gains: An Analysis of Cooperation on Global Climate Change, Ozone Depletion, and International Trade." *International Studies Quarterly* 50(4): 781–801.

Helm, Carsten and Detlef F. Sprinz. 2000. "Measuring the Effectiveness of International Environmental Regimes." *Journal of Conflict Resolution* 44(5): 630–652.

Hovi, Jon, Detlef F. Sprinz, and Arild Underdal. 2003a. "The Oslo-Potsdam Solution to Measuring Regime Effectiveness: Critique, Response, And Extensions." *Global Environmental Politics* 3(3): 74–96.

Hovi, Jon, Detlef F. Sprinz, and Arild Underdal. 2003b. "Regime Effectiveness and the Oslo-Potsdam Solution: A Rejoinder to Oran Young." *Global Environmental Politics* 3(3): 105–107.

Köppel, Martin and Detlef F. Sprinz. 2019. "Do Binding Beat Nonbinding Agreements? Regulating International Water Quality." *Journal of Conflict Resolution* 63(8): 1860–1888.

Sprinz, Detlef F. and Carsten Helm. 1999. "The Effect of Global Environmental Regimes: A Measurement Concept." *International Political Science Review* 20(4): 359–369.

Underdal, Arild. 1992. "The Concept of Regime 'Effectiveness'." *Cooperation and Conflict* 27(3): 227–240.

Young, Oran R. 2001. "Inferences and Indices: Evaluating the Effectiveness of International Environmental Regimes." *Global Environmental Politics* 1(1): 99–121.

Young, Oran R. 2003. "Determining Regime Effectiveness: A Commentary on the Oslo-Potsdam Solution." *Global Environmental Politics* 3(3): 97–104.

EMERGING COUNTRIES

Ana Flávia Barros-Platiau
University of Brasilia, Brazil

Amandine Orsini
Université Saint-Louis – Bruxelles, Belgium

In 1981, Antoine van Agtmael coined the term "emerging markets," in contrast to the "third world" concept. His idea was to point at the fact that several developing countries were in a period of transition, performing better economically than the rest of the South. According to the International Monetary Fund (IMF), the top ten emerging markets in 2018, therefore before the Coronavirus crisis which is likely to change the game were China, India, Brazil, Russia, Mexico, Indonesia, Turkey, Thailand, South Africa, and Malaysia. Some of these countries perform very well economically, but they also face social priorities (with low human development indexes) and are laggards with regards to environmental performance. Emerging countries therefore have mixed characteristics and challenge traditional concepts such as the North–South divide.

Emerging countries are considered rich in terms of biodiversity resources (Orsini and Nakanabo Diallo 2015), or megadiverse—as they host most of the world's biodiversity—and have traditional populations that own important knowledge that biotechnology companies can turn into commercial applications (pharmaceuticals, cosmetics, etc.). But they are also large polluters, the fastest growing greenhouse gas emitters and are vulnerable to natural **disasters** due to serious social problems and lack of **adaptation** policies. One should keep in mind that more

Indians and Chinese live under the poverty line than the population of all least developed countries put together.

From a global environmental perspective, emerging countries are interesting for two reasons. First, their respective fast-growing middle classes tend to have an increasing environmental footprint. Second, their economic performance led them to struggle for more assertiveness in major multilateral institutions, notably those concerning trade, financing, and development, particularly China.

Although there is no clear definition of the category of emerging countries, two broad emerging countries' **negotiating coalitions** active in economic governance have embraced environmental issues, namely the BRICS (Brazil, Russia, India, China, and South Africa) and the IBSA (India, Brazil, and South Africa). These loose coalitions actively support multilateral arenas linking development and environment, such as the 2015 Addis Ababa Action Agenda and the **Sustainable Development Goals** (SDGs).

Emerging countries can also organize in specific groups within particular negotiations. It was only in 2009, at the Copenhagen summit of the **climate change regime**, that emerging countries expressed themselves in a coalition specifically dedicated to climate change known as the BASIC group (Brazil, South Africa, India, and China) that has been prominent within climate negotiations (Hochstetler and Milkoreit 2015). In October 2019, in a collective declaration, BASIC members confirmed "their commitments to multilateralism in order to address the issue and to foster climate resilience and promote greenhouse gas emissions reduction, low-carbon and sustainable development." Yet, their specific plans for action are unclear.

Emerging countries share principles and values that enable them to work together, such as the right to development, and the **common but differentiated responsibilities** principle. Overall, they agree that high-income countries must take first responsibility for financing global environmental solutions. Still, they are inconsistent on a number of other issues. For instance, disparities between the members can be found in the biosafety regime and the genetic resources regime (Cullet and Raja 2004; Gupta and Falkner 2006), as well as in the ongoing biodiversity beyond national jurisdiction negotiations (see **Ocean protection**) and in the **Antarctic Treaty System** negotiations. It may also be argued that emerging countries have in common a frequently stark dissonance between their national policies and their foreign policy discourses. As a result, their international agenda is often limited by their poor environmental regulations at home (Economy 2006).

Finally, in global environmental politics, emerging countries are often inclined to maintain a status quo that plays in their favor (with principles such as **sovereignty** or common but differentiated responsibilities), rather than promoting major reforms (Hurrell and Sengupta 2012). A few aspects are changing—there are some indications that emerging countries are trying to embrace donor roles (see also **Aid**). While the balance between the environmental benefits and harms of the individual projects their development banks finance is not evident (Hochstetler 2019), they are recently actively engaging in multilateral funding schemes such as the International Development Finance Club for climate action (see also **Sustainable finance**).

References

Cullet, Philippe and Jawahar Raja. 2004. "Intellectual Property Rights and Biodiversity Management: The Case of India." *Global Environmental Politics* 4(1): 97–114.

Economy, Elizabeth. 2006. "Environmental Governance: The Emerging Economic Dimension." *Environmental Politics* 15(2): 171–189.

Gupta, Aarti and Robert Falkner. 2006. "The Influence of the Cartagena Protocol on Biosafety: Comparing Mexico, China and South Africa." *Global Environmental Politics* 6(4): 23–55.

Hochstetler, Kathryn. 2019. "South-South Relations and Global Environmental Governance: Brazilian International Development Cooperation." *Revista Brasileira de Política Internacional* 62(2): 1–22.

Hochstetler, Kathryn and Manjana Milkoreit. 2015. "Responsibilities in Transition: Emerging Powers in the Climate Change Negotiations." *Global Governance* 21(2): 205–226.

Hurrell, Andrew and Sandeep Sengupta. 2012. "Emerging Powers, North–South Relations and Global Climate Politics." *International Affairs* 88(3): 463–484.

Orsini, Amandine and Rozenn Nakanabo Ndiallo. 2015. "Emerging Countries and the Convention on Biological Diversity." In *Rising Powers and Multilateral Institutions*, Eds. Dries Lesage and Thijs Van de Graaf, 258–276. Basingstoke and New York, Palgrave Macmillan.

Papa, Mihaela and Nancy W. Gleason. 2012. "Major Emerging Powers in Sustainable Development Diplomacy: Assessing their Leadership Potential." *Global Environmental Change* 22(4): 915–924.

ENERGY TRANSITION

Espen Moe

Norwegian University of Science and Technology, Norway

An energy transition can be defined as a change in the structure of primary energy supply, or as a fundamental, long-term, structural change in the energy system. We often think of it as a transition away from fossil fuels toward a decarbonized system based primarily on renewables, but there have been many transitions. Hydropower experienced rapid improvements in the mid-eighteenth century, coal was the early nineteenth century miracle fuel, electricity was utilized from the late nineteenth century, oil became the world's engine in the early twentieth century, and nuclear was a potential, but stillborn, revolution after the mid-twentieth century. We may also distinguish between transitions from biomass to fossil fuels and from animate to inanimate prime movers. These transitions have had major economic, social, and political effects, driving the world economy, creating industries, re-shaping the organization of industry and labor, and changing the balance of power between states (Moe 2010; Smil 2017).

Transitions typically flow from the discovery and exploitation of a new source of abundant energy that rapidly becomes cheaper and more exploitable. Politically, transitions depend on overcoming energy incumbents and vested energy interests. Today, renewable energy is growing in the shadow of arguably the biggest and most powerful incumbents ever; the major petroleum companies have obvious interests in preserving the existing energy system, preventing rather than encouraging structural change (Moe 2010).

Aiding transition is the fact that we now have far more knowledge about transitions than before (see **Science**). The current transition however also crucially differs. Renewable energy is yet not substantively cheaper or more abundant than existing alternatives, and there is still no strong economic rationale for a transition (see **Green economy**). Thus, it has been politically rather than economically driven, fear of global warming the primary motivator. It also differs in that success is no longer the success of single countries, but of every country, lest the result is severe climate change consequences for all (see **Climate change regime**).

Do we have an energy transition? We do if new sources of energy *replace* rather than merely *supplement* existing sources. While increasing rapidly, solar and wind power still account for only 8.7% of global electricity production (27% when including hydropower, biopower, and geothermal) (2019 figures). However, renewable energy investments have been higher than fossil-fuel investments since 2006, and the renewable share of *annual additions* of power generating capacity has been above 50% since 2012. Thus, there are signs of a transition, if still in its infancy (REN21 2020).

The transition has progressed farthest in electricity, but global electricity production only accounts for 17% of total final energy consumption (TFEC). Transportation accounts for 32% (2017 figures). The influx of electric cars makes a transportation transition likely, and in Norway approximately half of regular car sales are already electric. But globally, by 2018, of the energy consumption in transportation the renewable electricity share was only 0.3%, and the transition is slow, because of the existing stock of gasoline cars and because solutions for ships and planes are more difficult. Biofuels may be a solution, accounting for another 3.4% (2018), but there is a clear trade-off between biofuels and food production (see **Agroecology**). Thus, the EU has capped the share of biofuels in transportation at 7%. For heating and cooling—51% of TFEC (2017 figures)—the renewable energy share is 10% (primarily bioenergy), but growing only slowly (REN21 2020; IEA 2020).

Some transition definitions comprise energy efficiency, and according to projections made by the International Energy Agency (IEA) it accounts for more than a third of the emissions cuts necessary for the 2°C climate target (IEA 2019). However, the logic behind energy efficiency is one of emissions reductions through more efficient energy use, i.e. optimizing energy use *within the existing structure*, which is fundamentally different from the logic of structural change and does not lead to a phase-in of renewables (see **Critical political economy**). Under certain conditions energy efficiency may even counteract a transition (Patt et al. 2019). Fossil fuel producers could for instance try to avoid structural change for as long as possible by fulfilling their climate goals through energy efficiency improvements.

Another general disagreement concerns human behavior. Thus, some believe that any transition must include a dramatic reduction in individual consumption—that is, a transition both on the *system level of analysis* and the *individual level* (i.e. Princen et al. 2015)—whereas others (i.e. Moe 2015) are adamant that regardless of individual behavior, energy transitions are fundamentally systemic events.

References

IEA. 2019. World Energy Outlook 2019. Paris, IEA Publications.

IEA. 2020. Tracking Clean Energy Progress. https://www.iea.org/topics/tracking-clean-energy-progress

Moe, Espen. 2010. "Energy, Industry and Politics." *Energy* 35(4): 1730–1740.

Moe, Espen. 2015. *Renewable Energy Transformation or Fossil Fuel Backlash.* Basingstoke, Hampshire, Palgrave Macmillan.

Patt, Anthony, Oscar Vliet, Johan Lilliestam, and Stefan Pfenninger. 2019. "Will Policies to Promote Energy Efficiency Help or Hinder Achieving a 1.5°C Climate Target?" *Energy Efficiency* 12(2): 551–565.

Princen, Thomas, Jack P. Manno, and Pamela L. Martin. 2015. *Ending the Fossil Fuel Era.* Cambridge, MA, MIT Press.

REN21. 2020. *Renewables 2020 Global Status Report.* Paris, REN21 Secretariat.

Smil, Vaclav. 2017. *Energy Transitions: Global and National Perspectives.* Santa Barbara, CA, Praeger.

ENVIRONMENTAL JUSTICE

Alexandre Gajevic Sayegh

Université Laval, Canada

Environmental justice refers to the fair distribution of environmental risks, burdens, and benefits between populations, as well as to the meaningful involvement of all people with regards to the development, implementation, and enforcement of environmental policies and laws (see **Compliance and implementation**). The term is used by social movements and studied in social sciences. While this definition applies to theoretical and practical developments of environmental justice, it should be stressed that environmental justice groups do not focus solely on distribution, but also on recognition, **participation**, and functioning (Schlosberg 2007).

Environmental justice movements aim to protect groups from unfair treatment and exclusion. Local movements, past and present, provide a powerful lens through which it is possible to make sense of global struggles. Consider the case of activists and local representatives in Richmond, California, who have had to repeatedly sue Chevron Corporation. While the fossil fuel giant still contributes to this day to 10% of the city's budget, residents of Richmond have been facing the dire consequences of air pollution emanating from Chevron's major refinery in the city for decades. Following an explosion in 2012, the third in as many decades, 15,000 residents had to seek treatment for respiratory difficulties. Now note that 80% of Richmond residents are non-whites. Fifteen percent live in poverty. Children in Richmond have twice the asthma rate as children of nearby counties. This is a case of environmental injustice: a disadvantaged population bearing a disproportionate share of environmental consequences resulting from industrial activity. An explicit connection between the environmental justice movement in the United States and the environmentalism in South America, Asia, and Africa has been established since the mid-1990s (Martinez-Alier et al. 2016). Today, the Global Atlas of Environmental Justice provides an inventory of global socio-environmental conflicts. Local conflicts thus raise these issues to the global level.

Many actors of global environmental justice are indigenous and traditional communities, as well as ethnically discriminated groups, often engaged in a fight against environmental racism (Martinez-Alier et al. 2016). Consider the case of First Nations groups in British Columbia, Canada, demanding meaningful inclusion in the consultation process over the Trans Mountain pipeline expansion project. This project aims at the transportation of diluted bitumen, which poses even greater environmental risks to drinking water and indigenous lands than crude oil carriage, since the spillages are considerably harder to clean. The project will also endanger local species such as the Southern Resident orcas from increased oil tanker traffic. **Indigenous people and local communities** in the Canadian province are arguing that as of 2019 the Federal Government has not fulfilled its constitutional duty to consult, thus illustrating that participation is an important component of environmental justice, which can be supported by environmental law.

Environmental justice theories and movements have also increasingly insisted on the importance of discussing the obligations that humans should have toward other living species, in particular animals (see **Ecocentrism**). The **migration** that will result from displacements of populations that suffer from sea-level rises, more frequent droughts, and wildfires highlights another case of global environmental justice.

Theories of environmental justice can also contain an intergenerational dimension. For an example of intergenerational environmental injustice, observe that future generations will suffer an unfair burden from the depletion of natural resources, the loss of **biodiversity**, unsafe waste disposal, and desertification (see also **Desertification Convention**). Current generations are using resources at a rate that is inconsistent with the regeneration of natural resources and are therefore imposing an unjust burden on future people (see also **Carrying capacities paradigm**). Theories of intergenerational environmental justice will formulate principles to determine what burdens should be placed on current generations to ensure decent life prospects for future generations (Caney 2014).

Climate justice is a complex and pressing case of environmental justice. Like environmental justice, climate justice refers to the fair distribution of climate risks, burdens, and benefits between populations, as well as to the meaningful involvement of relevant parties in the development, implementation, and enforcement of climate policies. Theories of climate justice often respond to a theoretical challenge, a global challenge, and an intergenerational challenge (Gardiner 2011), while discussing mitigation, **adaptation**, migration or **geoengineering**, among other issues. A central question of global climate justice concerns how the burdens of fighting climate change should be distributed between countries. The leading principle of "**common but differentiated responsibilities**" was formulated in 1992 at the Rio Summit. As the **climate change regime** evolved, more precise interpretations of this principle are surfacing (Gajevic Sayegh 2018). The Annex I/Non-Annex I governance approach, which opposes polluting developed nations and low-emissions developing nations, does not capture the reality of rapidly growing emissions in **emerging countries**. Principles for the distribution of responsibilities for climate change mitigation can thus be grounded on key normative notions, such as: historical responsibility, according to which not all countries are equally responsible for past greenhouse gases (GHG) emissions; and capacity, which is sensitive to nations' capacity to reduce emissions without jeopardizing their economy.

Any reasonable principle discussing adaptation to climate change will raise the central issue that not all countries will be impacted in the same way, and that not all countries have the same capability to respond to the problem. Many lower income countries, notably in South Asia and Africa, will face the consequences of sea-level rise, droughts, and food scarcity, while having not contributed meaningfully to climate change. These nations today are not only asking for countries to lower their GHG emissions, but also asking developed nations to fulfill their pledges of **aid**, reiterated in the Paris Agreement in 2015. Note that the general idea of assisting countries in meeting the cost of adaptation can be traced to the United Nations Framework Convention on Climate Change of 1992.

For economies that rely heavily on emissions-intensive industries (e.g. Australia, Canada, and India) just transition issues are increasingly becoming more apparent (Stern 2015). Novel theories will have to determine how the burdens of climate action should be distributed among governments, workers, corporations, and households. Consider the case of carbon pricing. Imposing a price on carbon creates an incentive for all sectors upon which the price is imposed to lower their emissions. As the price is generally reflected all the way down the consumer chain, consumers will feel the price increase of carbon-intensive goods. Also, workers might lose their jobs in carbon-intensive sectors. Should workers be entitled to training and support in the **green economy** transition? Should the revenues of carbon pricing be returned to lower income households? Should subsidies to polluting industries become conditional upon GHG emissions reduction? Theories of climate justice thus ought to speak to the distribution of burdens and benefits in the green economy transition.

References

Caney, Simon. 2014. "Climate Change, Intergenerational Equity and the Social Discount Rate." *Politics, Philosophy & Economics* 13(4): 320–342.

Gajevic Sayegh, Alexandre. 2018. "Climate Justice after Paris: A Normative Framework." *Journal of Global Ethics* 13(3): 344–365.

Gardiner, Stephen. 2011. *A Perfect Moral Storm*. Oxford, Oxford University Press.

Martinez-Alier, Joan, Leah Temper, Daniela Del Bene, and Arnim Scheidel. 2016. "Is There a Global Environmental Justice Movement?" *The Journal of Peasant Studies* 43(3): 731–755.

Schlosberg, David. 2007. *Defining Environmental Justice: Theories, Movements, and Nature*. Oxford, Oxford University Press.

Stern, Nicholas. 2015. *Why Are We Waiting? The Logic, Urgency and Promise of Tackling Climate Change*. Cambridge, MA, MIT Press.

EPISTEMIC COMMUNITIES

Mai'a K. Davis Cross

Northeastern University, United States

Epistemic communities are networks of experts who persuade others (usually elite decision-makers) of their shared norms and policy goals by virtue of their professional knowledge. Their reliance on shared expertise is what differentiates them from other actors that seek to influence policy. This expertise need not necessarily be derived from hard **science**, as knowledge in environmental law or **disasters** response, for example, is no less expertise-driven than knowledge in environmental science or biology. However, epistemic communities' policy goals must derive from their members' expert knowledge, not some other motivation, otherwise they may lose authority with their target audience. Epistemic communities are recognized as key actors in transnational global governance, especially environmental governance, and they are a major means by which knowledge translates into power, in a less formalized way than for **boundary organization**s.

The concept of epistemic communities did not become widely known in the environmental politics literature until Peter Haas's 1990 book on the Mediterranean Action Programme. Later, a 1992 special issue of *International Organization* entitled "Knowledge, Power, and International Policy Coordination" defined epistemic community as "a network of professionals with recognized expertise and competence in a particular domain and an authoritative claim to policy-relevant knowledge within that domain or issue area" (Haas 1992: 3). The various contributors to this special issue operationalized the concept, provided numerous case studies, and laid out a research program for the future, which dozens of scholars in disciplines as varied as education, management science, and history of science have since followed. International relations scholars have used it to explain the setup of several international **regimes** including on the ozone layer, acid rain, whaling, or the Mediterranean Sea (Peterson 1992; Toke 1999).

In recent years, the literature has gone beyond the special issue to rethink and explore the boundaries of the concept, particularly in light of increasing globalization and the emergence of new forms of transnational global governance (Cross 2013), of which cooperation in dealing with climate change is a prime example (Gough and Shackley 2001). Epistemic communities can be located both within governance structures as well as outside of them. Moreover, the reason why these groups of experts come together is not as important as how they behave once they form their network. An epistemic community is evident when its members act together beyond their formal mandate, meet frequently in informal settings, develop shared norms, and at times even push against any governmental instructions they might receive to try to influence policy based on their shared expertise. One innovation to the concept is the argument that epistemic communities do not simply exist or not exist, but have varying degrees of influence, depending on their political opportunities (Zito 2001), alliances with environmental **nongovernmental organizations** (NGOs) (Gough and Shackley 2001; Meijerink 2005), types of scientific knowledge communicated (Dimitrov

2006), stages of policymaking (Campbell Keller 2009), and internal cohesion as a group (Cross 2013). For example, in the case of international whaling, Peterson (1992) finds that whalers and NGOs had much more influence on the **International Whaling Commission** (IWC) than epistemic communities of cetologists, as the latter were not as close to decision-makers in government, and had major scientific disagreements within their group at precisely the time when their influence might have mattered.

In an increasingly globalized world, epistemic communities, along with other transnational and non-state actors, such as advocacy networks, multinational corporations, lobbying groups, interpretive communities, rhetorical communities, and communities of practice are of growing importance (see **Transgovernmental networks** and **Business and corporations**). Epistemic communities not only craft specific government policies, but also shape environmental governance more broadly. Meijerink (2005) examines the case study of Dutch coastal flooding policy from 1945 to 2003, and finds that strong advocacy coalitions of safety experts and environmentalists have worked alongside influential epistemic communities of civil engineers and ecologists to develop coastal engineering projects in the Netherlands for **adaptation**. In the area of climate change, Gough and Shackley (2001) find that members of environmental NGOs sometimes contribute to broader epistemic communities as their expertise grows. Indeed, they find that these NGOs may even be too engaged in the formal policy process, as they are increasingly being invited to the negotiation table, and losing touch with the constituents whose opinions they wish to represent in the first place.

The concept of epistemic community has faced some criticism, especially stemming from the tendency to neglect the politics and power dynamics that provide the context for knowledge production. Those in power who stand to lose or gain from policy decisions about the environment may easily politicize expert knowledge to suit their own ends (Litfin 1995; Toke 1999; Lidskog and Sundqvist 2002). This type of politicization of environmental knowledge has had a clear impact, such as failure to reach agreement in international environmental negotiations or beliefs in some sectors of the public that climate change is a hoax. Thus, while the concept of epistemic communities is valuable in structuring our understanding of the role of expertise in politics, the power context must be taken into account in each case study. Nonetheless, this significant body of research clearly shows that networks with recognized expertise, shared policy goals, and a willingness to act are often highly influential.

References

Campbell Keller, Ann. 2009. *Science in Environmental Policy: The Politics of Objective Advice.* Cambridge, MA, MIT Press.

Cross, Mai'a K. Davis. 2013. "Rethinking Epistemic Communities Twenty Years Later." *Review of International Studies* 39(1): 137–160.

Dimitrov, Radoslav. 2006. *Science and International Environmental Policy: Regimes and Nonregimes in Global Governance.* Lanham, MD, Rowman & Littlefield.

Gough, Clair and Simon Shackley. 2001. "The Respectable Politics of Climate Change: The Epistemic Communities and NGOs." *International Affairs* 77(2): 329–345.

Haas, Peter. 1990. *Saving the Mediterranean: The Politics of International Environmental Cooperation.* New York, Columbia University Press.

Haas, Peter. 1992. "Introduction: Epistemic Communities and International Policy Coordination." *International Organization* 46(1): 1–35.

Lidskog, Rolf and Göran Sundqvist. 2002. "The Role of Science in Environmental Regimes: The Case of LRTAP." *European Journal of International Relations* 8(1): 77–101.

Litfin, Karen, T. 1995. "Framing Science: Precautionary Discourse and the Ozone Treaties." *Millennium* 24(2): 251–277.

Meijerink, Sander. 2005. "Understanding Policy Stability and Change: The Interplay of Advocacy Coalitions and Epistemic Communities, Windows of Opportunity, and Dutch Coastal Flooding Policy 1945–2003." *Journal of European Public Policy* 12(6): 1060–1077.

Peterson, M.J. 1992. "Whalers, Cetologists, Environmentalists, and the International Management of Whaling." *International Organization* 46(1): 147–186.

Toke, David. 1999. "Epistemic Communities and Environmental Groups." *Politics* 19(2): 97–102.

Zito, Anthony. 2001. "Epistemic Communities, Collective Entrepreneurship and European Integration." *Journal of European Public Policy* 8(4): 585–603.

FISHERIES GOVERNANCE

Elizabeth R. Desombre
Wellesley College, United States

Fish are an important resource for human consumption, and play central roles in aquatic ecosystems. But they are frequently overharvested, according to a **tragedy of the commons** scenario, and most ocean fisheries are either overexploited or can withstand no additional harvesting (FAO 2018: 40). Governance of fishing resources on the high seas is provided by **regional governance** through Regional Fishery Management Organizations (RFMOs). These organizations generally have a regional focus, and often a species focus as well, as exemplified by the Indian Ocean Tuna Commission (IOTC).

Although each RFMO has its own rules of procedure, they have some common elements. Decisions about catch limits or permitted equipment are made through a regulatory process that takes place every year or two. Most RFMOs have scientific committees that either conduct or aggregate research. These committees generally make recommendations on sustainable levels of fish catches or other management approaches (see **Science**). Those recommendations are then voted on by a fisheries commission, in which each state has one vote. Often these commission decisions do not require unanimity, and therefore allow dissenting states to opt out of rules with which they disagree. In addition, the regulations passed by fisheries commissions are rarely as strict as scientific advice advocates (Barkin and DeSombre 2013: 72).

Under the best of circumstances, fisheries governance is a challenge. There is often uncertainty about the health of fish stocks and the level of fishing they can sustain. Those whose livelihoods depend on continuing fishing often have short time horizons, and advocate high catches in the short term (even though they are the ones that would most benefit from successful long-term **conservation and preservation**), creating political pressure for laxer rules. And because of the vastness of the ocean and the difficulty of monitoring, **compliance and implementation** of the rules that are created can be low (Barkin and DeSombre 2013: 21–22) (see also **Ocean protection**).

States can also decline to be bound by international regulations, whether by opting out of rules or by simply remaining outside of the international regulatory system. Fishing vessels can also register in "flags of convenience," adopting the flag of states that keep fees and level of regulation low. Since a ship is bound by the rules its registry state has taken on, registry states lure fishing vessel registration by refraining from joining RFMOs.

Fisheries governance is made more difficult by subsidies that many states give to support their domestic fishing industries, thereby generating greater fishing capacity than can be supported by global fish stocks (Sumaila and Pauly 2006). The regional system of fisheries regulation also does not fit well with the global nature of the fishing industry; when ships are prevented by regulation from fishing for a given species or in a particular region, ships can shift focus to a different species or region.

The regulated stock may be well protected, but at the cost of increased fishing pressure elsewhere.

References

Barkin, J. Samuel and Elizabeth R. Desombre. 2013. *Saving Global Fisheries.* Cambridge, MA, MIT Press.

Food and Agriculture Organization (FAO). 2018. *The State of World Fisheries and Aquaculture 2018.* Rome, Food and Agriculture Organization of the United Nations.

Sumaila, Ussif Rashid and Daniel Pauly (Eds.). 2006. *Catching More Bait: A Bottom-Up Re-estimation of Global Fisheries Subsidies.* Fisheries Centre Research Reports 14(6). Vancouver, University of British Columbia

GAIA THEORY

Karen Litfin

University of Washington, United States

Gaia theory emerged as a falsifiable scientific hypothesis which posits Earth as a living system whose biosphere, atmosphere, lithosphere, and hydrosphere create conditions conducive to the furtherance of life (Lovelock 1979). In contrast to conventional evolutionary theory, life co-creates rather than merely adapts to its environment. Gaia theory represents a paradigm shift from reductionism to scientific holism most evident in its contribution to Earth system science, the new integrative mega-discipline that has catalyzed the term "**Anthropocene**."

Yet Gaia theory's sociopolitical impact may be even greater. By endowing the ancient image of *anima mundi* (or living earth) with scientific credibility, Gaia theory undercuts modernity's anthropocentric and mechanistic conception of Earth as a vast storehouse of inert resources for human consumption. Gaia theory at once dissolves the dichotomy between humans and nature and highlights the entanglement of the human future with Earth's evolutionary future (Crist and Rinker 2010).

While Gaia theory's implications for global governance are unclear at this early juncture, some broad principles are discernible. Living systems, from the cell to Gaia, are constituted through interdependent symbiotic networks that transform waste into food even as they propel Gaia's geophysiology (Litfin 2012). The global economy, which drives matter and energy on a linear trajectory from resource extraction to waste is profoundly at odds with Gaia, which knows no waste (see **Carrying capacity paradigm**). Gaian governance would therefore regulate circular economies within the homeostasis of the Earth system. Unlike today's competitive global economy, actors in a Gaian economy would operate symbiotically to the benefit of both themselves and the whole.

One model of Gaian governance is a nested system of participatory democratic polities from the neighborhood to the global level (see **Global deliberative democracy**). The guiding principle would be subsidiarity, the idea that social and political decisions should be made at the lowest level practicable (see **Scale**). Ecologically, the question would be: *what functions are most appropriate to the global scale?* A global Internet might pass the test, but most trade and travel would not. Gaian governance would therefore entail some relocalization, but this alone would leave the primary levers of power in the hands of the powers that be. We need, therefore, to "think *and* act globally *and* locally." In a profoundly unequal world, this raises the enormous distributive question: how should economic development proceed in an ecologically full world? Gaian governance would also foreground procedural justice—*who gets to decide and how?*—on a planetary scale. Natural and social scientists are debating these questions in the emerging field of Earth-system governance (Biermann 2014).

Until now, Gaia has apparently operated without purpose or planning. Intentional self-regulation represents a fundamentally new state of Gaia: Gaia 2.0 (Lenton and Latour 2018). Gaia 2.0 could take many forms: from a globalized network of ecovillages and eco-cities (Wahl 2019) to an authoritarian "Climate Leviathan" (Wainwright and Mann 2018) to a Novacene governed by hyper-intelligent electronic beings (Lovelock and Appleyard 2019).

In a time when anxiety and despair threaten our capacity for positive action, Gaia reminds us that we are an integral part—and an astonishing result—of an evolutionary process that has unfolded on our home planet for 4.5 billion years. We are neither separate from nor masters of nature; rather, we are the means by which Gaia is growing into self-awareness. The ramifications of this insight will suffuse human culture and politics for generations to come.

References

Biermann, Frank. 2014. *Earth System Governance: World Politics in the Anthropocene.* Cambridge, MA, MIT Press.

Crist, Eileen and Bruce Rinker. (Eds.). 2010. *Gaia in Turmoil: Climate Change, Biodepletion, and Earth Ethics in an Age of Crisis*. Cambridge, MA, MIT Press.

Lenton, Timothy M. and Bruno Latour. 2018. "Gaia 2.0: Could Humans Add Some Level of Self-Awareness to Earth's Self-Regulation?" *Science* 361(6407): 1066–1068.

Litfin, Karen. 2012. "Thinking Like a Planet: Integrating the World Food System into the Earth System." In *International Handbook of Environmental Politics, 2nd edition*, Ed. Peter Dauvergne, 419–430. Cheltenham, Edward Elgar.

Lovelock, James 1979. *Gaia: A New Look at Life on Earth*. Oxford, Oxford University Press.

Lovelock, James and Bryan Appleyard. 2019. *Novacene: The Coming Age of Hyperintelligence*. Cambridge, MA, MIT Press.

Wahl, Daniel C. 2019. "Gaia Education's Resources for Creating Multipliers of Local SDG Implementation." *Sustainability* 12(2): 134–139.

Wainwright, Joel and Geoff Mann. 2018. *Climate Leviathan: A Political Theory of our Planetary Future*. London, Verso.

GEOENGINEERING

David R. Morrow

American University, United States

Some researchers argue that, as a supplement to cutting greenhouse gas emissions, societies could reduce climate risk (see also **Risk society**) through geoengineering, the deliberate modification of Earth systems to counteract climate change. Some geoengineering methods, known as solar geoengineering or solar radiation management, would reflect sunlight into space before it warms the planet. Proposals to achieve this include, among others, releasing particles into the stratosphere or spraying salt into marine clouds to brighten them (Keith 2013; Reynolds 2019). The term geoengineering is sometimes taken (including in some international legal contexts) to encompass another way of modifying Earth systems known as carbon dioxide removal, which involves capturing carbon dioxide from the air and sequestering it (Talberg et al. 2018; Buck 2019). Reflecting the trend away from counting carbon dioxide removal as geoengineering, this entry focuses on solar geoengineering.

The existing governance **regime** for solar geoengineering is one of "governance-by-default," in which "geoengineering is loosely governed in an unplanned manner by a mix of international agreements designed for other purposes" (Talberg et al. 2018: 247). A range of international and domestic laws and governance structures apply to certain aspects of solar geoengineering, but few address geoengineering directly and none provides comprehensive governance (Talberg et al. 2018, Flegal et al. 2019, Reynolds 2019). For example, the **transboundary air pollution regime** imposes obligations on states injecting particles into the stratosphere, the **ozone regime** governs some possible impacts of doing so, and the **Law of the Sea Convention** applies to brightening marine clouds.

Many commentators doubt that governance-by-default suffices to govern solar geoengineering. Solar geoengineering raises difficult risk-risk trade-offs (Chhetri et al. 2018) and difficult issues in international law, politics, and global justice. Some scholars fear this makes solar geoengineering "ungovernable" (Hulme 2014). Others see it as a reason to improve governance (Chhetri et al. 2018; Talberg et al. 2018; Reynolds 2019).

Some important debates about governing solar geoengineering include: the nature and balance of risks at various stages of research, development, and deployment, including the role of **precautionary principles**; the ultimate goal of any possible deployment (Keith 2013; Buck 2019; Reynolds 2019); the role of public deliberation (Flegal *et al.* 2019; see also **Global deliberative democracy**); the appropriate degree of **polycentricity** in governance; and near-term governance needs (Chhetri et al. 2018).

References

Buck, Holly J. 2019. *After Geoengineering: Climate Tragedy, Repair, and Restoration.* London, Verso.

Chhetri, Netra, Dan Chong, Ken Conca, Richard Falk, Alexander Gillespie, Aarti Gupta, Sikina Jinnah, Prakash Kashwan, Myanna Lahsen, Andrew Light, Catriona McKinnon, Leslie Paul Thiele, Walter Valdivia, Paul Wapner, David Morrow, Carolyn Turkaly, and Simon Nicholson. 2018. *Governing Solar Radiation Management.* Washington, DC, Forum for Climate Engineering Assessment, American University.

Flegal, Jane A., Anna-Maria Hubert, David Morrow, and Juan B. Moreno-Cruz. 2019. "Solar Geoengineering: Social Science, Legal, Ethical, and Economic Frameworks." *Annual Review of Environment and Resources* 44(1): 399–423.

Hulme, Mike. 2014. *Can Science Fix Climate Change? A Case against Climate Engineering.* Cambridge, Polity Press.

Keith, David W. 2013. *A Case for Climate Engineering.* Cambridge, MA, MIT Press.

Reynolds, Jesse. 2019. *The Governance of Solar Geoengineering: Managing Climate Change in the Anthropocene.* Cambridge, Cambridge University Press.

Talberg, Anita, Peter Christoff, Sebastian Thomas, and David Karoly. 2018. "Geoengineering Governance-by-Default: An Earth System Governance Perspective." *International Environmental Agreements: Politics, Law and Economics* 18(2): 229–253.

GLOBAL DELIBERATIVE DEMOCRACY

John Dryzek

University of Canberra, Australia

Global deliberative democracy as developed by (among others) Bohman (2007), then applied to environmental affairs by Baber and Bartlett (2009), involves application of ideas drawn from the theory and practice of deliberative democracy to global governance. As such it seeks to redeem the promise of **green democracy** at the global level. Deliberative democracy rests on the idea that democratic legitimacy depends on the right, capacity, and opportunity of those subject to a collective decision (or their representatives) to participate in consequential deliberation about the content of that decision. Deliberation in turn is a particular form of communication that involves mutual justification of and reflection upon the reasons for and considerations relevant to collective actions, though it is also open to a range of communications such as rhetoric and testimony, not just argument. Participants should strive to make sense to those who do not share their conceptual framework. So, for example, supporters of **deep ecology** should endeavor to reach those who subscribe to business-friendly versions of **sustainable development** such as **liberal environmentalism** or **ecological modernization**. Deliberative democratic ideas are more applicable to global politics than are conventional approaches to democracy that emphasize elections, which are currently hard to envisage being organized at the global level. The principles of deliberative democracy can be used to both evaluate existing practices such as **treaty negotiations** (normally a long way from the ideal) and inform prescriptions for institutional arrangements such as citizen forums and more informal practices such as the engagement of environmental **nongovernmental organizations** with each other and with established centers of power (Dryzek et al. 2019).

In an environmental context (at any level) many authors claim that deliberative democracy can produce more effective collective decisions, not just more legitimate ones (Smith 2003; Baber and Bartlett 2005). The specifically environmental case for deliberative democracy rests on several theoretical claims. The first is that deliberation provides an effective mechanism for integrating the perspectives of those concerned with different aspects of complex problems, be they experts, ordinary people, political activists, or public officials. The second is that deliberation brings collective as opposed to partial interests to the fore, because points made through reference to **global public goods** or generalizable interests are more powerful than those based on partial interests. Environmental conservation and the condition of commons resources therefore stand to benefit. The third is that **participation** in deliberation brings to mind the interests of those who are not present in a particular forum—and this can extend to future generations and nonhumans (see **Ecocentrism** and **Environmental justice**). The fourth is that deliberation is a particularly good way of incorporating feedback on the condition of social-ecological systems into collective decision processes. The fifth is that participation in deliberative forums helps make people better environmental citizens. The sixth is that deliberation is conducive to reflexivity: the capacity of structures, systems, or sets of ideas to question their own core commitments, and if necessary change themselves in response. Findings from micro-level studies of citizen forums offer empirical support to these claims, though more important is whether they can be redeemed in macro-level systems. Here the evidence is less conclusive, because such systems have rarely if ever been organized along deliberative lines.

From the point of view of deliberative democracy, global environmental governance currently looks problematic for several reasons (Stevenson and Dryzek 2014). The first is that communication often occurs among actors organized within enclaves of like-minded actors. Such enclaves might include various World Business Summits, and radical civil society forums such as Klimaforum09 organized in parallel with the UNFCCC Conference of the Parties in Copenhagen in 2009. The second is that the vitality of deliberative activity in the broader public sphere does not extend into the forums where global agreements are negotiated by the representatives of states (though the Open Working Group that finalized the content of the **Sustainable Development Goals** in 2015 is a partial exception). The third is that transnational networked environmental governance (such as the International Council for Local Environmental Initiatives (ICLEI), or the Clean Technology

Fund; see **transgovernmental networks** and **partnerships**) often features representation only from a limited range of governmental and market actors. In practicing, seemingly deliberative forums can fall short on inclusiveness and consequentiality, as Schouten et al. (2012) demonstrate for the cases of multi-stakeholder roundtables on responsible soy production and sustainable palm oil production. On the other hand, global environmental governance is not irredeemable in deliberative terms. Litfin's (1994) account of the force of the "ozone hole" idea in spurring agreement on the **ozone regime** 1987 Montreal Protocol suggests rhetoric can make a difference; and rhetoric is just one of the forms of persuasion that can be (conditionally) accepted in deliberative democracy.

In light of the current obvious deliberative deficiencies, a number of reforms have been proposed by deliberative democrats. Many have been implemented in environmental governance at different **scales** (local, regional, and national), but relatively few at the global level. One reform would be to introduce moments of citizen deliberation directly into the system. The most ambitious of such global attempts to date have been the World Wide Views processes conducted on the **climate change regime** in 2009, on the **biodiversity regime** in 2012, and on climate and energy in 2015 (Rask and Worthington 2015). In all three cases a forum of around 100 ordinary citizens using an identical design was conducted on the same day in 38 countries (on climate change) or 25 countries (biodiversity) or 76 countries (climate and energy). In almost all countries citizens supported stronger action than their governments were prepared to contemplate. The results were presented at subsequent international negotiations but had no obvious impact on the content of the negotiations. Baber and Bartlett (2009) suggest instead using citizen juries to deliberate hypothetical environmental issues in order to generate principles that could be added to a body of international common law; they have conducted pilots in several countries.

Other reform proposals target the system of global governance as a whole. They include promoting deliberation across as well as within enclaves in the broader public sphere. So, for example, we might seek engagement across gatherings in parallel to **summit diplomacy**, for instance organized by the World Business Council for Sustainable Development (WBCSD) and radical forums such as the Peoples Summit for Social and Environmental Justice during the United Nations Conference on Sustainable Development (Rio+20) in 2012. International **treaty negotiations** could be made more like deliberation than bargaining by reforming the process—for example, putting them under the auspices of a facilitator rather than a chair, following procedural guidelines of deliberation as opposed to rules of debate. Negotiators could be encouraged to make themselves accountable to civil society representatives in deliberative (two-way) as opposed to the more common narrative (one-way) style that characterizes government delegation briefings for their national media and NGOs at multilateral negotiations. Governance networks such as the Climate Technology Initiative's Private Financing Advisory Network could benefit from more contestatory activity involving activists and not just low-visibility communication among like-minded state and market actors. The role of expertise (such as that claimed by the Intergovernmental Platform on Biodiversity and Ecosystem Services) could be re-thought in ways that would involve validation by competent citizens—not just assertion of the authority of science as is the case for most **boundary organizations**. The deliberative qualities of the system as a whole might benefit from moments of disruption that force reflection and establish or drive home the seriousness of particular concerns. So, for example, the **shaming** strategy of the Climate Action Network's Fossil of the Day ceremony at UNFCCC negotiations can sometimes induce reflection and more considered justification of positions on the part of its recipients.

In global environmental governance no less than elsewhere, democratic legitimacy matters, and so does policy **effectiveness**. Global deliberative democracy is an attempt to realize these twin aims by seeking authentic, inclusive, and consequential deliberation.

References

Baber, Walter F. and Robert V. Bartlett. 2005. *Deliberative Environmental Politics: Democracy and Ecological Rationality*. Cambridge, MA, MIT Press.

Baber, Walter F. and Robert V. Bartlett. 2009. *Global Democracy and Sustainable Jurisprudence: Deliberative Environmental Law*. Cambridge, MA, MIT Press.

Bohman, James. 2007. *Democracy Across Borders: From Demos to Demoi*. Cambridge, MA, MIT Press.

Dryzek, John S., Quinlan Bowman, Jonathan Kuyper, Jonathan Pickering, Jensen Sass, and Hayley Stevenson. 2019. *Deliberative Global Governance*. Cambridge, Cambridge University Press.

Litfin, Karen T. 1994. *Ozone Discourses: Science and Politics in Global Environmental Cooperation*. New York, Columbia University Press.

Rask, Mikko and Richard Worthington. 2015. *Governing Biodiversity through Democratic Deliberation*. Abingdon, Routledge.

Schouten, Greetje, Pieter Leroy, and Pieter Glasbergen. 2012. "On the Deliberative Capacity of Private Multi-Stakeholder Governance: The

Round-tables on Responsible Soy and Sustainable Palm Oil." *Ecological Economics* 83: 42–50.

Smith, Graham. 2003. *Deliberative Democracy and the Environment*. London, Routledge.

Stevenson, Hayley and John S. Dryzek. 2014. *Democratizing Global Climate Governance*. Cambridge, Cambridge University Press.

GLOBAL ENVIRONMENT FACILITY

Raymond Clémençon

University of California, Santa Barbara, United States

The Global Environment Facility (GEF) has been providing critical financial support to developing countries for fighting global environmental problems since 1991. It is the formal financial mechanism for the UN Framework Convention on Climate Change (UNFCCC) and the Convention on Biological Diversity (CBD) (see **Biodiversity regime**), adopted in June 1992, and more recently for the **UN Convention to Combat Desertification** (UNCCD) and the **Stockholm Convention on Persistent Organic Pollutants**.

The GEF has funded more than 4,700 projects in 170 countries and, through its Small Grants Program, supported nearly 24,000 civil society and community initiatives in 128 countries. It is supporting national research, institutional and political capacity building, and national program strategies in its focal areas. GEF-financed projects have produced concrete environmental benefits, tested and demonstrated innovative and effective approaches, encouraged replication of the best solutions, and leveraged co-financing from a variety of sources (GEF IEO 2017). In particular, the GEF has been essential for expanding protected areas around the world (see **Conservation and preservation**), for spearheading early pilot projects in energy conservation and renewable energy technologies (see **Energy transition**), and fighting pollution in international waters (see **Transboundary water regime**).

The GEF was first set up as a voluntary pilot phase in 1991, with the **World Bank** (WB) serving as its trustee. Developing countries had demanded separate funding mechanisms directly controlled by the Parties to the Convention on Climate Change and Biodiversity, to avoid the World Bank's influence but donor countries opposed this (Clémençon 2006).

The GEF was formally established with its current governing structure in 1994. It has a small **secretariat** and a Council in which developed and developing countries are represented equally. The Council approves program tranches and programmatic strategies in line with Convention guidance. At the outset, the WB, United Nations Development Programme (UNDP) and the **United Nations Environment Programme** (UNEP) were mandated with developing and implementing projects in recipient countries. The number of implementing agencies has grown to 18 over the years, and now includes regional development banks, UN specialized agencies, and **nongovernmental organizations** such as Conservation International and the World Wildlife Fund (WWF).

Donor countries' original promise for the GEF was to provide financial grant resources "additional" to official development assistance that would be used to fund "incremental costs" of investments that could turn regular development projects into projects with global environmental benefits (Clémençon 2006). But the distinction between regular development cooperation and compensation for global environmental services rendered by developing countries has been lost over time, as most donor countries draw GEF contributions from their regular development cooperation budgets. Funding has also declined in real terms. GEF funding amounts to less than one US dollar a year per person in rich donor countries. In 2018 donor countries pledged US$4.1 billion for a seventh 4-year replenishment period before a difficult political background, a drop compared with US$4.34 billion (GEF-5) in 2014 and US$4.43 billion (GEF-6) in 2018.

Considered on its own merit the GEF is making a critical difference around the world. But before the background of dire global environmental decline reported by international scientific **assessments** on climate change and biodiversity, the GEF is also testament to a disturbing lack of commitment by the international community to solving global environmental problems that would require a massive scaling up of multilateral financial resources (see **Sustainable finance**).

References

Clémençon, Raymond. 2006. "What Future for the Global Environment Facility." *Journal for Environment and Development* 15(1): 50–74.
Global Environment Facility Independent Evaluation Office (GEF IEO). 2017. *OPS6 Report: The GEF in the Changing Environmental Finance Landscape.* Washington, DC, GEF IEO.

GLOBAL ENVIRONMENTAL GOVERNANCE STUDIES

Oran R. Young

University of California, Santa Barbara, United States

Governance is a social function centered on the development of mechanisms to steer societies toward socially desirable outcomes and away from socially undesirable ones. Because international society is anarchic in the sense that it lacks an overarching public authority or what is commonly thought of as a government, the challenge in addressing large-scale environmental concerns (e.g. the mitigation of climate change, the protection of biological diversity) is to establish governance systems that can operate effectively in the absence of a government. Over the course of the last fifty years, some efforts to address these concerns (e.g. the phasing out of ozone-depleting substances) have succeeded, whereas others (e.g. the reduction of greenhouse gas emissions) have failed. As we move deeper into an era of human-dominated systems (popularly known as the **Anthropocene**), the need to do better in responding to such concerns has risen in importance to become one of the most urgent issues of our times (Biermann 2014).

The growing body of global environmental governance studies addressing this subject, supported actively by the earth system governance community and reflected prominently in the contents of journals such as *Global Environmental Politics* and *International Environmental Agreements*, draws attention to several interrelated but distinct substantive themes. Initially, the research community focused on the determinants of success or failure in efforts to form environmental governance systems or **regimes** as they are often called. As a natural corollary, the research community moved on to address the **effectiveness** of international environmental regimes. Why do some regimes (e.g. the **ozone regime**) succeed in meeting the need for governance, while other regimes (e.g. the **climate change regime**) fail? From these core concerns, the field has branched out in several directions. Some analysts have directed attention to patterns of change in environmental governance systems, seeking to identify the combinations of internal and external drivers that determine how these institutional arrangements fare over time. Others have studied **institutional interactions**, including the consequences of interplay between environmental regimes and similar governance systems operating in other issues areas (e.g. the international trade regime).

Still others, struck by the changes associated with the onset of the Anthropocene, ask whether the requirements for success in this new era differ from earlier requirements. A major feature of this development involves an emphasis on governing systems that are increasingly complex in the sense that they are characterized by hyperconnectivity, feature nonlinear changes, exhibit directional rather than cyclical patterns of change, and give rise to emergent properties that take those concerned with issues of governance by surprise (Young 2017).

Cross-cutting these analytical concerns is an interest in improving our ability to design successful governance systems rather than simply treating regimes as a focus for research. Can we extract lessons from the study of environmental governance systems that will make it possible to design and implement more effective arrangements to address emerging needs for environmental governance in international society? This has given rise to a growing interest in what those working on such matters regard as institutional diagnostics, a procedure intended to identify and consider systematically options for addressing specific needs for governance.

The field of global environmental governance studies is eclectic with regard to methodology. The mainstream consists of theoretically grounded but qualitative case studies (Andresen et al. 2012). Hundreds of such case studies are now available. There is also a small but growing body of quantitative studies, conducted by empirically trained political scientists and economists, that make use of statistical procedures to develop empirical generalizations about environmental governance systems (Miles et al. 2002; Breitmeier et al. 2006). A notable feature of recent research in this field is a search for methods that permit the analysis of sizable numbers of cases, while probing the complex patterns of causality that are common in this field. An example is qualitative comparative analysis, which employs Boolean algebra to search for sets of factors that together are necessary or sufficient to explain outcomes of interest (Stokke 2012). Convergence in the findings emanating from several modes of analysis reinforces confidence in the validity of conclusions; divergence leads to the framing of new puzzles energizing the next phase of research. Today, this field remains a vibrant source of insights regarding efforts to address environmental problems.

References

Andresen, Steinar, Elin Lerun Boasson, and Geir Hønneland (Eds.). 2012. *International Environmental Agreements.* New York, Routledge.

Biermann, Frank. 2014. *Earth System Governance*. Cambridge, MA, MIT Press.

Breitmeier, Helmut, Oran R. Young, and Michael Zürn. 2006. *Analyzing International Environmental Regimes*. Cambridge, MA, MIT Press.

Miles, Edward L., Arild Underdal, Steinar Andresen, Jørgen Wettestad, Jon Birger Skjaerseth, and Elaine M. Carlin. 2002. *Environmental Regime Effectiveness: Confronting Theory with Evidence*. Cambridge, MA, MIT Press.

Stokke, Olav S. 2012. *Disaggregating International Regimes*. Cambridge, MA, MIT Press.

Young, Oran R. 2017. *Governing Complex Systems: Social Capital for the Anthropocene*. Cambridge, MA, MIT Press.

GLOBAL PACT FOR THE ENVIRONMENT

Véronique Fournier

Université Laval, Canada

Launched in June 2017 by Le Club des Juristes, a French think tank, the first draft of the Global Pact for the Environment (GPE) intends to create a global and legally binding instrument. It would include key principles, such as the **precautionary principle**, **polluter pays principle** (PPP), **preventive action principle**, **principle of non-regression**, the right to a clean environment (see **Human and environmental rights**), and **common but differentiated responsibilities** (CBDR). In the search for increasing **effectiveness** of international environmental law, the Pact would be applicable to states and relied upon in courts at national and international levels (see **Compliance and implementation**). Similar to the governance issues that the **World Environment Organization** was meant to address, the Pact's main objectives include creating a common core of legally binding principles to bring environmental **regimes** closer (see **Polycentricity**), reduce environmental law fragmentation, fill-in its gaps, and increase its implementation by states.

Some scholars consider that formally codifying environmental law principles can favor the achievement of the **Sustainable Development Goals** (Knox 2019). Others suggest that the Pact should also address current implementation deficiencies, act as mediator between environmental protection and other objectives, and identify future challenges not yet covered by international environmental law (Voigt 2019).

The negotiation mandate for the Pact was adopted in May 2018 at the United Nations General Assembly (UNGA). The United States and Russia were two out of the five votes against this adoption. They expressed concerns with respect to states' **sovereignty** over natural resources, the need to focus on implementing existing instruments instead of adding new ones, and the insufficient time allowed to discuss the project before submitting the resolution for its adoption.

One can be skeptical about the prospect of these **treaty negotiations** considering the inherent difficulties in reaching consensus. Criticisms arise both on the symbolic and operational levels: is centralization or fragmentation preferable for the effective environmental governance? Does the Pact raise the right issues by closing gaps in international environmental law or should it look at what is required from other fields of international law (e.g. trade) to remove obstacles for environmental action (Biniaz 2019)? Defining the concept of gaps, whether factual, technical, or normative, and identifying these gaps is a forefront debate (Kotzé and French 2018). Strong discussions also revolve around the risk of undermining existing environmental agreements by diverting attention toward the Pact (see **Institutional interactions**).

References

Biniaz, Susan. 2019. "The UNGA Resolution on a 'Global Pact for the Environment': A Chance to Put the Horse before the Cart." *Review of European, Comparative & International Environmental Law* 28(1): 33–39.

Knox, John H. 2019. "The Global Pact for the Environment: At the Crossroads of Human Rights and the Environment." *Review of European, Comparative & International Environmental Law* 28(1): 40–47.

Kotzé, Louis J. and Duncan French. 2018. "A Critique of the Global Pact for the Environment: A Stillborn Initiative or the Foundation for Lex Anthropocenae?" *International Environmental Agreements: Politics, Law and Economics* 18(6): 811–838.

Voigt, Christina. 2019. "How a 'Global Pact for the Environment' Could Add Value to International Environmental Law." *Review of European, Comparative & International Environmental Law* 28(1): 13–24.

GLOBAL PUBLIC GOOD

Sélim Louafi

Cirad, France

The concept of global public good (GPG) draws from at least two theoretical backgrounds. The first one relates to the extension to the global level of the public good theory developed in the 1950s by the economist and Nobel laureate Paul Samuelson. It builds on the two attributes of publicness (as opposed to private goods): non-rivalry (no one is affected by the consumption of these goods by others) and non-excludability (no one can be excluded from their consumption). In the case of GPG, these two attributes span across national boundaries: the public good has benefits that extend across national **sovereignty**, substantial cross-border externalities, and is consumed by all. Sunlight or climate stability are two classic illustrations of non-rival and non-excludable goods at the global level (for a discussion on non-excludable but rival goods, see **Tragedy of the commons**). With globalization and increased inter-dependence between countries, public goods increasingly acquire such global scope.

The second theory comes from the field of **critical political economy**. It focuses on the limitations of the current international architecture to address global challenges. Three gaps in global policy-making lead to the underprovision of GPGs (Kaul et al. 1999: 450): (1) a jurisdictional gap due to the discrepancy between the global scope of challenges and the territorial competencies of nation states; (2) a **participation** gap due to the under-representation of many stakeholders contributing to GPGs in international policymaking; and (3) an incentive gap due to the lack of sufficient inducement at the international level to cooperate for GPGs.

In the absence of one unique international government on global environmental governance, one individual **regime** or one **world environment organization**, collective actions between state and non-state actors at the global level are essential for the provision of GPGs. Transnational problems and international coordination to deal with them existed long before the GPG concept emerged (e.g. cholera epidemic containment in the nineteenth century). The concept, however, provided an analytical framework to address in a systematic manner issues with similar characteristics and previously only considered in a discrete or sectoral way, such as access to medicines and access to food (Segasti and Bezanson 2001: 1).

While some global issues have public characteristics by nature, many GPGs are constructed. In these cases, the distinction between privateness and publicness results from a political decision with regard to the allocation of property rights—and thus of rivalry and excludability. Plant genetic resources are not inherently global public goods but it was a decision of the member states to the International Treaty on Plant Genetic Resources for Food and Agriculture (ITPGRFA) to construct them this way. This raises many questions: How are collective preferences aggregated at the international level? How are GPGs to be financed? What is the role of international organizations in their provision?

This concept has raised extensive debates in the literature about its fuzziness and usefulness (Carbone 2007: 185). Despite its weaknesses, it helped in addressing real issues faced by the international community that were formalized in the **Sustainable Development Goals** (SDGs). It has also led to some major innovations that continue to shape current international discussions, such as the ITPGRFA or the **Law of the Sea Convention** (UNCLOS), and to new multi-**scale** governance approaches for development assistance, such as the funding of international agronomic research.

References

Carbone, Maurizio. 2007. "Supporting or Resisting Global Public Goods? The Policy Dimension of a Contested Concept." *Global Governance* 13(2): 179–198.

Kaul, Inge, Isabelle Grunberg, and Marc Stern (Eds.). 1999. *Global Public Goods: International Cooperation in the 21st Century.* New York, Oxford University Press.

Segasti, Francisco and Keith Bezanson. 2001. *Financing and Providing Global Public Goods: Expectations and Prospects.* Stockholm, Swedish Ministry of Foreign Affairs.

GRASSROOTS MOVEMENTS

Brian Doherty
Keele University, United Kingdom

Although the meaning of "grassroots" is debatable, there is broad agreement that grassroots movements share certain characteristics: they exist outside political institutions, that is they are not the creation of governments or political parties; they have informal organizations, without professional staff (which distinguishes them from **nongovernmental organizations**); participants are not for the most part powerful or well resourced; and their scope is mainly local, in that they usually mobilize or pursue issues within a specific locality.

Beyond these broad tendencies, there is a lack of systematic data on grassroots movements, in part because they are so numerous. For instance, thousands of grassroots campaigns on environmental issues are being pursued globally at any one time, so that it would be impossible for scholars to analyze or even record all of them. Empirically, grassroots environmental movements can be divided into four types: (1) the resistance of "affected communities" in the global South; (2) **environmental justice** campaigns in the global North; (3) direct action anarchistic green networks (mainly in the global North) sometimes inspired by **ecocentrism** or **deep ecology** (particularly in North America); and (4) more recently climate protest networks such as the climate strikes led by young people and Extinction Rebellion.

The first two of these types of grassroots movement typically emerge in reaction to a new threat or suddenly imposed grievance affecting a locality. In the past two decades the commodification of common resources has led to an upsurge of local resistance groups in the global South against mines, dams, and land grabbing. In Latin America in particular the struggles of **indigenous peoples and local communities** and the rural poor against a new extractivism, in the form of mining for minerals, oil, and gas has generated frequent clashes and a strong discourse of resistance organized around **critical political economy**.

The discourses, forms of mobilization, and action repertoires of grassroots groups are contingent on the context. For example, Doyle (2004) contrasts militant traditions of non-engagement with opponents by anti-mining activists in the Philippines with the lobby-based strategies and dialogue with mining companies or symbolic direct action favored by Australian activists. Discursively, grassroots movements engaged in conflicts over environmental issues more often define their identity as a defense of community rather than in the name of a global environmentalism. This also means that how they mobilize is shaped by a socially constructed sense of community. In an analysis of environmental justice campaigns in the United States, Lichterman (1996) contrasted more hierarchical organizations in communities of color, where support for the campaign was a taken for granted assumption, with the flatter structures of mainly white "green" groups, where becoming activists marked them out as different and in which, as a consequence, they needed to feel they were valued individually. Nor is it necessarily the case that grassroots groups are democratic; they often reproduce forms of inequality that exist in their locality.

The lack of resources of grassroots groups relative to their opponents means that their impact is often dependent on external factors—economic and political decisions that can make a project unviable (Rootes 2007)—or successful alliances with NGOs or other grassroots groups.

Place-based grassroots environmental movements are rarely bound wholly by their location and are linked to national politics and international political actors through network ties (Featherstone 2008; Hadden 2015). As a result, their discourses are more often pluri-vocal rather than being a simple defense of local autonomy and traditional knowledge against development or Western **science**. However, it can also be argued that such alliances with external actors, including environmental NGOs, run the risk that local agendas are recast to fit with the interests of national or international groups (Doherty and Doyle 2013).

The transnational wave of climate change protests in 2019 by young people walking out of school in climate strikes and the civil disobedience of Extinction Rebellion can be seen as indicative of a new twenty-first century form of movement organization in which "the communication networks become the political organization" (Bennett and Segerberg 2015: 375). This points to the role that social media now plays in providing spaces for the dissemination of repertoires of protest, discourses, and the creation of collective identity (Wahlstrom et al. 2019), reducing the reliance on large organizations with permanent staff as initiators and organizers of major campaigns. We seem therefore to be in a new era of grassroots movements, in which protests develop more quickly and often unpredictably. The challenge is whether these new kinds of movement can translate their demands into substantive political change.

References

Bennett, W. Lance and Alexandra Segerberg. 2015. "Communication in Movements." In *The Oxford Handbook of Social Movements*, Eds. Donatella Della Porta and Mario Diani, 367–382. Oxford, Oxford University Press.

Doherty, Brian and Timothy J. Doyle. 2013. *Environmentalism, Solidarity and Resistance: The Politics of Friends of the Earth International*. London, Palgrave MacMillan.

Doyle, Timothy J. 2004. *Environmental Movements in Majority and Minority Worlds: A Global Perspective*. New Brunswick, NJ, Rutgers University Press.

Featherstone, David. 2008. *Resistance, Space and Political Identities: The Making of Counter-Global Networks*. Oxford, Wiley-Blackwell.

Hadden, Jennifer. 2015. *Networks in Contention*. Cambridge, Cambridge University Press.

Lichterman, Paul. 1996. *The Search for Political Community: American Activists Reinventing Tradition*. Cambridge, Cambridge University Press.

Rootes, Christopher. 2007. "Acting Locally: The Character, Contexts and Significance of Local Environmental Mobilisations." *Environmental Politics* 16(5): 722–741.

Wahlström, Mattias, Moritz Sommer, Piotr Kocyba, Michiel de Vydt, and Joost De Moor (Eds.). 2019. Protest for a Future: Composition, Mobilization and Motives of the Participants in Fridays For Future Climate Protests on 15 March, 2019 in 13 European Cities. Keele University http://eprints.keele.ac.uk/6571/

GREEN DEMOCRACY

Robyn Eckersley

University of Melbourne, Australia

The idea of green democracy was developed by environmental political theorists in the 1990s out of a critique of the ecological failings of liberal democracy in the wake of the exponential growth in ecological problems in the post-World War II period. Whereas the "limits-to-growth" debate of the early 1970s (see **Carrying capacities paradigm**) had generated calls for an eco-authoritarian state as the only means of preventing ecological overshoot and collapse, advocates of green (or ecological) democracy argue that more, rather than less, democracy is needed to tackle the ecological crisis. Green democrats also highlight the many ways in which the modern environmental movement and green political parties have enriched liberal democracy.

Green democrats join liberal democrats in arguing that civil and political rights and free elections generally lead to better environmental protection compared with centrally planned economies managed by a one-party state. However, they do not treat this as an ecological vindication of liberal democracy. Rather, they argue that meeting the sustainability challenge requires a stronger and more ecologically informed democracy across all levels of governance, but especially at the national level (see **Scale**).

According to the green critique, liberal democracy is beset with a range of democratic deficits that favor short-term, well-organized private interests at the expense of the long-term, public good of environmental protection. These problems include the short-term horizons of election cycles, a distorted public sphere, and inequalities of political **participation** and bargaining power in the policymaking process. More fundamentally, liberal democracies are criticized for being ill-suited to an ecologically interdependent world because elected representatives do not have to answer to the constituencies affected by the transboundary and trans-temporal ecological consequences of their decisions (see **Environmental justice**). Nor do they provide any systematic representation of the interests of the nonhuman world (see **Ecocentrism**).

The primary goal of green democrats has been to defend and/or develop a range of supplementary rights, norms, laws, administrative procedures, institutions, and practices of political participation, deliberation, representation, and accountability that would enable more systematic consideration of long-range, transboundary, ecological concerns. These include new constitutional environmental rights, new forms of proxy representation for future generations and nonhuman species, new legal principles such as the **precautionary principle**, and new treaties that promote transboundary environmental procedural rights, such as the Aarhus Convention 1998.

Green democrats also defend deliberative or discursive democracy over strategic bargaining, cost-benefit analysis, or the aggregation of unreflective preferences because the critical, public exchange of reasons that is the essence of deliberation helps to weed out uninformed and purely self-interested arguments in favor of generalizable interests such as environmental protection (see **Global deliberative democracy**). Green democrats have defended "mini-publics," such as citizen juries, consensus conferences, and deliberative polls, as one means of institutionalizing deliberative democracy (e.g. Smith 2003).

Critics have argued that "proxy representation" for future generations and nonhuman species gives rise to new problems of accountability because the environmental representatives do not have to answer to their constituency. Others have pointed out that those who seek to represent future generations and nonhuman others would have their claims tested in the public sphere (O'Neill 2001). Meanwhile, green democrats welcome the rise of new grassroots democratic initiatives that seek to create new and more ecologically responsible material practices in collective, embodied, and prefigurative ways (Schlosberg and Craven 2019; Eckersley 2019) (see also **Grassroots movements**). However, they worry about the growing climate emergency discourse given its potential to legitimate a "state of exception" and the winding back of democratic rights.

References

Eckersley, Robyn. 2019. "Ecological Democracy and the Rise and Decline of Liberal Democracy: Looking Back, Looking Forward." *Environmental Politics*. Epub ahead of print March 19, 2019. https://doi.org/10.1080/09644016.2019.1594536

O'Neill, John. 2001. "Representing People, Representing Nature, Representing the World." *Environment and Planning C: Government and Policy* 19(4): 483–500.

Schlosberg, David and Luke Craven. 2019. *Sustainable Materialism: Environmental Practice and the Politics of Everyday Life*. Oxford, Oxford University Press.

Smith, Graham. 2003. *Deliberative Democracy and the Environment*. London, Routledge.

GREEN ECONOMY

David Gibbs

University of Hull, United Kingdom

The **United Nations Environment Programme** (2011: 16) defines a green economy as being:

> low carbon, resource efficient, and socially inclusive … growth in income and employment should be driven by public and private investments that reduce carbon emissions and pollution, enhance energy and resource efficiency, and prevent the loss of biodiversity and ecosystem services.

This combines environmental discourses with economic policy objectives in search of "win-win" **ecological modernization** solutions and an upward spiral of progress and prosperity. In response **business and corporations**, as well as policymakers, have focused on: renewable energy; green building and energy-efficiency technology; energy-efficient infrastructure and transportation; recycling and waste-to-energy. However, although this concedes that "business as usual" has resulted in ecological crisis, the green economy is often co-opted as a neoliberal project, proposing that it is government's role to create new **markets** for capital investment, especially for renewable energy and low carbon production, and to use markets to manage nature and climate change (see **Liberal environmentalism**). This provides temporary "environmental fixes" to economic growth problems which shift the problem into the future without major changes to existing institutions and power structures or disrupting the goal of continued economic growth.

In response, critics have called for changes in the way we conceptualize the economy, challenged the centrality of economic growth, and critiqued measures of economic prosperity such as gross domestic product (GDP) (see **Critical political economy**). Different approaches to the green economy, frequently termed **degrowth**, raise fundamental questions about the relationship between material prosperity and individual and social well-being, and emphasize spreading prosperity more equitably (D'Alisa et al. 2014). In contrast to a view that the green economy can be accommodated within existing economic and social structures, it is argued that new forms of social and economic organization need to be developed which redefine prosperity and quality of life, and that these should be decoupled from the demands of economic growth. Alternative approaches focus on sustaining people, communities, and nature, and from this perspective these should form the core goals of economic activity and not simply be the by-products associated with conventional GDP.

These two definitions point to two divergent views. The first is that green technologies, such as various forms of clean energy, are sufficient solutions for current global environmental problems. The implication is that this would also create wealth and thus address widespread poverty and social inequality. Second, a counter argument is that this is not enough and that there is a need to explicitly incorporate social equity and environmental quality aims in any definition. Rather than having a clear or stable end point, the green economy is therefore a contested discourse and an ongoing contest between different economic visions of the future (Gibbs and O'Neill 2017).

References

D'Alisa, Giacomo, Federico Demaria, and Giorgos Kallis. 2014. *Degrowth: A Vocabulary for a New Era*. London and New York, Routledge.

Gibbs, David and Kirstie O'Neill. 2017. "Future Green Economies and Regional Development: A Research Agenda." *Regional Studies* 51(1): 161–173.

United Nations Environment Programme. 2011. Towards a Green Economy: Pathways to Sustainable Development and Poverty Eradication. Nairobi, UNEP.

HAZARDOUS WASTES REGIME

Henrik Selin

Boston University, United States

The 1989 Basel Convention on the Control of Transboundary Movements of Hazardous Wastes and Their Disposal is the main global agreement governing the trade and management of wastes hazardous to human health and the environment. Examples of hazardous wastes range from discarded chemicals and household electronic goods to obsolete ships. It was mainly movements from industrialized to developing countries and related environmental and human health risks that led to **treaty negotiations** in the 1980s (Clapp 2001).

The Basel Convention is one of the first global environmental agreements to mandate "prior informed consent" where an exporting party must receive approval from the importing party before a shipment of hazardous wastes can proceed. A party can only trade with non-parties if movements are subject to an agreement that is at least as stringent as the requirements under the Basel Convention. Exports are prohibited to Antarctica and to parties that have adopted domestic import bans. The parties have developed technical guidelines for environmentally safe storage and disposal of hazardous wastes.

After the Basel Convention entered into force in 1992, some countries and **nongovernmental organizations** including Greenpeace and the Basel Action Network argued for stricter trade regulations to protect developing countries from unwanted imports (Kummer 1995). The 1995 Ban Amendment prohibits the export of hazardous wastes for final disposal and recycling from countries that are members of the Organisation for Economic Co-operation and Development (OECD) and the EU as well as Liechtenstein to all other parties. The Ban Amendment, after a lengthy ratification process, entered into force in 2019.

Developing countries have invested in **regional governance** to supplement the Basel Convention (Selin 2010). The 1991 Convention on the Ban of the Import into Africa and the Control of Transboundary Movements and Management of Hazardous Wastes within Africa (the Bamako Convention) prohibits imports of hazardous wastes from non-African countries. The 1991 Lomé IV Convention bans the trade in hazardous wastes between members of the EU and former colonies in Asia, the Caribbean, and the Pacific. The 1995 Waigani Convention bans the import of hazardous and radioactive wastes to island countries in the South Pacific region.

The 1999 Basel Convention Protocol on Liability and Compensation identifies who is financially responsible in case of an incident during the transport of hazardous wastes (see **Liability**). The protocol, however, has not yet received the necessary ratifications to enter into force. The parties created a **compliance and implementation** mechanism to monitor the generation and transnational transport of hazardous wastes as well as regional centers assisting parties on capacity building and **technology transfer** for improved waste handling (Selin 2012).

To strengthen governance, the parties in 2011 adopted a strategic framework on implementation outlining goals and performance indicators to better measure progress on waste management. The growing trade in electronic goods for reuse and/or recycling draws increased attention to hazardous wastes. Many people mainly in developing countries involved in the recovery business are exposed to a large number of toxic substances, involving important **environmental justice** issues (Pellow 2007). In addition, the parties in 2019 adopted an amendment to address certain plastic wastes.

References

Clapp, Jennifer. 2001. *Toxic Exports: The Transfer of Hazardous Wastes from Rich to Poor Countries.* Ithaca, NY, Cornell University Press.

Kummer, Katharina. 1995. *International Management of Hazardous Wastes: The Basel Convention and Related Legal Rules.* Oxford, Clarendon Press.

Pellow, David Naguib. 2007. *Resisting Global Toxics: Transnational Movements for Environmental Justice.* Cambridge, MA, MIT Press.

Selin, Henrik. 2010. *Global Governance of Hazardous Chemicals: Challenges of Multilevel Management.* Cambridge, MA, MIT Press.

Selin, Henrik. 2012. "Global Environmental Governance and Regional Centers." *Global Environmental Politics* 12(3): 18–37.

HIGH-LEVEL POLITICAL FORUM ON SUSTAINABLE DEVELOPMENT

Kenneth W. Abbott

Arizona State University, United States

Steven Bernstein

University of Toronto, Canada

The High-Level Political Forum on Sustainable Development (HLPF) is the United Nations' main political body for follow-up and review of the 2030 Agenda for **Sustainable Development**, including the **Sustainable Development Goals** (SDGs). It meets annually under the Economic and Social Council, and quadrennially, at head of state or government level, under the UN General Assembly. The 2012 UN Conference on Sustainable Development (Rio+20) created the HLPF following dissatisfaction with the performance of the UN Commission on Sustainable Development, which it effectively replaced, and demands to upgrade the **United Nations Environment Programme**. The HLPF's expansive mandate includes political leadership; an action-oriented agenda; addressing emerging issues; enhancing integration and coherence of the three dimensions of sustainable development, across the UN system and at all levels of governance (see **Scales**); follow-up and review of SDG implementation (see **Compliance and implementation**); enhancing civil society **participation** and evidence-based decision-making (see **Science**); and providing a platform for **partnerships**.

Despite its mandate and institutional status, the HLPF lacks independent resources, legal decision-making authority, and enforcement capability. It must therefore govern indirectly through orchestration: enlisting public and private actors with resources and direct levers of influence as intermediaries (Abbott and Bernstein 2015). In fact, it is an "orchestrator of orchestrators" (Bernstein 2017), as many other orchestrating institutions are engaged with particular SDGs, including UN agencies, international financial institutions, the Group of 20, and private or public-private partnerships. Because the 2030 Agenda focuses on national action and "leaving no one behind," the HLPF's success hinges on promoting bottom-up, country-driven, stakeholder-oriented change processes, especially through Voluntary

National Reviews (VNRs). In the first review cycle (2015–2019), 142 countries presented VNRs, with 50 more expected in 2020, some for the second time.

Strengths identified in the HLPF's first cycle (UN 2019; Beisheim 2018; UNDESA 2019) include participation in VNRs, providing a platform for discussion and learning, and generating momentum for the 2030 Agenda. But observers also identify important weaknesses, notably the lack of "political leadership, recommendations and guidance" in ministerial declarations (UN 2019: 2) and weak performance in promoting policy and institutional coherence.

Dimitrov (2019) condemns the HLPF as an "empty institution," like the defunct Commission on Sustainable Development. Others (Boas et al. 2016) see it potentially as an integrated steering body for all economic, social, and environmental aspects of sustainable development, able to promote a "nexus" approach to the SDGs, orchestrating integrated action within interdependent policy domains such as water-food-energy. Still others highlight its potential to promote accountability (Karlesson-Vinkhuyzen et al. 2018).

Reform proposals include more action-oriented political declarations; improved "thematic reviews" of SDG implementation, based on evidence-based inputs such as the Global Sustainable Development Report (Independent Group of Scientists 2019); greater civil society participation, specifically in VNRs; and improved learning and dissemination of best practices (UN 2019; Beisheim 2018; UNDESA 2019).

References

Abbott, Kenneth W. and Steven Bernstein. 2015. "The High-Level Political Forum on Sustainable Development: Orchestration by Default and Design." *Global Policy* 6(3): 222–233.

Beisheim, Marianne. 2018. *UN Reforms for the 2030 Agenda: Are the HLPF's Working Methods and Practices "Fit for Purpose"?* SWP Research Paper 2018/RP 09. https://www.swp-berlin.org/en/publication/un-reforms-for-the-2030-agenda/.

Bernstein, Steven. 2017. "The United Nations and the Governance of Sustainable Development Goals." In *Governance through Goals: New Strategies for Global Sustainability*, Eds. Norichika Kanie and Frank Biermann, 213–239. Cambridge, MA, MIT Press.

Boas, Ingrid, Frank Biermann, and Norichika Kanie. 2016. "Cross-Sectoral Strategies in Global Sustainability Governance: Towards a Nexus Approach." *International Environmental Agreements: Politics, Law and Economics* 16(3): 449–464.

Dimitrov, Radoslav S. 2019. "Empty Institutions in Global Environmental Politics." *International Studies Review*. Epub ahead of print June 12, 2019. https://doi.org/10.1093/isr/viz029

Independent Group of Scientists, appointed by the Secretary-General of the United Nations. 2019. *Global Sustainable Development Report: The Future is Now – Science for Achieving Sustainable Development.* New York, United Nations.

Karlsson-Vinkhuyzen, Sylvia, Athur L. Dahl, and Åsa Persson. 2018. "The Emerging Accountability Regimes for the Sustainable Development Goals and Policy Integration: Friend or foe?" *Environment and Planning C: Politics and Space* 36(8): 1371–1390.

UN. 2019. *Summary of Expert Group Meeting on Lessons learned from the First Cycle of the High-Level Political Forum on Sustainable Development.* May 6–7, 2019. New York. https://sustainabledevelopment.un.org/content/documents/23135Summary_of_EGM_on_HLPF_review_FINAL.pdf.

UNDESA. 2019. *Comprehensive HLPF Survey Results: Evaluation of the HLPF after 4 years.* https://sustainabledevelopment.un.org/content/documents/24802Comprehensive_HLPF_Survey_Results_FINAL.pdf.

HUMAN AND ENVIRONMENTAL RIGHTS

Sophie Lavallée

Université Laval, Canada

Environmental rights are composed of substantive rights and procedural rights, which are tools provided by law to achieve substantial rights.

Regarding substantive rights, in 1972, the Stockholm Declaration stated that a quality environment is essential if humans are to enjoy their other rights. Since then, the right to environment has been recognized in various instruments.

Although the first two generations of human rights, civil and political or economic, social, and cultural, are acknowledged in all universal human rights instruments, the right to environment is not. Despite the indivisibility of human rights, there are only two universal international conventions that recognize this right in specific circumstances. In the first of these, the Convention on the Rights of the Child of 1989, article 24, protects the right to environment in order to further the right of children to enjoy the best possible state of health. Convention 169 concerning Indigenous and Tribal Peoples in Independent Countries of 1989 also refers to the right to environment in article 4, which requires states to take special steps to protect the environment of their **indigenous peoples and local communities**.

It is in terms of **regional governance** that progress in this direction has been made. The 1981 African Charter on Human and Peoples' Rights (also known as the Banjul Charter) states that "All peoples shall have the right to a general satisfactory environment favorable to their development." This collective reference to the right of peoples is not found in the Additional Protocol to the American Convention on Human Rights in the Area of Economic, Social and Cultural Rights (Protocol of San Salvador). Despite this, some decisions made under the inter-American human rights system appear to be moving toward recognition for a collective approach to human rights (Francioni 2010: 51). The large and liberal interpretation of human rights by the Inter-American Court of Human Rights, in particular the right to a "dignified life" or the collective right to property of indigenous peoples, is likely to increase **environmental justice** for them despite certain limitations (Theriault 2015).

At the request of Colombia, the Inter-American Court of Human Rights issued an advisory opinion on February 7, 2018 giving the Court one of its first opportunities to refer extensively to state obligations arising from the need to protect the environment in accordance with the American Convention (paragraph 46). The Court clearly stated that the right to a healthy environment is not only an individual right, but also a collective right that is of universal interest and which is owed to both current and future generations (paragraph 59).

Neither the European Convention for the Protection of Human Rights (ECHR), adopted in the 1950s, nor its protocols, recognizes a right to environment. In the European system, individual environmental rights are regarded as an extension, by way of interpretation, of other expressly recognized human rights, such as the rights to life, health, private and family life, information, and consultation (De Sadeleer 2012). At the international level, the **Global Pact for the Environment** has been a failure.

A Regional Agreement on Access to Information, Public Participation and Access to Justice on Environmental Issues in Latin America and the Caribbean was adopted in Escazú, Costa Rica on March 4, 2018. Taking up the three classic pillars of the 1998 Aarhus Convention, the Agreement breaks new ground by enumerating the relevant environmental principles (article 3), such as the **principles of non-regression** and progressivity, intergenerational equity, and pro-independence. Similarly, article 4 (1) more broadly guarantees the right of everyone to live in a healthy environment. The Escazú Agreement also contains provisions specific to the Latin American and Caribbean region on the protection of human rights defenders in connection with the environment and vulnerable persons and groups. Its entry into force requires ratification by at least eleven countries by September 2020. As of November 24, 2019, twenty-one countries have signed it and five have ratified it.

For many authors, despite the anthropocentrism of human rights, the recognition of an autonomous right to environment is necessary (Anderson 1996; Atapattu 2002; Shelton 2007). First, because only a human right is universal enough to allow all individuals to benefit, however inactive their government is in terms of protecting the environment. By approaching environmental protection through rights, the right to environment obtains a preferential place in the hierarchy of legal norms, and moves out of the area of preferences that can be changed through policy, into the area of rights that must be compared and balanced among themselves. Second, a right is never fully guaranteed if victims have only an indirect recourse via other human rights. Even though the courts can interpret first-and second-generation rights in a way that punishes environmental violations, they will never be able to ensure optimum protection for the environment using this approach. Proving a causal link between environmental degradation and the undermining of a guaranteed right creates a major hurdle in terms of evidence (Shelton 2007).

A collective fundamental right to environment should therefore be considered. Indeed, if only the individual aspect of human rights is protected, this may be a factor for social regression. Individual human rights can only prevent the worst from happening, and do not allow for any kind of social progress. More work is needed in this direction to give the right a more collective dimension (Francioni 2010: 54–55).

References

Anderson, Michael R. 1996. "Human Rights Approaches to Environmental Protection: An Overview." In *Human Rights Approaches to Environmental Protection*, Eds. Alan Boyle and Michael Anderson, 1–24. Oxford, Clarendon Press.

Atapattu, Sumudu A. 2002. "The Right to a Healthy Life or the Right to Die Polluted?: The Emergence of a Human Right to a Healthy Environment under International Law." *Tulane Environmental Law Journal* 16(1): 65–126; and also in *Human Rights and the Environment*, Ed. Dinah Shelton, 57–118. Cheltenham, Edward Elgar.

De Sadeleer, Nicolas. 2012. "Enforcing EUCHR Principles and Fundamental Rights in Environmental Cases." *Nordic Journal of International Law* 81(1): 39–74.

Francioni, Francesco. 2010. "International Human Rights in an Environmental Horizon." *European Journal of International Law* 21(1): 41–55.

Shelton, Dinah. 2007. "Human Rights and the Environment: What Specific Environmental Rights Have Been Recognised?" *Denver Journal of International Law and Policy* 35(1): 129–171.

Thériault, Sophie. 2015. "Justice environnementale et peuples autochtones: les possibilités et les limites de la jurisprudence de la Cour interaméricaine des droits de l'homme." *Revue Québécoise de droit international*: 129–148.

INDIGENOUS PEOPLES AND LOCAL COMMUNITIES

Marc Hufty

Graduate Institute of International and Development Studies, Switzerland

Indigenous peoples and local communities represent a major category of actors in global environmental governance. Indigenous peoples were defined by the United Nations in the 1980s as those human groups who have a historical continuity in a territory, a distinct culture, and who recognize themselves as indigenous. This comprises up to 350 million people worldwide, 70% of them living in Asia. They occupy 22% of the world's land area. Local communities refers to communities embodying traditional lifestyles in close contact with their natural environment. It is a term sometimes used as a way to avoid the controversy over who is or is not indigenous.

Indigenous peoples and local communities have long been considered as an impediment to progress in a modern world led by nation-states. Their traditional ways of managing natural resources were believed to damage the environment by ignorance. Swidden agriculture was singled out as a major cause of deforestation. Therefore, the incorporation of indigenous and local communities into modern societies was seen as positive, necessary, and unavoidable.

A radical shift in this perception has occurred over time through a series of historical developments: first, indigenous peoples' political emergence in global environmental governance; second, an increasing importance given to local management; and third, the recognition that traditional knowledge may bring key contributions to some intractable problems of environmental governance.

Indigenous peoples gradually emerged as a major international category of actors in the twentieth century, first in defense of their lands, then in a more comprehensive way. The first interventions of indigenous representatives in the international arena date back to the early 1920s when the Iroquois (Haudenosaunee) Confederacy applied for membership of the League of Nations and appealed to the League in its dispute with Canada over its **sovereignty** (Ayana 1996). The initiative failed as the case was judged as a domestic affair involving an ethnic minority. Yet, indigenous representatives persisted in addressing the international community until they acquired a legal status and the issues they raised were considered.

A major development was the adoption of the International Labor Organization (ILO) Convention No. 107 in 1957, in response to reports of labor discrimination against indigenous peoples in Latin America. Later criticized for its paternalism, the Convention nevertheless situated their status within the context of colonialism and recognized, among other rights, their right to own the land they occupied, and to be compensated if dispossessed. In 1989, the treaty evolved into ILO Convention No. 169, today's major binding international instrument on indigenous peoples, ratified by 23 countries, mostly Latin American and European. Based on the principle of nondiscrimination, it recognizes the cultural specificities of indigenous peoples, while requiring that they be allowed to participate in a free, prior, and informed way in decisions that affect them, and be consulted in good faith (Tomlinson 2017).

Within the UN system, the debate took place in the Sub-Commission on Human Rights. It led to the authoritative "Martinez Cobo Report" (UN 1983) that concluded there was a generally low respect of human rights standards for the indigenous, and called for a new legal international instrument, paving the way to the landmark 2007 UN Declaration on the Rights of Indigenous Peoples (UNDRIP), which asserts, among other rights, their right to self-determination, and anchored the debate on indigenous and local communities' rights to the debate on human rights (Higgins 2019).

These developments occurred in parallel with the political awakening of indigenous peoples at the national level in many countries. Despite their many differences, indigenous peoples have created political networks at the national and international levels, as well as alliances with environmental and human rights **nongovernmental organizations**, demanding the recognition of their rights (see also **Human and**

environmental rights). Among these, territorial rights and autonomy are the most sensitive issues for republican states used to seeing their territories as indivisible. States have responded in diverse ways, from outright rejection to new constitutional models in which land rights are entrusted to communities. The demands for land rights and autonomy has followed a trend observed in environmental issues, strategic **litigation**, understood as turning to national and international courts to secure these rights (Gilbert 2017).

The rediscovery of traditional local institutions for the governance of natural resources provided a theoretical legitimacy for these rights. Studies demonstrated that besides the market and the state, some local institutions have enabled a sustainable management of natural resources, sometimes over very long periods of time (Ostrom 1990). A large body of studies emerged, calling attention to experiments, especially in nature conservation (see **Conservation and protection**), such as the CAMPFIRE Program in Zimbabwe.

It had become obvious that indigenous and local communities play a crucial role in environmental governance. There is for example a strong coincidence between the world's most biodiverse ecoregions and the presence and diversity of indigenous peoples. And while protected areas are admittedly the main effective mechanism to preserve biological diversity, it has been demonstrated time and again that natural areas managed by local communities are especially well preserved (see **Effectiveness**). They have gradually become key partners in the mechanisms aimed at nature conservation, as well as water and forest management (Kothari et al. 2012).

Finally, as the technical solutions based on modern **science** have reached their limits in some areas, traditional knowledge and practices are increasingly taken seriously in domains such as agriculture, pharmacology, and the management of ecosystems. This role has been formally recognized in the 1993 **biodiversity regime** Convention Article 8J. It is now understood that indigenous and local communities often have a deep understanding of the complex interactions of environmental cycles (see **Gaia theory**). This expertise could prove critical for example in **agroecology**, recognized by the Food and Agriculture Organization as having a role to play in future food security, or **adaptation** to climate change. They are now fully recognized as development partners by organizations such as the **World Bank**.

Yet, in spite of this hard-earned recognition, indigenous and local communities are still vulnerable, poor, and marginalized. The confrontation with the modern world is often at their expense. They continue to be expelled from their traditionally inhabited lands for the creation of parks, dams, or soy and oil palm plantations. Their **participation** in environmental governance is also too often reduced to mere attendance at informational meetings in top-down projects. Their potential contribution to global environmental governance has yet to be fully developed.

References

Ayana, James. 1996. *Indigenous Peoples in International Law*. Oxford, Oxford University Press.

Gilbert, Jérémie. 2017. *Strategic Litigation Impacts Indigenous Peoples' Land Rights*. New York, Open Society Foundations.

Higgins, Noelle. 2019. "Creating a Space for Indigenous Rights: The Universal Periodic Review as a Mechanism for Promoting the Rights of Indigenous Peoples." *The International Journal of Human Rights* 23(1–2): 125–148.

Kothari, Ashish, Colleen Corrigan, Harry Jonas, Aurélie Neumann, and Holly Shrumm (Eds.). 2012. *Recognising and Supporting Territories and Areas Conserved by Indigenous Peoples and Local Communities: Global Overview and National Case Studies*. Montreal, Secretariat of the Convention on Biological Diversity.

Ostrom, Elinor. 1990. *Governing the Commons: The Evolution of Institutions for Collective Action*. Cambridge, Cambridge University Press.

Tomlinson, Katryn. 2017. "Indigenous Rights and Extractive Resource Projects: Negotiations over the Policy and Implementation of FPIC." *The International Journal of Human Rights* 23(5): 880–897.

United Nations Economic and Social Council. 1983. *Study of the Problem of Discrimination against Indigenous Populations: Final Report*. New York, Commission on Human Rights.

INFLUENTIAL INDIVIDUALS

Bob Reinalda
Radboud University Nijmegen, Netherlands

In social history individuals may matter because of their critical ideas, but they need movements and organizations to become influential. Some people make a difference in world history because they become aware of certain dangers very early. Modern technology has often raised expectations, but it took people longer to notice and think through the negative consequences, such as the formation of smog in cities and the effects of the pesticide DDT (dichloro-diphenyl-trichloroethane) on wildlife in water. Physicist Harrison Brown warned of such dangers in his book *The Challenge of Man's Future* (1954) and biologist Rachel Carson did so in her *Silent Spring* (1962). However, when most people ignore their warnings, early awareness does not mean that these individuals are taken seriously. To become influential, critical ideas should be elaborated further and attract support. During the 1960s larger groups of young people and critical scientists began to question the assumption that nature could bear any burden human beings might place on it and set up organizations with identifiable spokespersons. Canadian journalist Robert Hunter changed from being a reporter to becoming an activist after his adventurous journey to the Gulf of Alaska, where the US was planning nuclear tests in 1971, and founded the activist **nongovernmental organization** Greenpeace International, which set off for locations where large-scale, but low-visibility, environmental abuses were taking place, to bring them to the world's attention through publicity stunts. In 1972 Donella and Dennis Meadows and their colleagues from the Massachusetts Institute of Technology modeled for the Club of Rome the use of natural resources and announced that the "limits to growth" would be reached within a century.

The increasing environmental consciousness affected the UN too, with a conference on the human environment in Stockholm and the creation of the **United Nations Environment Programme** (UNEP) in 1972. The conference became a stepping stone for private environmental organizations and encouraged multilateral diplomacy in various international organizations. Unlike in the previous phase of consciousness-raising by individuals and NGOs, an intergovernmental organization makes possible the creation, spread, and implementation of international standards (e.g. the 1972 **polluter pays principle** of the Organization for Economic Cooperation and Development) and programs. Among UNEP's leading executives two different leadership styles emerged. Canadian Maurice Strong, Secretary-General of the Stockholm conference, UNEP's first Executive Director (1973–1975), and Secretary-General of the 1992 Rio Conference on the Environment, as a leader proved to be an "initiator," someone with the competence and ability to set up operations, leaving their further development to others. He launched UNEP's Regional Seas Programme (with the 1975 Mediterranean Action Programme, in force in 1978), which later developed into a program for oceans and coastal areas.

Strong's successor, Egyptian microbiologist Mostafa Tolba, UNEP's Executive Director between 1976 and 1992, is known for his scientific arguments, persistent consultations with political leaders, and intergovernmental negotiating skills. His organizational leadership and ability to deliver results were shown by the adoption of the 1987 Montreal Protocol to the 1985 Vienna Convention for the Protection of the Ozone Layer that is part of the **ozone regime**; the creation of the Intergovernmental Panel on Climate Change (IPCC; 1988, together with the World Meteorological Organization (WMO)) and the permanent Ozone Secretariat (1989); and the adoption of the Basel Convention on the Control of Transboundary Movements of Hazardous Wastes and their Disposal (1989) that is part of the **hazardous wastes regime** (Tolba 1998). In 1992 in Rio Tolba helped successfully negotiate the framework conventions of the **biodiversity regime** and the **climate change regime** by his mastery of the subjects and diplomatic skills. Oran Young (1991) developed his concept of "entrepreneurial leadership" for his tripartite typology of political leadership (also structural and intellectual) on the basis of Tolba's role. Entrepreneurial leaders frame issues, devise mutually acceptable formulas, and broker the interests of key players in building support for these formulas.

Norwegian Gro Harlem Brundtland embodies the "intellectual leader" who generates new ideas. As chair of the World Commission on Environment and Development, established by the UN General Assembly in 1983, she combined political experience, environmental expertise, and intellectual leadership to develop a new political concept that helped overcome several deadlocks and opened up new venues for international political action. The Commission's 1987 report *Our Common Future*, also known as the "Brundtland report," called for a strategy that combined development with the environment, with the term **sustainable development** linking the needs of present and future generations.

Successful individual leadership is discussed more abstractly in the context of bureaucracies. Biermann and Siebenhüner argue in their *Managers of Global Change* (2009) that the **secretariats** (bureaucracies) of major international organizations with far-reaching mandates and extensive resources are more influential than the small secretariats of international environmental agreements with narrow mandates and limited resources. However, both act as knowledge brokers, negotiation facilitators, and capacity builders, who influence the behavior of political actors by changing their knowledge and belief systems and have a significant effect on the creation and **effectiveness** of **regimes**. Strong leadership by secretaries-general or senior staff depends on factors such as the staff's ability to generate and process knowledge and the set of commonly shared basic assumptions that result from previous organizational learning processes. Secretaries-general bring different types of leadership and combine specific qualities and capabilities, as is shown by personalities such as Strong, Tolba, and Brundtland. Strong leadership includes the "ability to rapidly gain acceptance and acknowledgement by employees and externals, to develop, communicate, and implement vision, and to learn and change routines" (Biermann and Siebenhüner 2009: 58).

Influence through the media is shown by activists who work as journalists and documentary makers and use their media exposure to promote environmental awareness, such as marine conservationist and filmmaker Jacques Cousteau and documentary maker Nicolas Hulot in France, zoologist and science broadcaster David Suzuki in Canada, "crocodile hunter" Steve Irwin in Australia, and maker of natural history programs for the BBC, David Attenborough. Former US Vice-President Al Gore made the film *An Inconvenient Truth* (2006) and, jointly with the IPCC, was awarded the 2007 Nobel Peace Prize. The first environmentalist to win the Nobel Peace Prize was Kenyan political activist Wangari Maathai for her contribution to sustainable development, democracy, and peace (2004).

Swedish Greta Thunberg (15 years old in 2018) believed that, despite the alarm bells, not much action on climate change was undertaken and started in 2018 to address international negotiators and policymakers while launching a worldwide school strike movement to combat climate change. Her actions, backed by public demonstrations and support from already-existing institutions, inspired young people around the world to become activists and aim at demonstrating that even weak actors can make a difference (Thunberg 2019).

References

Biermann, Frank and Bernd Siebenhüner (Eds.). 2009. *Managers of Global Change: The Influence of International Environmental Bureaucracies.* Cambridge, MA, MIT Press.

Thunberg, Greta. 2019. *No One Is Too Small to Make a Difference.* London, Penguin Books.

Tolba, Mostafa K. 1998. *Global Environmental Diplomacy: Negotiating Environmental Agreements for the World, 1973–1992.* Cambridge, MA, MIT Press.

Young, Oran. 1991. "Political Leadership and Regime Formation: On the Development of Institutions in International Society." *International Organization* 45(3): 281–308.

INSTITUTIONAL INTERACTIONS

Sebastian Oberthür

Vrije Universiteit Brussel, Belgium

Thijs Van de Graaf

Ghent University, Belgium

The number of international **regimes**, **private regimes**, and organizations has grown exponentially over the past decades. This institutional proliferation has led to the emergence in the 2000s of a new field of research within **global environmental governance studies** dealing with "institutional interactions," situations in which one institution affects the development or performance of another institution (Oberthür and Stokke 2011). We address here so-called "horizontal interactions" between international institutions (and do not cover vertical interplay across different **scales**).

Early research on institutional interaction focused heavily on developing conceptual taxonomies. Young (1996), for example, introduced a distinction between four types of what he terms regime interplay: "embeddedness" within overarching principles (such as **sovereignty**); "nesting" within broader institutional frameworks (such as the nesting of various **regional governance** regimes within the UN **Law of the Sea Convention** (UNCLOS)); "clustering" in institutional packages (such as the linked but differentiable components of the **Antarctic Treaty System**); and "overlap" between regimes in substantial but often unexpected ways (for instance, the phase-out of chlorofluorocarbons under the **ozone regime** prompted states to turn to substitutes, some of which are potent greenhouse gases to be curbed under the **climate change regime**).

Building on these conceptual foundations, several scholars have set out to identify the driving forces and effects of institutional interaction. Their research can be mapped along two dimensions (Oberthür and Stokke 2011). First, a basic distinction can be drawn between systemic and actor-centered research strategies. Systemic approaches focus on the relationship among institutions, so that the key variables of interest are located at the macro-level of institutions. Studies of the interaction between the global trade regime and multilateral environmental agreements provide an example of this approach. Actor-centered approaches, by contrast, see actors as either the independent variable or the dependent variable, locating other variables at the macro-level of institutions. It has been well documented, for example, that state and non-state actors sometimes engage in "forum shopping," "regime shifting," and competitive regime creation (Morse and Keohane 2014)

Second, scholars can focus on different kinds of interaction settings as units of analysis. At one end of the spectrum, research can explore dyadic relationships between two institutions examining the causal pathway through which influence runs from one to the other (Oberthür and Gehring 2006). One may, for example, study the mutual influence of the **biodiversity regime** (CBD) and the **World Trade Organization** (WTO). At the other end, more integrationist approaches explore broader interaction settings involving several dyadic cases of interaction and/or several institutions (e.g. the WTO and several or all multilateral environmental agreements). Such settings have been termed "governance architectures" (Biermann et al. 2009) or "regime complexes", defined as an "array of partially overlapping and non-hierarchical institutions governing a particular issue area" (Raustiala and Victor 2004). Studying sets of institutions may allow us to identify new properties that are not inherent in the individual components but emerge from their interrelationship. Keohane and Victor (2011), for example, study the range of institutions involved in global climate governance and argue that the climate change regime complex has greater flexibility and adaptability than a comprehensive regime could possibly have. Their view contrasts with others who see the fragmentation of institutional structures as at least potentially problematic.

Such research on broader interaction settings has become particularly prominent in the 2010s (Alter and Raustiala 2018). Exemplifying a more systemic approach, Johnson and Urpelainen (2012) argue that negative spill-overs encourage regime integration, whereas positive spill-overs foster regime separation. Negative spill-overs exist when cooperation in one issue area undermines the pursuit of objectives in another issue area. Adopting a more actor-centric approach, Van de Graaf (2013) has argued that the institutional capture of the International Energy Agency by fossil and nuclear energy interests spurred the creation of the International Renewable Energy Agency.

An important dimension of institutional interaction and complexes concerns their governance effects. While institutional interactions may in principle produce synergistic, cooperative/neutral or conflictive/disruptive outcomes (Oberthür and Gehring 2006; Biermann et al. 2009), most attention has been devoted to instances of conflict. A popular hypothesis has been that the WTO undermines the **effectiveness** of multilateral environmental agreements by "chilling" the negotiation of environmentally motivated trade-related obligations (Eckersley 2004). Nonetheless, a large-*n* study of institutional interaction found that a clear majority of cases of interaction creates synergy, whereas about one-quarter resulted in disruption (Oberthür and Gehring 2006: 12). While a focus of attention on conflictual interaction may be comprehensible, the significance of synergistic effects deserves particular consideration when thinking about options for improved governance of institutional complexes and fragmentation.

Such thinking about managing institutional complexes has been further advanced under the headings of "interplay management" (Oberthür and Stokke 2011) and "orchestration" (Abbott et al. 2015). The plea for the establishment of a **World Environment Organization** has in part been justified with problems of institutional interaction and can thus be considered part of related debates. Nevertheless, the governance of institutional interaction and complexes, including its potential and conditions, remains a prominent and promising research area.

References

Abbott, Kenneth W., Philipp Genschel, Duncan Snidal, and Bernhard Zangl (Eds.). 2015. *International Organizations as Orchestrators*. Cambridge, Cambridge University Press.

Alter, Karen J. and Kal Raustiala. 2018. "The Rise of International Regime Complexity." *Annual Review of Law and Social Science* 14(1): 329–349.

Biermann, Frank, Philipp Pattberg, Harro van Asselt, and Fariborz Zelli. 2009. "The Fragmentation of Global Governance Architectures: A Framework for Analysis." *Global Environmental Politics* 9(4): 14–40.

Eckersley, Robyn. 2004. "The Big Chill: The WTO and Multilateral Environmental Agreements." *Global Environmental Politics* 4(2): 24–50.

Johnson, Tana and Johannes Urpelainen. 2012. "A Strategic Theory of Regime Integration and Separation." *International Organization* 66(4): 645–677.

Keohane, Robert O. and David G. Victor. 2011. "The Regime Complex for Climate Change." *Perspectives on Politics* 9(1): 7–23.

Morse, Julia C. and Robert O. Keohane. 2014. "Contested Multilateralism." *The Review of International Organizations* 9(4): 385–412.

Oberthür, Sebastian and Thomas Gehring (Eds.). 2006. *Institutional Interaction in Global Environmental Governance: Synergy and Conflict among International and EU Policies*. Cambridge, MA, MIT Press.

Oberthür, Sebastian and Olav Schram Stokke (Eds.). 2011. *Managing Institutional Complexity: Regime Interplay and Global Environmental Change*. Cambridge, MA, MIT Press.

Raustiala, Kal and David G. Victor. 2004. "The Regime Complex for Plant Genetic Resources." *International Organization* 58(2): 277–309.

Van de Graaf, Thijs. 2013. "Fragmentation in Global Energy Governance: Explaining the Creation of IRENA." *Global Environmental Politics* 13(3): 14–33.

Young, Oran R. 1996. "Institutional Linkages in International Society: Polar Perspectives." *Global Governance* 2(1): 1–23.

INTERNATIONAL WHALING COMMISSION

Steinar Andresen

Fridtjof Nansen Institute, Norway

The objective of the International Convention for the Regulation of Whaling, administered by the International Whaling Commission (IWC), is to establish regulations for the purposes of conservation and utilization of whale resources (see also **Conservation and preservation**). The Schedule to the Convention is an integral part of the Convention and its purpose is to set the specific conservation regulations applicable. Amendments to the Schedule require a three-quarter majority vote. The Convention was adopted in 1946 and came into force in 1948, the first meeting of the International Whaling Commission (IWC) being held in 1949. The IWC has undergone sharp changes over time (Andresen 2019).

Until the mid-1960s, the IWC was for all practical purposes a "whalers club." It was marked by the depletion of most large whale species due to the predominance of short-term economic interests of the pelagic whaling nations. Advice from the Scientific Committee was disputed (see **Science**), and the scientists were not able to quantify the necessary reductions in the total quota. In the next stage, a more conservation-oriented approach was adopted, due in part to more consensual and advanced scientific advice, but primarily to the fact that depletion had made it impossible for whalers to fulfill their quotas. Most Antarctic whaling nations therefore closed down their pelagic whaling operations that, during this period, were only conducted by the Soviet Union and Japan. The more conservation-oriented approach was also due to a gradual increase in non-whaling members as the IWC was open to all states (Andresen 2000). Since the late 1970s, however, the IWC has adopted a protectionist-oriented approach.

Why did the IWC turn from a conservation organization to a protectionist body? The main reason was probably the rapid spread of a strong anti-whaling norm in major Western countries (Friedheim 2001). As a result of active environmental **nongovernmental organizations** campaigning, it was progressively seen as morally wrong to kill whales and **shaming** and blaming toward the few remaining whaling nations was strong (Epstein 2006). New anti-whaling nations became members, actively recruited by NGOs such as Greenpeace as well as the United States (DeSombre 2001). The anti-whaling majority was so strong that a moratorium against commercial whaling was adopted in 1982 and entered into force in 1985 for coastal whaling and for the 1986 pelagic season. By 1988 all commercial whaling had ended, due not least to threats of economic sanctions and political pressure from the United States. Aboriginal whaling was still allowed, although this type of whaling was not much different from small-scale commercial whaling. The United States is a major aboriginal whaling nation.

From the mid-1990s the pro-whaling forces recovered somewhat. The anti-whalers have a simple explanation for this development: active recruitment by Japan, believed to link its bilateral aid to recruitment and subsequent voting. That is, economic assistance was given to new IWC members voting for the pro-whaling stance (Miller and Dolsak 2007). Links to other international forums can also explain the relative decline in anti-whaling sentiment (see **Institutional interactions**). Important here are developments in the **CITES**, where sustainable use rather than protection is gaining ground, especially among developing countries. Furthermore, the anti-whaling norm has not been as successful as expected (Bailey 2008). Despite the fact that the moratorium is still in place, and is likely to be upheld in the foreseeable future, catches have been increasing since Norway and Iceland decided to resume commercial whaling. More recently, the political momentum in the IWC has been strongly reduced and the whaling issue has virtually disappeared from the international political agenda. This reduced political prominence is also reflected in the fact that while IWC meetings used to be every year they are now biennial. The IWC also used to be a favorite meeting place for the green community, which now has almost vanished from the scene (Andresen 2019). It remains to be seen whether the fact that Japan has now left the IWC and has resumed commercial whaling will change the IWC dynamics.

References

Andresen, Steinar. 2000. "The International Whaling Regime." In *Science and Politics in International Environmental Regimes: Between Integrity and Involvement*, Eds. Steinar Andersen, Tora Skodvin, Arild Underdal, and Jørgen Wettestad, 35–68. Manchester, Manchester University Press.

Andresen, Steinar. 2019. "Science and Policy in the International Whaling Commission." In *Contesting Global Environmental Knowledge, Norms and Governance*, Ed. M. J. Peterson, 110–124. London and New York, Routledge.

Bailey, Jennifer. 2008. "Arrested Development: The Prohibition of Commercial Whaling as a Case of Failed Norm Change." *European Journal of International Relations* 14(2): 289–318.

DeSombre, Elisabeth. 2001. "Distorting Global Governance: Membership, Voting and the IWC." In *Toward a Sustainable Whaling Regime*, Ed. Robert Friedheim, 183–200. Seattle, WA, University of Washington Press.

Epstein, Charlotte. 2006. "The Making of Global Environmental Norms: Endangered Species Protection." *Global Environmental Politics* 6(2): 32–54.

Friedheim, Robert (Ed.). 2001. *Toward a Sustainable Whaling Regime*. Seattle, WA, University of Washington Press.

Miller, Andrew and Nives Dolšak. 2007. "Issue Linkage in International Environmental Policy: The International Whaling Commission and Japanese Development Aid." *Global Environmental Politics* 7(1): 69–96.

INVESTMENT PROTECTION

Laurie Durel

Université Laval, Canada

In contrast to international trade law, there is no multilateral organization such as the **World Trade Organization** that regulates investors' rights. Instead, there is an extended web of international treaties such as bilateral investment treaties (BITs) and treaties with investment provisions (TIPs). According to the United Nations Conference on Trade and Development, in 2019, there are more than 3,000 BITs and TIPs in force. One of their particularities is that they often include an investor-state **dispute settlement** (ISDS) **mechanism** which provides monetary compensation for foreign investors whose rights have been violated (Gerstetter and Meyer-Ohlendorf 2013: 6).

Several ISDS cases were related to environmental issues (Gerstetter and Meyer-Ohlendorf 2013: 10). Among the most famous ones, there is *Chevron Corp. v. Ecuador*; *LG&E Energy Corp. v. Argentine Republic*; *MTD Equity Sdn. Bhd and MTD Chile S.A. v. Chile*; *Methanex Corp. v. United States*; *S.D. Myers Inc. v. Canada*; *Metalclad v. United Mexican States*; and *Ethyl Corp v. Canada* (Slater 2015: 146). In the last decade, two arbitrations between Vattenfall, a Swedish power utility, and Germany, filed pursuant to the Energy Charter Treaty, have raised attention. It is in part because Germany agreed to a less stringent environmental requirement for Vattenfall in order to settle the first dispute (Gerstetter and Meyer-Ohlendorf 2013: 10). Generally, some academics fear the provisions in BITs and TIPs may prevent states from implementing environmental regulations and others argue that ISDS may induce a regulatory chill due to governments' fear of being involved in a dispute (Gerstetter and Meyer-Ohlendorf 2013; Tienhaara 2018). Nevertheless, most arbitration proceedings are concluded in favor of the states.

BITs and TIPs often include environmental provisions that are meant to recognize Parties' right to adopt or maintain environmental regulations. A frequent provision in BITs and TIPs expressly requires states not to lower their environmental standards in order to attract foreign investments (Jacur 2018). While it is not clear to which extent these kinds of provisions allow for real flexibility when states implement environmental measures, many states such as Canada, the EU, and the United States have modernized their BITs model over the years to include new provisions and mechanisms to ensure they fully maintain their ability to adopt measures to protect the environment (Jacur 2018). For example, the EU and Canada have followed a new approach in the Investment chapter of the Comprehensive Economic and Trade Agreement between Canada and the EU (the CETA) with the addition of several provisions directly pertaining to the protection of the environment.

References

Gerstetter, Christiane and Nils Meyer-Ohlendorf. 2013. *Investor-State Dispute Settlement Under TTIP: A Risk for Environmental Regulation?* Berlin, Heinrich Böll Stiftung.

Jacur, Francesca Romanin. 2018. "Corporate Social Responsibility in Recent Bilateral and Regional Free Trade Agreements: An Early Assessment" *European Foreign Affairs Review* 23(4): 463–484.

Slater, Tamara L. 2015. "Investor-State Arbitration and Domestic Environmental Protection." *Washington University Global Studies Law Review* 14(1): 131–154.

Tienhaara, Kyla. 2018. "Regulatory Chill in a Warming World: The Threat to Climate Policy Posed by Investor-State Dispute Settlement." *Transnational Environmental Law* 7(2): 229–250.

KUZNETS CURVE (ENVIRONMENTAL)

David I. Stern

Australian National University, Australia

The environmental Kuznets curve (EKC) is a hypothesized inverted U-shape relationship between various environmental impact indicators and income per capita. In the early stages of economic growth, environmental impacts and pollution increase, but beyond some level of income per capita economic growth leads to environmental improvement. The name comes from the similar relationship between income inequality and economic development called the Kuznets curve. Grossman and Krueger (1991) introduced the EKC concept in an analysis of the potential environmental effects of the North American Free Trade Agreement (NAFTA). The EKC also featured prominently in the 1992 **World Bank** *World Development Report* and has since become very popular in policy and academic circles. The EKC is seen as empirical confirmation of the interpretation of **sustainable development** as the idea that developing countries need to get richer in order to reduce environmental degradation and eventually transition to a **green economy**.

However, the EKC is a controversial idea, and the econometric evidence that is claimed to support it is not very robust (Stern 2017). It is undoubtedly true that some dimensions of environmental quality have improved in developed countries as they have become richer. City air and rivers have become cleaner since the mid-twentieth century and, in some countries, forests have expanded. But the overall human burden on the global environment has continued to increase, and the contribution of developed countries to global problems such as climate change has not been much reduced. Carbon dioxide emissions have declined over recent decades in only a few European countries. Therefore, it does not seem to be generally true that economic growth eventually reduces environmental degradation. There is also evidence that **emerging countries** take action to reduce severe pollution. For example, Japan cut sulfur dioxide emissions in the early 1970s following a rapid increase in pollution. It became a leader in pollution reduction when its income was still below that of the developed countries (Stern 2005).

Alternatively, while the **scale** of economic activity increases environmental impacts, improvements in technology can reduce these impacts both locally and globally according to the famous IPAT identity

(*Impact = Population* × *Affluence* × *Technology*). In emerging countries, rapid economic growth might overwhelm the rate at which technology improved resulting in increasing impacts, while in developed countries, where economic growth is slower, technology improvements could outpace growth, and environmental impacts would decrease over time (Brock and Taylor 2010). Thus, the apparent EKC for some pollutants might be a result of slower economic growth at higher income levels rather than of growth itself becoming green.

References

Brock, William A. and M. Scott Taylor. 2010. "The Green Solow Model." *Journal of Economic Growth* 15: 127–153.

Grossman, Gene M. and Alan B. Krueger. 1991. *Environmental Impacts of a North American Free Trade Agreement*, National Bureau of Economic Research Working Paper 3914. Cambridge, NBER.

Stern, David I. 2005. "Beyond the Environmental Kuznets Curve: Diffusion of Sulfur-Emissions-Abating Technology." *Journal of Environment and Development* 14(1): 101–124.

Stern, David I. 2017. "The Environmental Kuznets Curve After 25 Years." *Journal of Bioeconomics* 19: 7–28.

LABELING AND CERTIFICATION

Benjamin Cashore
National University of Singapore, Singapore

Graeme Auld
Carleton University, Canada

Stefan Renckens
University of Toronto, Canada

Labeling and certification initiatives are two key components of generation-long efforts among selected environmental activists, **businesses**, government agencies, and resulting stakeholder **partnerships** to ameliorate environmental and social issues by targeting decisions made along global supply chains. By identifying appropriate responsible standards, these initiatives entice firms to follow these practices by offering market "carrots," such as increased prices, and economic "sticks," such as the threat of boycotts.

Labeling and certification initiatives are some of the most prominent types of a broader suite of **private regimes** and **corporate social responsibility** (CSR) instruments that have been promoted as more effective and efficient than governmental regulatory approaches. Organic farming and fair trade certifications emerged in the 1970s and 1980s to empower marginalized actors, such as Southern producers, within the global economy. The establishment of the Forest Stewardship Council (FSC) in 1993, which included strict rules designed to control firm behavior, triggered the proliferation of stakeholder certification systems to many sectors, including fisheries and the garment industry (Auld et al. 2015).

Two main features distinguish these programs from other CSR initiatives: (1) state actors do not direct the standard-setting process or impose their sovereign authority to require adherence to the standards; (2) their survival and authority depends on support from market actors along the supply chain (Cashore 2002). Most programs rely on a third-party auditor to verify compliance with the private rules and use an on-product label to identify certified products.

Scholars explain the emergence and development of certification programs in three ways. Some refer to information asymmetries between producers and customers and consider certification a means to increase responsible businesses' reputation (Potoski and Prakash 2009). Others focus on their emergence in areas of (inter)governmental regulatory failure and the power struggles between and among public and private actors (Bartley 2007; see also **Critical political economy**). Still others focus on the evolutionary logic of certification programs, which requires distinguishing strategic choices around the initial formation of these programs from effects (such as acquiring political legitimacy) that likely occur once institutionalization is complete (Bernstein and Cashore 2007).

Fitting within the norm of **liberal environmentalism**, some see these programs as a means to overcome the negative externalities of neoliberal globalization and the underprovision of **global public goods** (Ruggie 2004); others consider them as instruments perpetuating unsustainable capitalist production and consumption, or highlight their potential to perpetuate global political-economic North–South inequalities (Pattberg 2006). A major dilemma for certification programs is thus to ensure broad **participation** while maximizing their sustainability impacts (Cashore et al. 2007). Setting high standards might address the latter; however, it makes **compliance and implementation** difficult. Recent scholarship investigating rule implementation and on-the-ground impacts shows mixed results for environmental and social **effectiveness**, even when behavioral changes occur (Grabs 2020; van der Ven et al. 2018).

Recognizing these limits, contemporary research is increasingly focusing on the types of interactions—competitive, complementary, or neutral—among private and public rules in shaping governance processes (Eberlein et al. 2014). In certain areas, such as organic agriculture or biofuels, governments have overtaken private certification or integrated it into public policy (Renckens 2020). Certification is increasingly examined within larger institutional complexes where the **institutional interactions** of public and private rules may not only require orchestration for global governance to operate more effectively (Abbott et al. 2015), but also broader problem-focused analysis to assess when and how labeling and certification are most appropriate (Cashore et al. 2019).

References

Abbott, Kenneth W., Philipp Genschel, Duncan Snidal, and Bernhard Zangl. 2015. *International Organizations as Orchestrators*. Cambridge, Cambridge University Press.

Auld, Graeme, Stefan Renckens, and Benjamin Cashore. 2015. "Transnational Private Governance between the Logics of Empowerment and Control." *Regulation & Governance* 9(2): 108–124.

Bartley, Tim. 2007. "Institutional Emergence in an Era of Globalization: The Rise of Transnational Private Regulation of Labor and Environmental Conditions." *American Journal of Sociology* 113(2): 297–351.

Bernstein, Steven and Benjamin Cashore. 2007. "Can Non-State Global Governance be Legitimate? An Analytical Framework." *Regulation & Governance* 1(4): 347–371.

Cashore, Benjamin. 2002. "Legitimacy and the Privatization of Environmental Governance: How Non-State Market-Driven (NSMD) Governance Systems Gain Rule-Making Authority." *Governance* 15(4): 503–529.

Cashore, Benjamin, Graeme Auld, Steven Bernstein, and Constance McDermott. 2007. "Can Non-State Governance 'Ratchet Up' Global Environmental Standards? Lessons from the Forest Sector." *Review of European Community and International Environmental Law* 16(2): 158–172.

Cashore, Benjamin, Steven Bernstein, David Humphreys, Ingrid Visseren-Hamakers, and Katharine Rietig. 2019. "Designing Stakeholder Learning Dialogues for Effective Global Governance." *Policy and Society* 38(1): 118–147.

Eberlein, Burkard, Kenneth W. Abbott, Julia Black, Errol Meidinger, and Stepan Wood. 2014. "Transnational Business Governance Interactions: Conceptualization and Framework for Analysis." *Regulation & Governance* 8(1): 1–21.

Grabs, Janina. 2020. *Selling Sustainability Short: The Private Governance of Labor and the Environment in the Coffee Sector*. Cambridge, Cambridge University Press.

Pattberg, Philipp. 2006. "Private Governance and the South: Lessons from Global Forest Politics." *Third World Quarterly* 27(4): 579–593.

Potoski, Matthew and Aseem Prakash. 2009. "A Club Theory Approach to Voluntary Programs." In *Voluntary Programs: A Club Theory Perspective*, Eds. Matthew Potoski and Aseem Prakash, 17–39. Cambridge, MA, MIT Press.

Renckens, Stefan. 2020. *Private Governance and Public Authority: Regulating Sustainability in a Global Economy*. Cambridge, Cambridge University Press.

Ruggie, John Gerard. 2004. "Reconstituting the Global Public Domain—Issues, Actors, and Practices." *European Journal of International Relations* 10(4): 499–531.

van der Ven, Hamish, Catherine Rothacker and Benjamin Cashore. 2018. "Do Eco-Labels Prevent Deforestation? Lessons from Non-State Market Driven Governance in the Soy, Palm Oil, and Cocoa Sectors." *Global Environmental Change* 52: 141–151.

LIABILITY

Cymie R. Payne

Rutgers University, United States

Liability is a consequence of the breach of a legal obligation; it results in an obligation to provide reparation. Activities that can give rise to environmental liability include pollution of air, land, and water; violations of the law of war; release of genetically modified organisms (see **Biosafety**); and actions causing climate change.

To incur environmental liability a state must have an obligation to prevent or avoid harm but still cause such harm because of its activity. Ordinary liability generally applies only when the responsible party is at fault; strict (also called absolute) liability may apply when harm results from an ultrahazardous activity, like nuclear power or transport of hazardous waste, irrespective of fault. International treaties, customary international law, and domestic law are the sources of obligations such as the **preventive action principle**. These obligations may be owed to other states, the international community (obligations "*erga omnes*"), **indigenous peoples and local communities**, or future generations.

A state is liable when the harmful action or omission is attributable to it. An operator or its insurer may be liable, in particular under treaties such as the International Convention on Civil Liability (ICCL) for Oil Pollution Damage (see also **Ocean protection**). A state may be exempt from liability if it has taken all necessary and appropriate measures to secure effective compliance by those under its jurisdiction or control, a due diligence obligation (ITLOS, 2011: para. 181).

Reparations include financial compensation and restoration (International Law Commission 2001); criminal sanctions may also apply. Environmental liability incentivizes prevention of harm, provides accountability, allocates costs of damage, and ensures environmental restoration. Legal liability can also be a strategy to manage common resources (Sands and Peel 2012) (see **Tragedy of the commons**). Environmental liability was arguably first adjudicated in the Trail Smelter Arbitration awards for air pollution damage to fruit trees in the US from a Canadian smelter (see also **Transboundary air pollution regime**). This exemplifies application of the **polluter pays principle** (Fitzmaurice 2008).

Strategies to balance victim compensation and industry vigor include insurance and limited liability. The ICCL provides insurance-style compensation when oil tanker spills cause damage so that victims will receive some compensation. The ICCL and the Paris Convention on Nuclear Third-Party Liability cap the amount of compensation owed to victims, protecting the industries from costly reparations. Most treaties provide for joint and several liability where the damage caused by two or more parties is not divisible. This means one party can be responsible for the full measure of reparations; this is the case for instance under the Convention on International Liability for Damage Caused by Space Objects (see also **Space debris**).

Critiques of liability as a governance tool observe that procedural obstacles in proving causation and attribution are often insurmountable and that there are gaps in liability regimes. Also, foreign investment treaties sometimes limit liability for environmental damage caused by multinational **business and corporations** (Wolfrum et al. 2005; Faure and Ying 2008; see also **Investment protection**). The preventive and restorative roles of liability are diminished when limited liability and risk-spreading insurance are used to protect industry.

The scope of harm subject to environmental liability can include the cost of monitoring the injury, the value of lost use of resources from the time of injury to recovery, and the cost of response measures to mitigate the harm. The subjects of environmental liability have expanded from market-valued resources such as timber and tourism to "pure" environmental (or ecological) resources that are not traded in **markets**, such as wildlife, ecosystems, or other public environmental resources, and cultural heritage (Bowman and Boyle 2002; *Costa Rica v. Nicaragua*, ICJ 2018). The UN Compensation Commission's environmental claims category based substantial awards on these theories and valuation approaches for the first time in a large-scale international proceeding (Payne and Sand 2011).

This concept is particularly relevant to the protection of **global public goods**, such as the high seas, ecological function, and biodiversity. In such cases, the public interest is protected by the government as public trustee or guardian. Under the US Oil Pollution Act and the EU Liability Directive, the government is legally obligated to use compensation for the benefit of the public environmental interests that were harmed; the UN Compensation Commission created a follow-up program for this purpose (Payne and Sand 2011).

These issues pose challenges to new theories of liability. Climate change liability claims present causation problems and would strain the legal system because the activities that cause climate change are so pervasive in modern life. Damage from commercial GMOs may take a long time to appear, remedies may be inadequate, and attribution is likely to be difficult. Indigenous peoples and local communities continue to face judicial rejection of their cultural damage claims based on subsistence lifestyle. Claims on behalf of future generations and of nature itself have been largely symbolic, so far (see **Ecocentrism** and **Environmental justice**) (Anton and Shelton 2011).

References

Anton, Donald K. and Dinah L. Shelton. 2011. *Environmental Protection and Human Rights*. New York, Cambridge University Press.

Bowman, Michael and Alan Boyle. 2002. *Environmental Damage in International and Comparative Law: Problems of Definition and Valuation*. New York, Oxford University Press.

Faure, Michael and Song Ying (Eds.). 2008. *China and International Environmental Liability*. Cheltenham, Edward Elgar.

Fitzmaurice, Malgosia. 2008. "International Responsibility and Liability." In *The Oxford Handbook of International Environmental Law*, Eds. Daniel Bodansky, Jutta Brunnée, and Ellen Hey, 1010–1035. New York, Oxford University Press.

International Court of Justice (ICJ). 2018. *Certain Activities Carried Out by Nicaragua in the Border Area (Costa Rica v. Nicaragua); Compensation Owed by the Republic of Nicaragua to the Republic of Costa Rica*, 2 February 2018, ICJ Reports.

International Law Commission. 2001. "Report of the International Law Commission on the Work of its 53rd Session." *Yearbook of the International Law Commission*, 2001, *vol. II*, Part Two, as corrected, UN Doc A/56/10.

ITLOS. 2011. Seabed Disputes Chamber in Responsibilities and Obligations of States Sponsoring Persons and Entities with Respect to Activities in the Area. Advisory Opinion of February 1, 2011, 10 ITLOS Rep. 7. https:// www.itlos.org/fileadmin/itlos/documents/cases/case_no_17/adv_op_ 010211.pdf

Payne, Cymie R. and Peter H. Sand. 2011. *Gulf War Reparations and the UN Compensation Commission: Environmental Liability*. New York, Oxford University Press.

Sands, Philippe and Jacqueline Peel. 2012. *Principles of International Environmental Law*. Cambridge, Cambridge University Press.

Wolfrum, Rüdiger, Christine Langenfeld, and Petra Minnerop. 2005. *Environmental Liability in International Law—Towards a Coherent Conception*. Berlin, Erich Schmidt Verlag GmbH and Co.

LIBERAL ENVIRONMENTALISM

Steven Bernstein

University of Toronto, Canada

Liberal environmentalism describes the normative compromise in global governance that has predicated international environmental protection on the promotion and maintenance of a liberal economic order (Bernstein 2001). Environmental governance norms define how policy actors and political communities understand the appropriate purposes and means to which political action should be directed, with important implications for how they address the world's most serious environmental problems.

Liberal environmentalism reflects a historical North–South bargain generated from the interaction of policy ideas and evolving structural features in the wider international political economy. Whereas **critical political economy** scholars argue that economic actors and interests (e.g. finance capital) empowered by the structure of economic relations have driven practices of global environmental politics in a neoliberal direction, "liberal environmentalism" directs attention also to the enabling and constraining norms that generate and circumscribe the acceptable range of policy practices and the politics of their resiliency, contestation, and evolution.

Liberal environmentalism differs from the first wide-scale global responses to environmental problems in the late 1960s and early 1970s, which focused on the negative environmental consequences of unregulated industrial development, suspicions of economic growth, and planetary consciousness. The popularization of **sustainable development** by the 1987 Brundtland Commission to link environment and development marked a key turning point. It promised to integrate the environment, the economy, and societal needs under a single rubric, in part to address longstanding worries among developing country elites that environmental concerns would trump economic growth, poverty eradication, and access to the markets of wealthy countries. However, Brundtland's focus on intergenerational equity and human needs in its definition of sustainable development—"development that meets the needs of the present without compromising the ability of future generations to meet their own needs" (WCED 1987: 43)—proved, in hindsight, less influential than its proposition that action on the global environment rested on a foundation of liberal economic growth.

Meanwhile, policymakers in the North had increasingly examined their own environmental policies through economic lenses and sought ways to address environmental problems without disrupting economic priorities. This trend, characterized by some as **ecological modernization**, focused especially on internalizing environmental costs through the **polluter pays principle** and on developing market mechanisms, such as tradable emissions permits (see **Markets** and **Sustainable finance**), to address environmental problems. The 1992 UN Conference on Environment and Development in Rio de Janeiro brought these lines of thinking together (see **Summit diplomacy**). It institutionalized the view that liberalization in trade and finance is consistent with, and even necessary for, international environmental protection. It thus embraced and helped legitimize the new economic orthodoxy then sweeping North and South alike, which promoted open markets, deregulation, and working with the private sector to achieve policy goals.

While the 1992 Rio Declaration on Environment and Development includes a range of norms (see Bernstein 2001), liberal environmentalism characterizes its overall interpretation of sustainable development, which Rio Principle 12 articulates most clearly: "States should cooperate to promote a supportive and open international economic system that would lead to economic growth and sustainable development in all countries, to better address the problems of environmental degradation." This interpretation legitimated this understanding of sustainable development across the UN system, the Bretton Woods Institutions, and the **World Trade Organization**. For example, the 1994 WTO Ministerial Declaration on Trade and Environment approvingly cites Rio Principle 12.

The 2002 World Summit on Sustainable Development further reinforced liberal environmentalism when it promoted public–private **partnerships** to implement sustainable development, a practice now well institutionalized in the UN system. The **UN High-Level Political Forum on Sustainable Development** (HLPF) currently promotes partnerships as a primary means to implement the 2015 UN **Sustainable Development Goals** (SDGs) for which it is the main UN body responsible for leadership, follow up, and review. Partnerships also anchor SDG 17, which identifies the framework and targets for implementing the SDGs and the wider 2030 Agenda of global policy priorities (UNGA 2015).

A wide range of policies and practices continue to reflect liberal environmentalism, including to address climate change generally (Newell and Paterson 2010) and specifically transnational and experimental forms of climate change governance—especially the proliferation of carbon markets—largely outside of the multilateral **climate change regime** (Hoffmann 2011), and forest (Humphreys 2006), water (Conca 2005), and oceans governance (Jacques and Lobo 2018) (see **Ocean protection**).

While liberal environmentalism created the necessary political space for mainstreaming environmental protection in global policy, its support of markets and partnerships, for example, contributed to fragmentation of institutions and authority over the longer term, and the subordination of environmental goals to economic principles.

The formal consensus on norms consistent with liberal environmentalism nonetheless masks ongoing contestation over their meanings and how to implement them (see **Compliance and implementation**). Debate persists, for example, on the meaning of the **polluter pays principle**, which implies internalizing costs for some, but responsibility of industrialized countries "to pay" for their historical pollution for others, while the increasingly contested norm of **common but differentiated responsibilities** and respective capabilities for developed and developing countries highlights similar ongoing differences over distributive and historical justice that could challenge liberal environmentalism (Bernstein 2019; see **Environmental justice**). Meanwhile, the SDGs show evidence of both reinforcing liberal environmentalism and potentially being transformative. They display a tension between "balance" and "integration" of the three dimensions of sustainable development in addressing issues ranging from poverty, employment, and gender equality to water and sanitation, energy access, and climate change. Notably, the negotiations over proposed Goal 8—on "sustained, inclusive and sustainable economic growth" and employment—included a compromise to include "sustained" and "sustainable" in the goal, but rejected a proposed reference to planetary boundaries despite general scientific agreement that sustainable development should incorporate such limits (Griggs et al. 2013). Meanwhile, the 2019 Global Sustainable Development Report (Independent Group of Scientists 2019), a mandated scientific input for SDGs implementation, focuses on a more integrative and transformative agenda, but whether its ideas will be adopted or work with or against liberal environmentalism is an open question.

References

Bernstein, Steven. 2001. *The Compromise of Liberal Environmentalism*. New York, Columbia University Press.

Bernstein, Steven. 2019. "The Absence of Great Power Responsibility in Global Environmental Politics." *European Journal of International Relations* 26(1): 8–32.

Conca, Ken. 2005. *Governing Water: Contentious Transnational Politics and Global Institution Building*. Cambridge, MA, MIT Press.

Griggs, David, Mark Stafford-Smith, Owen Gaffney, Johan Rockström, Marcus C. Öhman, Priya Shyamsundar, Will Steffen, Gisbert Glaser, Norichika Kanie, and Ian Noble. 2013. "Sustainable Development Goals for People and Planet." *Nature* 495: 305–307.

Hoffmann, Matthew J. 2011. *Climate Governance at the Crossroads: Experimenting with a Global Response after Kyoto*. New York, Oxford University Press.

Humphreys, David. 2006. *Logjam: Deforestation and the Crisis of Global Governance*. London and Sterling, VA, Earthscan.

Independent Group of Scientists (appointed by the Secretary-General of the United Nations). 2019. *Global Sustainable Development Report 2019: The Future is Now – Science for Achieving Sustainable Development*. New York, United Nations.

Jacques, Peter J. and Rafaella Lobo. 2018. "The Shifting Context of Sustainability: Growth and the World Ocean Regime." *Global Environmental Politics* 18(1): 85–106.

Newell, Peter and Matthew Paterson. 2010. "The Politics of the Carbon Economy." In *The Politics of Climate Change: A Survey*, Ed. Maxwell T. Boykoff, 80–99. New York, Routledge.

United Nations General Assembly (UNGA). 2015. Transforming Our World: The 2030 Agenda for Sustainable Development. A/RES/70/1, seventieth session, 25 September.

World Commission on Environment and Development (WCED). 1987. Report of the World Commission on Environment and Development: Our Common Future. https://sustainabledevelopment.un.org/content/documents/5987 our-common-future.pdf.

LITIGATION

Christina Voigt

University of Oslo, Norway

Environmental litigation before international courts and tribunals (ICTs) has become a dynamic field of global environmental governance. Initially, international environmental cases were sparse (Maljean-Dubois 2017), but with the rise of climate change and other international environmental challenges, a move toward international litigation can be observed. In the absence of a special international environmental court, disputes or claims with environmental relevance come up across a wide spectrum of ICTs and in a wide range of circumstances (Stephens 2009).

Environmental cases hold a number of particular challenges that are not (all) present in other areas of law (Voigt 2019). In particular, ICTs need to tread a thin line between adherence to state **sovereignty** over natural resources on one side and the protection of common interests in the environmental asset at stake or the prevention of transboundary environmental harm on the other (Bodansky 2009). Because of their independence, ICTs can ensure the strength, quality, and longevity of environmental protection against other interests pursued by states. In that way, they can be defenders of existing environmental laws and norms. They can also act proactively, at the forefront of norm development.

ICTs play multiple roles in global environmental governance (Voigt 2013; Voigt and Makuch 2018). In environmental cases, their primary role is to adjudicate disputes between states, or between states and other actors, arising out of the interpretation and application of international law with respect to environmental protection. They legitimize states' claims, clarify legal positions, and announce consequences that arise from breaches of treaties or acts and omissions that do not correspond to legal duties. In doing so, they hold states accountable to their respective international legal obligations and help to ensure compliance by those subject to the rules (Young 2017; see also **Compliance and implementation**).

150

Some ICTs, such as the International Court of Justice, the Inter-American Court on Human Rights, or the International Tribunal for the Law of the Sea, are also competent to give advisory opinions on questions of international law. This is especially important in international environmental law, where many norms are vague and ambiguous. ICTs can determine what the law requires by providing authoritative interpretations, and adapt the law to new circumstances through dynamic and evolutionary interpretation. Especially with respect to expanding the environmental dimension of human rights, the European Court of Human Rights (Council of Europe 2012) as well as the IACtHR (IACtHR 2017) the whole scope of (IACtHR 2017) have been particularly active.

In order to grasp the whole scope of international litigation on the environment, it is necessary to investigate the various ways and means by which different international and regional courts and quasi-judicial bodies deal with environmental claims.

References

Bodansky, Daniel. 2009. *The Art and Craft of International Environmental Law*. Cambridge, MA, Harvard University Press.

Council of Europe. 2012. *Manual on Human Rights and the Environment*, 2nd edition. Strasbourg, Council of Europe Publishing.

Inter-American Court on Human Rights. 2017. The Environment and Human Rights (State Obligations in Relation to the Environment in the Context of the Protection and Guarantee of the Rights to the Life and to Personal Integrity-Interpretation and Scope of Articles 4(1) and 5(1) of the American Convention on Human Rights, Advisory Opinion. www.corteidh.or.cr/docs/opiniones/seriea_23_esp.pdf (in Spanish).

Maljean-Dubois, Sandrine. 2017. "International Litigation and State Liability for Environmental Damages: Recent Evolutions and Perspectives." In *Climate Change Liability and Beyond*, Ed. Jiunn-rong Yeh, 27–60. Taipei, National Taiwan University Press.

Stephen, Tim. 2009. *International Courts and Environmental Protection*. Cambridge, Cambridge University Press.

Voigt, Christina (Ed.). 2013. *Rule of Law for Nature*. Cambridge, Cambridge University Press.

Voigt, Christina. 2019. "Introduction." In *International Judicial Practice on the Environment*. Ed. Christina Voigt, 1–21. Cambridge, Cambridge University Press.

Voigt, Christina and Zen Makuch (Eds.). 2018. *Courts and the Environment*. Cheltenham, Edward Elgar Publishing.

Young, Oran R. 2017. *Governing Complex Systems: Social Capital for the Anthropocene*. Cambridge, MA, MIT Press.

MARKETS

Matthew Paterson

University of Manchester, United Kingdom

Environmental governance has seen innovation in recent decades with a policy instrument involving creating new markets (see **Sustainable finance**). These markets operate by creating rights or credits to do with the environmental problem concerned that can be traded among actors within that domain. They started in the US in the 1970s, but expanded in particular from the 1990s onwards, notably within the **climate change regime**.

From the 1960s onwards, several environmental economists argued that markets could be used to control pollution at lower cost than with traditional regulatory approaches. Governments would focus on setting overall goals for environmental policy, and thus on "internalizing environmental externalities"—those impacts of an activity that are not contained in its market price.

Achieving this could be done either by directly internalizing those costs, via a **taxation** mechanism, or by creating scarcity in the rights to cause environmental damage. Environmental markets arise from the latter strategy. Coase (1960) was the first to argue that externality problems were best understood as problems of imperfect property rights, and that assigning such rights was the best means to internalize external costs. Dales (1968) extended this argument to argue for the establishment of emissions trading systems (ETS) to manage environmental problems (Gormon and Solomon 2002).

In an ETS, an authority allocates rights to emit pollution or use a specific environmental resource, and then enables the rights holders to trade those rights. Within a specific time frame each permit holder would have to hold an amount of permits equivalent to the environmental damage he or she causes. The logic is that while all economic actors thus have an incentive to reduce their damage, those polluters that find it relatively cheap to do so will engage in more aggressive abatement in order to realize profits from the sale of surplus permits, while those that find it relatively expensive will be able to purchase those extra permits rather than reduce their own pollution. The system overall therefore is intended to create incentives both for reduced consumption of particular pollution-producing goods, and for research and development and investments in alternatives.

During the 1970s and 1980s there were a number of experiments, notably in programs to phase out leaded gasoline and chlorofluorocarbons (Gormon and Solomon 2002: 294). The most prominent experiment came in the US Clean Air Act amendments of 1990. These established an ETS in the US for sulfur dioxide emissions. More recently, environmental markets have been established in wetlands (Robertson 2004; Swyngedouw 2007) and in the emergence of payment for **ecosystem services**. Also important were key conceptual innovations, notably the idea of offsets. With offsets, instead of allocating emissions rights, polluters can invest elsewhere in projects to compensate for their polluting activity.

By far the largest environmental marketization project has been in the development of carbon markets. These were mooted early on in the debates about climate change (e.g. Grubb 1989). They became institutionalized in the Kyoto Protocol, agreed in 1997, which established three market mechanisms. One is an ETS, whereby industrialized states' obligations to reduce their emissions were transformed into a series of tradable permits, known as Assigned Amount Units. The other two are offset markets, where investment by country A in country B in emissions reductions can be used against the obligations of country A to reduce its own emissions. Joint Implementation involves investments among industrialized countries, while the Clean Development Mechanism (CDM) involves investments by industrialized countries in developing countries. The Paris Agreement on Climate Change, agreed in 2015, replaced the Kyoto Protocol with a new regime design. Article 6 of the Paris Agreement provides the basis for a market mechanism, although negotiations on the details have not at the time of writing (2019) been completed.

The Kyoto Protocol was followed by a number of ETS at national or **regional governance** levels, as well as some private sector internal schemes (see Betsill and Hoffmann 2011 for the fullest survey). The rate of growth of these systems slowed during the 2010s, and carbon **taxation** grew more quickly in this period, but nevertheless new carbon markets were established in South Korea and China, and other developing countries continue to consider them (World Bank 2019).

The EU Emissions Trading System (EU ETS) remains the largest market. Its impact on emissions is disputed, with some crediting it for contributing to emissions reductions and others regarding it as a dangerous distraction. The EU also allowed companies regulated under the EU ETS to purchase credits from the CDM and surrender them against their ETS obligations. This made the EU ETS the principal driver of demand for credits from the CDM and thus from offset projects. Most of this investment has gone to **emerging countries**, notably China and India.

Environmental markets, in particular carbon markets, have come under sustained criticism. They are variously criticized for the basic idea of commodifying the atmospheric **global public goods**, for being "climate fraud," "carbon colonialism," and other problems (see for example Lohmann 2006).

Carbon markets have arguably gained traction in policy worlds precisely because of their economic attractiveness to a range of **business and corporations**, irrespective of their **effectiveness** in resolving climate change or other environmental problems (Newell and Paterson 2010). Nevertheless, despite criticisms, carbon markets have continued to expand around the world, and there are also pushes to extend the market logic to other areas of environmental governance.

References

Betsill, Michele and Matthew J. Hoffmann. 2011. "The Contours of 'Cap and Trade': The Evolution of Emissions Trading Systems for Greenhouse Gases." *Review of Policy Research* 28(1): 83–106.

Coase, Ronald. 1960. "The Problem of Social Cost." *Journal of Law and Economics* 3(1): 1–44.

Dales, John H. 1968. *Pollution, Property and Prices*. Toronto, University of Toronto Press.

Gorman, Hugh S. and Barry D. Solomon. 2002. "The Origins and Practice of Emissions Trading." *Journal of Policy History* 14(3): 293–320.

Grubb, Michael. 1989. *The Greenhouse Effect: Negotiating Targets*. London, Royal Institute of International Affairs.

Lohmann, Larry. 2006. "Carbon Trading: A Critical Conversation on Climate Change, Privatization and Power." *Development Dialogue* (48): 1–356.

Newell, Peter and Matthew Paterson. 2010. *Climate Capitalism: Global Warming and the Transformation of the Global Economy*. Cambridge, Cambridge University Press.

Robertson, Morgan M. 2004. "The Neoliberalization of Ecosystem Services: Wetland Mitigation Banking and Problems in Environmental Governance." *Geoforum* 35(3): 361–373.

Swyngedouw, Erik. 2007. "Dispossessing H_2O: The Contested Terrain of Water Privatization." In *Neoliberal Environments: False Promises and Unnatural Consequences*, Eds. Nik Heynen, James McCarthy, Scott Prudham, and P. Robbins, 51–62. London, Routledge.

World Bank. 2019. *State and Trends of Carbon Pricing 2019*. Washington, DC, World Bank.

MIGRANTS

François Gemenne

FNRS/The Hugo Observatory, Université de Liège, Belgium

Throughout history, environmental changes have always been key drivers of human migration. Both environmental **disasters** and more gradual changes such as climate change have led to massive population movements, shaping the distribution of the population on the planet as we know it today. Yet, until the mid-2000s, both scholars and policymakers had overlooked this important driver of human migration, focusing mostly on economic and political drivers. However, in the past decade, massive population displacements have often been described among the most dramatic consequences of climate change, and environmental disruptions have been increasingly recognized as a major driver of migration. Over time, migration has become instrumental in the discourses and representations of climate change, and migrants have often been portrayed as the "human faces of climate change," the first witnesses and victims of the impacts of global warming (Gemenne 2011a). This perception, however, often contradicts the empirical realities of environmental migration.

The definition of environmental migration remains disputed in the literature. The concept was coined by environmental scholars in the late 1970s: along with many **nongovernmental organizations** and think tanks such as the Worldwatch Institute, they initially described environmental migration as a new and distinct category of migration, an unavoidable by-product of climate change. Migration scholars, however, first insisted on the multi-causality of migration, and on the impossibility of isolating environmental factors from other migration drivers (Kibreab 1997). It is, however, now usually acknowledged that environmental migrants are:

> persons or groups of persons, who, for compelling reasons of sudden or progressive changes in the environment that adversely affect their lives or living conditions, are obliged to leave their habitual homes, or choose to do so, either temporarily or permanently, and who move either within their country or abroad.
>
> (International Organization for Migration 2007)

The number of environmental migrants remains extremely difficult to estimate, partly because most do not cross an international border and are therefore not accounted for in statistical databases. Every year since 2008, there have been more people displaced by **disasters** than people displaced by violence and war (IDMC 2019). This figure, however, does not include those who migrate as a result of slow-onset changes, and whose number is almost impossible to estimate today (Gemenne 2011b). The importance of environmental disruptions in migration dynamics is likely to increase dramatically in the future as a result of climate change.

The concept of "environmental migrants" encompasses a wide array of diverse environmental changes, but also of migration patterns. Key environmental disruptions that can induce migration include flash floods, earthquakes, droughts, storms, and hurricanes, but also slow-onset changes such as sea-level rise, desertification, or deforestation (see **Desertification Convention** and **REDD+**). Large development or conservation projects, such as dams and natural reserves, are sometimes included as well. These disruptions lead to diverse forms of migration, requiring different policy responses. Empirical research shows that most of these migration movements occur over short distances, often within national boundaries (Foresight 2011). Contrary to a frequent assumption, those who migrate are usually not the most vulnerable populations. These are often trapped and immobile when faced with environmental changes, as they do not have access to the resources, networks, and information that would enable them to relocate to safer areas (Foresight 2011). Though most of these migrations occur in the least developed countries, and particularly in South Asia, Southeast Asia, and sub-Saharan Africa, developed countries can also experience them, as evidenced by the massive population displacements resulting from hurricane Katrina in the south of the US, or the Fukushima disaster in Japan, or the 2019–2020 bushfires in Australia.

Environmental migration remains inadequately addressed by international law. The 1951 Geneva Convention, which defines refugee status, does not take into account environmental factors: "environmental refugees" is therefore a misnomer. Though some scholars had initially favored a new treaty that would have created a refugee status for environmental migrants, many have deemed this solution inadequate or unrealistic, and other policy responses are now preferred (McAdam 2011), such as the Nansen Initiative, a process of intergovernmental consultations that resulted in a global protection agenda for those displaced across borders by **disasters**, endorsed by 110 governments in 2015. Rather than a binding treaty, this protection agenda is a series of good principles and recommendations elaborated on the basis of consultations with different governments, and upheld by a new intergovernmental organization created as a follow-up to the Nansen Initiative, the Platform on Disaster Displacement (PDD). **Regional governance** solutions have also been promoted, especially in Asia-Pacific, the region most affected by environmental migration (Asian Development Bank 2012). These gaps in international law also mean that no UN agency is specifically mandated to assist those displaced by environmental changes, though different organizations and agencies, such as the UN High Commissioner for Refugees (UNHCR), the International Organization for Migration (IOM), and the PDD, conduct humanitarian interventions and/or policy projects on a regular basis.

Many have also turned to the negotiations related to the **climate change regime** as a suitable forum to design policy responses. Whereas environmental migration was initially viewed as a solution of last resort, a failure to adapt to environmental changes, it is now increasingly recognized as a possible **adaptation** strategy (Black et al. 2011), but also as an immaterial loss that should be compensated under the "Loss and Damage" program. Finally, debates on the security implications of climate change have also resulted in migration being presented as a **security** threat, a view that has been refuted by scholars (Gemenne 2011a).

References

Asian Development Bank. 2012. *Addressing Climate Change and Migration in Asia and the Pacific.* Manila, ADB.

Black, Richard, Stephen R.G. Bennett, Sandy M. Thomas, and John R. Beddington. 2011. "Climate Change: Migration as Adaptation." *Nature* 478(7370): 447–449.

Foresight. 2011. *Migration and Global Environmental Change.* Final Project Report. London, Government Office for Science.

Gemenne, François. 2011a. "How They Became the Human Face of Climate Change: Research and Policy Interactions in the Birth of the 'Environmental Migration' Concept." In *Migration and Climate Change*, Eds. Etienne Piguet, Antoine Pécoud, and Paul de Guchteneire, 225–259. Cambridge and Paris, Cambridge University Press/UNESCO.

Gemenne, François. 2011b. "Why the Numbers Don't Add Up: A Review of Estimates and Predictions of People Displaced by Environmental Changes." *Global Environmental Change* 21(S1): 41–49.

International Displacement Monitoring Centre (IDMC). 2019. *Global Report on Internal Displacement.* Geneva, Internal Displacement Monitoring Centre.

International Organization for Migration (IOM). 2007. *Discussion Note: Migration and the Environment.* Geneva, International Organization for Migration, MC/INF/288.

Kibreab, Gaim. 1997. "Environmental Causes and Impact of Refugee Movements: A Critique of the Current Debate." *Disasters* 21(1): 20–38.

McAdam, Jane. 2011. "Swimming against the Tide: Why a Climate Change Displacement Treaty is Not the Answer." *International Journal of Refugee Law* 23(1): 2–27.

MILITARY CONFLICTS

Maya Jegen

Université du Québec à Montréal, Canada

The history of war is replete with examples of environmental degradation. To fight off Napoleon and Hitler, Russian and Soviet armies adopted the "scorched earth" policy, destroying all of their resources that could be used by the enemy, including food, land, and people. During World War I, European forces used mustard gas to poison the air around trenches. In Vietnam, the US sprayed the herbicide "Agent Orange" to defoliate forests, thus exposing and starving guerillas (Zierler 2011). In 1991, Iraq released oil into the Persian Gulf to prevent a landing of US ground forces, severely damaging the marine ecosystem, curtailing fishery, threatening a desalinization plant and thus potable water sources.

The impact of military conflicts on the environment can be intentional or unintentional. We speak of intentional damage, or environmental warfare, when the environment is manipulated for hostile military purposes. Arthur H. Westing (1985), one of the main thinkers on the environmental impact of war, reminds us that, historically, energy stored in forests or water held by dams has often been used strategically for destructive purposes in wars. One of the most devastating examples of environmental warfare occurred during the Second Sino-Japanese War, when the Chinese army destroyed the Huayuankow dike on the Yellow River in an attempt to stop the Japanese invasion. Several thousand Japanese soldiers drowned, as did 750,000 Chinese civilians. Millions of Chinese were left homeless, and millions of hectares of arable land were destroyed by the flood.

Although hypothetical, the most radical scenario of environmental warfare would be the "nuclear winter." According to Sagan and Turco (1993), a global nuclear conflict would not only destroy our physical environment through its blast, fire, and radioactive fallout; it would also have an adverse effect on the Earth's climate, reducing temperatures and destroying human activity (Gleditsch 1998). From an ecocentric perspective, some authors would then speak of "ecocide" (see **Ecocentrism**).

Yet armed forces will often cause environmental damage unintentionally: the environment is the victim of collateral damage. For instance, NATO's air bombing of a petrochemical factory in 1999, ostensibly to deny fuel to Serbian forces, released highly toxic chemicals into the air and the waterways, causing one of the biggest **disasters** in volume and toxicity in recent history.

Two trends can be observed that mitigate the impact of military conflicts on the environment. First, there is the timid rise of normative consciousness as indicated by, for instance, the UN 1976 Environmental Modification Convention that limits the use of environmental modification as a method of warfare, or the inclusion of two provisions in the 1977 Additional Protocol I to the Geneva Convention of 1949 that limit the environmental damage permitted during international armed conflict (Schmitt 2000: 88). Likewise, Principle 5 of the 1982 World Charter for Nature holds that "Nature shall be secured against degradation caused by warfare or other hostile activities." Second, some armed forces such as NATO's are beginning to incorporate environmental **assessment** in their management practices (safeguarding hazardous materials, treating waste water, or reducing energy consumption). Some authors call for the creation of an interdisciplinary field of study—warfare ecology— to investigate the relationship between warfare and the environment (Machlis and Hanson 2008).

Causal relationships between environmental **scarcity and conflicts** remain contested, as is the role of climate change as a threat multiplier. For instance, the Syria climate conflict thesis, which considers human-induced climate change as a main driver of the civil war, has been seriously disputed (Selby et al. 2017). There is however no doubt that wars cause major environmental degradation. Intentional damage is most visible, but collateral damage is more difficult to assess and mitigate.

References

Gleditsch, Nils Petter. 1998. "Armed Conflict and the Environment: A Critique of the Literature." *Journal of Peace Research* 35(3): 381–400.

Machlis, Gary E. and Thor Hanson. 2008. "Warfare Ecology." *BioScience* 58(8): 729–736.

Sagan, Carl and Richard P. Turco. 1993. "Nuclear Winter in the Post-Cold War Era." *Journal of Peace Research* 30(4): 369–373.

Schmitt, Michael N. 2000. "War and the Environment: Fault Lines in the Prescriptive Landscapes." In *The Environmental Consequences of War*, Eds. Jay E. Austin and Carl E. Bruch, 87–136. Cambridge, Cambridge University Press.

Selby, Jan, Omar S. Dahi, Christiane Fröhlich, and Mike Hulme. 2017. "Climate Change and the Syrian Civil War Revisited." *Political Geography* 60: 232–244.

Westing, Arthur H. 1985. "Environmental Warfare." *Environmental Law* 15: 645–666.

Zierler, David. 2011. *The Invention of Ecocide: Agent Orange, Vietnam, and the Scientists Who Changed the Way We Think about the Environment.* Athens, GA, University of Georgia Press.

MINAMATA CONVENTION

Azusa Uji

Kyoto University, Japan

The Minamata Convention on Mercury was adopted by over 140 countries in 2013 and entered into force in 2017. The Convention aims to protect human health and the environment from anthropogenic emissions and releases of mercury and mercury compounds. This Convention was named after the Minamata disease in Japan, a major mercury poisoning incident that caused severe nerve damages, deformations, and deaths (see **Disasters**). The incident indicated to the world the importance of preventing repeats of the incident in the future.

The Convention stipulates the appropriate management and reduction of emissions through the entire lifecycle of mercury, including mining, use in products and manufacturing processes, emission to the atmosphere, and disposal as waste. Geographically, mercury emissions in eastern and southern Asia account for almost half of global emissions, and the largest anthropogenic sources are artisanal and small-scale gold mining (ASGM) and coal burning (37% and 24%, respectively, in 2010; see UNEP 2013). ASGM, mainly located in the developing countries in Asia, Latin America, and Africa, is a highlighted area of capacity building under the Convention.

The institutional design of the Convention is widely regarded as a remarkable achievement in terms of behavioral rule and **implementation and compliance**. The Convention has legally binding rules for emission reduction and it has established a compliance mechanism and an independent fund called the Specific International Program to promote capacity building. Several analysts argue that multilateral **negotiations** for the adoption of the Convention played an important role in establishing the arrangements that were not agreed on under other chemicals conventions (Andresen et al. 2013; Templeton and Kohler 2014; Uji 2019).

Three other chemical conventions (BRS conventions), namely, the Basel Convention, the **Rotterdam Convention**, and the **Stockholm Convention**, have influenced the Minamata Convention (see also **Hazardous wastes regime**). Difficulties in capacity building and compliance under the BRS conventions strongly affected the institutional design of the Minamata Convention. Article 14 of the Convention states that cooperation and coordination with BRS conventions "should be sought to increase the **effectiveness** of technical assistance and its delivery." For example, the Special Program to support institutional strengthening at national level for chemicals and wastes management promotes the implementation of the Minamata Convention in conjunction with the BRS conventions. However, the Convention has its own independent **Secretariat** and conference of parties (COP), which are separate from the integrated Secretariat and the Triple COPs of the BRS conventions (Allan et al. 2018). It remains to be seen how the Convention will fulfill its objectives in collaboration with the BRS conventions.

References

Allan, Jen Iris, David Downie, and Jessica Templeton. 2018. "Experimenting with TripleCOPs: Productive Innovation or Counterproductive Complexity?" *International Environmental Agreements: Politics, Law and Economics* 18(4): 557–572.

Andresen, Steinar, Kristin Rosendal, and Jon Birger Skjærseth. 2013. "Why Negotiate a Legally Binding Mercury Convention?" *International Environmental Agreements: Politics, Law and Economics* 13(4): 425–440.

Templeton, Jessica, and Pia Kohler. "Implementation and Compliance under the Minamata Convention on Mercury." 2014. *Review of European, Comparative & International Environmental Law* 23(2): 211–220.

Uji, Azusa. 2019. "Institutional Diffusion for the Minamata Convention on Mercury." *International Environmental Agreements: Politics, Law and Economics* 19(2): 169–185.

UNEP. 2013. *Global Mercury Assessment 2013: Sources, Emissions, Releases and Environmental Transport.* Geneva, Switzerland, UNEP Chemicals Branch.

NEGOTIATING COALITIONS

Pamela Chasek

Manhattan College, United States

A coalition is an ad hoc grouping of nations united for a specific purpose. Coalitions offer countries a way to increase their relative strength—a position presented on behalf of multiple countries is given more weight than a position presented by a single country (Wagner et al. 2012). Coalitions also create the necessary structure to simplify **treaty negotiations** by reducing the number of speakers. A country's ability to contribute constructively relies on size of delegation, negotiator skill, and influence, which can be enhanced when countries enter into coalitions (Gupta 2000).

When forming a coalition, negotiators must first recognize an issue or issues that require attention. The degree of success or effectiveness of a coalition depends largely on its type (majority versus minority coalitions, general versus issue-specific) and on the nature and precision of its objectives. Coalitions may strive for an optimal or merely satisfactory agreement or they may seek to deprive the outcome of certain clauses, conditions, or rules that their members do not want (Dupont 1996). There can be shifts in positions and membership depending on the issues under negotiation. Goals may be general (e.g. a satisfactorily worded resolution or decision coming out of an international conference) or very specific in terms of the contents of the agreement (e.g. agreement to ban a chemical). Assessments of the **effectiveness** of a coalition are influenced by bargaining strength and its evolution over time, role of the coalition in the negotiations, size of the coalition, leadership, cohesion, organization, and strategies (Dupont 1996).

In environmental negotiations, coalitions are often based on level of development, or shared geopolitical or socioeconomic interests. The Group of 77 (G77), which was formed in 1964 by seventy-seven countries, is the largest coalition, now including more than 130 developing countries. The G77 usually coordinates with China, for example, in arguing that environmental rules should not hinder economic development. Thus, since the early 1990s, developing countries have called for financial assistance, **technology transfer**, and capacity building to help them implement multilateral environmental agreements (MEAs). In addition, over the years the G77 and China maintain that the historical responsibility for climate change lies with industrial countries, which should bear the main responsibility for correcting the problem according to **common but differentiated responsibilities**.

However, differences between developing countries are often pronounced. Defining countries' common interests is increasingly difficult, resulting in the formation of smaller coalitions. In the climate change negotiations, the G77 has been fractured by radically different national interests and priorities (Barnett 2008). At one end of the spectrum lie the members of the Alliance of Small Island States (AOSIS), which are particularly vulnerable to climate change because sea-level rise will destroy or render uninhabitable all or part of their territory. At the other end lie the members of the Organization of Petroleum Exporting Countries (OPEC), which stand to lose substantial revenue from measures to avert climate change (Chasek and Rajamani 2002).

In recent years many sub-coalitions of developing countries have emerged. Some are general coalitions that focus on many issues. For example, the least developed countries are concerned with ensuring their development needs are taken into consideration. Land-locked developing countries advocate for their special development challenges, arising from their lack of territorial access to the sea and geographical remoteness from international markets. Members of **regional governance** groups also often speak as a coalition on many issues, especially the African Group, the Arab Group, and the Latin American and Caribbean Group. Some are more issue specific, such as the Like-Minded Megadiverse Countries, which was established in 2002 to promote interests and priorities related to **conservation and preservation**.

Numerous coalitions have developed in the **climate change regime** negotiations, in addition to AOSIS and OPEC. For example, the Association of Independent Latin American and Caribbean states was established in 2012 to launch an ambitious case for low-carbon development (Roberts and Edwards 2012) and advocate for developing countries not to hide behind the principle of common but differentiated responsibilities and respective capabilities (CBDR-RC), but instead to assume responsibility both at home and abroad to demonstrate leadership on climate change and stimulate negotiations (Blaxekjæra and Nielsen 2014).

The BASIC Group (Brazil, South Africa, India, and China), formed in November 2009 (Olsson et al. 2010), supports recognition of the needs and special circumstances of developing countries in implementing the Paris Agreement, in accordance with the principle of CBDR-RC, in light of different national circumstances. The Bolivarian Alliance for the Peoples of Our America was formed in 2005 and takes a hard line on many issues, including opposition to the use of **market** mechanisms to control carbon emissions and also calls for reparations from developed states to compensate for damage that has already been caused and to meet the adaptation needs of those who are most vulnerable to the effects of climate change (Wagner et al. 2012; Edwards and Roberts 2015).

Moreover, there are two issue-specific developed country coalitions that operate in the climate change negotiations. One is a loose coalition of non-EU developed countries called the Umbrella Group, which is usually made up of Australia, Belarus, Canada, Iceland, Israel, Japan, Kazakhstan, New Zealand, Norway, Russian Federation, Ukraine, and the United States. This coalition works to ensure that climate agreements do not contain language that is antithetical to their energy and economic interests and often shares an insistence that developing countries should undertake emission reduction commitments along with developed countries. The other is the Environmental Integrity Group (EIG), comprising Mexico, Liechtenstein, Monaco, the Republic of Korea, Switzerland, and Georgia. This coalition of non-EU developed countries seeks a more progressive approach than that advocated by the Umbrella Group.

The largest developed country coalition is regional: the European Union (EU). Unlike most coalitions, the EU as a regional economic integration organization is a party in its own right to many MEAs and its members are legally bound together. The twenty-seven members (following the United Kingdom's withdrawal) usually speak with a single voice at environmental negotiations.

A second general developed country coalition was formed when Japan and the United States began consulting with the CANZ group (Canada, Australia, and New Zealand) in 1995, creating JUSCANZ (Newell 1997). Switzerland, Norway, and several other non-EU Organisation for Economic Co-operation and Development (OECD) countries (Iceland, Andorra, Republic of Korea, Liechtenstein, Mexico, San Marino, Turkey, and Israel) also occasionally consult with this group, often referred to as JUSSCANNZ to reflect participation beyond the original five countries. This coalition usually seeks to balance the power of the EU in various environmental negotiations.

Another general coalition consists of the Russian Federation, former Soviet republics that are not G77 members, and non-EU Eastern European countries. These countries are often referred to as "countries with economies in transition" (Wagner et al. 2012). Their goal is to ensure that their interests are not lost in **treaty negotiations** that are often dominated by the EU, JUSSCANNZ, and the G77.

Multiple memberships in both broad coalitions and small ones appear to confer greater leverage: while the small, issue-focused groups help define, voice, and protect the shared interests of their members, such as the specific needs of the landlocked developing countries, the broad coalitions, such as the G77, may offer more general support and more power through a larger coalition across negotiations. On the other hand, sometimes multiple coalition memberships can lead to a conflict of interest, such as AOSIS's concern with climate change when the G77 (to which all AOSIS members belong) is dominated by its more powerful members who may be defending their fossil fuel-dominated economies.

References

Barnett, Jon. 2008. "The Worst of Friends: OPEC and G-77 in the Climate Regime." *Global Environmental Politics* 8(4): 1–8.

Blaxekjær, Lau Øfjord and Tobias Dan Nielsen. 2014. "Mapping the Narrative Positions of New Political Groups under the UNFCCC." *Climate Policy* 15(6): 751–766.

Chasek, Pamela and Lavanya Rajamani. 2002. "Steps toward Enhanced Parity: Negotiating Capacity and Strategies of Developing Countries." In *Providing Global Public Goods: Managing Globalization*, Ed. Inge Kaul, 245–262. New York, Oxford University Press.

Dupont, Christoph. 1996. "Negotiation as Coalition Building." *International Negotiation* 1(1): 47–64.

Edwards, Guy and J. Timmons Roberts. 2015. *A Fragmented Continent: Latin America and the Global Politics of Climate Change*. Cambridge, MA, MIT Press.

Gupta, Joyeeta. 2000. *On Behalf of My Delegation, … A Survival Guide for Developing Country Climate Negotiators*. Washington, DC, Center for Sustainable Development in the Americas.

Newell, Peter. 1997. "A Changing Landscape of Diplomatic Conflict: The Politics of Climate Change Post-Rio." In *The Way Forward: Beyond Agenda 21*, Ed. Felix Dodds, 37–46. London, Earthscan.

Olsson, Marie, Aaron Atteridge, Karl Hallding, and Joakim Hellberg. 2010. *Together Alone? Brazil, South Africa, India, China (BASIC) and the Climate Change Conundrum*. Policy Brief. Stockholm, Stockholm Environment Institute.

Roberts, Timmons and Guy Edwards. 2012. "A New Latin American Climate Negotiating Group: The Greenest Shoots in the Doha Desert." *UpFront* Brookings Institution. www.brookings.edu/blogs/up-front/posts/2012/12/12-latin-america-climate-roberts.

Wagner, Lynn M., Reem Hajjar, and Asheline Appleton. 2012. "Global Alliances to Strange Bedfellows: The Ebb and Flow of Negotiating Coalitions." In *The Roads from Rio: Lessons Learned from Twenty Years of Multilateral Environmental Negotiations*, Eds. Pamela Chasek and Lynn Wagner, 85–105. New York, RFF Press.

NONGOVERNMENTAL ORGANIZATIONS

Michele M. Betsill

Colorado State University, United States

Nongovernmental organizations (NGOs) are a prominent force in global environmental politics. For example, in the realm of **summit diplomacy**, more than 900 NGOs participated in the 2012 United Nations Conference on **Sustainable Development**. Scholars of global environmental governance use the term "NGO" in reference to a broad spectrum of formal non-profit organizations that are independent of governments and are committed to the provision of **global public goods** (Betsill and Corell 2008). While this clearly excludes political parties, organizations that advocate violence, as well as **business and corporations**, non-profit associations representing particular industrial sectors occupy a gray area. NGOs are diverse and work at and across different levels of social and political organization (often in coalitions or networks with other NGOs), focus on a broad set of issues, and engage in a variety of activities from research to lobbying to project development. Global environmental governance scholars often differentiate between NGOs' role as advocates for particular policies and their role as global governors (Betsill and Corell 2008).

NGOs became a focus of global environmental governance research in the 1990s, prompted in part by their visibility at the 1992 United Nations Conference on Environment and Development, and by broader debates on the role of non-state actors in world politics, the changing nature of state–society relations, and the importance of norms and ideas (e.g. Wapner 1996). Global governance scholars contend that non-state actors (including NGOs) represent a new form of authority whose interactions constitute alternative public spaces for confronting global issues. Today, NGOs are seen as valuable partners in addressing global environmental problems, especially in light of globalization processes that challenge the ability of nation-states to deal with these problems themselves.

Many NGOs advocate for particular policies and practices (Betsill and Corell 2008; Newell 2008). They frequently target states, either in multilateral fora such as environmental **treaty negotiations** or international economic institutions, or through domestic channels. At the international level, NGOs often interact directly with state decision-makers by serving on national delegations or participating as observers to negotiation processes. Where such direct access is blocked (or as a complement to these activities), NGOs engage in public protests or **shaming** public awareness campaigns to put pressure on states via the public and the media. NGOs also target multinational **corporations** through consumer boycotts and shareholder activism (Wapner 1996; Newell 2008). Specialized knowledge and expertise along with appeals to moral arguments are key sources of leverage in NGO advocacy work (see **Science**). Whether they achieve their goals depends on several factors related to both the nature of NGO strategies and resources as well as the institutional context in which the advocacy takes place (Allan and Hadden 2017). Even when they fail to achieve their specific goals, NGO advocacy may contribute to changes in norms and ideas about global environmental governance (Chatterton et al. 2012).

NGOs increasingly are recognized as global environmental governors. States routinely delegate specific governance functions to NGOs, such as monitoring and **reporting** or capacity building. In addition, NGOs (often with other types of actors) are involved in establishing **private regimes** for global environmental governance, such as **labeling and certification** schemes and public–private **partnerships** (Pattberg 2005; Bernstein and Cashore 2007). This raises questions about how NGOs come to be seen as authoritative actors. In contrast to state actors, whose authority to govern is often taken for granted, NGOs must justify their authority to those who are being governed and often do so by once again appealing to moral arguments as well as their specialized knowledge and expertise.

In theory, NGOs could contribute to "better" decisions and environmental outcomes. They have knowledge and expertise to deal with complex global environmental problems, and by representing diverse stakeholder interests (see **Participation**), they confer legitimacy on decision-making processes, making **compliance and implementation** more likely (Bernstein and Cashore 2007; Bernauer and Gampfer 2013). In practice, this link between NGO participation and outcomes is mediated by political debates about knowledge claims and/or whose voices and interests are being represented (or not).

Arguably, NGOs make global environmental governance more democratic. In creating new forms of governance, NGOs open up alternative space, such as **global deliberative democracy**, for reasoned argument and persuasion. They enhance participatory democracy by giving voice to a wide range of stakeholders whose interests may otherwise be under-represented in decision-making. NGO participation along with monitoring and reporting activities help affected publics hold decision-makers to account (Newell 2008). Again, NGOs are susceptible to criticism about their own democratic character. While NGOs often claim to speak on behalf of marginalized populations, do these groups have any say in who represents their interests and how? Is there recourse if NGO programs have negative impacts on a community's livelihoods? There are also concerns about North–South dynamics and NGO participation in global environmental governance (Duffy 2013). These issues suggest a need to develop strategies for enhancing deliberation, participation, and accountability within NGOs.

Some critical scholars challenge the assumption that NGOs are a positive force in global environmental governance, arguing that they may perpetuate environmental degradation by reinforcing the neoliberal economic order (Duffy 2013). NGOs reproduce this dominant ideology, and thereby serve the interests of the global elite, by contributing to the shift toward non-state and market-based forms of environmental governance (see **Markets**). In turn, this makes it difficult for weak states in the developing world to exercise **sovereignty** over their natural resources. From this perspective, NGOs must become a counter-hegemonic force for global transformation.

References

Allan, Jen Iris and Jennifer Hadden. 2017. "Exploring the Framing Power of NGOs in Global Climate Politics." *Environmental Politics* 26(4): 600–620.

Bernauer, Thomas and Robert Gampfer. 2013. "Effects of Civil Society Involvement on Popular Legitimacy of Global Environmental Governance." *Global Environmental Change* 23(2): 439–449.

Bernstein, Steven and Benjamin Cashore. 2007. "Can Non-State Global Governance be Legitimate? An Analytical Framework." *Regulation and Governance* 1(4): 347–371.

Betsill, Michele M. and Elisabeth Corell (Eds.). 2008. *NGO Diplomacy: The Influence of Non-Governmental Organizations in International Environmental Negotiations.* Cambridge, MA, MIT Press.

Chatterton, Paul, David Featherstone, and Paul Routledge. 2012. "Articulating Climate Justice in Copenhagen: Antagonism, the Commons, and Solidarity." *Antipode* 45(3): 602–620.

Duffy, Rosaleen. 2013. "Global Environmental Governance and North-South Dynamics: The case of CITES." *Environment and Planning C: Politics and Space* 31(2): 222–239.

Newell, Peter. 2008. "Civil Society, Corporate Accountability and the Politics of Climate Change." *Global Environmental Politics* 8(3): 122–153.

Pattberg, Philipp. 2005. "The Institutionalization of Private Governance: How Business and Nonprofit Organizations Agree on Transnational Rules." *Governance* 18(4): 589–610.

Wapner, Paul. 1996. *Environmental Activism and World Civic Politics*. Albany, NY, SUNY Press.

NONREGIMES

Radoslav S. Dimitrov

Western University, Canada

A nonregime is defined as "transnational public policy arenas characterized by the absence of multilateral agreements for policy coordination" (Dimitrov et al. 2007: 231). In the simplest sense, nonregimes are policy problems without treaties. Today there are no multilateral policy agreements to combat global deforestation or coral reefs degradation (Dimitrov 2006); UN agencies do not regulate biofuels production (Lima and Gupta 2013); and governments have discussed Arctic haze but never attempted to negotiate formal solutions (Wilkening 2011) (see **Arctic Council**). As most environmental **treaty negotiations** succeed, the failure of talks on such prominent problems is an interesting and remarkably understudied topic.

Identifying a case as a nonregime is not a straightforward matter and requires precise definitions. The number of empirical cases is potentially infinite. For example, states do not cooperate on noise pollution or street litter. Nonregimes are puzzling only when theories create expectations of **regime** creation. A case is relevant only if the potential for mutual gains and conducive conditions are present.

In some cases, negotiations have commenced and failed, and in other cases they never began. Arctic haze and coral reefs degradation, for instance, have not triggered formal discussions on policy coordination (Dimitrov 2002; Wilkening 2011). Global forest policy, on the other hand, was under bitter negotiations between 1990 and 2000 that failed to produce a convention (Davenport 2005; Dimitrov 2006).

At what point do we label a case a nonregime rather than a regime in the making? International negotiations sometimes last decades and remain in deadlock for years. At a particular point in time, the outcome may not be clear. Negotiations on the post-2012 **climate change regime** began in 2007 and failed repeatedly before they produced the

2015 Paris Agreement on Climate Change. In 2014, the case could have been labelled a nonregime and even today scholars disagree on the strength of the outcome and whether weak policy accords constitute regimes. It is reasonable to regard ineffective regimes as regimes nonetheless but the matter is open to debate.

It is also useful to distinguish public and private nonregimes. Most studies adopt a state-centric approach and focus on the absence of formal policy agreements between states (Dimitrov 2006; Wilkening 2011). Alternatively, the absence of transnational corporate or NGO initiatives on a problem would constitute a private nonregime (see **Private regimes** and **Nongovernmental organizations**).

The attempt to investigate cases of non-occurrence immediately raises the methodological question: How can we study something that is not "there"? The task is less challenging than it appears since all nonregimes feature sociopolitical processes involving public discourse, national decision-making, multilateral consultations, and occasionally formal negotiations. These processes can be studied in the same manner we study processes of successful regime formation. Although the outcome makes the cases interesting, what we actually investigate is the process. Thus, we study nonregimes in the same way we explore regimes (Dimitrov et al. 2007).

A fundamental question for nonregimes research pertains to the potential symmetry between theories of success and failure. Should regime theory be able to explain also nonregimes? Embracing the notion of symmetry implies that a comprehensive theory must account for successes and failures, and requires structured comparisons of regime and nonregime cases (Young and Osherenko 1993; Dimitrov 2006). Investigation of "negative" cases could test regime theories and help build more complete theoretical explanations of collective action.

Alternatively, no single theory may be able to capture both outcomes and nonregime studies could produce novel and original interpretations of regime making. For instance, the presence of private regimes may explain the absence of state regimes. Private regimes have arisen to provide solutions to numerous transnational problems in a void left by governments' inability or unwillingness to cooperate. The increasing prevalence of private governance may offer governments rationale for eschewing interstate regimes.

Beyond theoretical consideration, nonregime research has added value for practical reasons. It can help identify obstacles to negotiations and produce policy recommendations where progress is urgently needed.

References

Davenport, Deborah. 2005. "An Alternative Explanation of the Failure of the UNCED Forestry Negotiations." *Global Environmental Politics* 5(1): 105–130.

Dimitrov, Radoslav S. 2002. "Confronting Nonregimes: Science and International Coral Reef Policy." *Journal of Environment and Development* 11(1): 53–78.

Dimitrov, Radoslav S. 2006. *Science and International Environmental Policy: Regimes and Nonregimes in Global Governance.* Lanham, MD: Rowman & Littlefield.

Dimitrov, Radoslav S., Detlef Sprinz, Gerald DiGiusto, and Alexander Kelle. 2007. "International Nonregimes: A Research Agenda." *International Studies Review* 9(2): 230–258.

Lima, Mairon G. Bastos and Joyeeta Gupta. 2013. "The Policy Context of Biofuels: A Case of Non-Governance at the Global Level?" *Global Environmental Politics* 13(2): 46–64.

Wilkening, Kenneth. 2011. "Science and International Environmental Nonregimes: The Case of Arctic Haze." *Review of Policy Research* 28(2): 125–148.

Young, Oran R. and Gail Osherenko (Eds.). 1993. *Polar Politics: Creating International Environmental Regimes.* Ithaca, NY: Cornell University Press.

OCEAN PLASTICS CHARTER

Marcus Haward

University of Tasmania, Australia

Increased attention is being directed at the problem of marine plastic pollution (Borrelle et al. 2017; Haward 2018). Annually between 4.8 and 12.7 million tonnes of plastic is estimated to be dumped in the world's seas and oceans (UNEP 2017). A vast majority of marine plastic pollution (over 80%) derives from land-based sources. While this is a global problem—plastics reach the sea from all coastal states—83% of land-based sourced marine plastic pollution originates from 20 of the world's 192 coastal states and the "top 20 polluting rivers were mostly located in Asia" (Löhr et al. 2017: 91). This can be explained in part as plastic waste is correlated to size of population (Löhr et al. 2017), but many developed countries have exported plastics to a number of Asian states for recycling (O'Neill 2019).

A key issue is the problem of micro-plastics either derived from small (1 μm–1 mm) and nano-sized (<1 μm) particles from specific use or applications of plastics, or produced through the breakdown of larger items (Haward 2018). Micro-plastics are being consumed by marine

171

life that confuses them with food sources (Borrelle et al. 2017, see also **Ocean protection**). Responding to the problem of marine plastic pollution is challenging. A range of proposals including new international agreements, stronger state action, increased focus on reducing single use plastics, and working with **business and corporations** on circular economy approaches, have been proposed (Haward 2018: 2; see also **Green economy**).

The Ocean Plastics Charter, a nonbinding agreement negotiated under the Group of 7 (G7) was signed by five (UK, Canada, France, Germany, Italy, and the European Union) of its members in 2018. The G7 had focused on marine pollution at previous meetings and member states had been active in multilateral forums such as the Rio+20 meeting in 2012, but the development of the Oceans Plastics Charter is an example of "minilateralism"—where agreements are developed among a small number of states instead of through larger United Nations processes (see, for example, Naím 2009). The signatories agreed

> to take a lifecycle approach to plastics stewardship on land and at sea [and] to avoid unnecessary use of plastics and prevent waste, and to ensure that plastics are designed for recovery, reuse, recycling and end-of-life management to prevent waste through various policy measures.
>
> (Morath 2019: 49)

Another sixteen governments and sixty-three businesses and organizations have since endorsed the Charter. The Ocean Plastics Charter addresses twenty-three actions across five core areas: (1) Sustainable design, production, and after-use **markets**; (2) Collection, management, and other systems and infrastructure; (3) Sustainable lifestyles and education; (4) Research, innovation, and new technologies; and (5) Coastal and shoreline action.

The Ocean Plastics Charter is a response to a complex problem in environmental governance that is difficult to resolve by traditional state-centered measures. As one example of a collective problem calling for joint solutions, the Ocean Plastics Charter focuses on information sharing, monitoring, and suasion between state and non-state actors. Such "sunshine methods" (Mitchell 2009: 142) provide opportunities to build compliance and avoid the limitation of formal state-centered hard law instruments (see **Compliance and implementation**).

References

Borrelle, Stephanie B., Chelsea M. Rochman, Max Liboiron, Alexander L. Bond, Amy Lusher, Hillary Bradshaw, and Jennifer F. Provencher. 2017. "Opinion: Why We Need an International Agreement on Marine Plastic Pollution." *Proceedings of the National Academy of Sciences of the United States of America* 114(38): 9994–9997.

Haward, Marcus. 2018. "Plastic Pollution of the World's Seas and Oceans as a Contemporary Challenge in Ocean Governance." *Nature Communications* 9(1): 667.

Löhr, Ansje, Heidi Savelli, Raoul Beune, Marci Kalz, Ad Rags and Frank Van Belleghem. 2017. Solutions for Global Marine Litter Pollution." *Current Opinion in Environmental Sustainability* 28: 90–99.

Mitchell, Ronald B. 2009. *International Politics and the Environment.* London, SAGE Publications.

Morath, Sarah J. 2019. "Our Plastic Problem." *Natural Resources & Environment* 33(4): 45-49.

Naím, Moisés. 2009. "Minilateralism". *Foreign Policy* 173: 135–136.

O'Neill, Kate. 2019. "As More Developing countries Reject Plastic Waste Exports, Wealthy Nations Seek Solutions at Home" *The Conversation,* June 6, 2019." https://theconversation.com/as-more-developing-countries-reject-plastic-waste-exports-wealthy-nations-seek-solutions-at-home-117163

United Nations Environment Programme. 2017. *Towards a Pollution-Free Planet: Background Report.* Nairobi, Kenya, United Nations Environment Programme.

OCEAN PROTECTION

Alice Vadrot

University of Vienna, Austria

Ocean protection covers activities in two types of area: *within* and *beyond* national jurisdiction. It seeks to reduce serious pressures on the marine environment, such as: overfishing, ocean acidification, climate change, and pollution (see **Ocean Plastics Charter**).

The ocean itself is a complex social-ecological system, a dense network of carbon, heat, plankton, and fish. The "cumulative results of our actions is a serial decline in the ocean's health and resilience" (IPSO 2013: 3), for human activities are rapidly expanding, including deep-water fisheries, deep-seabed mining, and deep-water oil and gas drilling, which may cause tremendous harm to ecosystems. The ocean is interconnected, thus extra-regional sources of pollution may exert significant impacts, including in polar areas. For this reason, ocean protection targets activities detrimental to the marine environment both in the ocean and on land.

From a legal perspective, ocean protection is a "common concern of humankind" (Harrison 2017: 2). Article 192 of the United Nations **Law of the Sea Convention** requires states to protect and preserve the marine environment. This is complemented by sectoral treaties, such as the Fish Stocks Agreements and conventions under the International Maritime Organization concerning navigation and shipping.

In 2018, governments began to negotiate a legally binding instrument for the protection and sustainable use of marine biodiversity beyond national jurisdiction (BBNJ), which is supposed to fill legal gaps related to, for example, Area-Based Management Tools including Marine Protected Areas and Environmental Impact **Assessments** (De Santo et al. 2019). BBNJ belongs to the "global commons," a particular class of international problem involving resources that do not fall under sovereign national jurisdiction. At present, these are regulated differently in different maritime zones. The "**Common heritage of humanity**" principle, for instance, governs activities in the "Area" (seabed, ocean floor, and subsoil beyond the limits of national jurisdiction) but not in the water column above it, where "Freedom of the High Seas" applies.

The application of different legal principles and norms to different zones and resources is a challenge for ocean protection. Consequently, scholars are exploring connections between politics and policy at all levels—local, national, international, and global (Harris 2019) (see **Scale**). They have become sensitive to the role of knowledge, primarily because of significant gaps in ocean **science**, increasing recognition of traditional knowledge, and striking imbalances between the Global North and South. This resonates with **critical political economy** approaches viewing the ocean as a social conflict space that reveals the disconnect between economic incentives and sustainable use (Steinberg 2001).

References

De Santo, Elizabeth, Aslaug Asgeirsdottir, Ana Barros-Platiau, Frank Biermann, Leandra Regina Gonçalves, Rakhyun E. Kim, Elizabeth Mendenhall, Ronald B. Mitchell, Elizabeth Nyman, Michelle Scobie, Kai Sun, Rachel Tiller, D.G. Webster and Oran Young. 2019. "Protecting Biodiversity in Areas

Beyond National Jurisdiction: An Earth System Governance Perspective." *Earth System Governance* 2. https://doi.org/10.1016/j.esg.2019.100029

Harris, Paul G. (Ed.). 2019. *Climate Change and Ocean Governance: Politics and Policy for Threatened Seas*. Cambridge, Cambridge University Press.

Harrison, James. 2017. *Saving the Oceans through Law: The International Legal Framework for the Protection of the Marine Environment*. Oxford, Oxford University Press.

International Programme on the State of the Ocean (IPSO). 2013. *Implementing the Global State of the Oceans Report*. www.stateoftheocean.org/science/state-of-the-ocean-report/

Steinberg, Philip E. 2001. *The Social Construction of the Ocean*. Cambridge and New York, Cambridge University Press.

ORBITAL SPACE DEBRIS

Steven Freeland

Western Sydney University, Australia

Space debris—sometimes referred to as "space junk"—and their cascading effects represent one of the greatest challenges for the long-term sustainability of space activities. According to estimates on the European Space Agency website, as of January 2019, there were in Earth orbit more than 128 million pieces of debris smaller than 1 cm, about 900,000 pieces of debris 1–10 cm in length, and around 34,000 pieces larger than 10 cm. Given the orbital velocity of even the smallest piece of debris, any collision with another space object would almost certainly result in the destruction of that object and the production of further pieces of debris. This increases the possibility of what has been termed the "Kessler Syndrome," and ultimately a **tragedy of the commons** that is outer space (Kellman 2014; Salter 2015).

Space debris principally comprises those space objects (satellites) that have reached their end of life, various launch stages (for example, rocket bodies, upper stages of launch vehicles), and the remnants of space objects from explosions, conjunctions, or deliberate destruction, but will also include other items that are deliberately or accidentally released during a space mission. If a piece of debris that causes damage can be definitively identified, it may also constitute a "space object" within the terms of the **liability** for damage regime under international space law.

175

Although the volume of space debris orbiting the Earth has for long given rise to significant concern and debate at the international level (Kessler and Cour-Palais 1978), there is as yet no universally accepted or legally binding definition of orbital space debris. The United Nations Committee on the Peaceful Uses of Outer Space (UNCOPUOS), which is considered as the main multilateral forum for addressing issues relating to the exploration and use of outer space, has developed a definition of space debris—incorporating debris both in Earth orbit but also in the process of "de-orbiting"—as follows: "[A]ll man-made objects including fragments and elements thereof, in Earth orbit or re-entering the atmosphere, that are non-functional" (paragraph 1).

This definition comes from voluntary guidelines for the mitigation of space debris, reflecting the existing practices as developed by a number of national and international organizations (Shackelford 2014). The importance of developing appropriate practices with respect to orbital space debris has recently (June 2019) been further emphasized by the adoption within UNCOPUOS of the Preamble and 21 Guidelines for the Long-Term Sustainability of Outer Space Activities.

While it is generally regarded that a lack of functionality is (one of) the defining criteria of space debris, some contend that even a seemingly useless and inoperative space object may constitute a valuable asset for the state of registry, which retains jurisdiction over it even after it ceases to be functional by virtue of the registration regime under international space law. This could for instance be the case with a satellite placed "in reserve" for future operations, or objects that no longer operate but carry classified information.

If that were the case, then "objective" functionality may thus constitute an insufficient criterion for the evaluation of an object's "status" as debris, and that therefore the determination that an object in orbit is, indeed, space debris, can only be made by the state of registry itself.

References

Kellman, Barry. 2014. "Space: The Fouled Frontier: Adjudicating Space Debris as an International Environmental Nuisance." *Journal of Space Law* 39(2): 227–274.

Kessler, Donald J., and Burton G. Cour-Palais. 1978. "Collision Frequency of Artificial Satellites: The Creation of a Debris Belt." *Journal of Geophysical Research: Space Physics* 83(A6): 2637–2646.

Salter, Alexander William. 2015. "Space Debris: A Law and Economics Analysis of the Orbital Commons." *Stanford Technology Law Review* 19(2): 221–238.

Shackelford, Scott J. 2014. "Governing the Final Frontier: A Polycentric Approach to Managing Space Weaponization and Debris." *American Business Law Journal* 51(2): 429–513.

OZONE REGIME

David L. Downie

Fairfield University, United States

The international **regime** to protect stratospheric ozone is one of the most effective cases of global environmental policy. Naturally occurring ozone helps to shield the Earth from harmful ultraviolet radiation emitted by the sun. Destroying this "ozone layer" would be disastrous and a significant depletion would dramatically increase skin cancers and eye cataracts, weaken immune systems, harm many plants and animals, and damage certain food crops and ecosystems.

In the 1970s, scientists discovered that chlorofluorocarbons (CFCs) release chlorine into the stratosphere, which then destroys ozone (Molina and Rowland 1974). CFCs were widely used as coolants in air-conditioning and refrigeration systems and in many other applications. Subsequent research discovered other ozone depleting substances (ODS), including: halons, widely used and effective fire suppressants; methyl bromide, a cheap and toxic pesticide; and HCFCs, which are less ozone damaging CFC-substitutes.

Formal global negotiations on protecting stratospheric ozone did not begin until 1982 and only after major EC countries secured agreement that the talks would seek only a framework convention. The resulting agreement, the 1985 Vienna Convention for the Protection of the Ozone Layer, called for international cooperation in monitoring and protection but did not specify regulatory action nor even mention CFCs.

Discovery of severe ozone depletion above Antarctica, often called the ozone hole, allowed lead states to argue successfully that negotiations on a control Protocol were needed, despite the lack of firm evidence linking the hole to CFCs (see **Science**). The new negotiations resulted in the landmark 1987 Montreal Protocol on Substances that Deplete the Ozone Layer, the centerpiece of global ozone policy.

The Montreal Protocol established binding requirements that industrialized countries reduce their production and use of the five most widely used CFCs and freeze production of three halons. Developing countries had to take the same action but were given 10-year extensions to allow them to use CFCs for economic development. The Protocol also includes important and precedent-setting **reporting** requirements, prohibitions on trade of control substances with countries that did not ratify the agreement, and procedures for reviewing the treaty's **effectiveness** and strengthening its controls, including periodic reports by Scientific, Environmental Effects, and Technology **Assessment** Panels. New chemicals can be added and other changes made to the Protocol by standard amendment procedures, which require formal ratification to take effect. However, the treaty also allows the Meeting of the Parties (MOP) to adjust control measures on chemicals already listed in the Protocol without an amendment. Such adjustments take effect immediately, without the need for time-consuming ratification. Since 1987, parties have used these mechanisms to strengthen the Protocol significantly in response to new scientific information regarding the ozone layer and new commercial developments regarding ODS replacements, including important amendments and adjustments agreed to in 1990, 1992, 1995, 1997, 1999, 2007, and 2016. Today, the Protocol requires parties to eliminate their production and use of all commercially produced ODS. Different chemicals have different phase-out schedules. Exemptions allow parties to use small amounts of some substances for limited periods. Broad and controversial exemptions permit the continued use of methyl bromide for many agricultural uses.

Via a historic amendment in 1990, the Protocol also obligates industrialized countries to provide technical and financial assistance to developing countries to help them switch to non-ozone-depleting chemicals and fulfill other regime obligations. The Multilateral Fund has disbursed more than US$3 billion to support capacity building, technical assistance, **technology transfer**, training, and industrial conversion projects in 145 countries. The different phase-out schedules for developing countries and creation of the Multilateral Fund were explicit acknowledgements of the principle of **common but differentiated responsibilities**. The 1990 London Amendment also created an unprecedented non-compliance procedure that reviews, in a largely facilitative manner, failures by states to meet regime terms and makes recommendations to the MOP for further action (see **Compliance and implementation**).

The Montreal Protocol is the only global environment treaty to achieve universal ratification. The production and use of new CFCs, halon, carbon tetrachloride, and methyl chloroform have been almost entirely eliminated. Methyl bromide and HCFC production have declined significantly. Ozone depletion has essentially stabilized and if all countries implement their obligations (something that is not guaranteed), the ozone layer should return to normal levels later this century. A 2015 amendment expanded the regime by mandating reductions in HFCs, an important group of CFC alternatives that do not deplete stratospheric ozone but are strong greenhouse gases (see **Institutional interactions**).

Several sets of causal factors played central roles in the creation, content, expansion, and extent of success of the ozone regime. Advancing scientific knowledge played an important but not a determinative role (Benedick 1998; Parson 2003; Downie 2015). It gave rise to the issue in the first place, undercut European opposition to starting negotiations, and assisted countries advocating for creating and later strengthening the controls. A relatively influential **epistemic community** that understood the scientific and technological issues also influenced the process (Haas 1992), including framing certain discourses and introducing precautionary and intergenerational perspectives (Litfin 1994).

The economic interests of states and key **business and corporations**, including perceptions of costs and benefits that changed over time, also played central roles. Not surprisingly, economic interests often impeded efforts to create stronger ODS controls, most recently in the creation of broad exemptions for methyl bromide and relatively lengthy phase-out periods for HCFCs. However, during several crucial periods economic interests assisted efforts to strengthen the ozone regime. This included the initial US support for a global treaty to give its industry the same rules as competitors in countries that had not adopted domestic controls, the dramatic policy shifts by major CFCs manufacturers and their governments once they discovered effective alternatives, and the impact of the Multilateral Fund (Downie 2015).

UNEP greatly assisted efforts to get the issue on the global agenda, to start formal negotiations, and to reach agreement on the Protocol and 1990 Amendment (Chasek and Downie 2021; Benedick 1998). The evolving structure of the Montreal Protocol itself also proved critical (Chasek and Downie 2021; Downie 2015). The regime could not have been strengthened so quickly if parties had not been able to adjust as well as formally amend the Protocol. The allowance for exemptions prevented isolated interests from keeping a country from joining the regime or blocking its strengthening. Trade restrictions prohibiting parties from exporting ODS to non-Parties provided powerful incentives for importing countries, especially smaller countries, to join the regime. The Multilateral Fund attracted the **participation** of large developing countries, assisted developing countries to meet and sometimes exceed the phase-out schedules, and created supporters of ODS control among actors that received funding and transitioned to alternatives. The requirement that parties review the adequacy of control measures was made more impactful by the Assessment Panels and the regime principle that control measures should be guided by scientific understanding of threats to the ozone layer in the way of the **precautionary principle**.

The ultimate success of the Montreal Protocol is not guaranteed, however. Global ozone policy faces challenges that could delay or even prevent full recovery. These include completing the HCFC and methyl bromide phase-outs, eliminating halon exemptions, preventing new future ODS production, and ensuring that CFCs trapped in obsolete equipment and insulating foam do not reach the atmosphere (Downie 2015).

References

Benedick, Richard E. 1998. *Ozone Diplomacy*. Cambridge, MA, Harvard University Press.

Chasek, Pamela and David Downie. 2021. *Global Environmental Politics*, 8th Edition. Abingdon, Routledge.

Downie, David. 2015. "Still No Time for Complacency: Evaluating the Ongoing Success and Continued Challenge of Global Ozone Policy." *Journal of Environmental Studies and Sciences* 5(2): 187–194.

Haas, Peter. 1992. "Banning Chlorofluorocarbons, Epistemic Community Efforts to Protect Stratospheric Ozone." *International Organization* 46(1): 187–224.

Litfin, Karen. 1994. *Ozone Discourses, Science and Politics in Global Environmental Cooperation*. New York, Columbia University Press.

Molina, Mario and F. Sherwood Rowland. 1974. "Stratospheric Sink for Chlorofluoromethanes: Chlorine Atomic Catalyzed Destruction of Ozone." *Nature* 249(5460): 810–812.

Parson, Edward A. 2003. *Protecting the Ozone Layer, Science and Strategy*. Oxford, Oxford University Press.

PARTICIPATION

Philippe Le Prestre
Université Laval, Canada

International environmental governance rests on the activities of a variety of actors that do not restrict their action to one level of governance or one issue area. The United Nations (UN) takes it for granted that broad public **participation** in decision-making is a fundamental prerequisite for the achievement of **sustainable development**. Accordingly, Agenda 21 in 1992, recognized that the "major groups" (local authorities, workers and unions, **indigenous peoples and local communities**, farmers, **business and corporations**, the scientific and technological community, women, children, and youth, and **nongovernmental organizations**) have a right to participate in decisions that affect them or touch upon values they promote. Indeed, the UN has given civil society a significant role since its creation, a role that has kept expanding although its dimensions vary greatly among agencies and organizations.

The basis for strengthening participation of civil society in environmental policymaking lies in Principle 10 of the Rio Declaration and in Agenda 21 (see **Summit diplomacy**). At the regional level, the 1998 Aarhus Convention (see also **Transparency**) aims to encourage states to put into place procedures for effective public participation at the early stages of legislations, policies, and program development. Its theoretical roots are diverse, including pluralist, institutional, and **global deliberative democracy** theories. Its pragmatic roots are also diverse, ranging from the fear of capture of the bureaucracy by organized interests, to the experience of aid agencies and international development banks with controversial projects. Participation is supposed to strengthen democratic values, promote **environmental justice**, and improve **effectiveness**. It is intended to create a sense of ownership of the solution, help reconcile global expectations with local demands, and increase the legitimacy of the decisions and policies adopted. In sum, participation transforms policy subjects into stakeholders.

Though participation is now viewed as a necessity rather than a privilege, the goals it should pursue, how it should be conducted, and its impacts remain contested. A first set of questions touches upon representativeness, process, and its instrumental function.

First, who should participate? In international forums, participation faces logistical, equity, and legitimacy problems. There is always a risk of the process being captured by better organized groups and interests. Indeed, preferences do not automatically translate into group formation. In addition, who should select the participants and the criteria used to assess representativeness? In some developed countries, indigenous peoples and local communities have been granted significant policy roles, which often translates into privileges at the international level, such as membership in national delegations. Their spokespersons in international forums, however, represent group interests before they do knowledge. Can we also assume that most local problems have local solutions and that local communities always know better? Conversely, how much weight should be given to the majority opinion of representatives of local communities against that of an organized minority financially supported by foreign interests?

Second, what does participation encompass? Is it a process of providing information to affected parties, of convincing people of the soundness of decisions made elsewhere, of identifying emergent needs and demands, or of integrating the perspectives of groups into the definition of the problems and of solutions? Which issues should be given priority and under what conditions? In one extreme example, the UN Declaration on the Rights of Indigenous Peoples grants indigenous peoples the rights to exploit natural resources according to their needs, and to participate in the decision-making process of institutions charged with managing these natural resources. These principles are not binding on nation-states, however, and groups vary considerably in terms of the levels of authority they enjoy within bilateral or multilateral institutions. In some cases, representatives of indigenous groups are granted access to closed meetings or, as in the case of the **biodiversity regime**, even co-chair some ad hoc working groups. The Inuit Circumpolar Conference (ICC) has been an active participant in the scientific committees of the **Arctic Council** and thus able to influence the contents of its reports.

Third, how can one control for the unintended if not perverse effects of participation or prevent it from becoming a tool used for other political ends? Participation can increase inequalities by strengthening the power of local elites acting as go-betweens linking the community with donors or political authorities. For the same reasons, it can exacerbate political conflicts by empowering new individuals at the expense of established hierarchies, as seen in the context of so-called "development brokers." Finally, participation may be used to impose a particular viewpoint (through the selection of participants) and thus steer policy dynamics in a preferred direction.

A second set of questions pertains to the impacts of participation on environmental outcomes. Provisions for public participation may make issues more intractable. There is indeed a debate whether participation encourages gridlock or, rather, helps shift the power balance in favor of more stringent environmental policies (Green 1997; Beierle and Cayford 2002). Even then, there exists a potential trade-off between the environmental soundness of decisions and the **effectiveness** of their implementation (see **Compliance and implementation**) (Fritsch and Newig 2012). The impact of participation thus depends on its context (the political structure, the existence of clear targets, and obligations, for example) and on the nature of the issue.

Public participation requirements alone are not sufficient to foster environmental sustainability and environmental justice. Arguably it is not participation that shapes politics but the other way around. The key to international influence may well lie at home, where strong segments of civil society can use domestic channels in order to gain influence at the international level.

References

Beierle, Thomas C. and Jerry Cayford. 2002. *Democracy in Practice: Public Participation in Environmental Decisions.* Washington, DC, Resources for the Future.

Fritsch, Oliver and Jens Newig. 2012. "Participatory Governance and Sustainability: Findings of a Meta-Analysis of Stakeholder Involvement in Environmental Decision-Making." In *Reflexive Governance for Global Public Goods*, Eds. Eric Brousseau, Tom Dedeurwaerdere, and Bernd Siebenhüner, 181–203. Cambridge, MA, MIT Press.

Green, Andrew J. 1997. "Public Participation and Environmental Policy Outcomes." *Canadian Public Policy* 23(4): 435–458.

PARTNERSHIPS

Liliana Andonova, Manoela Assayag, and Dario Piselli

Graduate Institute of International and Development Studies, Switzerland

The term "partnerships" is a broad umbrella. It covers governance arrangements of various characteristics—more or less decentralized and voluntary; and more or less formal (Andonova 2017). Partnerships lack traditional top-down steering and regulation and involve actors at global as well as local **scales**. Their collaborative dynamics may entail agreements between the private sector and civil society organizations, such as the product line of natural cosmetics developed by Brazilian company Natura in partnership with community groups and **nongovernmental organizations** in the Amazon region of Brazil; initiatives carried out jointly by public organizations and non-state actors, for instance the climate finance instruments facilitated by the **World Bank**, governments, and the private sector; and larger multi-stakeholder arrangements like the Global Alliance for Clean Cookstoves. Partnerships are thus agreements between different actors, public (including national governments, agencies, subnational governments, and intergovernmental organizations) and non-state (including foundations, **Business and corporations**, and nongovernmental organizations), which establish common norms, rules, objectives, decision-making processes, and implementation procedures for a set of pressing policy problems. From this perspective, a partnership can be seen as a form of experimentalist institution, which seeks to advance cooperation on sustainability objectives through novel governance instruments that are often non-legalized and based on learning-by-doing approaches (Andonova 2017; De Burca et al. 2014).

Since the 1990s, this mode of environmental governance has proliferated rapidly—from the about 200 partnerships registered as official Type II outcomes of the 2002 Johannesburg Summit to the thousands listed since 2012 on the "Partnerships for the **Sustainable Development Goals**" **(SDGs)** platform created by the United Nations. Today, the landscape of partnerships ranges from global initiatives facilitated by international organizations and UN specialized agencies, for instance the Climate and Clean Air Coalition to reduce short-lived climate pollutants, to a plethora of arrangements at the regional, national, and subnational level, such as the joint initiative by US Dow Chemical and The Nature Conservancy on ecosystem services valuation or the ActionLAC partnership set up to accelerate climate action in Latin America. Furthermore, their critical role as instruments of governance is now enshrined in the 2030 Agenda for **Sustainable Development**, which depicts them as key means of implementation of the SDGs through their contribution to the mobilization and dissemination of knowledge (see **Science**), expertise, technology, and financial resources (see **Sustainable finance**).

The increased complexity of collective action problems, the changing nature of multilateralism (coupled with the emergence of powerful transnational actors) and the preferences of Western countries have all been described as leading explanations for the rapid proliferation and diversity of partnerships (Reinsberg and Westerwinter 2019). At the same time, partnerships have also been seen as embodying a range of potentially conflicting expectations and discourses, and their rise has prompted a search for cumulative understanding around three core and interrelated questions. Who governs through partnerships, to what effect, and with what degree of accountability? We consider these three layers of partnership politics in turn.

The rise in the power and mobilization of transnational non-state actors has been an important driver of new collaborative governance. The "business case" for partnerships, for instance, includes managing political and business risks associated with environmental externalities and scrutiny; improving community relations; developing new markets for green products or services; and ultimately increasing corporate reputation and maintaining license to operate in a complex world. The business administration literature distinguishes, however, between more integrative corporate partnerships, which combine environmental or social purpose with the core business of the company, and those that remain largely philanthropic or not necessarily associated with the core environmental impacts of company operations (Austin and Seitanidi 2014; Porter and Kramer 2006). An example of the first type of partnership is the Natura cosmetics line developed in collaboration with Amazon communities. By contrast, while the Dow partnership with The Nature Conservancy supports research by the environmental organization to inform the incorporation of natural capital values into corporate strategies, it does not pertain directly to the company's core business of chemical production.

For nongovernmental organizations, partnerships are means to engage in direct governance to advance specific normative or implementation agendas. Partnerships also facilitate access to powerful actors such as states, intergovernmental organizations, and companies and opportunities to establish a common collaborative purpose. The Amazon Protected Areas Partnership in Brazil for instance entails a substantial reworking of relations between the government, the World Wildlife Fund (WWF), the World Bank, and other actors toward a large-scale program of biodiversity conservation and sustainable use in the Brazilian Amazon (Andonova 2014) (see **Conservation and preservation**). WWF has also facilitated corporate partnerships such as Climate Savers, whereby partner companies commit to specific carbon footprint reductions.

The visible non-state agency in partnerships has hardly derogated public institutions to insignificance, however. As partnerships evolved in number, purpose, and governance tools over the last three decades, intergovernmental organizations have continuously legitimized partnerships as a mode of governance and remain among the most important entrepreneurs of collaborative governance, drawing on agency agendas and autonomy, technical expertise, and normative capital (Andonova 2017; Bäckstrand and Kylsäter 2014). States, and in particular donor countries, provide a significant share of the financial resources that are essential for experimentation with partnership governance (Andonova 2018). The agency of developing countries has also been essential for the implantation and increasing leadership of partnerships initiatives. Rather than retreating, states with some institutional capacity have re-articulated to engage non-state actors in national and subnational initiatives (Andonova 2014).

What motivates public and private governors to foster partnerships has important implications for the effects such initiatives produce. Data on partnership effects, although still limited, suggest a potentially dramatic variation. There are governance niches such as clean energy, biodiversity, climate finance, and risks from chemicals and industrial accidents, where partnerships have produced a range of behavioral or environmental outcomes. In clean energy, for instance, the San Cristóbal Wind Power partnership facilitated the deployment of wind power on the island, reducing by 50% its dependence on imported fossil fuels and mitigating environmental risk in the fragile ecosystem of the Galápagos Islands. Moreover, its achievements gave broader political impetus to an Ecuadorian government strategy aiming at the decarbonization of the archipelago and demonstrated the feasibility of ambitious clean energy projects in similarly challenging scenarios. The collaborative initiatives financed through the **Global Environment Facility** Small Grants Programme have similarly contributed to improved access to efficient and cleaner technologies for buildings, cooking, and agriculture of thousands of communities around the developing world.

Paradoxically, however, such instances of partnership success also highlight major hurdles to **effectiveness**. More than half of the partnerships that had been registered before 2012, for example, were found to be non-functional (Bäckstrand and Kylsäter 2014). At the same time, the effectiveness of the rest is often variable and highly dependent on the specificity of partnership arrangements (Beisheim and Liese 2014), as well as on the commitment of resources by powerful actors (Pattberg et al. 2012). Successful initiatives remain unevenly clustered, often bypassing least developed countries and vulnerable populations that lack capacity or voice to engage partners. Successful partnership experiments have not yet been brought up to scale to make a global dent in pressing issues such as access to clean energy, water, and other environmental services.

Partnerships as modes of governance are thus closely embedded in broader institutional and policy structures. The extent and audiences of partnership accountability (powerful partner constituencies vs. affected populations or national publics) has been an issue for contestation and analysis. The level of **transparency** between partnerships and their policy environment, along with appropriate means for peer, **market**, and procedural accountability, appear to be necessary elements of a complex accountability dynamic. While collaborative governance does not provide a comprehensive or standard solution to global problems, it often creates significant pockets of implementation capacity, new ideas, and extraordinary reach across appropriate scales of action. The frontier of partnerships research has to move beyond the rise and nature of hybrid authority to account for the differential impacts, accountability, and conditions for broader and more equitable up-scaling of successful partnership practices for the environment.

References

Andonova, Liliana B. 2014. "Boomerangs to Partnerships? Explaining State Participation in Transnational Partnerships for Sustainability." *Comparative Political Studies* 47(3): 481–512.

Andonova, Liliana B. 2017. *Governance Entrepreneurs: International Organizations and the Rise of Global Public-Private Partnerships*. Cambridge, Cambridge University Press.

Andonova, Liliana B. 2018. "The Power of the Public Purse: Financing of Global Health Partnerships and Agenda Setting for Sustainability." *Chinese Journal of Population Resources and Environment* 16(3): 186–196.

Austin, James E. and M. May Seitanidi. 2014. *Creating Value in Nonprofit–Business Collaborations: New Thinking and Practice*. San Francisco, CA: Jossey-Bass.

Bäckstrand, Karin and Mikael Kylsäter. 2014. "Old Wine in New Bottles? The Legitimation and Delegitimation of UN Public–Private Partnerships for Sustainable Development from the Johannesburg Summit to the Rio+20 Summit." *Globalizations* 11(3): 331–347.

Beisheim, Marianne and Andrea Liese (Eds.). 2014. *Transnational Partnerships: Effectively Providing for Sustainable Development?* Basingstoke and New York, Palgrave Macmillan.

De Burca, Gráinne, Robert O. Keohane, and Charles F. Sabel. 2014. "Global Experimentalist Governance." *British Journal of Political Science* 44(3): 477–486.

Pattberg, Philipp, Frank Biermann, Sander Chan, and Aysem Mert. 2012. *Public-Private Partnerships for Sustainable Development: Emergence, Influence, and Legitimacy.* Cheltenham, Edward Elgar.

Porter, Michael E. and Mark R. Kramer. 2006. "Strategy and Society: The Link between Competitive Advantage and Corporate Social Responsibility." *Harvard Business Review* 84(12): 78–92.

Reinsberg, Bernhard and Oliver Westerwinter. 2019. "The Global Governance of International Development: Documenting the Rise of Multi-stakeholder Partnerships and Identifying Underlying Theoretical Explanations." *Review of International Organizations*: 1–36.

POLYCENTRICITY

Tiffany H. Morrison

James Cook University, Australia

At the beginning of the new millennium, global environmental governance (GEG) was still in the throes of the decentralization and collaboration wave. Dozens of countries and transnational organizations decentralized and democratized environmental governance in pursuit of gains in efficiency, justice, **participation**, and accountability (Andersson and Ostrom, 2008; see **Effectiveness**). However, by 2010, the infatuation with decentralization and collaboration was over. Rapid and increasingly complex environmental change, including climate change, and an increasingly diversified polity called for a different kind of governance, focusing more on diverse responses and action at multiple **scales**. Analysts variously described this new kind of governance as multilevel, networked, fragmented, or polycentric. Out of all of these, the concept of polycentric governance, and its defining features of self-organization and mutual adjustment, best captured the zeitgeist.

Considered a promising alternative to both top-down and bottom-up systems, polycentric systems comprise many centers of authority interacting coherently for a common governance goal. Advocates suggest that polycentric governance encourages equal representation from different social actors, facilitates policy innovation and **policy diffusion**, and provides flexibility through rapid reconfiguration of alliances to achieve specific goals. Polycentric governance also allows specialization, division of tasks between central, regional (see **Regional governance**), and local levels, and tailoring of interventions to local-regional circumstances and community preferences, thus improving the efficiency of environmental governance by matching interventions to the context and scale of the problem. Many analysts also regard polycentric systems as more robust because their high degree of overlap and redundancy means that if one part of the system fails, others may take over their functions. In addition, the multiple causal factors and symptoms of contemporary environmental problems, the high levels of uncertainty about the set of solutions, and the lack of definitive answers as to who is responsible for the solution mean that alternative approaches are often impossible. Polycentricity is now "a fact of life" for many environmental governance **regimes**, including the global **climate change regime**, **biodiversity regimes**, **fisheries governance**, and the **REDD+** regime.

Polycentricity is not a new concept, dating back to Polanyi's classic 1951 text, *The Logic of Liberty*. In the 1960s, Vincent Ostrom employed the concept to understand how public goods and services could be efficiently provided across multiple metropolitan governments in the United States (Ostrom et al. 1961). Then, at the turn of the century, Elinor Ostrom extended the concept to focus on how interactions across multiple levels and boundaries could resolve cooperation problems in the **tragedy of the commons**. Ostrom's reflections in 2010 on the failure of top-down climate solutions triggered a surge in popularity of the concept (Ostrom 2010). This popularity coincided with the rise of sustainability **science**, and the borrowing of ecological concepts (e.g. ecological complexity, response diversity, and functional diversity) and network approaches and methods (e.g. **transgovernmental networks** (TGNs), social network analysis) to understand complex environmental governance.

Today, different strands of the concept are evident across the disciplines of political science, institutional economics, and sustainability science. Political science (along with international relations, EU studies, and federalism studies) tends to view polycentric governance as a "regime complex" with the costs and benefits of coordination manageable through nonhierarchical steering or "orchestration" (Abbott 2012). Institutional economists and analysts of public policy, administration, and governance prefer to employ polycentric governance as a diagnostic for understanding problems of cooperation in environmental governance (Berardo and Lubell 2019; Ostrom 2010). Sustainability scientists tend to employ the concept more normatively, advocating polycentric governance as a new opportunity for multiple actors at multiple levels to take responsibility for initiating and implementing environmental solutions. Across all of the fields, the use of network approaches and methods to map and analyze structural patterns of polycentric governance is in ascendance (Kim 2019).

Despite initial enthusiasm, most studies have shown that polycentric governance is more useful as a diagnostic and a description than a panacea for solving the multiple challenges of global environmental change (Andersson and Ostrom 2008). Indeed, many polycentric governance systems are struggling to cope with the growing risks of rapid social and environmental change. Documented problems include low **transparency**, high transaction costs, inconsistencies, freeloading, unanticipated effects, gridlock, and ultimate **compliance and implementation** failure.

A third wave of polycentricity studies is beginning to highlight how **effectiveness** is not explainable by structural analysis alone. Indeed, recent analysts have successfully claimed that the concept of polycentricity is plagued by inherent contradictions and assumptions, and some big gaps in knowledge remain. For example, there is still little understanding of the inner workings of polycentric systems, especially how power is exerted by the various actors involved, the **institutional interactions** in polycentric governance, and how polycentric governance feeds back into environmental politics (Morrison 2017; Jordan et al. 2018). Polycentric governance has also been shown to be not as robust as once assumed. Resolving these issues will be critical to moving polycentric governance from a concept to a theory and practice for addressing global environmental change.

References

Abbott, Kenneth W. 2012. "The Transnational Regime Complex for Climate Change." *Environment and Planning C: Government and Policy* 30(4): 571–590.

Andersson, Krister P. and Elinor Ostrom. 2008. "Analyzing Decentralized Resource Regimes from a Polycentric Perspective." *Policy Sciences* 41(1): 71–93.

Berardo, Ramiro and Mark Lubell. 2019. "The Ecology of Games as a Theory of Polycentricity: Recent Advances and Future Challenges." *Policy Studies Journal* 47(1): 6–26.

Jordan, Andrew, Dave Huitema, Harro Van Asselt, and Joanna Forster. 2018. *Governing Climate Change: Polycentricity in Action?* Cambridge, Cambridge University Press.

Kim, Rakhyun E. 2019. "Is Global Governance Fragmented, Polycentric, or Complex? The State of the Art of the Network Approach." *International Studies Review*. Epub ahead of print September 18, 2019. https://doi.org/10.1093/isr/viz052

Morrison, Tiffany H. 2017. "Evolving Polycentric Governance of the Great Barrier Reef." *Proceedings of the National Academy of Sciences* 114(15): E3013-E3021.

Ostrom, Elinor. 2010. "Polycentric Systems for Coping with Collective Action and Global Environmental Change." *Global Environmental Change* 20(4): 550–557.

Ostrom, Vincent, Charles M. Tiebout, and Robert Warren. 1961. "The Organization of Government in Metropolitan Areas: A Theoretical Inquiry." American Political Science Review 55: 831–842.

POLICY DIFFUSION

Katja Biedenkopf

University of Leuven, Belgium

Policy diffusion describes the process through which policies spread among a group of jurisdictions or even globally. It can be observed at and across different **scales** of governance, from the local to the global. Authors distinguish several causal mechanisms and a number of scope conditions. Mechanisms describe a sequence of events that explains how one policy triggers or influences a policy change in another jurisdiction. Whereas the number and types of mechanisms differ between studies, a growing consensus on coercion, competition, learning, and emulation has emerged (Gilardi 2012: 460–461).

Coercion is the imposition of a policy change by one jurisdiction on another, mainly by means of sanctions and conditionality. This includes trade sanctions but also incentives in the form of payments or admission to, for example, an international organization as reward for a demanded policy change. Countries wanting to join the European Union (EU) (see **Regional governance**) must fulfill the condition of adopting the Union's entire set of environmental laws. In the case of the Central and Eastern European countries that acceded in the 2000s, this obligation was accompanied by incentivizing financial and administrative capacity-building measures (Andonova 2003: 6–9).

Competition is based on jurisdictions' struggle to retain or attract resources and investment. If one jurisdiction weakens its environmental regulation so that doing business becomes cheaper, it might attract more investment (see **Dumping**). In response, another jurisdiction could equally weaken its environmental regulation to compete for the same investment, which is commonly labeled a "race to the bottom."

Yet, the globalization of production chains and sales **markets** can also lead to the opposite effect: a "race to the top." If a jurisdiction with a large and attractive market adopts ambitious environmental regulation, all companies that are active in this market must comply. Out of efficiency considerations, some companies can decide to apply the more stringent requirements to all of their products. Having made the initial **compliance** investments, companies can decide to actively advocate policy change in other jurisdictions where they operate to level the playing field with domestic competitors that otherwise would not make the investments (Vogel 1997: 561–563). In 1960, California enacted a standard for limiting car emissions, which led to the adoption of an identical federal standard five years later. In the 1970s, the European Economic Community and Japan adopted similar standards to the US. The global nature of car manufacturing is often cited as the main reason for this race to the top (Carlson 2008).

Learning means drawing lessons from another jurisdiction's experiences. Policymakers use other jurisdictions' experiences and material for inspiration and to gauge the consequences of possible policy options. Environmental ministries and agencies have diffused rapidly since the 1970s. Busch and Jörgens (2005: 875) argue that international communication and exchange of experiences contributed to this diffusion process, through for instance **transgovernmental networks** and **epistemic communities**. Learning only leads to policy diffusion if the result of the process is the conclusion that adopting a similar policy is beneficial.

Emulation is the adoption of policy similar to another jurisdiction's policy based on normative grounds. Viewing a certain policy as appropriate and legitimate is the motivation for this process. Jurisdictions follow others' policy examples because of their adherence to the same norms, their high esteem for the jurisdiction that adopted the policy first, and as a result of socialization efforts by the early adopters of the respective policy. For example, eco-labels (see **Labeling and certification**) were first introduced in the 1970s by a few countries. In the late 1980s/early 1990s, their diffusion rate surged rapidly. One explanation for this can be found in the international cooperation and socialization among the adopting countries (Tews et al. 2003: 583–585). Empirically, emulation and learning are difficult to distinguish.

Diffusion can occur through a combination of mechanisms, which can reinforce or weaken each other. One example of mutual reinforcement is an EU law that requires electronic products to be (re)designed so as to eliminate certain hazardous substances (apart from designated exemptions; see **Hazardous wastes regime**). Through the competition mechanism, the EU has leverage over countries such as China, which produces many electronics components for global supply chains. Leading by example, the EU additionally influenced China's own regulation on the restriction of hazardous substances through learning and, to a lesser degree, emulation (Biedenkopf 2012).

Diffusion only occurs under certain conditions. These can pertain to the first-adopting jurisdiction, the follower jurisdiction(s), their relationship, and the diffused policy's properties. In the above-mentioned example of substance restrictions, the structure of the Chinese economy, China's administrative capacity, and its legal system explain why the Chinese regulation that resulted from the diffusion process has not only similarities to but also differences from the EU law (Biedenkopf 2012).

Policy diffusion has been used in a plethora of studies, analyzing a vast array of policies and jurisdictions, which has led to inconsistencies in the ways in which the mechanisms are conceptualized and measured. Moreover, domestic factors in follower jurisdictions can be idiosyncratic and are difficult to generalize. This patchwork and its inconsistencies render comparison of studies and findings difficult (Maggetti and Gilardi 2016).

Many policy diffusion studies take little account of agency. The role of individuals and organizations in fostering or impeding diffusion processes is often overshadowed by structural variables. For this reason, the politics of diffusion remain rather understudied. This relates to the broader question of how actors could strategically use policy as a governance tool (Biedenkopf and Dupont 2013: 190–192).

Despite the growing academic interest in policy diffusion, it has a strong bias for the Global North. Studies of how and why policies diffuse among jurisdictions in the Global South are rare. One exception is Knoblauch et al.'s (2018) analysis of plastic bag policy diffusion in the Global South, which finds distinct drivers of diffusion for the Global North compared to the Global South and detects that plastic bag policies tend to be more stringent in the Global South than the Global North (see also **Ocean Plastics Charter**).

References

Andonova, Liliana B. 2003. *Transnational Politics of the Environment: The European Union and Environmental Policy in Central and Eastern Europe.* Cambridge, MA, MIT Press.

Biedenkopf, Katja. 2012. "Hazardous Substances in Electronics: The Effects of European Union Risk Regulation on China." *European Journal of Risk Regulation* 3(4): 477–488.

Biedenkopf, Katja and Claire Dupont. 2013. "A Toolbox Approach to the EU's External Climate Governance." In *Global Power Europe*, Eds. Astrid Boening, Jan-Frederik Kremer, and Aukje van Loon, 181–199. Heidelberg, Springer.

Busch, Per-Olof and Helge Jörgens. 2005. "The International Sources of Policy Convergence: Explaining the Spread of Environmental Policy Innovations." *Journal of European Public Policy* 12(5): 860–884.

Carlson, Anne E. 2008. *California Motor Vehicle Standards and Federalism: Lessons for the European Union*, Working Paper 2008(4). Berkeley, CA, Institute of Governmental Studies.

Gilardi, Fabrizio. 2012. "Transnational Diffusion: Norms, Ideas, and Policies." In *Handbook of International Relations*, Eds. Walter Carlsnaes, Thomas Risse, and Beth A. Simmons, 453–477. London, Sage.

Knoblauch, Doris, Linda Mederake, and Ulf Stein. 2018. "Developing Countries in the Lead—What Drives the Diffusion of Plastic Bag Policies?" *Sustainability* 10(6): 1994.

Maggetti, Martino and Fabrizio Gilardi. 2016. "Problems (and Solutions) in the Measurement of Policy Diffusion Mechanisms." *Journal of Public Policy* 36(1): 87–107.

Tews, Kerstin, Per-Olof Busch, and Helge Jörgens. 2003. "The Diffusion of New Environmental Policy Instruments." *European Journal of Political Research* 42(4): 569–600.

Vogel, David. 1997. "Trading Up and Governing Across: Transnational Governance and Environmental Protection." *Journal of European Public Policy* 4(4): 556–571.

POLLUTER PAYS PRINCIPLE

Nicolas de Sadeleer

Université Saint-Louis – Bruxelles, Belgium

The use of environmental goods typically gives rise to what economists call externalities where social costs linked to environmental degradation are passed on to the community. In accordance with the theory of externalities developed by English economist Pigou, such external costs should be internalized: that is, integrated into the price of the goods or services in question, by charging those responsible for them. As long as these costs remain hidden, **markets** will react to distorted price signals and make inefficient economic choices. Against this background, the polluter pays principle (PPP) mirrors an economic rule of cost allocation whose source lies precisely in the theory of externalities. Accordingly, it requires polluters to take responsibility for the external costs arising from their pollution (de Sabran-Pontevès 2007).

Besides having been endorsed since the 1970s by the Organisation for Economic Co-operation and Development (OECD) and the European Union (EU), the PPP has been expressly enshrined either in the preamble or in the operative provisions of a number of environmental agreements, the majority of which aim at protecting regional seas (Sands and Peel 2012; see also **Regional governance**). At the 1992 Rio Conference, the principle was proclaimed in the Declaration on Environment and Development, albeit in aspirational rather than obligatory terms:

> National authorities should endeavor to promote the internalization of environmental costs and the use of economic instruments, taking into account the approach that the polluter should, in principle, bear the cost of pollution, with due regard to the public interest and without distorting international trade and investment.
>
> (Principle 16)

In contrast to other parts of the world where the principle has never been endorsed, it has been gathering momentum within EU countries, most of which are imposing environmental charges on polluters (de Sadeleer 2020). In addition, several national lawmakers (France, Belgium, Italy, Germany) have expressly recognized it as a guiding norm or a fundamental principle of their environment policy in enshrining it in their framework legislation. The PPP has been regularly invoked in court **litigations**, in **liability**, and in tax cases. Several European courts have been reviewing tax arrangements in light of the PPP combined with the principle of proportionality.

The history of the PPP reflects a gradual shift in meaning. At first, the principle was carved out by both the OECD and the EU in the course of the 1970s as a means of preventing the distortion of competition (instrument of harmonization intended to ensure the smooth functioning of the internal market); later, in the course of the 1980s it formed the basis both for internalizing chronic pollution (instrument of redistribution through the use of environmental funds) and preventing it (instrument of prevention through the use of **taxation**); finally, it served more recently to guarantee the integrated reparation of damage (curative instrument thanks to liability schemes).

Last, the PPP juxtaposes two terms whose meanings appear self-evident at first glance but become more elusive as one attempts to define them. The act of definition is thus best approached from two different angles. First: who is the polluter? And second: how much must the polluter pay? The polluter should be the person who causes pollution. However, in the case of diffuse pollution, where multiple causes produce single effects and single causes produce multiple effects, the identification of the polluter would be somewhat difficult. Once identified, the polluter will have to pay, but it still remains to agree on a price. Furthermore, the question arises as to whether the polluter pays principle entails a full or a partial internalization of externalities. However, pricing environmental costs remains embroiled with controversies.

References

de Sabran-Pontevès, Elzéar. 2007. *Les transcriptions juridiques du principe pollueur-payeur*. Aix-en-Provence, Presses universitaires d'Aix-Marseille.

de Sadeleer, Nicolas. 2020. *Environmental Principles*. 2nd edition. Oxford, Oxford University Press.

Sands, Philippe and Jacqueline Peel. 2012. *Principles of International Environmental Law*. Cambridge, Cambridge University Press.

POPULATION SUSTAINABILITY

Diana Coole

Birkbeck University of London, United Kingdom

Population sustainability may be construed in three ways. First, it concerns the demographic viability of a particular population: does it have sufficient critical mass, resilience, and fecundity to maintain itself over time? Second, it refers to the material capacity of the external environment to support existing or projected numbers. This is sometimes related to a third, more prescriptive sense in which a sustainable population is equated with an optimum population. During the 1920s there were attempts at fixing an optimal range and this is still sometimes related to the **carrying capacities paradigm**, although critics regard definite numbers as overly rigid.

The second meaning is most pertinent to environmental sustainability. In pre-modern cultures there is evidence of populations disappearing as they outgrew natural resources. The issue emerged more forcefully during Europe's fertility transition when Malthus, in 1798, cited famine, disease, and war as consequences of exponential demographic growth. During the 1960s and 1970s these warnings were reignited by a post-war baby boom that amplified the West's rising per capita consumption, triggering concerns over resource shortages and environmental degradation. Paul Ehrlich's *The Population Bomb* (1972) and the Club of Rome's *Limits to Growth* (Meadows et al. 1972) recommended population stabilization and a steady state economy. The UN Conference on the Human Environment (Stockholm 1972) refers in its fifth proclamation to continuous population growth as a source of problems for environmental preservation (see **Conservation and preservation**) and its sixteenth principle recommends appropriate demographic policies where population growth rates or concentrations adversely affect the environment, provided these respect human rights (see **Human and environmental rights**).

The topic of unsustainable population growth subsequently fell into abeyance as population control policies became politically toxic, the growth rate slowed, and neoliberals seized upon anti-Malthusian demographic revisionism. This argues that more people are a spur to economic growth and technological innovation, thereby rendering resources elastic while increasing the revenue for managing **ecosystem services** more effectively (Coole 2018). At the Rio Earth Summit (1992), an eighth principle merely tacked "appropriate demographic policies" onto eliminating unsustainable patterns of production and consumption. Since 1994, the "Cairo Consensus" reached at the final International Conference on Population and Development has effectively replaced demographic concerns with a focus on development that foregrounds women's rights, health, and empowerment. This is credited with reducing fertility rates without relying on contentious population policies. By Rio+20 (2012), demographic policies had disappeared entirely from the **sustainable development** toolbox.

That said, almost all countries do have policies for raising or reducing fertility rates and numbers, depending on their stage of demographic transition and economic development. Least developed nations are likely to equate high fertility rates with impediments to economic growth (World Bank 2015), while emergent economies are suspending neo-Malthusian approaches in order to maintain bulges of working-age people: their "demographic dividend." Most developed countries, meanwhile, are trying to raise fertility (and immigration) in order to sustain (working) numbers in the face of population aging. Economic growth, rather than environmental considerations, drives such policies. But given continuing population growth in some **emerging countries** and worldwide (the UN projects nearly 11 billion by 2100), a rising global middle class, and evidence of an anthropogenic climate emergency plus chronic biodiversity loss, demographic concerns have recently begun to reemerge as part of the sustainability challenge (The Royal Society, 2012). Satisfying unmet needs for contraception, incentivizing small family norms, and promoting gender equality are recognized as cost-effective ways to mitigate an environmental **tragedy of the commons**.

References

Coole, Diana 2018. *Should We Control World Population?* Cambridge, Polity.

Ehrlich, Paul. 1972. *The Population Bomb*, 2nd edition. London, Pan/Ballantine.

Meadows, Donella H., Dennis L. Meadows, Jorgen Randers, and William W. Behrens III. 1972. *The Limits to Growth*. New York, Universe Books.

The Royal Society. 2012. *People and the Planet*. London, The Royal Society.

World Bank. 2015. *Africa's Demographic Transition. Dividend or Disaster?* Washington, DC, World Bank.

POST-ENVIRONMENTALISM

Chiara Certomà

Ca' Foscari University of Venice, and Ghent University, Belgium

The post-environmentalism theory emerged in the 1990s as part of a larger corpus of theoretical critiques pointing out the weakness of the **sustainable development** paradigm and the inefficacy of mainstream environmental politics (see also **Critical political economy**). It affirms that from the 1980s onward **summit diplomacy**, **business and corporations**, and large **nongovernmental organizations** (NGOs) put forward a process of de-politicization of environmental issues in the pursuit of establishing consensus-seeking global environmental governance. This process went together with the search for technical solutions to environmental problems that have weakened the sociopolitical strengths of environmental claims, disempowered social agency, and produced largely ineffective policy measures, such as tradable permits and other **market**-based solutions.

The term post-environmentalism was introduced into the political philosophy debate by John Young (1992) and a few years later it was picked up by the critical philosopher Klaus Eder (1996), who envisages post-environmentalism as a master frame for a further development of the cognitive and moral modern rationality in the public space.

By critically building upon the mentioned contributions, political scientist Ingolfur Blühdorn (2000) proposed a theoretical advancement from post-environmentalism to *post-ecologism*, in order to overcome the conventionally accepted definition and practices of environmentalism itself. He claims that the full acceptance of strictly environmental values is incompatible with the practices of modern capitalist consumer democracies and this determines a no-way-out situation for mainstream environmental politics (Blühdorn 2011). In order to disclose the paradox determined by the coexistence of the hyper-ecologism of declaratory commitments toward sustainability goals and the immutable faith of infinite growth, he advances a critical analysis of the social construction of environmental issues proposed by the **ecological modernization** theory and reveals it to be a mere peacekeeping strategy with no real consequences.

In 2004 consultants Michael Shellenberger and Ted Nordhaus published a pamphlet titled "The Death of Environmentalism" that gave rise to a large debate in the US public policy sector and in the environmental sociology field (Latour 2008). They criticized environmental movements for not making any effort to link with other social movements and thus for determining their marginalization in the political debate. Post-environmentalism claims that the naïve presentation of environmental issues as merely pertaining to nature **conservation and preservation** undermined their high political and social relevance and the possibility for environmental campaigns to be successful (Certomà, 2016), exemplarily represented by the failure to tackle the climate change emergency.

References

Blühdorn, Ingolfur. 2000. *Post-Ecologist Politics: Social Theory and the Abdication of the Ecologist Paradigm*. London, Routledge.

Blühdorn, Ingolfur. 2011. "The Politics of Unsustainability: COP15, Post-Ecologism and the Ecological Paradox." *Organization and Environment* 24(1): 34–53.

Certomà, Chiara. 2016. *Postenvironmentalism. A Material-Semiotic Perspective on Living Spaces*. New York, Palgrave McMillan.

Eder, Klaus. 1996. *The Social Construction of Nature*. London, Sage.
Latour, Bruno. 2008. "'It's the Development, Stupid!' or How Can we Modernize Modernization?" www.bruno-latour.fr/node/153.
Young, John. 1992. *Post-Environmentalism*. London, Belhaven Press.

PRECAUTIONARY PRINCIPLE

Aarti Gupta

Wageningen University, Netherlands

The precautionary principle is often touted as one of the most important principles of global environmental governance. Its central premise is that scientific uncertainty about the nature and extent of environmental or human health risks and harm should not be a reason for policy inaction (see **Science**) (Foster et al. 2000). One of the most well-known articulations of the precautionary principle is that contained in the Rio Declaration adopted during the 1992 Earth Summit (see **Summit diplomacy**). Principle 15 of this declaration states that "Where there are threats of serious or irreversible damage, lack of full scientific certainty shall not be used as a reason for postponing cost-effective measures to prevent environmental degradation."

The policy domain of global environmental and risk governance has seen the most intense debates over precaution, given persisting scientific uncertainties about cause, impact, and distribution of harm and risk (Pellizzoni and Ylönen 2008). The historical antecedents of the precautionary principle go back to the German notion of *Vorzorgeprinzip*, first articulated in a domestic context in the 1970s, and implying the need for preventive and forward-looking (rather than reactive) action on environmental problems (O'Riordan and Jordan 1995). Much scholarly attention has focused since then on the challenges of defining and operationalizing the precautionary principle, particularly in an international context (Löfstedt et al. 2001).

The principle has continued to generate controversy in both scholarly and policy debates over the last decades, with strong advocates (Sachs 2011) and equally strong and influential detractors (Sunstein 2005). One reason for such contrary reactions relates to the proliferating definitions of the concept, with resultant uneven and contested policy implications. Many scholars have noted that at least fourteen definitions are identifiable in various international declarations and treaties (Foster et al. 2000). This definitional diversity implies that there is little shared understanding of key elements of the precautionary principle, including appropriate triggers for precautionary action or where the burden of proof should lie in claiming harm or lack thereof. This lack of shared understanding extends to whether precaution should even be considered a "principle" or merely an "approach" to environmental policymaking. While the United States (US) prefers this latter characterization, the European Union (EU) has long been a strong advocate for the precautionary principle as a cornerstone of its regional environmental policy (see **Regional governance**) (Pellizzoni and Ylönen 2008).

A longstanding scholarly debate turns on whether the precautionary principle's "vagueness" and openness to multiple interpretations is its key strength or a fatal flaw. While some claim that the precautionary principle "will remain politically potent as long as it continues to be tantalizingly ill-defined" (O'Riordan and Jordan 1995: 193), others view the lack of definitional clarity as leaving the principle open to abuse. These definitional debates are also linked to identifying and critiquing "weak" versus "strong" versions of the precautionary principle. Strong versions include those that seem to call for zero risk or "full" scientific certainty. In a cogent critique, Sunstein (2005) argues that strong versions of the precautionary principle that preclude taking (uncertain) risks are paralyzing since, taken to their logical conclusion, they permit neither action nor inaction, given that both carry with them corresponding risks and forgone opportunities. From such a perspective, the precautionary principle as a guide to policy is useless.

Others allege that its vagueness allows the precautionary principle to serve as a front to further protectionist trade agendas. For example, the principle has been implicated in the transatlantic conflict between the US and EU over trade in genetically modified organisms (GMOs), given that the EU evokes the precautionary principle to justify its restrictions on GMO imports from the US (Tait 2001). This conflict is linked to similar longstanding disputes and **institutional interactions** over how precaution is being conceptualized in international environmental versus trade **regimes**. One of the most closely analyzed relationships is that between the international environmental treaty governing GMO transfers, the Cartagena Protocol on Biosafety negotiated under the **biodiversity regime**, and the science-based regulation of environmental risks and safety under the **World Trade Organization**'s Agreement on Application of Sanitary and Phytosanitary Measures (SPS Agreement).

The SPS Agreement requires that national sanitary and phytosanitary standards relating to plant, animal, and human health and safety have a scientific justification, to prevent their becoming non-tariff barriers to trade. Article 5.7 of the SPS Agreement allows, however, that:

> in cases where relevant scientific evidence is insufficient, a Member may provisionally adopt ... [restrictive] measures [while seeking] to obtain the additional information necessary for a more objective **assessment** of risk, and review the sanitary or phytosanitary measure accordingly within a reasonable period of time.

Thus, the SPS Agreement permits recourse to trade restrictive precautionary measures, including for GMOs, as long as these are time-bound and efforts are under way to generate concrete scientific evidence of harm. In contrast, the 2000 Cartagena Protocol appears to provide greater leeway to countries to take precautionary action, insofar as it does not require a review of precautionary measures within a specified period of time. Nonetheless, scholarly debates persist about how to interpret the articulation of the precautionary principle in each global regime (Gupta 2001).

The United Nations Framework Convention on Climate Change (UNFCCC) in its Article 3 also evokes a version of the precautionary principle in mandating that "lack of full scientific certainty should not be used as a reason for postponing ... [climate mitigation] measures" (see **Climate change regime**). This issue area highlights, as do many others, a need to go beyond definitional conflicts to embed operationalization of precaution into the growing institutionalization of science and (different types of) uncertainty in global environmental governance (Pellizzoni and Ylönen 2008).

References

Foster, Kenneth R., Paolo Vecchia, and Michael H. Repacholi. 2000. "Science and the Precautionary Principle." *Science* 288(5468): 979–981.

Gupta, Aarti. 2001. "Advance Informed Agreement: A Shared Basis for Governing Trade in Genetically Modified Organisms?" *Indiana Journal of Global Legal Studies* 9(1): 265–281.

Löfstedt, Ragnar E., Baruch Fischhoff, and Ilya R. Fischhoff. 2001. "Precautionary Principles: General Definitions and Specific Applications to Genetically Modified Organisms." *Journal of Policy Analysis and Management* 21(3): 381–407.

O'Riordan, Timothy and Andrew Jordan. 1995. "The Precautionary Principle in Contemporary Environmental Politics." *Environmental Values* 4(3): 191–212.

Pellizzoni, Luigi and Marja Ylönen. 2008. "Responsibility in Uncertain Times: An Institutional Perspective on Precaution." *Global Environmental Politics* 8(3): 51–73.

Sachs, Noah M. 2011. "Rescuing the Strong Precautionary Principle from its Critics." *University of Illinois Law Review* 4: 1285–1338.

Sunstein, Cass. 2005. *Laws of Fear: Beyond the Precautionary Principle*. New York, Cambridge University Press.

Tait, Joyce. 2001. "More Faust than Frankenstein: The European Debate about the Precautionary Principle and Risk Regulation for Genetically Modified Crops." *Journal of Risk Research* 4(2): 175–189.

PREVENTIVE ACTION PRINCIPLE

Hélène Trudeau

Université de Montréal, Canada

The principle of preventive action is associated with the concept of **sustainable development**. This principle means that states should take necessary measures to protect the environment and to prevent harm caused by activities on their territory, not only from a transboundary perspective but also from a global one. These measures can include, for example, the regulation of products and activities that can be toxic or harmful and the **assessment** and authorization of projects that could generate risks for the environment.

It is important to distinguish the **precautionary principle** from the principle of preventive action. Although connected because preventive measures and action can be warranted in face of all risks (Trouwborst 2009), the principle of preventive action applies more specifically to known risks to the environment (see **Risk society**). The precautionary principle is an advanced articulation of prevention that applies to risks framed with scientific uncertainty (De Sadeleer 2002) (see **Science**).

The principle of preventive action finds its origin in the rules governing state **liability**. In 1941, in the Trail Smelter dispute, Canada was held responsible for the damage caused to American farmers by emissions emanating from a plant on the Canadian side of the border. The arbitral tribunal said that a state is not allowed to use its territory in a way that can harm the territory of another state.

In international law, states have a responsibility to prevent damages they can cause outside their territory, in spite of their **sovereignty** over their natural wealth and resources. With respect to the protection of the environment, a correlating duty has emerged imposing on states the responsibility to control and correctly manage activities based

203

on their territory if they can impact on the territory of another state (Sands 1995; Paradell-Trius 2000; Trouwborst 2009). This obligation is limited to a conduct of "due care" or "due diligence": a state will not be held liable for damages if it took reasonable measures to prevent them from happening (Crawford et al. 2010). That duty has been articulated during **summit diplomacy** in both Principle 21 of the Stockholm Declaration and Principle 2 of the Rio Declaration. It has found application in situations of transboundary harm and pollution and has been clearly stated as a customary rule of international law in several international **litigations** and **dispute settlement mechanisms** (Trail Smelter, Lac Lanoux, Gabcikovo-Nagymaros, Certain Activities Carried Out by Nicaragua in the Border Area (*Costa Rica v. Nicaragua*) and Pulp Mills on the River Uruguay (*Argentina v. Uruguay*)).

Its precise normative content is provided for in bilateral and multilateral treaties such as the Convention on Environmental Impact Assessment and the **transboundary air pollution regime**, which formulate concrete measures of prevention applicable between states (**assessments**, consultation, cooperation, monitoring sources of potential transboundary harm). Water law treaties also provide such obligations. Moreover, in 2001, the International Law Commission (ILC) codified the specific elements resulting from that due care obligation in the Draft Articles on Prevention of Transboundary Harm from Hazardous Activities (Barboza 2011).

References

Barboza, Julio. 2011. *The Environment, Risk and Liability in International Law*. Leiden, Boston, Martinus Nijhoff Publishers.

Crawford, James, Alain Pellet, and Simon Olleson. 2010. *The Law of International Responsibility*. Oxford, Oxford University Press.

de Sadeleer, Nicolas. 2002. *Environmental Principles*. Oxford, Oxford University Press.

Paradell-Trius, Lluis. 2000. "Principle of International Environmental Law: An Overview." *Review of European, Comparative and International Environmental Law* 9(2): 93–99.

Sands, Philippe. 1995. *Principles of International Environmental Law*. Manchester, Manchester University Press.

Trouwborst, Arie. 2009. "Prevention, Precaution, Logic and Law: The Relationship between the Precautionary Principle and the Preventative Principle in International Law and Associated Questions." *Erasmus Law Review* 2(2): 105–127.

PRINCIPLE OF NON-REGRESSION

Lynda Collins

University of Ottawa, Canada

The principle of non-regression has both ecological and legal dimensions: it can be defined as a prohibition on state conduct that results in environmental degradation (e.g. increased pollution, biodiversity loss) or in the weakening of environmental laws. Depending on the jurisdiction, non-regression may also be known as "non-degradation," "the standstill doctrine," or the obligation not to "backtrack" from environmental commitments (Collins and Boyd 2016: 294–300). The non-regression principle originates in international human rights law (Prieur 2012: 54) and may be viewed as "a negative obligation inherent in all positive obligations associated with fundamental rights" (Hachez 2008: 195, own translation) including **human and environmental rights**. It has been recognized in the UN Framework Principles on Human Rights and the Environment (Knox 2018: para 33). More than 130 countries have also recognized the principle of environmental non-regression through international investment agreements (Mitchell and Munro 2019: 627).

At the theoretical level, non-regression is closely related to other key tenets of environmental governance including the **precautionary principle**, **sustainable development**, the principle of intergenerational equity, and the right to a healthy environment (Prieur 2012: 54). In practice, non-regression would ensure that environmental gains are not reversed with changes in governmental, social, or economic circumstances. States have adopted the principle of environmental non-regression through national constitutions, legislation, and judicial decision-making. In particular, non-regression has been understood as an aspect of the constitutional right to a healthy environment, recognized in at least 147 constitutions around the world (Collins and Boyd 2016: 298–300). Non-regression has also received significant support in several important non-binding instruments of international environmental law (e.g. GA Res. 66/288 "The Future We Want").

Most recently, non-regression has evolved into an even stronger environmental principle known as the *progression principle*, meaning the continuous improvement of environmental legislation. Significantly, the progression principle is included in the Paris Agreement on climate change. It is integrated in the draft **Global Pact for the Environment** (GPE).

References

Collins, Lynda and David Boyd. 2016. "Non-regression and the *Charter* Right to a Healthy Environment." *Journal of Environmental Law and Practice* 29: 285–304.

Hachez, Isabelle. 2008. *Le principe de standstill dans le droit des droits fondamentaux: une irréversibilité relative.* Brussels, Bruylant.

Knox, John. 2018 "Framework Principles on Human Rights and the Environment." A/HRC/37/59. United Nations Human Rights Office of the High Commissioner. https://www.ohchr.org/EN/Issues/Environment/SREnvironment/Pages/FrameworkPrinciplesReport.aspx.

Mitchell, Andrew D. and James Munro. 2019. "No Retreat: An Emerging Principle of Non-Regression from Environmental Protections in International Investment Law." *Georgetown Journal of International Law* 50: 627.

Prieur, Michel. 2012. "Non-regression in Environmental Law." *S.A.P.I.E.N.S* 5(2): 53.

PRIVATE REGIMES

Jessica F. Green

University of Toronto, Canada

States are no longer the sole actors responsible for governing global environmental problems. Increasingly, private regimes, which are transnational rules created by non-state actors (including **nongovernmental organizations**, **business and corporations**, and **partnerships**), are managing environmental issues (Andonova 2017; Green 2014; see also **Regimes**).

The trend toward private regimes can be traced, in part, back to the 1992 Conference on Environment and Human Development, where states called on non-state actors to promote environmental protection through partnerships and other activities. The most prominent type of private regime takes the form of environmental **labeling and certification**. These are rules created by non-state actors that set standards for the environmental attributes of various products. For example, these private regimes decide what constitutes "sustainable" fish or "organic" food. These are driven by **market** logic: consumers from developed nations demand products that have a reduced environmental impact, for which they are willing to pay a premium (Cashore et al. 2004).

Codes of conduct for **corporate social responsibility** (CSR) are examples of self-regulation, which can also be considered a type of private regime. The chemical industry created the Responsible Care program to improve the environmental safety and public accountability of chemical manufacturers. The majority of global chemical producers are now members, and have adopted principles of behavior to improve their conduct.

Information-based standards are a third form of private regime. They require organizations—usually firms—to collect and report their activities with respect to some environmental practice (see **Audits**). Thus, the Global Reporting Initiative (GRI) (see **Reporting**) provides a framework for organizations to report on the economic, social, and environmental impacts of their activities. The Carbon Disclosure Project (CDP) does the same, but is focused largely on carbon emissions. Environmental management systems, such as ISO14001, can also be considered a private regime: these standards are created by private actors to improve their internal operations (Prakash and Potoski 2006). They are process-based rules, and as such do not have any requirements about outcomes.

There are a few different views about why private regimes emerge; ultimately, the answer depends in part on who creates the rules and who adopts them. Private regimes constituted by and for business often confer some benefit to members. This may include an improved corporate reputation, or the ability to forestall more stringent public regulation. Others see private regimes, especially labeling and certification, as the result of globalization. Supply chains now span the length of the globe and cannot be regulated by any single nation; private regimes have emerged to fill this gap. Since fish sold in the United States may have been caught in one nation and processed in another, no single nation can regulate this product. Thus, the demand for these private regimes may come from consumers or from firms. In other cases, the demand comes from NGOs who seek to reduce the environmental impacts of firms (Bartley 2007).

Since private regimes are voluntary, and not required by law, they have been critiqued as being weak and ineffective. Weak regimes are viewed as a form of "greenwashing"—making claims about improving environmental quality without really doing so (Dauvergne and Lister 2013). Even with strong rules, private regimes may also be ineffective, since they cannot compel organizations to join. For example, although the Marine Stewardship Council (MSC) now certifies almost one-tenth of the world's fish catch, most of the world's fisheries are still dangerously overexploited despite the parallel existence of **fisheries**

governance. Recently, studies have begun to examine whether and how private regimes can be strengthened through governmental action. For example, many EU nations now accept timber certified by forest labeling schemes such as the Forest Stewardship Council (FSC) (Overdevest and Zeitlin 2014). This public policy creates more demand and, in theory, enhances the **effectiveness** of labeling schemes. Of course, if governments are needed for the proper functioning of private regimes, this raises the question of whether they are really necessary forms of governance.

Private regimes are also vulnerable to legitimacy critiques. Since they are not endowed with authority by the state, there is a question of whether non-state actors are viewed as rightful rule-makers (Bernstein and Cashore 2007). Perceptions of legitimacy are closely tied to the ability to govern, since legitimacy provides private actors with authority. Some works discuss the specific measures that private regimes have adopted to cultivate legitimacy, including **transparency** and **participation** procedures to ensure that they are held accountable to those that they regulate, and to the public at large.

Despite these potential problems, private regimes are growing rapidly. Their growth raises questions about competition: what happens when multiple regimes compete to regulate the same issue (see **Institutional interactions**)? Since private regimes are voluntary, actors can choose not to join or to join those regimes with weak rules. Thus, a big question in research on private regimes is whether competition among standards can produce a "ratcheting up" effect, so that weak regimes are either driven out of business or are forced to strengthen their rules, or a "race to the bottom," where private regimes weaken their rules to compete for adherents. Thus far, the findings on the question of the **policy diffusion** of private regimes are mixed.

References

Andonova, Liliana. 2017. *Governance Entrepreneurs: International Organizations and the Rise of Global Public-Private Partnerships*. Cambridge, Cambridge University Press.

Bartley, Tim. 2007. "Institutional Emergence in an Era of Globalization: The Rise of Transnational Private Regulation of Labor and Environmental Conditions." *American Journal of Sociology* 113(2): 297–351.

Bernstein, Steven and Benjamin Cashore. 2007. "Can Non-State Global Governance be Legitimate? An Analytical Framework." *Regulation and Governance* 1(4): 347–371.

Cashore, Benjamin William, Graeme Auld, and Deanna Newsom. 2004. *Governing through Markets: Forest Certification and the Emergence of Non-State Authority.* New Haven, CT, Yale University Press.

Dauvergne, Peter, and Jane Lister. 2013. *Eco-Business: A Big-Brand Takeover of Sustainability.* Cambridge, MA, MIT Press.

Green, Jessica F. 2014. *Rethinking Private Authority: Agents and Entrepreneurs in Global Environmental Governance.* Princeton, NJ, Princeton University Press.

Overdevest, Christine and Jonathan Zeitlin. 2014. "Assembling an Experimentalist Regime: Transnational Governance Interactions in the Forest Sector." *Regulation & Governance* 8(1): 22–48.

Prakash, Aseem and Matthew Potoski. 2006. *The Voluntary Environmentalists: Green Clubs, ISO 14001, and Voluntary Environmental Regulations.* Cambridge, Cambridge University Press.

REDD+

Heike Schroeder

University of East Anglia, United Kingdom
Institute for Advanced Sustainability Studies, Germany

With their dwindling forest cover, the problem of massive deforestation in tropical forest countries has come center stage in addressing climate change, accounting for 13–17% of annual global greenhouse gas emissions (van der Werf et al. 2009). After the newly formed Coalition for Rainforest Nations (CfRN) lobbied for addressing deforestation in the post-Kyoto negotiations under the **climate change regime** and Stern (2007) famously framed reforestation as a cheap mitigation option, avoiding deforestation was adopted as international climate change policy in the Bali Action Plan in 2007.

The Bali Action Plan launched the designing of a mechanism to compensate tropical forest countries for keeping forests standing and thereby to reduce emissions from deforestation and forest degradation (REDD) as part of the ongoing post-2012 climate change negotiations. The 2009 Copenhagen Accord committed to funding activities toward REDD as well as conservation, sustainable management of forests, and enhancement of forest carbon stocks (REDD+). The 2010 Cancun Agreements include provisional language on social and environmental safeguards and provide guidance on REDD+ readiness activities. During 2011 and 2012, much attention was focused on finance and developing guidelines for measuring, **reporting**, and verifying reductions in deforestation (Lyster et al. 2013).

Meanwhile, funds have been flowing to tropical forest countries to develop capacity on the ground, experiment with various schemes, and gain a head start in finding ways to reduce emissions while providing benefits to forest-dependent people. UN-REDD supports countries in developing and implementing national REDD+ strategies and the **World Bank** Forest Carbon Partnership Facility (FCPF) funds partner countries to get ready for REDD+. In addition, several bilateral, transnational, and nongovernmental schemes and pilot projects are being carried out (Angelsen et al. 2018). The 2015 Paris Agreement sends a strong signal in favor of REDD+ in dedicating one whole article (Article 5) to the role of forests in addressing climate change (Korhonen-Kurki et al. 2019).

It has been widely acknowledged that governance issues are the central challenge for REDD+ (Corbera and Schroeder 2011). REDD+ will not be effective in avoiding deforestation without causing social and environmental harm unless a number of crucial governance challenges at levels of international design, global consumption, and in-country implementation are sufficiently addressed (see **Scale**). These include the problem of leakage, i.e. forest saved in one location may lead to deforestation elsewhere if the global and/or domestic drivers of deforestation are not addressed at the same time; permanence, i.e. how to engage with recipient country stakeholders on donor countries' demands for long-term contracts over avoiding deforestation; and additionality, i.e. how to calculate sufficiently precisely the degree of difference to the business-as-usual trajectory of deforestation that the international payment has enabled.

References

Angelsen, Arild, Erlend A.T. Hermansen, Raoni Rajão, and Richard van der Hoff. 2018. "Results-based Payment: Who Should be Paid, and for What?" In *Transforming REDD+: Lessons and New Directions*, Eds. Arild Angelsen, Christopher Martius, Veronique De Sy V, Amy E. Duchelle, Anne M. Larson, and Pham Thu Thuy, 41–54. Bogor, CIFOR.

Corbera, Esteve and Heike Schroeder. 2011. "Governing and Implementing REDD+." *Environmental Science and Policy* 14(2): 89–99.

Korhonen-Kurki, Kaisa, Maria Brockhaus, Jenniver Sehring, Monica Di Gregorio, Samuel Assembe-Mvondo, Andrea Babon, Melaku Bekele, Vanessa Benn, Maria Fernanda Gebara, Harmann W. Kambire, Felicien Kengoum,

Cynthia Maharani, Mary Menton, Moira Moeliono, Robert Ochieng, Naya Sharma Paudel, Pham Thu Thuy, Guy Patrice Dkamela, and Almeida Sitoe. 2019. "What Drives Policy Change for REDD+? A Qualitative Comparative Analysis of the Interplay between Institutional and Policy Arena Factors." *Climate Policy* 19(3): 315–328.

Lyster, Rosemary, Catherine MacKenzie, and Constance McDermott. 2013. *Law, Tropical Forests and Carbon: The Case of REDD*. Cambridge, Cambridge University Press.

Stern, Nicholas. 2007. *The Economics of Climate Change*. Cambridge, Cambridge University Press.

Van der Werf, Guido, Douglas C. Morton, Ruth S. DeFries, Jos G.J. Olivier, Prasad S. Kasibhatla, Robert B. Jackson, Jim Collatz, and James T. Randerson. 2009. "CO_2 Emissions from Forest Loss." *Nature Geoscience* 2: 737–738.

REGIMES

Amandine Orsini
Université Saint-Louis – Bruxelles, Belgium

Jean-Frédéric Morin
Université Laval, Canada

The concept of international regimes is not specific to, but frequently used in, the study of global environmental governance. Building on the definition by Stephen Krasner, specialists have defined environmental regimes as institutions that give rise to social practices, assign roles, and govern interactions to address situations of ecosystem degradation through overuse (for instance **fisheries governance**) or through pollution (for instance the **climate change regime**) (Young et al. 2008). Regimes occupy an intermediary position: they are shaped by structures in place, including power distribution or prevailing ideas, but they also guide and constrain the behavior of actors.

International regimes are not necessarily centered on a formal treaty or an intergovernmental organization. For example, no universal intergovernmental organization and no multilateral treaty is dedicated to fresh water, but there is arguably a **transboundary water regime** made of a set of implicit rules that lay out actors' expectations. However, most regimes are formalized by international treaties. In environmental governance, **treaty negotiations** tend to evolve in a path dependency

211

manner: from political declarations to framework conventions, to protocols, follow-up annexes, and decisions.

Research on environmental regimes started in the 1980s. Initially, scholars focused on the reasons and the conditions leading to the establishment of such regimes. They found that **science** and the agency of **epistemic communities** were instrumental in explaining the adoption of environmental regimes such as the acid rain regime, the **ozone regime**, or the Mediterranean Sea regime.

In the 1990s, while scholars in other fields abandoned the concept of international regimes to its detractors, researchers in environmental governance worked to adapt it in several manners (Vogler 2003). First, to answer the critics that viewed regime analysis as functionalist, environmental scholars demonstrated that "issue areas," as defining criteria of regimes, depended on social and cognitive constructions. Second, in reaction to the accusation of state centrism, experts of global environmental governance studied in detail the **participation** of non-state actors and the development of **private regimes**. Third, against the claim that regime theory was biased in favor of positive cases, environmental scholars developed extensive regime databases to identify recurring patterns (Breitmeier et al. 2006) and looked at **nonregimes** to refine scope conditions.

In the 2000s, environmental scholars developed conceptual and methodological tools to assess regime **effectiveness**. They show that regimes have various impacts, including on neighboring regimes. Regimes can collide, compete against each other, develop synergies, or even merge. Since the beginning of the 2010s, regime analysts have been investigating **institutional interactions** between different regimes known as "regime complexes." This concept announces a rebirth of regime analyses in global environmental governance (Orsini et al. 2013).

References

Breitmeier, Helmut, Arild Underdal, Oran R. Young, and Michael Zürn. 2006. *Analyzing International Environmental Regimes: From Case Study to Database.* Cambridge, MA, MIT Press.

Orsini, Amandine, Jean-Frédéric Morin, and Oran Young. 2013. "Regime Complexes: A Buzz, a Boom, or a Boost for Global Governance." *Global Governance* 19: 27–39.

Vogler, John. 2003. "Taking Institutions Seriously: How Regime Analysis can be Relevant to Multilevel Environmental Governance." *Global Environmental Politics* 3(2): 25–39.

Young, Oran, Leslie L. King, and Heike Schroeder. 2008. *Institutions and Environmental Change: Principal Findings, Applications, and Research Frontiers.* Cambridge, MA, MIT Press.

REGIONAL GOVERNANCE

Tom Delreux

University of Louvain, Belgium

In the environmental sphere, "governance" refers to "structures of authority that manage collective environmental problems and resolve conflicts between stakeholders" (Elliott and Breslin 2011: 3). Such structures are developed not only at the global, state, or sub-state **scales**, but also at the regional level, where they are called "regional governance." Although there is no commonly accepted definition of "region," political scientists agree that a region implies a limited number of states within geographical proximity and exposed to a certain degree of interdependence.

It is generally acknowledged that regional governance constitutes an important component of the international environmental politics architecture. When the national or the global level do not provide the appropriate scale for tackling a particular environmental problem, the regional level may emerge as an in-between solution to effectively deal with these challenges. Indeed, regional governance initiatives can contribute to solving common action problems where national or intrastate action is not sufficient, mostly due to the transboundary nature of the environmental problem at stake. Furthermore, they often emerge when the global level fails or when global environmental governance is deadlocked. The **compliance and implementation** problems faced by several multilateral environmental agreements, the lowest common denominator outcomes of global negotiations, the fuzziness of the distribution of work between various **regimes**, or the fatigue in environmental **summit diplomacy** all raise questions about the continued feasibility of negotiating agreements at the global level and open the door for an increased belief in regional initiatives (Conca 2012). Environmental issues such as fresh water, nature, pollution, and habitats are more frequently dealt with in regional arrangements than in global ones (Balsiger and Prys 2016).

Besides regional governance initiatives that establish **transgovernmental networks** and structures of authority between public and private actors such as **partnerships**, most regional environmental governance arrangements are concluded between adjacent states. The two main instruments of regional environmental governance are regional agreements and regional organizations.

Regional environmental agreements are treaties between states on environmental issues, mostly touching upon ecologically defined geographical areas such as river basins, mountain ranges, or regional seas, yet also dealing with transboundary problems such as air pollution (Haas 2016). Several hundreds of regional environmental agreements have been concluded since the Second World War, and their number is still growing substantially (Balsiger and VanDeveer 2012; Balsiger and Prys 2016) (see also **Arctic Council** or **Antarctic Treaty System**). Although single-issue environmental agreements are still the norm, many regional economic integration organizations have adopted environmental agreements. In North America, for instance, environmental concerns are addressed not only in the North American Free Trade Agreement (NAFTA) itself, but also in a separate side-treaty to NAFTA, the North American Agreement on Environmental Cooperation (NAAEC).

Regional environmental organizations are international governmental organizations, which include states from a single region among their membership and which are created through an international agreement. Regional environmental organizations can be found around the globe and they take many different forms. Some regional environmental organizations were especially created to deal with environmental issues, such as the International Commission for the Protection of the Danube River (ICPDR) (operative since 1998), whereas others initially were focused on economic or security integration but gradually began to develop activities in the environmental domain, such as the European Union (EU) or the Association of Southeast Asian Nations (ASEAN).

Regional organizations can be a forum for environmental policy and an actor in global environmental politics. First, organizations such as the EU or to a lesser extent also ASEAN have harmonized environmental policies or practices of their member states. Whereas environmental cooperation in a regional organization such as ASEAN is characterized by non-binding agreements, non-interference in domestic politics of its member states, and project-based cooperation (Elliott 2012), the EU has adopted a broad range of legally binding environmental policies with a deep impact on the policy autonomy of its member states. Having adopted hundreds of pieces of environmental legislation, it has the strongest and most comprehensive regional environmental regulatory framework in the world, covering almost all environmental issues, including chemicals, biodiversity, waste, noise, and climate change (Delreux and Happaerts 2016). Whereas EU environmental policy has for a long time been characterized by a top-down regulatory approach, yet also with implementation problems in the member states, an evolution toward more freedom for the member states and toward softer instruments of environmental governance can be gradually observed.

Second, regional organizations can be important actors in global environmental negotiations. The EU is again the most illustrative example here. Since the 1990s, the EU has been a major force in promoting strong environmental protection at the international level and has ratified more than sixty multilateral environmental agreements. The EU has attempted to play a leadership role in many **regimes** and **treaty negotiations**. Although the EU's leadership ambitions are certainly not limited to this area, it has been most visible and most widely discussed in the literature with regard to negotiations under the **climate change regime** (Wurzel et al. 2016). EU leadership was badly damaged at the 2009 Copenhagen climate change conference, although the EU seems to have found a new bridge-building and coalition-making role in the following conferences. Scholars currently debate to what extent the EU is still able to lead in international environmental politics and what the scope conditions are under which a regional organization such as the EU is able to exert actorness and to be influential in global negotiations.

References

Balsiger, Jorg and Miriam Prys. 2016. "Regional Agreements in International Environmental Politics." *International Environmental Agreements* 16(2): 239–260.

Balsiger, Jörg and Stacy D. VanDeveer. 2012. "Navigating Regional Environmental Governance." *Global Environmental Politics* 12(3): 1–17.

Conca, Ken. 2012. "The Rise of the Region in Global Environmental Politics." *Global Environmental Politics* 12(3): 127–133.

Delreux, Tom and Sander Happaerts. 2016. *Environmental Policy and Politics in the European Union*. London, Palgrave Macmillan.

Elliott, Lorraine. 2012. "ASEAN and Environmental Governance: Strategies of Regionalism in Southeast Asia." *Global Environmental Politics* 12(3): 38–57.

Elliott, Lorraine and Shaun Breslin. 2011. Comparative Environmental Regionalism. Abingdon, Routledge.

Haas, Peter. 2016. "Regional Environmental Governance." In *The Oxford Handbook of Comparative Regionalism*, Eds. Tanja Börzel and Thomas Risse, 430–456. Oxford, Oxford University Press.

Wurzel, Rüdiger, James Connelly, and Duncan Liefferink (Eds.). 2016. *The European Union in International Climate Change Politics. Still Taking a Lead?* Abingdon, Routledge.

REPORTING

Klaus Dingwerth

University of St. Gallen, Switzerland

Cornis van der Lugt

University of Stellenbosch, South Africa

As environmental policymaking has matured since the 1980s, information-based policy instruments have become increasingly prominent. As one such instrument, reporting involves the disclosure of information about environmental performance in a specified format and covering an agreed time period. Such information is seen to be valuable for the reporting organizations themselves—it allows them to identify strengths and weaknesses in their performance—as well as for a variety of stakeholders who can sanction poor and reward good performance. By addressing information asymmetry, reporting holds the promise to promote both performance and accountability and to help informed markets and economies to function better.

Environmental reporting is used in both intergovernmental and transnational environmental governance. At the intergovernmental level, reporting is closely tied to monitoring and verification of environmental performance, either in relation to treaties or to overarching goals like the UN **Sustainable Development Goals** (SDGs). Reporting adds a degree of reflexivity that can inform the regular review and further development of treaty systems (Raustiala 2001).

Treaty provisions require member states to report on their **compliance and implementation** of goals set in environmental agreements. Such multilaterally negotiated **transparency** includes requirements for reporting data on the release, use, or trade of substances listed in treaty annexes as well as on domestic measures put into place to implement an international agreement. Most treaty systems require contracting parties to report to the treaty **secretariat** annually using prescribed reporting templates. Data quality varies greatly, across states and treaty systems, as does the degree to which national reports are independently verified (Wettestad 2007).

While self-reporting is often challenged as unreliable, national reporting can nonetheless help to provide a focal point for discussing a state's performance for policy learning across states. It can also help to legitimate internationally agreed environmental policy goals in policy circles and the bureaucratic apparatus at home (Bodansky 2010: 238–240). In climate governance, the 2015 Paris Agreement puts reporting, monitoring, and verification center stage as it requires state parties to regularly update and raise their own emissions targets in light of what others have contributed.

Like their intergovernmental peers, transnational reporting schemes do not set explicit environmental performance targets (see **Private regimes**). Rather, they set standards of organizational performance management that are intended to be used by business and other types of organizations (see **Business and corporations**). This is often linked to **corporate social responsibility** efforts. Examples are the Global Reporting Initiative (GRI), International Integrated Reporting Council (IIRC), Carbon Disclosure Project (CDP), and Taskforce on Climate-related Financial Disclosures (TCFD) of the Financial Stability Board (FSB). Founded in 1997 by the Coalition for Environmentally Responsible Economies and the **United Nations Environment Programme**, the multi-stakeholder GRI issues sustainability reporting standards such as environmental performance indicators. Founded in 2010 by the GRI and other partners including the accounting profession, the IIRC issues a framework for "integrated reporting," a new type of reporting that takes elements of annual financial and sustainability reporting to present a synthesis document (Rinaldi et al. 2018). The IIRC does not recommend indicators, but requires reporting on the use of diverse resources, including natural capital. Financial stakeholders are primary target audiences in initiatives such as the CDP and TCFD. Under the CDP, institutional investors demand information on emissions, energy, and related environmental issues from investee corporations (Hahn et al. 2015). Making the link between financial stability and climate change as systemic phenomena, the TCFD represents an effort by central banks to require financial institutions and heavy industries to report on the climate risks they face (Eccles and Krzus 2018).

Over the last two decades a growing number of governments and **market** regulatory authorities have introduced mandatory requirements for disclosure of information on certain environmental topics and broader non-financial reporting by notably large and listed corporations. Initiatives have also been started to link guidance from transnational reporting standards with indicators and targets related to the SDGs. Today most large multinational corporations do sustainability reporting based on the GRI guidelines, and use of the IIRC framework is growing.

As independent verification is voluntary, researchers and report users point to shortcomings in the quality, reliability, and comparability of disclosed data (Ciplet et al. 2018). Market-based approaches have also led to a critique that the private standards involved reflect regulatory capture and that the reported information is focused on investors at the cost of other stakeholders (Dingwerth and Eichinger 2014; Flower 2015).

Setting the parameters for "regulation by revelation" (Durant 2017), governments find themselves in a managerial position of having to collaborate with multiple actors on a complex agenda. However, the transformative potential of reporting remains more limited than is often portrayed. Critical studies on transnational schemes for information disclosures thus conclude either that such schemes need to improve to prevent market failure or that they display merely symbolic action to appease stakeholders (Ciplet et al. 2018; Kramarz and Park 2019). Amid complexity, the digital age offers new opportunities for smart regulation in which reporting as information-instrument will figure prominently.

References

Bodansky, Daniel. 2010. *The Art and Craft of International Environmental Law.* Cambridge, MA, Harvard University Press.

Ciplet, David, Kevin M. Adams, Romain Weikmans, and J. Timmons Roberts. 2018. "The Transformative Capability of Transparency in Global Environmental Governance." *Global Environmental Politics* 18(3): 130–150.

Dingwerth, Klaus and Margot Eichinger. 2014. "Tamed Transparency and the Global Reporting Initiative: The Role of Information Infrastructures." In *Transparency in Global Environmental Governance*, Eds. Aarti Gupta and Michael Mason, 225–247. Cambridge, MA, MIT Press.

Durant, Robert. 2017. "Regulation-by-Revelation." In *Environmental Governance Reconsidered: Challenges, Choices, and Opportunities*, Eds. Robert F. Durant, Daniel J. Fiorino, and Rosemary O'Leary, 337–367. Cambridge, MA, MIT Press.

Eccles, Robert G and Michael P. Krzus. 2018. "Why Companies Should Report Financial Risks from Climate Change." *MIT Sloan Management Review* 59(3): 1–6.

Flower, John. 2015. "The International Integrated Reporting Council: A Story of Failure." *Critical Perspectives on Accounting* 27: 1–17.

Hahn, Ruediger, Daniel Reimsbach, and Frank Schiemann. 2015. "Organisations, Climate Change, and Transparency: Reviewing the Literature on Carbon Disclosure." *Organisation and Environment* 28(1): 80–102.

Kramarz, Teresa and Susan Park (Eds.). 2019. *Global Environmental Governance and the Accountability Trap*. Cambridge, MA, The MIT Press.

Raustiala, Kal. 2001. *Reporting and Review Institutions in 10 Multilateral Environmental Agreements*. Nairobi, UNEP.

Rinaldi, Leonardo, Jeffrey Unerman and Charl de Villiers. 2018. "Evaluating the Integrated Reporting Journey: Insights, Gaps and Agendas for Future Research." *Accounting, Auditing & Accountability Journal* 31(5): 1294–1318.

Wettestad, Jørgen. 2007. "Monitoring and Verification." In *Oxford Handbook of International Environmental Law*, Eds. Daniel Bodansky, Jutta Brunnée, and Ellen Hey, 974–994. Oxford. Oxford University Press.

RISK SOCIETY[1]

Ulrich Beck

Ludwig Maximilian University Munich, Germany

Environmental **disasters** such as Chernobyl, 9/11, global financial crises, and climate change are manufactured uncertainties and incalculable global risks resulting from the triumphs of modernity and mark the human condition at the beginning of the twenty-first century. Speaking very generally, the theorem of "(world) risk society" (Beck 1986, 2009) is conceived of as a radicalized form of the dynamic of modernization that is dissolving the familiar formulae of "first" modernity. The first—the "classical" or "high"—modernity associated specifically with industrial society was characterized by a logic of organization and action that involved the establishment of extremely fine divisions between categories of people and of activities and the distinctions between spheres of action and forms of life such as to facilitate an unambiguous institutional ascription of competence, responsibility, and jurisdiction. Today, the limitations of this logic of fine division and unambiguousness are becoming ever more evident. The *logic of unambiguousness*—one might speak here, metaphorically, of a "Newtonian" social and political theory of the first modernity—is now being replaced by a *logic of ambiguity*—which one might envisage, to extend the metaphor, in terms of a new "Heisenbergian fuzziness" of the social and the political.

For the institutions of advanced societies, the transition to a "second" modernity entails the challenge of developing a new logic of action and decision-making, which finds its orientation no longer in the principle "either this or that" but rather in the principle "this and that both." In various spheres—from **science** and technology through the state and the economy, individualized life-worlds, and social structures right up to the level of the present debates and confrontations regarding the new ordering of global politics—one thing is becoming ever clearer: that great body of distinctions, standardizations, norms, and role-systems essential to the very institutions of the first modernity can no longer be treated as valid; they describe ever less adequately the current normal condition of societies, of nation-states, and of interstate relations. The reality we face today is rather that of a (more or less) acknowledged plurality in respect of forms of work, of family life, of lifestyle, of political **sovereignty**, and of politics in general. We live—to recur to a metaphor already current in the social sciences—in the "era of flows": of capital flow, of cultural flow, of flows of human beings, information, and risks.

The collapse of boundaries and the new mobility of risks (Arnoldi 2009; Rosa et al. 2014) have fundamental implications for the social sciences inasmuch as it helps us to the insight that sociology (as well as historiography, political science, economics, jurisprudence, etc.) remains bogged down in a "methodological nationalism." Methodological nationalism rests on the assumption that "modern society" and "modern politics" are synonymous with a society and a politics organized in terms of nation-states. The state is understood as creator, supervisor, and guarantor of society. Societies (the number of which is equal to the number of nation-states) are understood as mere containers, arising and subsisting in a space defined by the power of the state.

Note

1. This contribution is a reproduction of the original one published in the 2015 edition of this book. The editors simply updated the citations.

References

Arnoldi, Jakob. 2009. *Risk: An Introduction*. Cambridge, Polity Press.
Beck, Ulrich. 1992 [1986]. *Risk Society: Towards a New Modernity*. London, Sage.

Beck, Ulrich. 2009. *World at Risk*. Cambridge, Polity Press.

Beck, Ulrich. 2015. "Emancipatory Catastrophism: What Does it Mean to Climate Change and Risk Society?" *Current Sociology* 63(1): 75–88.

Rosa, Eugene A., Ortwin Renn, and Aaron M. McCright. 2014. *The Risk Society Revisited: Social Theory and Governance*. Philadelphia, PA, Temple University Press.

ROTTERDAM CONVENTION ON THE PRIOR INFORMED CONSENT PROCEDURE IN TRADE

Peter Hough

Middlesex University London, United Kingdom

The 1998 Rotterdam Convention on the Prior Informed Consent Procedure for Certain Hazardous Chemicals and Pesticides in International Trade, which came into force in 2004, commits exporters of chemicals restricted in their own countries to notify importers of this through a prior informed consent procedure (PIC). As of 2019 there were 161 parties to the Convention, including all major chemical exporters bar the US. Under PIC exporters are obliged to provide Decision Guidance Documents detailing the environmental and health grounds for the domestic restriction of chemicals such as dichloro-diphenyl-trichloroethane (DDT) and parathion. The Convention created a legally binding character to Article 9 of the voluntary Food and Agriculture Organization's (FAO) 1986 International Code of Conduct on the Distribution and Use of Pesticides, inspired by the 1984 Bhopal chemical plant **disaster** in India. Thousands of people died as a consequence of the disaster, resulting from the leak of the chemical methyl isocyanate, a substance completely unknown to the Indian Government hosting the plant owned by the US multinational corporation Union Carbide. The establishment of PIC as a binding international rule was sealed by eventually gaining the support of the chemical industry in the early 1990s, after initial opposition, after a civil society campaign led by the Pesticide Action Network (PAN), an alliance of **nongovernmental organizations**. The reason for this U-turn by the industry was a fear of the alternatives, such as an outright prohibition of the export of certain pesticides, as debated in a bill in the US Congress during 1991–1992 (Hough 1998).

The Rotterdam Convention features a Chemical Review Committee, which considers proposals from Parties or NGOs for including new chemicals to the automatically triggered PIC list (Annex III). By 2019, this contained fifty-three chemical formulations. Inclusion on the list requires the unanimous agreement of the Parties. Progress in adding chemicals to Annex III has been slow as **business and corporations** have often persuaded national delegations to block this. Most notoriously the listing of chrysotile (white) asbestos, a known carcinogen responsible for over 100,000 deaths a year worldwide, has been resisted by delegations of major exporters such as India and Russia. Governance hence has inched forward, in line with Rotterdam's "sister" regimes, the **persistent organic pollutants** (POPs) regime and the **hazardous wastes regime**, whose secretariats and Conferences of the Parties were merged in 2013. However, the sheer existence of these regimes has created a discourse on global chemical safety and helped expose displays of blatant vested interest. In particular, the public naming of chemicals subject to national bans has tended to serve as something of a de facto international ban by influencing the evolution of domestic systems in Global South countries (Jansen and Dubois 2014).

References

Hough, Peter. 1998. *The Global Politics of Pesticides: Forging Consensus from Conflicting Interests*. London, Earthscan.

Jansen, Kees and Milou Dubois. 2014. "Global Pesticide Governance by Disclosure: Prior Informed Consent and the Rotterdam Convention." In *Transparency in Global Environmental Governance: Critical Perspectives*, Eds. Aarti Gupta and Michael Mason, 107–131. Cambridge, MA, MIT.

SCALE

Kate O'Neill

University of California at Berkeley, United States

Scale in global environmental governance (GEG) is defined in different ways. The concept applies to different levels at and across which governance can occur. These are often jurisdictional: local, national, regional, and global. It is also used in the sense of scaling out, capturing how phenomena and events broaden out to or manifest at scales from micro (individuals, see **Influential individuals**, or communities) to macro levels (regional, see **Regional governance**, or global). Researchers who study scale often examine vertical linkages between and across scales, and movement of ideas, policies, and actors between scales (as opposed to horizontal linkages such as **institutional interactions**). Some also examine the social construction of scales (Marston 2000). It has become an important concept in GEG because of the emergence of institutions that operate at different scales and because of the growing interest in the role of local and regional knowledge, politics, and communities in the instigation, **compliance and implementation** of GEG (Andonova and Mitchell 2010).

Several examples demonstrate how scale and vertical linkages matter in contemporary GEG. For example, the role of city governments in climate governance is one area where local actors are, through **transgovernmental networks**, reaching the global scale (Betsill and Bulkeley 2006; Vaz and Reis 2017). Conversely, regional centers that implement terms of the chemicals agreements at local levels are another way in which vertical linkages are made across jurisdictional levels (Selin 2010). Global flows of goods, resources, and risks are shaped and governed by actors and institutions across scales. Changing global market conditions have rapid knock-on effects right down to the level of local communities. To give an example, China's decision in 2018 to halt plastic scrap imports re-shaped recycling regulations in **cities** and neighborhoods across the US, in other words, what households put out on the curbs each week (O'Neill 2019). Cases of the incorporation of **indigenous peoples**' knowledge into **regimes** such as the **biodiversity regime** highlight how ideas and knowledge flow upwards to the global level as well as down (Jasanoff and Martello 2004).

Although it is often a hard concept to pin down and operationalize, the development and use of scale has pushed researchers to engage more effectively with a new generation of GEG initiatives. Scale and vertical linkages are important in understanding various dimensions of some of the more complex environmental issues we face, including climate change, biodiversity, and deforestation, their governance, and their socioeconomic impacts (see **Climate change regime** and **REDD+**). They shed light on dynamics of transnational activism and policymaking, and on practical questions of how global governance institutions can connect to local communities and actors.

References

Andonova, Liliana B. and Ronald B. Mitchell. 2010. "The Rescaling of Global Environmental Politics." *Annual Review of Environment and Resources* 35(1): 255–282.

Betsill, Michele M. and Harriet Bulkeley. 2006. "Cities and the Multilevel Governance of Global Climate Change." *Global Governance* 12(2): 141–159.

Jasanoff, Sheila and Marybeth Long Martello (Eds.). 2004. *Earthly Politics: Local and Global in Environmental Governance*. Cambridge, MA, MIT Press.

Marston, Sallie A. 2000. "The Social Construction of Scale." *Progress in Human Geography* 24(2): 219–242.

O'Neill, Kate. 2019. *Waste*. London, Polity Press.

Selin, Henrik. 2010. *Global Governance of Hazardous Chemicals: Challenges of Multilevel Management*. Cambridge, MA, MIT Press.

Vaz, Domingos Martins and Liliana Reis. 2017. "From City-States to Global Cities: The Role of Cities in Global Governance." *JANUS.NET e-journal of International Relations* 8(2): 13–28.

SCARCITY AND CONFLICTS

Alexis Carles

Université libre de Bruxelles, Belgium

The assumption that environmental scarcity leads to interstate conflicts has become prevalent, notwithstanding numerous contributions putting into question this inference. Despite specific case studies' analyses and concrete theoretical inputs, the debate on whether or not environmental scarcity is a triggering factor of conflicts still divides the academic world.

Historical contributions suggest this causal relation dates back to the works of Malthus under the **carrying capacities paradigm**, who predicted that at some point in time the world's population would exceed the food supply, leading to conflicts over resource allocation. Garrett Hardin's theorization of the **tragedy of the commons** in the 1960s also predicted environmental conflicts in the case of overexploitation of common environmental resources. The modern debate started during the last years of the Cold War, along with the redefinition of the traditional concept of security to include environmental **security**.

Thomas Homer-Dixon (1994, 1999) is one of the pioneering authors linking environmental scarcity to conflicts. Informed by realist approaches shaped by neo-Malthusian geopolitical thoughts, he argues that the consequent social changes due to environmental scarcity trigger or exacerbate tensions between parties sharing the same resource. According to him, environmental scarcity embeds three dimensions: resource degradation and depletion (supply scarcity); higher socioeconomic and demographic needs (demand scarcity); and unequal distribution (structural scarcity). These lead to both a decline in economic productivity and an increase in the number of **migrants**, which eventually generate ethnic, socioeconomic, or political conflicts. For example, Homer-Dixon showed that land scarcity combined with flooding gave rise to massive migrations of Bengalis to India in the 1980s, which critically altered inter-ethnic relations, land distribution arrangements, and power relations in the border regions.

The main criticism of neo-Malthusian assumptions is their overly deterministic character. Some advocates of this perspective overlook other social and economic variables driving environmental resources' management, such as **market** mechanisms and technological innovation (Haas 2002). First, the neglect of market mechanisms implies that neo-Malthusians do not take into account the variations of prices and thus the potential for social **adaptation** to scarcity. The recent boom of sustainable energies is as much the consequence of price signals from markets of traditional energy sources, as of the growing awareness of environmental issues worldwide (see also **Energy transition**). Second, humans have historically proven to be innovative in the face of scarcity, either by developing new technologies, or by using other resources to substitute for traditional ones. For instance, the development of drip irrigation—watering agricultural products through a drop-by-drop system—saves tremendous amounts of water. Likewise, the progressive replacement of copper wires (land lines) by fiber optics and satellite technologies shows that a resource given as disappearing at some point in time (such as copper in the mid-1970s) can subsist thanks to substitution through innovation.

"Cornucopians," or "resource optimists," view scarcity as an opportunity for states to cooperate. Their theoretical assumptions are close to liberal and neoliberal institutionalist authors. If they acknowledge that there is an inherent risk in resource scarcity, they argue that humans will rather cooperate, notably through creation of institutions for resource allocation (Simon 1998). Recent theoretical and empirical findings on the role of regional and international institutions as catalysts of cooperation offer a window of opportunity to minimize the influence of environmental scarcity as a component of international conflicts. Scarcity should be grasped as an issue of common interest, a motivation for creating **regimes** on shared environmental resources in order to coordinate actors' arrangements toward rational win–win solutions. The Southern African Development Community (SADC), one of the most advanced regional integration processes after the European Union, was founded on cooperation over **transboundary water regimes**. Water is very unevenly distributed in the region, and the first SADC protocol was on shared watercourse systems. The SADC is now driven by twenty-six protocols on various issues (e.g. trade, mining, health). Following that stance, some argue that cooperation on resource scarcity is a catalyzing factor for deeper cooperation on other issues.

Most empirical contributions on the subject are qualitative case studies. They often refer to transboundary water issues, which are grasped as one of the riskiest resources, despite a clear empirical trend in favor of cooperation. A few studies revealed that water scarcity, under specific circumstances, could contribute to enhancing the probability of violent conflict occurring, thereby supporting Homer-Dixon's arguments (Hauge and Ellingsen 1998). It has been notably the case in India in 2019 where extreme water scarcity led to local violence and tensions with Pakistan.

Other studies argue that other political and socioeconomic factors are more significant explanatory independent variables for conflicts to occur. Theisen et al. (2012), for instance, showed that drought has minimal impact on civil conflicts in Africa, compared with political and economic marginalization of ethnic groups. Peter Haas's statement that "no one has been killed in direct international conflict over any resource" (Haas 2002: 7) still seems accurate.

Despite these different viewpoints, most academics agree that resource scarcity can sometimes contribute to catalyzing existing sociopolitical tensions. Lowi strongly doubted that there could be war over water in the Middle East but admitted that it could happen in extreme cases where the resource is in short supply, where adversarial parties are highly dependent on the same resource, and where geographical positions and power configurations limit their autonomy (Lowi 1999: 385). The growing impact and unpredictability of climate change adds an additional layer of uncertainty. Finally, for some scholars, environmental scarcity may actually be the consequence rather than the cause of conflicts (see **Military conflicts**).

References

Haas, Peter M. 2002. "Constructing Environmental Conflicts from Resource Scarcity." *Global Environmental Politics* 2(1): 1–11.

Hauge, Wenche and Tanja Ellingsen. 1998. "Beyond Environmental Scarcity: Causal Pathways to Conflict." *Journal of Peace Research* 35(3): 299–317.

Homer-Dixon, Thomas F. 1994. "Environmental Scarcities and Violent Conflict: Evidence from Cases." *International Security* 19(1): 5–40.

Homer-Dixon, Thomas F. 1999. *Environment, Scarcity, and Violence*. Princeton, NJ, Princeton University Press.

Lowi, Miriam R. 1999. "Water and Conflict in the Middle East and South Asia: Are Environmental Issues and Security Issues Linked?" *The Journal of Environment & Development* 8(4): 376–396.

Simon, Julian L. 1998. *The Ultimate Resource II: Peoples, Materials and Environment*. Princeton, NJ, Princeton University Press.

Theisen, Ole M., Holtermann Helge, and Halvard Buhaug. 2012. "Climate Wars? Assessing the Claim that Drought Breeds Conflict." *International Security* 36(3): 79–106.

SCENARIOS

Stacy VanDeveer
University of Massachusetts, Boston, United States

Simone Pulver
University of California, Santa Barbara, United States

Scenarios are a set of techniques designed to think about how the world might be in the future and are often commissioned with the stated goal of aiding decision-makers (in the public, private, and civil society sectors) in envisioning, understanding, and planning for the future. Commonly defined as "plausible, challenging and relevant stories about how the future might unfold" (Raskin 2005: 36), scenarios generally combine quantitative biophysical and economic models and qualitative storylines of social and political shifts. The quantitative modeling elements ensure internal consistency and impose structural limitations, for example maximum possible rates of technology replacement, while the narrative storylines accommodate the possibility of rapid social transformation, for example the collapse of the Soviet Union or unexpected events such as disasters.

Scenario techniques were first developed and deployed in national **security** and business communities (Raskin 2005; see also **Business and corporations**), but over the past four decades they have become a ubiquitous part of environmental politics, policymaking, and social learning, from global to local governance **scales**. Prominent examples in the global environmental arena include the various emissions scenarios issued by the Intergovernmental Panel on Climate Change (IPCC) (see **Boundary organizations**), global resource and biodiversity scenarios (e.g. Sala et al. 2000), and global **energy transition** scenarios (e.g. Child et al. 2018). Decision-makers use scenarios in three ways (Van Notten et al. 2003). First, forecasting scenarios are used to envision multiple likely futures. For example, efforts to predict changes in global biodiversity over the next century seek to identify key drivers of biodiversity decline and opportunities to intervene through better policies (Pereira et al. 2010). Second, backcasting scenarios, such as the IPCC's special report on *Global Warming of 1.5°C* (IPCC 2018), identify possible pathways to a single chosen future. Third, scenarios can be used to assess the robustness of a decision across a range of likely and unlikely possible futures. In all three uses, scenario exercises achieve dual outcomes: a process of social and organizational learning based on dialogue across diverse perspectives; and a final product that summarizes the results of the scenario exercise. Scenario exercises tend to emphasize one or the other goal. For example, the primary goal of early IPCC scenarios was to create a set of emissions trajectories that could be "plugged into" a host of other climate change and energy-related modeling, scenarios, and assessment exercises. In the Millennium Ecosystem Assessment (MEA) (see **Assessments**), scenarios were used to bring together people from diverse disciplinary, sectoral, educational, and/or social backgrounds to "think through" identified issues and explore opportunities to learn via processes of scenarios construction and output production (O'Neill et al. 2008).

Despite the remarkable spread of scenarios in environmental governance (Pulver and VanDeveer 2009), including their continuing use by states, international organizations, and firms, scenario analysis remains a relatively unexamined methodology. Unlike purely quantitative modeling exercises, whose limitations have been explored (Craig et al. 2002), systematic analysis of the application of scenarios and their impact on policy outcomes remains in its early stages. Scholars and practitioners disagree on the usefulness of information generated through scenarios, on how to characterize and interpret uncertainty in scenario outcomes, and on how to best structure scenario processes (Anderson 2019; Jewel 2019). Current research focuses on formalizing expert input to developing storylines, on techniques to estimate likelihoods associated with scenario outcomes, on the political and social dynamics of scenarios as knowledge processes and objects, and on the actual use of scenarios in decision-making (Wright et al. 2013).

References

Anderson, Kevin. 2019. "Wrong Tool for the Job" *Nature* 573(7774): 348–348.

Child, Michael, Otto Koskinen, Lassi Linnanen, and Christian Breyer. 2018. "Sustainability Guardrails for Energy Scenarios of the Global Energy Transition." *Renewable and Sustainable Energy Reviews* 91: 321–334.

Craig, Paul P., Ashok Gadgil, and Jonathan G. Koomey. 2002. "What Can History Teach Us? A Retrospective Examination of Long-term Energy Forecasts for the United States." *Annual Review of Energy and the Environment* 27(1): 83–118.

IPCC. 2018. *Global Warming of 1.5°C*, Eds. Valérie Masson-Delmotte, Panmao Zhai, Hans-Otto Pörtner, Debra Roberts, Jim Skea, Priyadarshi R. Shukla, Anna Pirani, Wilfran Moufouma-Okia, Clotilde Péan, Roz Pidcock, Sarah Connors, J. B. Robbins Matthews, Yang Chen, Xiao Zhou, Melissa I. Gomis, Elisabeth Lonnoy, Tom Maycock, Melinda Tignor, and Tim Waterfield. Geneva, Switzerland, IPCC.

Jewell, Jessica. 2019. "Clarifying the Job of IAMs" *Nature* 573(7774): 349–349.

O'Neill, Brian, Simone Pulver, Stacy VanDeveer, and Yaakov Garb. 2008. "Where Next with Global Environmental Scenarios?" *Environmental Research Letters* 3(4): 045012.

Pereira, Henrique M., Paul W. Leadley, Vânia Proença, Rob Alkemade, Jörn P.W. Scharlemann, Juan F. Fernandez-Manjarrés, Miguel B. Araújo, Patricia Balvanera, Reinette Biggs, and William W.L. Cheung. 2010. "Scenarios for Global Biodiversity in the 21st Century." *Science* 330(6010): 1496–1501.

Pulver, Simone and Stacy D VanDeveer. 2009. " 'Thinking about Tomorrows': Scenarios, Global Environmental Politics, and Social Science Scholarship." *Global Environmental Politics* 9(2): 1–13.

Raskin, Paul. 2005. "Global Scenarios in Historical Perspective." In *Ecosystems and Human Well-Being: Scenarios – Findings of the Scenarios Working Group Millennium Ecosystem Assessment Series*, Eds. Stephen Carpenter, Prabhu Pingali, Elena Bennett, and Monica Zurek, 35–44. Washington, DC, Island Press.

Sala, Osvaldo E., F. Stuart Chapin, Juan J. Armesto, Eric Berlow, Janine Bloomfield, Rodolfo Dirzo, Elisabeth Huber-Sanwald, Laura F. Huenneke, Robert B. Jackson, and Ann Kinzig. 2000. "Global Biodiversity Scenarios for the Year 2100." *Science* 287(5459): 1770–1774.

van Notten, Philip, Jan Rotmans, Marjolein Van Asselt, and Dale Rothman. 2003. "An Updated Scenario Typology." *Futures* 35(5): 423–443.

Wright, George, George Cairns, and Ron Bradfield. 2013. "Scenario Methodology: New Developments in Theory and Practice." *Technological Forecasting and Social Change* 80(4): 561–565.

SCIENCE

Tim Forsyth

London School of Economics and Political Science, United Kingdom

Science in global environmental governance refers to underlying authoritative knowledge about environmental problems. The main political controversies for science, however, arise from the legitimacy and authority it has within political debates. For many environmental scholars, scientific debates have to be clearly demarcated from political debates in order to gain a politically neutral understanding of environmental change, and to provide a compelling basis for environmental policy (Pielke 2007). But many other analysts—including both supporters of environmental policy and those resistant to it—argue that science has either been misused by political interests, or cannot escape from political and social influences. Consequently, various analysts argue there is a need to make science more transparent and open to governance. This requirement also applies to the expert groups that produce or summarize research such as **epistemic communities** or certain **boundary organizations**.

One key theme of debate is scientific certainty. Many environmental analysts argue environmental policy needs to be based on scientific certainty about the existence of environmental problems and human influences on them. Sometimes, the standards for certainty are relaxed under the **precautionary principle** when causal links are not yet certain, but when there is consensus that potential risks are sufficiently worrying. On certain occasions, scientific statements of certainty have been challenged as motivated by political interests, and skeptics have invoked contrasting science. For example, the skeptic Global Warming Policy Foundation uses a chart of twenty-first-century global average temperatures to suggest that no overall temperature rise has taken place. On a parallel theme, the US has also challenged the European Union in the **World Trade Organization** to demonstrate that its restrictions on importing genetically modified crops should be based on "sound science" rather than the precautionary principle (see **Biosafety**).

These debates about scientific certainty rarely take place without some reference to the credibility and legitimacy of the science and scientific organizations speaking. During the "Climate-gate" scandal of 2009, climate change skeptics used emails hacked from the University of East Anglia Climate Research Centre to imply that scientists had deliberately manipulated data in order to maintain evidence for the proposed "hockey stick" chart of rising global temperatures (these claims were refuted). The aim of this strategy was to cast doubt on the ethics and politics of climate change scientists and the Intergovernmental Panel on Climate Change (IPCC). Yet, simultaneously, environmental political scientists have also argued that most information challenging climate science has been shaped by conservative think tanks, and have questioned the accuracy of their claims (Jacques et al. 2008).

Consequently, other scholars have argued that the debate about science in global environmental governance should look more holistically at how facts and normative values are connected. Scholars in science and technology studies (STS) for example, argue that scientific certainty should not just refer to statistical trends, but to the social and political forces that stabilize public debate about which statistics to gather, or the meaning given to observed trends. Accordingly, STS scholars analyze the social conditions that give rise to the generation of science, and to the perceived status of experts and organizations that legitimize science. This approach does not question the possibility of worrying environmental changes, or the need to regulate human activities, but it suggests that diverse societies will always disagree about the objectives and legitimacy of scientific measurement (Hulme 2009). STS therefore asks two important questions: what visions of social order are reproduced when scientific information is presented as universally accurate and applicable for all society? And, which normative perspectives or options for physical environmental management are excluded when science is presented as politically neutral and not open to public debate?

An important example is the use of national statistics of climate change emissions to indicate the political responsibility for undertaking climate change policy (see **Scenarios**). For example, the Indian think tank, the Centre for Science and Environment, famously argued that simply comparing national statistics of emissions overlooked per capita usage, the number of years that countries have been industrialized, and whether developed countries had already cut down forests in order to expand agricultural land (Agarwal and Narain 1991; Beck 2011).

Moreover, climate models that focus on atmospheric greenhouse gas concentrations overlook the role of social vulnerability and resilience on the ground that is related to levels of development or international assistance (Forsyth 2012). The implications here are that "global" representations of risk or crisis sometimes understate the diversity by which different societies or individuals respond to environmental change (see **Risk society**). Hence, using climate change models or frameworks such as the hockey stick to indicate risk universally might impose assumptions about social identity and behavior upon different societies in ways that do not address their experience of risk or undermine trust in **treaty negotiations** (Jasanoff and Martello 2004).

Analysts therefore debate how to govern hybrid scientific and policy-advocacy bodies and scientific assessments that engage across the boundaries between science and politics. STS scholars see "boundary work" as the means by which science is rendered non-political, and consequently no longer open to public debate. Earth-system scientists, however, see boundary work as the ways scientists can interact with policymakers without appearing biased. The IPCC, for example, has been urged to make data more transparent, and to establish clearer procedures for considering information from non-peer-reviewed sources (InterAcademy Council 2010).

Another theme is the social **participation** within **assessments**, where the objective is to diversify social perspectives on complex environmental problems in order to increase the relevance of policies for different stakeholders (this has been discussed, for example, in the Intergovernmental Science-Policy Platform on Biodiversity and Ecosystem Services (IPBES) and under the **biodiversity regime**).

References

Agarwal, Anil and Sunita Narain. 1991. *Global Warming in an Unequal World*. Delhi, Center for Science and Environment.

Beck, Silke. 2011. "Moving beyond the Linear Model of Expertise? IPCC and the Test of Adaptation." *Regional Environmental Change* 11(2): 297–306.

Forsyth, Tim. 2012. "Politicizing Environmental Science Does Not Mean Denying Climate Science Nor Endorsing it Without Question." *Global Environmental Politics* 12(2): 18–23.

Hulme, Michael. 2009. *Why We Disagree about Climate Change: Understanding Controversy, Inaction and Opportunity*. Cambridge, Cambridge University Press.

InterAcademy Council. 2010. *Climate Change Assessments: Review of the Processes and Procedures of the IPCC*. Committee to Review the Intergovernmental Panel on Climate Change. Amsterdam, InterAcademy Council.

Jacques, Peter, Riley E. Dunlap, and Mark Freeman. 2008. "The Organization of Denial: Conservative Think Tanks and Environmental Scepticism." *Environmental Politics* 17: 349–385.

Jasanoff, Sheila and Marybeth Martello. 2004. *Earthly Politics: Local and Global in Environmental Governance*. Cambridge, MA, MIT Press.

Pielke, Roger A. 2007. *The Honest Broker: Making Sense of Science in Policy and Politics*. Cambridge, Cambridge University Press.

SECRETARIATS

Bernd Siebenhüner

Carl von Ossietzky University of Oldenburg, Germany

Almost all international environmental treaties foresee a secretariat to fulfill fundamental administrative and some executive functions in implementing the agreement (see **Compliance and implementation**). They are mandated to organize meetings and conferences, prepare documentation and monitoring, and implement practical projects and campaigns. In the field of global environmental governance, secretariats play a particularly prevalent role given the absence of a strong **World Environment Organization**. However, there is substantial variation with regard to the scope of their actual activities and related influence in international environmental governance. While some like the Secretariat of the Agreement on the Conservation of the Populations of European Bats have only a few staff members, others employ hundreds of international civil servants, such as the secretariat of the **climate change regime**.

Following Biermann and Siebenhüner (2009: 6), convention secretariats take the form of international bureaucracies that can be defined as:

> Agencies that have been set up by governments or other public actors with some degree of permanence and coherence and beyond formal direct control of single national governments (notwithstanding control by multilateral mechanisms through the collective of governments) and that act in the international arena to pursue a policy.

In most cases, treaty secretariats as international bureaucracies are characterized through a hierarchically organized group of international civil servants with a given mandate, given resources, identifiable boundaries, and a set of formal rules and procedures within the context of a policy area.

Different approaches argue about the actual influence of treaty secretariats (Bauer et al. 2016). For instance, political realism in the field of international relations theory views international bureaucracies as derivatives of different national governmental interests with almost no independent influence. More recent studies from the field of sociological

233

institutionalism find significant autonomy with international bureaucracies of major UN agencies (Barnett and Finnemore 2004). A particular source of influence is found in expertise and knowledge that is provided by the secretariats to negotiators and other stakeholders (e.g. Haas 1990). Other institutional approaches identified fields of influence in the area of fostering international agreements and norm-setting since international secretariats prepare, organize, and often arrange **treaty negotiations** (Biermann and Siebenhüner 2009). Explanatory schemes for this influence refer to the characteristics of the underlying environmental problem such as political salience and visibility, to economic incentive structures as conceptualized in principal–agent approaches, or to personalities involved. The actor quality in international bureaucracies is often focused in their top executives, such as the executive secretaries who lend their faces to this bureaucratic personality (Andresen and Agrawala 2002; Depledge 2007) (see **Influential individuals**). Considering perspectives from organizational theory, it is also the organizational culture, the institutional setting in which it acts, and the processes it performs that make the difference for the effects an international bureaucracy such as an environmental treaty secretariat has (Bauer et al. 2009; Jinnah 2014).

Key examples can be drawn from the issue areas of climate change and biodiversity governance. Both global UN processes were launched in 1992 with the **climate change regime** and the **biodiversity regime** mandating secretariats with key administrative tasks. While the climate regime was seen as an independent process with a secretariat only accountable to the respective Conference of the Parties and the UN General Assembly, the Convention on Biological Diversity process remained formally under the responsibility of the **United Nations Environment Programme**. However, the mandates for both affiliated secretariats are almost equal whereas the actual performance and influence differ significantly (Bauer et al. 2009).

Since its formal establishment in 1996, the climate secretariat, located in Bonn, has only slowly developed some influence on the negotiation processes in the climate field. Its main function has been to translate parties' political agreements into functioning technical systems and procedures. However, during the negotiation processes, parties increasingly relied on the secretariat to provide consensus documents and texts that find the common ground of all parties. The secretariat has been reluctant to promote an own political agenda, like other secretariats. It was only in the preparation of the Paris Agreement in 2015 that it became successful in putting through particular issues in the negotiations

(Hale 2016). So far, the climate secretariat has focused less on shaping discourses related to the regime and has limited itself to disseminating largely factual and descriptive information to stakeholders.

By contrast, the biodiversity secretariat, located in Montreal, enjoys a reputation among parties and is trusted as a credible and balanced facilitator of international cooperation. Governments as well as **non-governmental organizations** changed their behavior because of their experiences with the work of the secretariat. In general, the biodiversity secretariat helps to organize the negotiations rather inclusively and thereby facilitates the implementation of the convention. Since it does not interfere autonomously with any discourses related to the regime, it can be described as an environmentalist facilitator.

By way of explanation, this variation can be attributed in part to the problem structure that involves significantly higher stakes in the climate regime than any other international environmental agreement. These high stakes have motivated parties to be extremely wary of any of the secretariat's activities and, by imposing considerable constraints on the secretariat, to rule out initiatives by the secretariat. In the case of the biodiversity secretariat, its organizational and conceptual expertise constitutes an important source of influence that has earned it the reputation of a trusted provider of information and knowledge at large.

References

Andresen, Steinar and Shardul Agrawala. 2002. "Leaders, Pushers and Laggards in the Making of the Climate Regime." *Global Environmental Change* 12(1): 41–51.

Barnett, Michael N. and Martha Finnemore. 2004. *Rules for the World: International Organizations in Global Politics*. Ithaca, NY, Cornell University Press.

Bauer, Michael W., Christoph Knill, and Steffen Eckhard (Eds.). 2016. *International Bureaucracy: Challenges and Lessons for Public Administration Research*. London, Springer.

Bauer, Steffen, Per-Olof Busch, and Bernd Siebenhüner. 2009. "Treaty Secretariats in Global Environmental Governance." In *International Organizations in Global Environmental Governance*, Eds. Frank Biermann, Bernd Siebenhüner, and Anna Schreyögg, 174–191. London and New York, Routledge.

Biermann, Frank and Bernd Siebenhüner (Eds.). 2009. *Managers of Global Change: The Influence of International Environmental Bureaucracies*. Cambridge, MA, MIT Press.

Depledge, Joanna. 2007. "A Special Relationship: Chairpersons and the Secretariat in the Climate Change Negotiations." *Global Environmental Politics* 7(1): 45–68.

Haas, Ernst B. 1990. *Where Knowledge is Power: Three Models of Change in International Organizations.* Berkeley, CA, University of California Press.

Hale, Thomas. 2016. "'All Hands on Deck': The Paris Agreement and Nonstate Climate Action." *Global Environmental Politics* 16(3): 12–22.

Jinnah, Sikina. 2014. *Post-Treaty Politics: Secretariat Influence in Global Environmental Governance.* Cambridge, MA, MIT Press.

SECURITY

Hiroshi Ohta

Waseda University, Japan

The concept of security as such is elusive and open to many different interpretations. Arnold Wolfers summed up succinctly: "security, in an objective sense, measures the absence of threats to acquired values, [and] in a subjective sense, the absence of fear that such values will be attacked" (Wolfers 1962: 150). With the two oil crises of the 1970s, the end of the Cold War, and the 1992 Rio Earth Summit, it became clear that the acquired values to be protected go beyond strict military concerns and cover economic, energy, food, and environmental benefits as well.

Reflecting both sides of Wolfers' definition, Floyd (2013) epistemologically divides environmental security studies into empirical studies on how ecological security matters in practice and critical or/and normative studies on the conditions of environmental security. While the former positivist environmental security studies focus on research about causal relations between resource scarcity (or abundance) and acute conflicts (see **Scarcity and conflicts**), the latter critical ecological security studies interact with various security concerns such as environmental security, human security, and climate security.

An example of the second perspective is the Copenhagen School (Buzan et al. 1998). One of the key concepts developed by this school is "securitization." When we attach the term "security" to specific issues, such as climate security and human security, and if they are accepted by a concerned community, whether national or international, those issues take politics beyond the established rules and they are framed as a special kind of politics that can generate an emergency response. However, both climate security and human security have not necessarily shown securitization effects. One of the greatest beneficiaries of securitization of environmental change would be the military in developed nations, particularly when "environmental refugees" from developing countries are perceived as threats to national security (see **Migrants**) (Dalby 2009). More appropriate responses to environmental issues may be preventive approaches and risk management based on the logic of a **risk society**.

The last few decades have witnessed a significant number of theoretical and empirical studies on environmental security (Matthew 2014). The **scale** and speed of environmental changes caused by human activities are unprecedented. Biodiversity is on a rapid decline, plastic litter and microplastics are floating in the oceans (see **Ocean Plastics Charter**), and ice sheets are melting. In the geological age of the **Anthropocene**, humans are undermining their ecological foundation. The human species facing the danger of extinction is now both the subject and the object of security concerns.

References

Buzan, Barry, Ole Wæver, and Jaap de Wilde. 1998. *Security: A New Framework for Analysis*. Boulder, CO, Rienner.

Dalby, Simon. 2009. *Security and Environmental Change*. Cambridge, Polity.

Floyd, Rita. 2013. "Analyst, Theory and Security: A New Framework for Understanding Environmental Security Studies." In *Environmental Security: Approaches and Issues*, Eds. Rita Floyd and Richard A. Matthew, 21–34. London, Routledge.

Matthew, Richard A. (Ed.). 2014. *Environmental Security*, 4 Volumes. London, SAGE.

Wolfers, Arnold. 1962. *Discord and Collaboration: Essays on International Politics*. Baltimore, MD, Johns Hopkins University Press.

SHAMING

Charlotte Epstein
The University of Sydney, Australia

"Shaming" refers to a set of strategies mobilized by international actors in order to obtain that states honor their international obligations, notably with regards to environmental protection (see **Compliance and implementation**). This behavior speaks to the anarchical structure of the international system, which lacks a centralized political authority. Indeed, in the absence of an overarching enforcement mechanism, in a peaceful international system, actors cannot be forced into a course of action. They can, however, be shamed into complying with their obligations; for example, to avert the extinction of a species (see **CITES**). Human rights and the environment constitute the main issue areas where shaming has been deployed and studied (see **Human and environmental rights**).

The targets of shaming strategies have included states and multinational **business and corporations**. For example, in their campaign against biopiracy, a coalition of **nongovernmental organizations** (NGOs) have brought pharmaceutical companies into the limelight by awarding them the Captain Hook Award for profiteering of **indigenous peoples and local communities**' genetic resources. The actors deploying the strategies range from NGOs to international organizations or states, which can use international fora to shame other states into complying with international norms. An example constitutes the annual meetings of the **International Whaling Commission** (IWC), where a coalition of anti-whaling states, together with anti-whaling NGOs, have sought over the last three decades to shame Japan into halting its commercial and scientific whaling activities (see Epstein 2017, 2008).

Conceptually, "shaming" has been analyzed through both rationalist and constructivist accounts of international politics. Rationalist explanations focus on the material effects of shaming strategies, whether on their costs to actors who are shamed (Lebovic and Voeten 2009) or on their benefits to international cooperation (Franklin 2008). Shaming enters into the neoliberal institutionalist analysis of cooperation as a corollary to the interest-based analysis of reputation and the effect of the shadow of the future upon interstate interactions (Hafner Burton 2008).

However, insofar as it involves complying with normative behavior, shaming beckons constructivist accounts that emphasize the intrinsic power of norms. Here, two lines of enquiry have been pursued successively: how shaming strategies operate, and why they are successful. With regards to the first, shaming constitutes the linchpin to "leverage politics" applied upon states (Keck and Sikkink 1998) or a key mechanism of their socialization into international norms. In seeking to understand why states actually respond to this form of leverage the second foregrounds the role of identities. States are sensitive to shaming because of the moral damage to their self-images and identities (Epstein and Barclay 2013).

References

Epstein, Charlotte 2008. *The Power of Words in International Relations: Birth of an Anti-Whaling Discourse*. Cambridge, MA, MIT Press.

Epstein, Charlotte. 2017. "Stop Telling Us How to Behave: Socialization or Infantilization?" In *Against International Relations Norms: Postcolonial Perspectives*, Ed. Charlotte Epstein, 74–86. Abingdon, Routledge.

Epstein, Charlotte and Kate Barclay. 2013. "Shaming to 'Green': Australia–Japan Relations and Whales and Tuna Compared." *International Relations of the Asia-Pacific* 13(1): 195–123.

Franklin, James C. 2008. "Shame on You: The Impact of Human Rights Criticism on Political Repression in Latin America." *International Studies Quarterly* 52(1): 187–211.

Hafner Burton, Emilie M. 2008. "Sticks and Stones: Naming and Shaming the Human Rights Enforcement Problem." *International Organization* 62(4): 689–716.

Keck, Margaret E. and Kathryn Sikkink. 1998. *Activists beyond Borders: Advocacy Networks in International Politics.* Ithaca, NY, Cornell University Press.

Lebovic, James H. and Erik Voeten. 2009. "The Cost of Shame: International Organizations and Foreign Aid in the Punishing of Human Rights Violators." *Journal of Peace Research* 46(1): 79–97.

SOVEREIGNTY

Jean-Frédéric Morin
Université Laval, Canada

Amandine Orsini
Université Saint-Louis – Bruxelles, Belgium

"The Earth is one but the world is not" begins the Brundtland Report of the World Commission on Environment and Development (WCED) (1987: 27). Indeed, states are divided whereas the biosphere exists as a unit. This fact makes environmental politics an interesting case of reflection for the principle of sovereignty.

In the 1960s, during the decolonization process, developing countries insisted upon controlling their natural resources. Many were suspicious of Western environmental intentions, fearing a form of neocolonialism (see **Critical political economy**). In 1962, they strongly advocated for the adoption of the United Nations Resolution 1803 on the *Permanent Sovereignty Over Natural Resources*, recognizing "the inalienable right of all states freely to dispose of their natural wealth and resources in accordance with their national interests." Still today, developing countries frequently refer to this principle and make sure that negotiated texts explicitly recall it (Conca 1994; Hochstetler et al. 2000).

Some environmentalists see the biosphere as one entity and fear that a full, exclusive, and supreme state sovereignty impedes environmental protection. Under this line of reasoning, two options are frequently mentioned as means to limit sovereignty and favor environmental protection. The first consists in extending the **common heritage of humanity**. This would allow, for example, for the establishment of a global system of inspection and **taxation** for resources traditionally under state sovereignty. The second route for a post-Westphalian order is to increase the rights of non-state actors: **nongovernmental organizations**, **business and corporations**, **epistemic communities**, or **indigenous peoples and local communities** (Shadian 2010).

However, the supremacy of state sovereignty is not universally accepted as an impediment to environmental protection. International law already includes principles that limit sovereignty. Following the **preventive action principle**, for example, a state cannot use its territory in a way that damages the environment of another state. It was politically endorsed in the Stockholm (1972) and the Rio (1992) Declarations (see **Summit diplomacy**), and legally recognized by the International Court of Justice (ICJ) (Sands 1995).

Moreover, international treaties qualify sovereignty rights by assigning specific obligations to states (Schrijver 1997). The **Law of the Sea Convention**, for example, extends sovereignty rights to 200 nautical miles from the coasts but provides for environmental duties. This led some legal experts to affirm that sovereign rights "over certain environmental resources are not proprietary, but fiduciary" (Sand 2004: 48). Here, sovereignty can be seen as a form of public trusteeship granted to states with specific obligations and limitations.

Other requirements also create conditions that push states toward cooperation and joint action. For instance, several environmental treaties prohibit trade with non-parties. The Montreal Protocol (see **Ozone regime**) bans imports, even from non-parties, of products containing substances that are harmful to the ozone layer. The **hazardous wastes regime** bans imports and exports of toxic wastes with non-parties. Consequently, a country whose firms produce sprays or process toxic wastes has a high incentive to respect these treaties (DeSombre 2005). Global interdependence prevents regulatory autarky.

With time, it appeared that sovereign rights could even consolidate environmental cooperation. As the **tragedy of the commons** suggests, a clear definition of rights can provide incentives for the **conservation and preservation** of natural resources. For example, the 1992 **biodiversity regime** and its 2010 Nagoya Protocol placed genetic resources under national sovereignty, rejecting the common heritage principle that was formerly found in the 1983 FAO International Undertaking on Plant Genetic Resources. Through their sovereign rights, states can now control access to their biodiversity and ask biotechnology **business and corporations** to compensate for the use of their national genetic resources.

Arguably, concerning **effectiveness**, states are often the best actors to enforce and control environmental measures. Not only are they able to impose regulations, levy taxes, offer subsidies, and define education programs, they also have the political and legal capacity to challenge actors that damage their natural resources. Fish stocks are unsustainably fished and extra-atmospheric space hazardously over-polluted partly because of the lack of national sovereignty over these resources.

The debates between sovereignty as an obstacle or as a means for environmental protection could be somewhat resolved by breaking down the concept. Karen Litfin (1997) divides sovereignty into authority, control, and legitimacy. She argues that states engage in "sovereignty bargains" along these dimensions. For instance, tying emission targets to domestic ownership of green technology could increase autonomy but reduce legitimacy, while delegating emission targets to an internationally recognized scientific body (see **Boundary organizations**) could increase legitimacy but decrease autonomy. Here, sovereignty is not understood as an absolute attribute but as a multidimensional concept in constant flux, and in constant social redefinition (Conca 1994; Chayes and Chayes 1998; Hochstetler et al. 2000).

To further understand the complex interaction between the principle of sovereignty and environmental protection, it might be useful to differentiate environmental problems. The quality of scientific knowledge (see **Science**), the level of ecological interdependence, the availability of international institutions, and the type of natural resources might affect the desirability for a strong sovereignty norm and the bargains settled between sovereignty dimensions. One hypothesis is that the protection of local resources benefits from the direct involvement of transnational and supranational actors, whereas transboundary resources are better protected when states guard their sovereign rights.

References

Chayes, Abram and Antonia H. Chayes. 1998. *The New Sovereignty: Compliance with Treaties in International Regulatory Regimes.* Cambridge, MA, Harvard University Press.

Conca, Ken. 1994. "Rethinking the Ecology-Sovereignty Debate." *Millennium* 23(3): 701–711.

DeSombre, Elizabeth R. 2005. "Fishing under Flags of Convenience: Using Market Power to Increase Participation in International Regulation." *Global Environmental Politics* 5(4): 73–94.

Hochstetler, Kathryn, Ann Marie Clark, and Elisabeth J. Friedman. 2000. "Sovereignty in the Balance: Claims and Bargains at the UN Conference on the Environment, Human Rights, and Women." *International Studies Quarterly* 44(4): 591–614.

Litfin, Karen T. 1997. "Sovereignty in World Ecopolitics." *Mershon International Studies Review* 41(2): 167–204.

Sand, Peter H. 2004. "Sovereignty Bounded: Public Trusteeship for Common Pool Resources." *Global Environmental Politics* 4(1): 47–71.

Sands, Philippe. 1995. *Principles of International Environmental Law.* Manchester, Manchester University Press.

Schrijver, Nico. 1997. *Sovereignty over Natural Resources: Balancing Rights and Duties.* Cambridge, Cambridge University Press.

Shadian, Jessica, 2010. "From States to Polities: Reconceptualizing Sovereignty through Inuit Governance." *European Journal of International Relations* 16(3): 485–510.

United Nations World Commission on Environment and Development. 1987. *Our Common Future.* Oxford, Oxford University Press.

STOCKHOLM CONVENTION ON PERSISTENT ORGANIC POLLUTANTS

Jessica Templeton

London School of Economics and Political Science, United Kingdom

Adopted in 2001, the Stockholm Convention on Persistent Organic Pollutants (POPs) is a legally binding global agreement designed to protect human health and the environment from exposure to certain hazardous, transboundary chemical pollutants. POPs fall into three categories: pesticides, such as DDT (dichloro-diphenyl-trichloroethane);

industrial chemicals, such as the flame retardant PFOA (perfluorooctanoic acid); and unintended by-products of combustion and industrial processes, such as dioxins.

The concept of a POP is socially constructed; POPs include only those chemicals that are subject to long-range environmental transport and thus pose threats to human health and the environment on a global **scale** (Selin 2010). This characteristic necessitates global collective action to protect people from exposure to these substances, which tend to concentrate in the Arctic (Downie and Fenge 2003). POPs are also toxic, bioaccumulative (increasing in concentration as they move through the food chain), and persistent (breaking down very slowly in the environment).

Decisions to ban or limit production and use of POPs are based on **science**. Substances nominated for regulation are evaluated by the POPs Review Committee, a subsidiary body composed of thirty-one technical experts affiliated with parties to the Convention (see **Epistemic communities**). The committee reflects a variety of areas of expertise, as well as regional and gender diversity. Kohler (2006) argues that such diversity is essential to the perceived legitimacy of **boundary organizations** which work at the interface of science and policy.

The Stockholm Convention is one of three treaties that address global chemical pollution; the other two are the Basel Convention on **hazardous wastes** and the **Rotterdam Convention** on prior informed consent in trade. While these conventions are legally autonomous, an unprecedented "synergies" initiative by the **United Nations Environment Programme** has formalized administrative and programmatic linkages among them. The three **secretariats** have merged to increase administrative efficiency, and the biennial meetings of the Conferences of the Parties to the conventions are held back-to-back to enhance the cooperation of these instruments in overlapping areas of responsibility (see **Institutional interactions**). These changes have strengthened the vertical and horizontal linkages among the chemicals and wastes conventions, including through integration of technical assistance to developing countries to support implementation. However, strengthening linkages can also confuse issues and create obstacles to agreement; for example, when controversy in one forum spills over to another (Selin 2010) or when delegates engage in cross-treaty deal-making and brinksmanship (Allan et al. 2018).

References

Allan, Jen Iris, David Downie, and Jessica Templeton. 2018. "Experimenting with TripleCOPs: Productive Innovation or Counterproductive Complexity?" *International Environmental Agreements* 18(4): 557–572.

Downie, David Leonard and Terry Fenge (Eds.). 2003. *Northern Lights against POPs: Combatting Toxic Threats in the Arctic.* Montreal, McGill-Queen's University Press.

Kohler, Pia. 2006. "Science, PIC and POPs: Negotiating the Membership of the Chemical Review Committees under the Stockholm and Rotterdam Conventions." *Review of European Community and International Environmental Law* 15(3): 293–303.

Selin, Henrik. 2010. *Global Governance of Hazardous Chemicals: Challenges of Multilevel Management.* Cambridge, MA, MIT Press.

SUMMIT DIPLOMACY

Arild Underdal

University of Oslo and CICERO, Norway

In the study of international relations, a "summit" is usually defined as a meeting involving heads of state or government (typically presidents or prime ministers) in direct face-to-face communication in the same room (Dunn 1996: 16ff.). Meetings of this format have a long history, but Winston Churchill seems to have been the first, in 1950, to label them "summits."

Churchill used this label restrictively for (rare) meetings where the leaders of the Great Powers negotiated important high politics issues such as World War II strategies, trade relationships, and peace settlements. Over the past five to six decades summit diplomacy has expanded and become more institutionalized. Leaders of the most important states still meet in exclusive club-like settings, notably G7 and G20, but now they meet regularly, most of the "clubs" are larger, and their agendas are more diverse. Moreover, meetings of heads of state or government have become an integral component of the political system of several regional organizations including the European Union (EU) and the African Union (AU), and of forums such as the Asia-Pacific Economic Cooperation (APEC) (see **Regional governance**). Most of these meetings cover multiple issues, but over time attention to environmental concerns seems to have been growing.

These developments have led to a more diverse setting. Today, two main types of summits play important but different roles in environmental governance. First, regional organizations such as the EU have over time engaged themselves more actively in a wider range of environmental *protection* policies. Some critics dismiss the achievements made in these settings as focusing primarily on policies for economic growth and stability rather than on environmental protection. Yet, if we measure importance in terms of environmental *consequences*, summits that take place within these settings and despite focus also on economic issues will often—for better or worse—be the most important arena available. The EU's importance is further boosted by its direct involvement in a broad range of policymaking and by its unique institutional capacity.

The second important type of summit is associated with club-like forums such as the G20 and occasional other meetings. These summits usually have a broad agenda, and their contributions to environmental governance vary significantly (see **Ocean Plastics Charter**). In a longer time perspective, governmental efforts to develop cooperative environmental policies take place mostly in the context of international **regimes** and UN global conferences. Prominent examples of the latter include the 1972 Stockholm Conference on the Human Environment, the 1992 Rio Conference on Environment and Development (also known as the Earth Summit), the 2002 Johannesburg World Summit on Sustainable Development, the 2012 Rio Conference on Sustainable Development, and the 2015 Paris Agreement. Common to all these meetings is the emphasis on *universal* **participation**. The setting is traditionally dominated by *environmental* ministries, agencies, experts (often forming **epistemic communities**), and **nongovernmental organizations**. What these actors presumably have in common is a genuine commitment to environmental values, and a weak mandate to intervene in the human activities that threaten these values. The active involvement of heads of government or state may be thought of as particularly important to ensure that environmental values and policies in fact penetrate also *other* policy domains. Available evidence confirms that meetings of leaders indeed can provide unique opportunities for enhancing environmental policies (Young 2011). The current institutional reform of the **High-Level Political Forum on Sustainable Development** is an attempt to take advantage of such opportunities. However, particularly in its present format of mega-gatherings with sprawling agendas and a rich flora of side events, global conference diplomacy can hardly provide a conducive setting for some of the most important leadership functions that *summit*s are supposed to serve (Victor 2011).

Let us nevertheless begin on the bright side. First, global conferences often serve as an effective tool for raising awareness, setting political agendas, and simultaneously focusing the attention of governments and stakeholders worldwide on the same problem (Young 2011; Seyfang and Jordan 2002). All these effects are amplified, sometimes substantially, if the conference includes a summit attended by presidents or prime ministers of the most important states. In fact, preparations for such meetings often lead to *unilateral* upgrading of a state's policies and/or its institutional capacity (Meyer et al. 1997). Second, summit diplomacy generates, particularly for the leaders involved, positive stakes in its own success. Summits thus provide windows of opportunity for environmental ministries, agencies, and NGOs to influence policy (Seyfang and Jordan 2002), and they usually end with some kind of *joint declaration*. Third, the active participation of heads of government and state enhances *aggregation capacity*. These leaders can modify positions, link issues, and make trade-offs that their ministers, let alone ordinary ambassadors, have no mandate to make. In short, at its best, summit diplomacy can cut deadlocks and strike deals that qualify as important breakthroughs for global environmental governance (Caramerli 2012).

Alas, summit diplomacy also involves significant risks. First, plenary sessions with political leaders in the spotlight provide fertile ground for ideological posturing. Particularly in areas characterized by stark asymmetries between large groups of countries ("North" and "South"), leaders can use such meetings to mobilize domestic support. Under these circumstances, the risk of deadlock over basic principles and beliefs may *increase* when leaders meet. Second, high public expectations sometimes create strong incentives for leaders to (over)emphasize achievements. Announcements of lofty goals with no implementation plans attached are a common symptom of this "disease." Third, to deliver what is expected, leaders depend heavily on the preparations made at lower levels. When these preparations fail to come up with coherent texts or clear policy alternatives, leaders may respond by some combination of withdrawal and improvisation. Fourth, as seen from the perspective of seasoned diplomats, summitry inevitably involves some risk of *magnifying* mistakes. These risks are inherent in the institutional order itself, as heads of states face few institutional constraints.

For these and other reasons, enthusiasm for global conference summitry is muted in many of the assessments of environmental governance published by scholars (e.g. Susskind 1994; Victor 2011) as well as practitioners (e.g. Tolba and Rummel-Bulska 2008).

References

Caramerli, Angela. 2012. "Summit Diplomacy: Positive and Negative Aspects". *Acta Universitatis Danubius* 5(1): 23–30.

Dunn, David H. 1996. *Diplomacy at the Highest Level*. Basingstoke, Macmillan.

Meyer, John W., David J. Frank, Ann Hironaka, Evan Schofer, and Nancy B. Tuma. 1997. "The Structuring of a World Environmental Regime, 1870–1990." *International Organization* 51(4): 623–651.

Seyfang, Gill and Andrew Jordan. 2002. "The Johannesburg Summit and Sustainable Development: How Effective are Mega-Conferences?" In *Yearbook of International Co-operation on Environment and Development 2002–2003*, Eds. Olav S. Stokke and Øystein B. Thommessen, 19–26. London, Earthscan.

Susskind, Lawrence E. 1994. *Environmental Diplomacy: Negotiating More Effective Global Agreements*. Oxford, Oxford University Press.

Tolba, Mostafa K. and Iwona Rummel-Bulska. 2008. *Global Environmental Diplomacy*. Cambridge, MA, MIT Press.

Victor, David G. 2011. *Global Warming Gridlock – Creating More Effective Strategies for Protecting the Planet*. Cambridge, Cambridge University Press.

Young, Oran R. 2011. "Effectiveness of International Environmental Regimes: Existing Knowledge, Cutting-Edge Themes, and Research Strategies." *PNAS Direct Submission* 108(50): 19853–19860.

SUSTAINABLE DEVELOPMENT

Edwin Zaccai

Université libre de Bruxelles, Belgium

Sustainable development was defined in the Brundtland Report in 1987 as "development that meets the needs of the present without compromising the ability of future generations to meet their own needs" (World Commission on Environment and Development 1987: 43). This has remained, for more than 30 years, the best known definition, even though the World Conservation Strategy was one of the first to use the term (IUCN et al. 1980). The Brundtland report is a product of the World Commission on Environment and Development, an international expert panel that was commissioned by the UN General Assembly in 1983 to define a new type of global development that reconciles environment and development in both the North and the South.

In this definition *intergenerational equity* stands out as the clearest specificity of sustainable development, compared with former formulas of development (see **Environmental justice**). The expression *future generations* encompasses not only the next generation, but several generations, obliging one to consider a time frame well beyond that of current policy decisions. The capacities to be sustained in order to meet people's needs (with a priority for essential needs) in the distant future are not limited to the environment, but include economic, social, and institutional aspects as well. Brundtland's approach to sustainable development recognizes also that there are limits to be set in the exploitation of the environment (see **Carrying capacities paradigm**), but these have to be dealt with in combination with technical developments and social equity.

As regards global governance, the major historic step in the sustainable development discourse was the United Nations Conference on Environment and Development (Rio, 1992), also referred to as the Earth Summit (see **Summit diplomacy**). It was held shortly after the end of the East–West divide, and attracted high expectations. The Rio Declaration includes prominent environmental governance principles, such as the **polluter pays principle**, the **preventive action principle**, or the **precautionary principle**. In addition, it contains a major principle often used in international negotiations, namely one arguing for **common but differentiated responsibilities** between states.

The academic literature provides a multiplicity of definitions of sustainable development and often describes the concept as being fuzzy (Lélé 1991). Broadly a general objective, it is specified by different actors depending on their context: whether **ecological modernization**, more suitable in industrial countries (Mol et al. 2009); greener forms of development in agrarian developing countries (Adams 2008); or local projects in towns or regions under the banner of Local Agenda 21, and more recently sustainability transitions (see **Energy transition**). In any case the symbolic and political value of the concept should be highlighted. It is consensual, federating a number of interests, previously seen as in conflict, at least potentially. Arguably, it enabled a broad participation in the conferences and institutions that were dedicated to sustainable development, rallying **business and corporations**, developing countries, institutions for economic development, or associations of workers or of environmentalists.

After the mid-1990s the concept of sustainable development has been increasingly understood as a balance between environmental, social, and economic pillars, dimensions, or objectives. In practice, the balance between these objectives remains contingent on the indicators used, the time scale chosen, or the actors that are included or excluded, which reflects on the policies put in place (Zaccai 2012). A turning point in the definition of sustainable development is the setting of seventeen **Sustainable Development Goal**s (SDGs), in order to clarify its operationality (Sachs 2015). These goals are increasingly referred to in many contexts such as environmental, climate change (including by the Intergovernmental Panel on Climate Change), or economic reports.

From the start, the sustainable development formula set the stage, among other "win–win" objectives, for reconciling environmentalism and business and corporations' interests. One of the chapters of the Brundtland report is entitled *Producing More with Less*, which illustrates this environment–business tandem. The Business Council for Sustainable Development, which later became the World Business Council for Sustainable Development, is a group of major global transnational corporations that was founded before the Rio Conference in order to participate actively in the discussions, and has influenced these orientations. A multitude of links have developed between corporate sustainable development and **corporate social responsibility**.

Economists interested in sustainable development introduced a distinction between strong and weak sustainability (Pearce 1993). Weak sustainability assumes substitutability between various forms of capital (economic capital, but also natural capital, several forms of social or even cultural capitals). The most common substitution would be if a decrease in natural capital (i.e. deforestation) were compensated by an increase in economic capital. Under the weak sustainability paradigm, development is considered successful when the total capital stock grows, no matter its composition. In contrast, strong sustainability considers some natural capital to be "critical," which implies limited substitutability and the need for certain nature conservation at any cost.

In a synthesis paper Hopwood et al. (2005) present a classification and "mapping" of different trends of thought on sustainable development along two broad axes. One is the ability of using technological solutions in order to solve environmental problems versus the conservation of a more intact environment. The other axis relates to the degree of presence of inequality or social concerns within the work of the authors that are considered. The Organisation for Economic Co-operation and Development, the EU, or the Ecological Modernizers stand not too far from each other on one side of the figure, in modes of sustainable development that may fit with **liberal**

environmentalism. At the opposite side we find environmental justice or anti-capitalist movements, which might also refer occasionally to sustainable development, emphasizing transformational change. In the middle of the figure stand the Brundtland Report and mainstream environmental groups, among others.

A controversial issue in the sustainability discourse that has been debated at length is the compatibility between economic growth and sustainable development (Jackson 2009) (see **Degrowth**). Some ecological economists consider sustainable development, and especially sustainable growth, to be an oxymoron, based on the argument that a development path based on ever-increasing production cannot be sustainable in a finite world. On the other hand, the Brundtland Report draws a strong distinction between economic growth and development. Within the SDGs economic growth is now only part of one of the seventeen objectives, namely Objective 8 on "Decent work and economic growth."

References

Adams, Bill. 2008. *Green Development: Environment and Sustainability in a Developing World*. London, Routledge.

Hopwood, Bill, Mary Mellor, and Geoff O'Brian. 2005. "Sustainable Development: Mapping Different Approaches." *Sustainable Development* 13(1): 38–52.

IUCN, UNEP, WWF. 1980. *World Conservation Strategy: Living Resource Conservation for Sustainable Development*. Gland, IUCN.

Jackson, Tim. 2009. *Prosperity without Growth*. London, Routledge.

Lélé, Sharachchandra. 1991. "Sustainable Development: A Critical Review." *World Development* 19 (6): 607–621.

Mol, Arthur P.J., David A. Sonnefeld, and Gert Spaargaren (Eds.). 2009. *The Ecological Modernisation Reader: Environmental Reform in Theory and Practice*. London and New York, Routledge.

Pearce, David W. 1993. *Blueprint 3, Measuring Sustainable Development*. London, Earthscan.

Sachs, Jeffrey D., 2015. *The Age of Sustainable Development*. New York, Columbia University Press

United Nations World Commission on Environment and Development. 1987. *Our Common Future*. Oxford, Oxford University Press.

Zaccai, Edwin. 2012. "Over Two Decades in Pursuit of Sustainable Development: Influence, Transformation, Limits." *Environmental Development* 1(1): 79–90.

SUSTAINABLE DEVELOPMENT GOALS

Elham Seyedsayamdost

American University, Dubai

The Sustainable Development Goals (SDGs) are a series of seventeen goals and 169 targets that aim to eradicate poverty, promote peace and prosperity, and protect the planet by the year 2030. The SDGs were first introduced in the United Nations General Assembly Resolution 70/1 "Transforming our world: the 2030 Agenda for Sustainable Development," which was adopted by all UN member states in September 2015. Focusing on people, planet, prosperity, peace, and **partnerships**, the SDGs integrate the economic, social, and environmental dimensions of **sustainable development**; are indivisible and universally applicable; and aspire to leave no one behind. Having followed on the Millennium Development Goals (MDGs), a set of eight goals and twenty-one targets that expired in 2015, the SDGs are considerably different. The MDGs constituted a limited agenda, developed by a small group (see **Treaty negotiations**), with goals and targets relevant for developing countries primarily. The SDGs, on the other hand, constitute a global agenda, resulting from a three-year consultative and participatory process (see **Participation**), and contain a long list of goals addressing global challenges from poverty to inequality, gender equality to governance, and climate change to sustainable **cities**, among others.

The mandate to develop a proposal on the SDGs was included in the Rio+20 outcome document, "The Future We Want," in June 2012. As a result, the UN Secretary-General appointed a **High-Level Political Forum** (HLPF) to provide political leadership and guidance, which has since become the central platform for review of the SDGs, where states voluntarily share reports on their progress in the forum's annual meetings. The deliberative body that prepared the proposal on the SDGs was the inter-governmental Open Working Group (OWG) of the General Assembly, which involved seventy countries. The OWG drew on the expertise of stakeholders in civil society, the private sector, and international organizations while global, regional, and national consultations around the world attempted to expand the deliberations beyond the UN headquarters. Nevertheless, member states were ultimately the primary architects of the SDGs. The creation of these tools and innovations of multilateralism to facilitate global negotiations around the SDGs have been highlighted by some as a paradigm shift in global governance (Kamau et al. 2018).

Since their launch, the SDGs have been the target of both praise and criticism. The inclusive goal-setting process and the Herculean task of getting 193 member states to unanimously adopt the 2030 Agenda have been widely applauded (Biermann et al. 2017). In addition, by uniting development and environment, the SDGs are considered to be transformative, in particular due to their emphasis on interlinkages among the SDGs. This has been highlighted as the SDGs' potential to contribute to integrated policy design across different issue areas (Le Blanc 2015). For example, SDG 2—while erroneously dubbed "zero hunger"—in reality transcends hunger to emphasize malnutrition in all its forms (including micronutrient deficiency and obesity), ensure sustainable food production systems, and promote **agroecology**, among others. Finally, the SDGs have been mobilizing actors across different sectors and at different **scales** of governance, due to the all-encompassing nature of the goals.

Despite these positive attributes, the SDGs are not without flaws. The same participatory process of negotiations that put member states in the driver's seat has been faulted for the long list of targets, which are very costly to measure, let alone to implement. In the same vein, no priorities have been assigned to the goals of this holistic and broad agenda, both raising questions as to which goals might receive policy attention and resources and generating conflicts among the goals (Fukuda-Parr 2016). For example, "trade-offs" exist between responsible consumption and production (SDG 12) and life on land (SDG 15), where progress in one goal might translate into obstacles in achieving the other goal (Pradhan et al. 2017). The non-binding nature of the SDGs has also been scrutinized, as it makes **compliance and implementation** voluntary for states (Young 2017). This has been further exacerbated by the lack of a strong global review mechanism, "giving primacy to nationally organized follow-up, which is subject to institutional capacity and political will" (Bexell and Jönsson 2017: 25).

Nevertheless, the 2030 Agenda for Sustainable Development and the SDGs have come to embody an umbrella framework for not only states and international organizations but also civil society and private sector actors. They represent a blueprint for collective action on the most pressing global challenges of our time.

References

Bexell, Magdalena and Kristina Jönsson. 2017. "Responsibility and the United Nations' Sustainable Development Goals." *Forum for Development Studies* 44(1): 13–29.

Biermann, Frank, Norichika Kanie, and Rakhyun E. Kim. 2017. "Global Governance by Goal-setting: The Novel Approach of the UN Sustainable Development Goals." *Environmental Sustainability* 26–27: 26–31.

Fukuda-Parr, Sakiko. 2016. "From the Millennium Development Goals to Sustainable Development Goals: Shifts in Purpose, Concept, and Politics of Global Goal Setting for Development." *Gender and Development* 24(1): 43–52.

Kamau, Macharia, Pamela Chasek, and David O'Connor. 2018. *Transforming Multilateral Diplomacy: The Inside Story of the Sustainable Development Goals.* Abington, Routledge.

Le Blanc, David. 2015. "Towards Integration at Last? The Sustainable Development Goals as a Network of Targets." *Sustainable Development* 23(3): 176–187.

Pradhan, Prajal, Luis Costa, Diego Rybski, Wolfgang Lucht, and Juergen P. Kropp. 2017. "A Systematic Study of Sustainable Development Goal (SDG) Interactions." *Earth's Future* 5(11): 1169–1179.

Young, Oran. 2017. *Governing Complex Systems: Social Capital for the Anthropocene.* Cambridge, MA, MIT Press.

SUSTAINABLE FINANCE

Dirk Schoenmaker

Rotterdam School of Management, Erasmus University, The Netherlands

Sustainable finance, also called green or environmental finance, refers to allocating investment and lending to sustainable governmental institutions, **corporations**, and projects. This accelerates the transition to a low-carbon, circular, and inclusive economy (see also **Green economy**). The financial system moves from a traditional investment and lending approach that maximizes financial value subject to risk, often in a narrow and short-term way, toward investing and lending for long-term value creation that optimizes financial, social, and environmental value subject to risk. Sustainable finance thus involves considering environmental and social value, alongside financial value.

Traditional finance assumes efficient **markets**, which means that all available information is incorporated in (stock) market prices. Investors just invest in the market index, which contains all available stocks providing a diversified portfolio. However, there is evidence that carbon risks are not fully reflected in stock prices. Rather, the adaptive markets hypothesis (Lo 2017) provides a better framework, as it recognises the limitations to market efficiency and the need for market participants to adapt to new information, such as social and environmental factors.

Varying methods to include environmental, social, and governance (ESG) information into investment and lending decisions have developed (Schoenmaker and Schramade 2019). At one end of the spectrum, investors and lenders are increasingly using ESG ratings to incorporate the social and environmental dimensions. However, these external ratings rely on scanty and sometimes conflicting data and provide limited information on material ESG factors. At the other end of the spectrum, investors and lenders follow an active investment approach, based on fundamental analysis of companies' ESG factors and engagement with investee companies on material ESG factors. The aim is to uncover and realize companies' social and environmental value next to their financial value.

Fundamental investing leads to more concentrated portfolios and alternative measures of investment performance (away from market benchmarks). The incorporation of ESG information into stock prices is an adaptive process, the success of which is dependent on the number of fundamental analysts and the quality of their learning.

What happens to financial returns? If we attach a positive probability to the **scenario** that the transition toward **sustainable development** will (partly) happen, then sustainable investing in and lending to companies that are preparing for this transition will generate a proper return. Finance can thus help in making production more sustainable, accelerating **ecological modernization**. By contrast, a business-as-usual **scenario** may lead to stranded assets.

Green bonds are a recent but fast-growing phenomenon (Zerbib 2019). Green bonds are bonds that finance green projects (projects that provide environmental or **climate change** benefits), but are otherwise the same as other bonds. The energy sector is the main sector involved, accounting for almost half of outstanding green bonds.

References

Lo, Andrew W. 2017. *Adaptive Markets: Financial Evolution at the Speed of Thought.* Princeton, NJ, Princeton University Press.

Schoenmaker, Dirk and Willem Schramade. 2019. *Principles of Sustainable Finance.* Oxford, Oxford University Press.

Zerbib, Olivier D. 2019. "The Effect of Pro-Environmental Preferences on Bond Prices: Evidence from Green Bonds." *Journal of Banking & Finance* 98: 39–60.

TAXATION[1]

Bernard P. Herber

University of Arizona, United States

Taxation not only provides government revenues, but it may also promote economic efficiency by internalizing unpriced externalities back into the price system (see **Polluter pays principle**). These taxation functions normally occur within a sovereign nation, but technological progress and globalization have made them increasingly important between nations due to the emergence of major inter-nation externalities. In environmental governance, such externalities include pollution of the global oceans and excess carbon emissions into the global atmosphere, the latter resulting in global warming with its destructive climate change effects. Externalities distort economic efficiency since they escape market pricing.

Two policy instruments proposed by economists to reduce carbon emissions are the carbon tax and carbon market (cap and trade) devices (Nordhaus 2007; Metcalf and Weisbach 2009; Aldy and Stavins 2012; also, see **Markets**). The carbon tax, an excise form of sales tax, is normally levied upon the mining or distribution of fossil fuels, which emit carbon in providing energy for economic production and consumption. It is a Pigovian tax that enters the prices of fossil fuels, thus "internalizing" previously unpriced carbon pollution costs into the prices of the economic goods that the fuels produce.

An ideal carbon tax design would levy a tax rate that is highest on coal, which has the highest carbon content per unit of energy produced, a lower rate on oil, which has less carbon content than coal, and lowest on the least carbon-emitting fuel, natural gas. A carbon tax attacks the core of the climate change problem by reducing carbon emissions. Meanwhile, its revenues may be used for such purposes as **adaptation** to already existing climate change effects and for the creation of a global trust fund to address normative inter-nation distributional issues associated with a global carbon tax.

Implementation of such a tax is a formidable undertaking (see **Compliance and implementation**). Taxation is inherently unpopular due to its "compulsory" nature, compared with the "free choice" nature of market transactions. Moreover, it faces even greater resistance at the supranational level where sovereign political authority is absent. Efforts to compensate for this void often utilize international treaties, whereby nations "delegate" **sovereignty** to a supranational entity via binding agreements (see **Treaty design**). However, treaty decision-making is hindered by the unwieldy consensus-voting rule (see **Treaty negotiations**).

Optimally, a sovereign "global political authority" that corresponds to the "global geographical space" of climate change externalities would levy the tax (Herber 1992). Otherwise, significant free-rider incentives would arise if only one, or a few, nations, or even a regional affiliation of nations, levy the tax. Yet, the world has no sovereign global political body nor is it likely to create one in the foreseeable future.

Nonetheless, a "second-best" approach, albeit one using the flawed treaty mechanism, could establish a functional "de facto" global carbon tax (Cooper 2008; Silverstein 2010; Nordhaus 2011). The treaty would delegate sovereignty from national governments to a nonsovereign supranational government for the purpose of harmonizing a network of national carbon taxes across national political boundaries. This supranational entity could be either an existing body, such as the United Nations, or a newly created nonsovereign supranational government. The resulting tax domain would correspond to the geographical scope of global climate change externalities.

Although such a treaty would face considerable opposition, the gravity of the climate change threat—as voiced by a large majority of global climate scientists—lends support for strong action. Moreover, the tax could be made more acceptable if nations were allowed to retain some of the revenues generated by the tax. Meanwhile, a policy framework for definitive global climate policy already exists in the **climate change regime** (Skovgaard et al. 2019). Furthermore, a conceptual foundation for such policy, the **common heritage of humanity** principle, is part of international law in the **Law of the Sea Convention**.

Note

1. This contribution is a reproduction of the original one published in the 2015 edition of this book. The editors simply updated the citations.

References

Aldy, Joseph and Robert Stavins. 2012. "The Promise and Problems of Pricing Carbon: Theory and Experience." *Journal of Environment and Development* 21(2): 152–180.

Cooper, Richard. 2008. *The Case for Charges on Greenhouse Gas Emissions.* Discussion Paper 08–10, Harvard Project on International Climate Agreements. Cambridge, MA, Harvard Kennedy School.

Herber, Bernard. 1992. *International Environmental Taxation in the Absence of Sovereignty.* WP/92/104. Washington, DC, International Monetary Fund.

Metcalf, Gilbert and David Weisbach. 2009. "The Design of a Carbon Tax." *Harvard International Law Review* 33: 499–556.

Nordhaus, William. 2007. "To Tax or Not to Tax: Alternative Approaches to Slowing Global Warming." *Review of Environmental Economics and Policy* 1(1): 26–44.

Nordhaus, William. 2011. "The Architecture of Climate Economics: Designing a Global Agreement on Global Warming." *Bulletin of the Atomic Scientists* 67(1): 9–18.

Silverstein, David. 2010. A Method to Finance a Global Climate Fund with a Harmonized Carbon Tax. Munich Personal RePEc Archive, Paper No. 27121. https://mpra.ub.uni-muenchen.de/27121/

Skovgaard, Jakob, Sacks Ferrari Sofia, and Åsa Knaggård. 2019. "Mapping and Clustering the Adoption of Carbon Pricing Policies: What Polities Price Carbon and Why?" *Climate Policy* 19(9): 1173–1185.

TECHNOLOGY TRANSFER

Joanna I. Lewis

Georgetown University, United States

Achieving environmental goals frequently requires the utilization of specific technology: for instance pollution control technology, low emission technology, or energy efficient technology. As many of these environmental technologies originate in the industrialized world but must be implemented in the developing world in order to achieve global environmental goals, such technology must be transferred from the North to the South. It is this phenomenon that has historically dominated the discussion of technology transfer in the global environmental governance literature, although the concepts of "South–South" and even "South–North" technology transfer are gaining interest with the rise of the emerging economies and their increasingly prominent role in environmental technology development and deployment (see **Emerging countries**).

Technology transfer is closely tied to the concept of "technology leapfrogging," or the skipping of some generations of technology or stages of development. The concept has particular resonance in the area of climate change mitigation, suggesting that developing countries might be able to follow more sustainable, low carbon development pathways and avoid the more emissions-intensive stages of development that were previously experienced by industrialized nations. Low carbon technology transfer is thus a key focus of global climate mitigation efforts and related research (Rai and Funkhouser 2015; Kirchherr and Urban 2018).

Technology transfers may be facilitated by the efforts of government, international organizations, research institutes, or **business and corporations**, and can occur through many different models, including technology licensing, mergers and acquisitions, joint development, and foreign direct investment. Barriers to the transfer of environmental technologies have been documented across multiple industries and technologies. Cases have demonstrated that the transfer of technology without supplemental "know-how" or tacit knowledge may detract from the lasting **effectiveness** of the technology transfer, and that "absorptive capacity," or the ability to adopt, manage, and develop new technologies, is an important indicator of the technology recipient's ability to fully implement an effective technology transfer (IPCC 2000).

The role of intellectual property protections in facilitating or inhibiting technology transfers has been examined extensively. There is some evidence that stronger protection in developing countries facilitates technology transfer from industrialized countries through exports, foreign direct investment, and licensing by limiting the risk for foreign firms of intellectual property theft or imitation (Hall and Helmers 2010). The high costs of accessing intellectual property have been demonstrated to obstruct technology transfer in some cases, including when technology is still in pre-commercial stages and the initial investor has not yet recovered the initial research and development investments. In other cases, however, intellectual property rights have not served as a significant barrier to technology transfer (Lewis 2013).

Almost all multilateral environmental agreements (MEAs) contain some provision to facilitate technology transfer to developing countries in order to assist them in meeting their obligations. For example, technology transfer is encouraged by the **climate change regime**, the **hazardous wastes regime**, the **ozone regime**, and the **biodiversity regime**, and is a key aim of the **Global Environment Facility (GEF)**. Due to differences in treaty objectives and the types of technologies involved, there is no universal framework for the transfer of environmental technologies under MEAs. While most agreements provide for developed countries to make some effort to promote the transfer of technology to developing countries, in most cases the specific obligations are rather vague, making **compliance and implementation** challenging (Shepherd 2007).

Perhaps the most successful technology transfer mechanism to date was the one created by the parties to the Montreal Protocol to assist developing countries in phasing out their use of ozone-depleting substances (see **Ozone regime**). A Multilateral Fund, managed by both developed and developing countries and funded by contributions from developed countries, was created to finance the implementation of developing countries' obligations to phase-out their use of ozone-depleting substances on an agreed schedule. While much of the successful technology transfer under the Montreal Protocol was directed at industrial conversion projects, it has also supported a variety of technical assistance, training, and capacity building activities.

The **climate change regime** has taken a different approach to technology transfer from that of the Montreal Protocol, primarily due to the complexity of the climate challenge, the wide range of technologies needed for mitigation, and the enormous costs involved. Many years of technology transfer negotiations produced a Technology Mechanism, strengthened in the Technology Framework of the Paris Agreement. The climate change regime involves a wide variety of activities that may facilitate technology transfer, primarily by linking actors across countries and regions from the public and private sectors, and facilitating training, capacity building, and international **partnerships**.

While climate change presents perhaps the largest opportunity for environmental technology transfer to date, the scale of the low carbon transformation required stretches the limits of existing frameworks and systems for understanding and facilitating such transfers.

References

Hall, Bronwyn H. and Christian Helmers. 2010. *The Role of Patent Protection in (Clean/Green) Technology Transfer.* Working Paper 16323. Washington, DC, National Bureau of Economic Research.

Intergovernmental Panel on Climate Change (IPCC). 2000. *Methodological and Technological Issues in Technology Transfer.* Bert Metz, Ogunlade R. Davidson, Jan-Willem Martens, Sascha N.M. van Rooijen, and Laura Van Wie McGrory (Eds.). Cambridge, Cambridge University Press.

Kirchherr, Julian, and Frauke Urban. 2018. "Technology Transfer and Cooperation for Low Carbon Energy Technology: Analysing 30 Years of Scholarship and Proposing a Research Agenda." *Energy Policy* 119(C): 600–609.

Lewis, Joanna I. 2013. *Green Innovation in China: China's Wind Power Industry and the Global Transition to a Low-Carbon Economy.* New York, Columbia University Press.

Rai, Varun and Erik Funkhouser. 2015. "Emerging Insights on the Dynamic Drivers of International Low-Carbon Technology Transfer." *Renewable and Sustainable Energy Reviews* 49: 350–364.

Shepherd, James. 2007. "The Future of Technology Transfer Under Multilateral Environmental Agreements." *Environmental Law Reporter* 37(7): 10547–10561.

THERMOECONOMICS

Kozo Mayumi

University of Tokushima, Japan

Thermoeconomics usually refers to applying thermodynamics to engineering or socioeconomic systems with the aim of improving energy efficiency and of reducing economic cost. The concept has been used in global environmental governance because thermoeconomics at the global scale covers, not only the thermodynamic application to these systems, but also the material circulation aspects of **ecosystem services** including mineral resources that maintain **sustainable development**. Frederick Soddy was one of the first to use thermodynamic analysis for global governance to distinguish biophysical wealth (available energy) from monetary wealth (Soddy 1926). Nicholas Georgescu-Roegen (1971) extended Soddy's work by placing the entropy law at center stage of the economic process. Entropy is a general index of unavailable energy. Available energy is irrevocably transformed into unavailable energy: after burning oil, it is impossible to recover the dissipated energy. Georgescu-Roegen claimed that energy shortage and scarcity of mineral resources ultimately limit human survival (see also **Carrying capacities paradigm**). Factors such as the oil shocks of the 1970s, concern about peak oil, and climate change have triggered scientific investigations and theories about how to tackle entropy and material circulation for sustainability. To make quantitative **assessments** of energy quality on a global **scale**, Charlie Hall (Hall et al. 1986) proposed the energy return on investment (EROI) concept that was originally designed as surplus energy by Fred Cottrell (Cottrell 1955). EROI is the ratio of energy produced from an energy-gathering activity to the energy used in that process. It indicates whether a fuel is a net energy gainer or loser.

On the other hand, industrial ecology, a branch of thermodynamics for global scale, initiated by Ayres and Kneese (1969), emphasizes the importance of the first law of thermodynamics (conservation of energy and matter) in the economic process. On a global level, industrial ecology is the study of material and energy flows through a network of industrial systems. One important question of how the Earth as a whole has been functioning was investigated by Atsushi Tsuchida (Tsuchida and Murota 1987, see **Gaia theory**). The Earth is an open system with respect to energy but is closed materially, so it would be useful to describe a mechanism by which the Earth could discard dissipated energy due to various activities including economic ones into outer space. According to Tsuchida, the Earth can be regarded as a big thermal engine powered by the temperature difference between the sun and outer space. Water in a vapor form is much lighter than air; therefore our planet could effectively discard dissipated thermal energy into outer space through water and air circulating systems. Yet global climate change is a threat to this important mechanism.

At least five practical problems appear when applying thermoeconomics in practice. First, a thermodynamic consideration per se does not necessarily produce useful scientific information. For example, *exergy* (maximum obtainable mechanical work) cannot be used as a benchmark value for practical purposes because environmental conditions are continuously changing and the system in question moves among those various environmental conditions. Second, EROI by itself is not enough to judge the virtues or vices of particular fuels or energy sources because, as Georgescu-Roegen emphasized, the roles of mineral resources and energy must be simultaneously incorporated into thermoeconomics. Third, industrial systems need different forms of energy carriers such as fuels, process heat, and electricity (or biomass for rural society), depending on where these industrial systems are situated. Fourth, energy efficiency is an important consideration for thermodynamic systems, but improving energy efficiency does not necessarily lead to a reduction in the total amount of energy carriers used for socioeconomic systems (Jevons paradox). Fifth, the material circulation aspect of ecology (closing circle concept) proposed by Barry Commoner (1971) is not fully reached for industrial ecology. Actually, the current bandwagon of circular economy (see also **Green economy**) supported by the United Nations and the European Union misunderstands and overlooks the role of natural processes and the biosphere in recycling materials used by the economy (Mayumi and Giampietro 2019).

References

Ayres, Robert U. and Allen V. Kneese. 1969. "Production, Consumption, and Externalities." *The American Economic Review* 59(3), 282–297.

Commoner, Barry. 1971. *The Closing Circle*. New York, Alfred A. Knopf.

Cottrell, Fred. 1955. *Energy and Society*. Westport, CT, Greenwood Press.

Georgescu-Roegen, Nicholas. 1971. *The Entropy Law and the Economic Process*. Cambridge, MA, Harvard University Press.

Hall, Charles A., Cutler J. Cleveland, and Robert Kaufmann. 1986. *Energy and Resource Quality: The Ecology of the Economic Process*. New York, John Wiley.

Mayumi, Kozo and Mario Giampietro. 2019. "Reconsidering 'Circular Economy' in Terms of Irreversible Evolution of Economic Activity and Interplay between Technosphere and Biosphere." *Romanian Journal of Economic Forecasting* 22(2): 196–206.

Soddy, Frederick. 1926. *Wealth, Virtual Wealth and Debt*. London, George Allen and Unwin Ltd.

Tsuchida, Atsushi and Takeshi Murota. 1987. "Fundamentals in the Entropy Theory of Ecocycle and Human Economy." In *Environmental Economics: The Analysis of a Major Interface*, Eds. G. Pillet and T. Murota, 11–35. Geneva, R. Leimgruber.

TRAGEDY OF THE COMMONS

Thomas Falk

International Crops Research Institute for the Semi-Arid Tropics, India

Björn Vollan

University of Marburg, Germany

Michael Kirk

University of Marburg, Germany

The "tragedy of the commons" is a social dilemma arising from a situation in which members of a group make independent rational decisions that lead to the depletion of a resource, even though this will eventually result in a welfare loss for every group member. Garrett Hardin (1968) stimulated this discussion by emphasizing the increasing pressure on natural resources, expressing doubts that technology will solve their management challenges. To shape his arguments he introduced the parable of a pasture jointly used by a group of herders implicitly assuming the absence of any coordination between the users. Each individual herder of the group will receive all of the profits from his or her own animals. Simultaneously, the negative consequences of pasture degradation caused by the animals will be shared by all group members. With too many cows on the pasture competing for fodder, the animals will give less milk, lose weight, and the ecosystem will be disturbed. Thus, each add-itional cow causes harm to other herders. The rational herder concludes that the only sensible course to pursue is to add another animal to his or her herd—and another, and another. This is the conclusion reached by each herder resulting in an overexploitation of the resource. Therein is the tragedy of the commons (Hardin 1968). Hardin's example of a social dilemma can be applied to various common pool resources such as fisheries or forests, as well as to the problem of maintaining and con-tributing to **global public goods** such as clean air (see **Fisheries governance**).

Ostrom (1990) defines common pool resources as resource systems marked by (1) high costs of exclusion and (2) the subtractability of resource use. Difficulties to exclude emerge for instance in the case of large-scale resources with undefined borders and mobile resource units, such as the atmosphere or the sea. The degree of subtractability describes how strongly one person's resource use affects other people's ability to use the resource. The difference between a common pool resource (e.g. a pasture) and a public good (e.g. the atmosphere) is that public goods can be enjoyed by everyone without decreasing the utility of other users (low subtractability of resource use).

The main criticism of Hardin's argumentation refers to equating the commons with a situation of open access management. Open access describes a management system where no property rights are assigned and no institutions regulate relations between users (Gordon 1954). Open access is, however, a rare case in reality. Many common pool resources are managed as common property regimes that give owner-ship over resources to a user group. It is important to note that common pool resources can be owned by individuals, a group of people (common property), or the government. Part of the confusion around the commons emerges from the ambiguous use of the term as it is sometimes used for common pool resources and sometimes for common property.

Hardin's misinterpretation led to the conclusion that all commons under scarcity will inevitably be overused unless the state controls resource use or private property rights are assigned to them. In the first case, complete and bundled property rights are supposed to be assigned to a powerful state that effectively regulates resource use (Hardin 1968;

Ophuls 1973). In the second case, farmers hold individual rights on the pasture and through **markets** the use rights are distributed to the most productive farmers while the others are compensated. The exclusive use rights provide incentives for the farmers to maintain the productive capacity of the pasture over time.

While markets and state coordination can in many situations be appropriate mechanisms, Nobel laureate Elinor Ostrom argued that in many cases users of common pool resources can avoid its overexploitation on the basis of self-organization (Ostrom 1990). Under self-organization and common property regimes as the third governance alternative, a group of people hold rights of use in a resource system and effectively exclude non-group members, thereby preventing the tragedy of the commons and allowing the capture of future benefit streams to the collective. Formal and informal institutions such as bylaws or customary community norms regulate each member's resource use even though no individual rights to particular resource units are usually given to group members.

It is possible to find examples of both success or failure of state, private, and common property regimes (Ostrom 1990). Ostrom (2007) highlighted that no governance regime is per se superior to the other and that there are no panaceas to prevent the tragedy of the commons. The coordination mechanism needs to fit to the context. In the case of common pool resources, high costs of exclusion make it difficult to assign private property rights to related benefits which is a precondition for a good functioning of **markets**. State monitoring and enforcement of management regulations is costly too. Especially in cases of common pool resources of moderate scale, self-organization or common property regimes have often advantages.

Common property regimes have mainly been studied on the local **scale** and there is skepticism of the degree to which experiences can be applied to **global public goods** (Berkes 2006). One approach is to treat nations as unitary actors. Similar to local level self-organization, agreements such as **CITES** are reached on the basis of informal strategies such as subtle social sanctions for achieving **compliance and implementation** (Dietz et al. 2003). On the basis of such global agreements, national **sovereign** governments apply state mechanisms to govern global commons. Increasingly, also market-based instruments such as **REDD+** or other **payments for ecosystem services** are applied. It is important to take an undogmatic view which acknowledges the advantages of different coordination mechanisms, allowing the solutions that best fit the specific context to be found.

References

Berkes, Fikret. 2006. "From Community-Based Resource Management to Complex Systems: The Scale Issue and Marine Commons." *Ecology and Society* 11(1): 45.

Dietz, Thomas, Elinor Ostrom, and Paul C. Stern. 2003. "The Struggle to Govern the Commons." *Science* 302(5652): 1907–1912.

Gordon, Scott H. 1954. "The Economic Theory of a Common-Property Resource: The Fishery." *The Journal of Political Economy* 62(2): 124–142.

Hardin, Garrett. 1968. "The Tragedy of the Commons." *Science* 162: 1243–1248.

Ophuls, William. 1973. "Leviathan or Oblivion?" In *Toward a Steady-State Economy*, Ed. Herman E. Daly, 215–230. San Francisco, CA, Freeman & Company.

Ostrom, Elinor. 1990. *Governing the Commons—The Evolution of Institutions for Collective Action.* Cambridge, Cambridge University Press.

Ostrom, Elinor. 2007. "A Diagnostic Approach for Going beyond Panaceas." *Proceedings of the National Academy of Science* 104(39): 15181–15187.

TRANSBOUNDARY AIR POLLUTION REGIME

Delphine Misonne

Université Saint-Louis – Bruxelles, Belgium

Air pollution means the introduction by humans, directly or indirectly, of substances or energy into the air resulting in deleterious effects of such a nature as to endanger human health, harm living resources, ecosystems, and material property, and impair or interfere with amenities and other legitimate uses of the environment (Geneva Convention on Long-Range Transboundary Air Pollution (CLRTAP), art.1). Because air pollution knows no borders and because it has impacts and causes far away from its physical origin, answers need to embrace a transboundary dimension.

One would expect a global comprehensive **regime** on air pollution, including on its transboundary dimension, but there is none today, except for the significant role the World Health Organization plays, with its indicative guidelines on ambient air pollution, in influencing debates and policies across the world.

For historical reasons, there is a disconnect between the worldwide **climate change regime** and regional transboundary air pollution regimes, while both concern emissions into the atmosphere, often by the same sources of pollution (industry, vehicles, housing, agriculture). Such divide impacts the choice of instruments (**markets**' mechanisms vs. emissions and concentration standards), the definition of governing principles (no **common but differentiated responsibilities** in transboundary air quality regimes), and the type and distribution of obligations.

The transboundary impact of air pollution (on forests, on agriculture, on people) was first addressed in a landmark arbitration case between Canada and the United States (Trail Smelter, 1949), which provided the foundation of today's customary no-harm principle, according to which states are responsible, notwithstanding their **sovereignty** over their own resources, to ensure that activities within their jurisdiction or control do not cause damage to the environment of other states or of areas beyond the limits of national jurisdiction.

In 1979, the need to combat acid rain (Palmer 2017) forced the adoption of the CLRTAP. That convention gathered together fifty-one parties, all located in the United Nations Economic Commission for Europe region, around the need to install cooperation mechanisms and to share knowledge (Wettestad 2002). The Convention was meant as a dynamic framework. It led to the adoption of eight protocols and played a major role in efforts to reduce acidification, photochemical smog, ground-level ozone, and eutrophication (Byrne 2015), but significant challenges remain. Among its core policy concepts are the "critical load" concept, addressing the **carrying capacity** of ecosystems and the "national emissions ceiling" concept, fixing the maximum amount of a substance expressed in kilotons that may be emitted from a party in a calendar year. Discretion left to national public authorities did not ease **compliance and implementation**.

Regional action on transboundary air pollution also exists in other parts of the world, such as in South Asia, where an Agreement on Transboundary Haze Pollution was adopted in 2002 (see **Regional governance**).

Fundamentally, air pollution is a sensitive stake. On the one hand, states tend to resist the adoption of strict rules that could impact their sovereignty and industrial activity. On the other hand, air quality is a matter of health protection, fundamental rights, and environmental equity, and a transboundary and intercontinental (Yamineva and Romppanen 2017) approach is necessary in a world of industrial competition and trade globalization. So far, current regimes are still insufficient and poorly implemented. But times are changing due to the pressure of citizen movements and the rise of public interest **litigation**, which make the recognition of a fundamental right to clean air a core claim.

References

Byrne, Adam. 2015. "The 1979 Convention on Long-Range Transboundary Air Pollution: Assessing its Effectiveness in a Multilateral Environmental Regime after 35 Years." *Transnational Environmental Law* 4(1): 37–67.

Palmer, Paul. 2017. *The Atmosphere: A Very Short Introduction*. Oxford, Oxford University Press.

Wettestad, Jørgen, 2002. *Clearing the Air: European Advances in Tackling Acid Rain and Atmospheric Pollution*. Aldershot, Ashgate.

Yamineva, Yulia and Seita Romppanen. 2017. "Is Law Failing to Address Air Pollution? Reflections on International and EU Developments." *Review of European, Comparative and International Environmental Law* 26(3): 189–200.

TRANSBOUNDARY WATER REGIME

Shlomi Dinar

Florida International University, United States

Pundits, policymakers, and prominent international figures have long prophesied that the next war will likely be over water. Water is not only necessary for all of humanity's needs, but is becoming increasingly scarce, is unequally distributed, and is often transboundary in nature. Transboundary fresh water refers to water bodies such as lakes and rivers that are shared between two or more states thus making conflict over the allocation or management of the resource possible (see **Scarcity and conflicts**). While there have been a number of militarized disputes over shared water resources, the last war over water took place 4,500 years ago between the city-states of Lagash and Umma in modern day Iraq over the Tigris River (Wolf and Hamner 2000).

The more impressive history regarding international hydro-politics is that of cooperation in the form of international water agreements (see **Regional governance**). This is not to suggest that the past is devoid of instances of non-violent conflict over water. Examples abound of political disputes from Europe (e.g. Rhine Basin) to Asia (e.g. Indus Basin) over pollution and unilateral dam projects, respectively. Nor does the impressive record of agreements suggest that cooperation has been without incident or perhaps even taken other forms, less formalized or conventional. Scholars have pointed to inequity and strategic maneuvering enabled by power differentials (Zeitoun and Warner 2006) while other researchers have highlighted alternative forms of coordination and water governance such as networks of professionals, social movements, and international legal principles (Conca 2005). Some scholars have pointed to nuance related to the efficacy of treaties or have casted overall doubt on a treaty's ability to improve water relations among states (Bernauer and Kalbhenn 2010). Still, the sheer number of interstate agreements (more than 400 since 1820) is impressive and the cooperation these treaties engender (governing issues such as flood control and hydroelectric production) is noteworthy, suggesting that the characteristics that explain conflict over water may also explain interstate cooperation.

The hydro-politics literature is rich with case studies. Too numerous to mention here, they have covered almost every region and major river basin in the world (e.g. Elhance 1999). More recently, large-n (or quantitative) studies have proliferated. Many of these published works have utilized the theories developed in the aforementioned case-study literature to examine hypotheses allowing for more generalizable inferences. Water scarcity, for example, has been identified as an important variable. Scholars studying conflict have uncovered some inconclusive results regarding scarcity and militarized conflicts between states yet have found some evidence to suggest that countries with low average rainfall are at more risk of interstate conflict (Gleditsch et al. 2006). Those studying cooperation have found more conclusive results suggesting that increased water scarcity motivates formalized international cooperation (Tir and Ackerman 2009). Still, very high scarcity levels (and very low scarcity levels) lead to decreased instances of cooperation (Dinar et al. 2011). Other sociopolitical, economic, and geographic variables have also been examined in these quantitative studies (see Dinar et al. 2013 for a survey of many of these works).

Given the effects of climate change on international rivers, researchers have turned to investigating the impact of water variability, floods, and droughts (see **Disasters**). Some have argued that such environmental effects will have adverse social consequences (Chellaney 2011). Yet others have focused on the ability of river basin states to adapt to the effects of climate change by considering the treaties governing the basin and their make-up—a measure of institutional capacity (Drieschova et al. 2008). In fact, since institutions could potentially play an important role in mitigating conflict and enhancing cooperation, research on water **treaty design** has explored a variety of water treaty mechanisms including side-payment and issue-linkage stipulations as well as enforceability, information sharing, and monitoring instruments, among others (Dinar et al. 2015; Mitchell and Zawahri 2015). Most recently scholars have also explored how context (in this particular case, the number of treaty signatories) impacts treaty design and the extent of treaties (Dinar et al. 2019).

References

Bernauer, Thomas and Anna Kalbhenn. 2010. "The Politics of International Freshwater Resources." In *The International Studies Encyclopedia*, Eds. Robert A. Denemark and Renée Marlin-Bennett, 5800–5821. Malden, MA, Wiley-Blackwell.

Chellaney, Brahma. 2011. *Water: Asia's New Battleground*. Washington, DC, Georgetown University Press.

Conca, Ken. 2005. *Governing Water: Contentious Transnational Politics and Global Institution Building*. Cambridge, MA, MIT Press.

Dinar, Ariel, Shlomi Dinar, Stephen McCaffrey, and Daene McKinney. 2013. *Bridges over Water: Understanding Transboundary Water Conflict, Negotiation, and Cooperation*. Singapore, World Scientific.

Dinar, Ariel, Lucia De Stefano, Getachew Nigatu, and Neda Zawahri. 2019. "Why Are There So Few Basin-Wide Treaties? Economics and Politics of Coalition Formation in Multilateral International River Basins." *Water International* 44(4): 463–485.

Dinar, Shlomi, Ariel Dinar, and Pradeep Kurukulasuriya. 2011. "Scarcity and Cooperation along International Rivers." *International Studies Quarterly* 55(3): 809–833.

Dinar, Shlomi, David Katz, Lucia De Stefano and Brian Blankespoor. 2015. "Climate Change, Conflict and Cooperation: Global Analysis of the Effectiveness of International River Treaties in Addressing Water Variability." *Political Geography* 45: 55–66.

Drieschova, Alena, Mark Giordano, and Itay Fischhendler. 2008. "Governance Mechanisms to Address Flow Variability in Water Treaties." *Global Environmental Change* 18(2): 285–295.

Elhance, Arun. 1999. *Hydropolitics in the 3rd World: Conflict and Cooperation in International River Basins*. Washington, DC, United States Institute of Peace Press.

Gleditsch, Nils Petter, Kathryn Furlong, Håvard Hegre, Bethany Lacina, and Taylor Owen. 2006. "Conflict over Shared Rivers: Resource Scarcity or Fuzzy Boundaries." *Political Geography* 25(4): 361–382.

Mitchell, Sara and Neda Zawahri. 2015. "The Effectiveness of Treaty Design in Addressing Water Disputes." *Journal of Peace Research* 52(2): 187–200.

Tir, Jaroslav and John Ackerman. 2009. "Politics of Formalized River Cooperation." *Journal of Peace Research* 46(5): 623–640.

Wolf, Aaron and Jesse Hamner. 2000. "Trends in Transboundary Water Disputes and Dispute Resolution." In *Water for Peace in the Middle East and Southern Africa*, Ed. Green Cross International, 55–66. Geneva, Green Cross International.

Zeitoun, Mark and Jerown Warner. 2006. "Hydro-hegemony: A Framework of Analysis of Transboundary Water Conflicts." *Water Policy* 8(5): 435–460.

TRANSGOVERNMENTAL NETWORKS

Harriet Bulkeley

Durham University, United Kingdom

As the study of global environmental governance has moved beyond a focus on **regimes** scholars have sought to understand the alternative ways in which governance is undertaken and coordinated transnationally. Transnational governance is undertaken not only through **private regimes** and **partnerships** of **business and corporations** and **nongovernmental organizations**, but also through networks of state-based actors that operate transnationally—transgovernmental networks.

Although work on transnational networks began to be explored in the 1990s, it has only been over the past decade that it has grown to be a major theme within the study of global environmental governance (GEG). This research has found that traditional transgovernmental networks consisting of interactions between national level state authorities have limited reach in this domain. Bäckstrand (2008: 91) finds that transgovernmental networks gathering the specialized agencies of national governments in the climate change domain were "represented by voluntary agreements between governments involving cooperation for clean technology, renewable energy, clean coal and carbon sequestration" (see **Climate change regime**). Analysis by Bulkeley et al. (2014) also found such networks were relatively rare in the transnational climate governance arena. This suggests that, at least in the climate change domain, such networks of nation-state-based actors are either to be found only in regimes or that transgovernmental networks of this type are relatively rare, with collaboration usually involving other non-state actors and generating a more heterodox landscape of transnational governance.

While originally developed to analyze national level governmental agencies and their transboundary activities, the term "transgovernmental" can also be applied to those networks that have been formed between subnational state-based agencies (Bäckstrand 2008) (see **Scale**). Since the early 1990s, researchers have documented a growing number of transnational networks organized by and orchestrated through subnational tiers of government—regions and municipalities—that have mobilized in response to climate change (see **Cities** and **Regional governance**) (Betsill and Bulkeley 2006; Kern and Bulkeley 2009). Such transgovernmental networks are regarded as important in mobilizing subnational responses because they have provided a sense of collective purpose, political support, access to knowledge, and the sharing of best practice. In some cases, transgovernmental networks have also offered a means through which specific policies and tools are developed and deployed, and access to financial resources secured. During the past two decades, the number of such networks has grown and their membership has diversified. At the same time, networks have sought to distinguish themselves from one another while also coordinating their actions. The result is a complex "ecology" of transgovernmental networks at work within and between cities and regions. While these networks have predominantly emerged in the climate change domain, the broad way in which climate change is approached has meant that a number of urban development challenges—from poverty and development to air pollution, transportation, and energy security—are now being governed not only locally and nationally, but transnationally through the work of transgovernmental networks.

In the climate change domain transgovernmental activity is therefore often the result of cooperation between local and subnational governments and not necessarily arising from cooperation between nation-states. This form of transnational governance appears to be on the decline as alternative private and hybrid forms proliferate. In their comprehensive analysis, Roger et al. (2017) find that while transgovernmental arrangements dominated the transnational governance of climate change until 1998, since that time their role has been reduced such that they now make up only 14% of the total of transnational governance arrangements. Although transnational governance has yet to be developed to the same extent in other issue areas of environmental governance, the trend appears to point in the same direction with new initiatives and governance arrangements most often involving either networks of subnational and local actors or the participation of private and civil society organizations. The role and power of transgovernmental networks in environmental politics seems to be on the wane.

References

Bäckstrand, Karin. 2008. "Accountability of Networked Climate Governance: The Rise of Transnational Climate Partnerships." *Global Environmental Politics* 8(3): 74–102.

Betsill, Michele M. and Harriet Bulkeley. 2006. "Cities and the Multilevel Governance of Global Climate Change." *Global Governance* 12(2): 141–159.

Bulkeley Harriet, Liliana Andonova, Michele M. Betsill, Daniel Compagnon, Thomas Hale, Matthew Hoffmann, Peter Newell, Matthew Paterson, Charles Roger, and Stacy VanDeveer. 2014. *Transnational Climate Change Governance.* New York, Cambridge University Press.

Kern, Kristin and Harriet Bulkeley. 2009. "Cities, Europeanization and Multilevel Governance: Governing Climate Change through Transnational Municipal Networks." *Journal of Common Market Studies* 47(2): 309–332.

Roger, Charles, Thomas Hale, and Liliana Andonova. 2017. "The Comparative Politics of Transnational Climate Governance." *International Interactions* 43(1): 1–25.

TRANSNATIONAL CRIME

Lorraine Elliott

Australian National University, Australia

Transnational environmental crime (TEC)—one of the fastest growing areas of cross-border criminal enterprise—is the knowing violation of international prohibition or regulation **regimes** or of national criminal law by individuals, private actors, and sometimes by public entities for illegal gain. It includes the trafficking of illegally logged timber, the smuggling of endangered species, the black market in ozone-depleting substances, the transboundary dumping of toxic and hazardous waste, and the illegal exploitation of marine living resources (see Nellemann 2016; Elliott and Schaedla 2016). Criminal actors have also been attracted to the potential for fraudulent gains in carbon markets (see **Sustainable finance**) (Gibbs and Cassidy 2016). These crimes are serious because of their environmental consequences, because of their various links with violence, corruption, and a range of cross-over crimes such as money-laundering, and because they undermine the rule of law and good governance at local, national, and global levels (Elliott 2012).

TEC challenges conventional assumptions that criminal activity is managed through hierarchical cartels and mafia-type organizations. Rather, those engaged in this clandestine sphere rely on the operational advantages offered by network structures: that they are flexible, decentralized, "highly resistant to decapitation and more difficult to contain" (Williams 2001: 73). TEC involves commodity-specific smuggling networks, criminal groups involved in other forms of illegal activity, and, in some cases, politically motivated organizations such as militia groups for whom TEC generates illicit income. For example, timber illegally logged in the Congo Basin, sometimes with militia involvement, is transported via Burundi, Rwanda, and Uganda to the EU, the Middle East, China, and other Asian countries with support from financiers in the US (Nellemann 2012: 6).

The global governance complex (see **Institutional interactions**, **Polycentricity** and **Scale**) for TEC constitutes a form of multilevel governance, characterized by effort across multiple national, regional, and international agencies and sites of authority. No international treaty specifically prevents, suppresses, or punishes the kinds of trafficking and smuggling that constitute TEC. Existing transnational crime agreements such as the 2000 UN Convention against Transnational Organized Crime and the 2003 UN Convention against Corruption pay little attention to environmental crime. Key multilateral environmental agreements (MEAs) such as **CITES**, the **ozone regime**, and the **hazardous wastes regime** were designed to strengthen environmental protection, not to address transnational crime.

Parties to these various MEAs have nevertheless moved to take illegal trade and associated criminal activity more seriously. Agencies such as the World Customs Organization (WCO), INTERPOL, and the UN Office on Drugs and Crime (UNODC) have made TEC more prominent in their individual agendas, responding to a key global governance principle that "networked threats [such as TEC] require a networked response" (Slaughter 2004: 160). However, this proposition is yet to be tested fully with respect to TEC. In pursuit of effective policy and operational responses, governments and other actors have adopted regional arrangements such as wildlife enforcement networks (see **Regional governance**) and formal and informal **partnerships** between MEA **secretariats** and international organizations. The

International Consortium on Combating Wildlife Crime is one such example, established in 2010 as a collaborative effort between CITES, INTERPOL, the WCO, the **World Bank**, and UNODC to support national and regional wildlife and illegal logging enforcement efforts. TEC also offers an empirical lens on the role of **nongovernmental organizations** and a conceptual lens on forms of agency beyond the state. NGO participation in coordination and knowledge network arrangements with governments and intergovernmental organizations extends the boundaries of relevant **epistemic communities**. Their work in coordinating undercover operations and intelligence gathering of the kind usually taken to be the responsibility of governments (see Environmental Investigation Agency 2019, for example) further challenges assumptions about global (environmental) governance as the primary preserve of states.

References

Elliott, Lorraine. 2012. "Fighting Transnational Environmental Crime." *Journal of International Affairs* 66(1): 87–104.

Elliott, Lorraine and William H. Schaedla (Eds.). 2016. *Handbook of Transnational Environmental Crime*. Cheltenham, Edward Elgar Publishing.

Environmental Investigation Agency. 2019. *Running Out of Time: Wildlife Crime Justice Failures in Vietnam*. London, Environmental Investigation Agency.

Gibbs, Carole and Michael Cassidy. 2016. "Crimes in the Carbon Market." In *Handbook of Transnational Environmental Crime*, Eds. Lorraine Elliott and William H. Schaedla, 235–254. Cheltenham, Edward Elgar Publishing.

Nellemann, Christian (Ed.). 2012. *Green Carbon, Black Trade: Illegal Logging, Tax Fraud and Laundering in the World's Tropical Forests, a Rapid Response Assessment*. Arendal, Norway, UNEP, GRID-Arendal.

Nellemann, Christian (Ed. in Chief). 2016. *The Rise of Environmental Crime: A Growing Threat to Natural Resources Peace, Development and Security*. Nairobi, United Nations Environment Programme and RHIPTO Rapid Response–Norwegian Center for Global Analyses.

Slaughter, Anne-Marie. 2004. "Disaggregated Sovereignty: Towards the Public Accountability of Global Government Networks." *Government and Opposition* 39(2): 159–190.

Williams, Phil. 2001. "Organizing Transnational Crime: Networks, Markets and Hierarchies." In *Combating Transnational Crime: Concepts, Activities and Responses*, Eds. Phil Williams and Dimitri Vlassis, 57–87. London, Frank Cass.

TRANSPARENCY

Michael Mason

London School of Economics and Political Science, United Kingdom

Right-to-know is a legal principle affording individuals an entitlement to information from governmental authorities and private entities. Mandatory disclosure of information is now a widespread requirement for state actors in democratic political systems, with extensive but selective use in the private sector, notably company **reporting** rules and **labeling** obligations. Right-to-know laws have been adopted by more than eighty countries (see **Policy diffusion**): they are both an alternative and a supplement to other regulatory instruments, and are most apposite where information deficits or asymmetries are related to welfare losses, including environmental degradation. Uptake of right-to-know legislation includes national examples with broad scope, such as in India and South Africa (covering both public and private sector actors), and also more restrictive applications, notably the Chinese freedom of information legislation designed to promote efficient decision-making.

Environmental information may be covered within the general provisions of right-to-know legislation, but environment-specific information access is set out in substantive laws prescribing disclosure about particular pollutants or harmful chemicals. In democratic political systems, right-to-know about toxic chemicals normally means different disclosure responsibilities within and outside the workplace. Pollution inventories or registers are a common institutional embodiment of right-to-know norms, applied to the release and transfer of selected chemicals. These inventories are found both in advanced economies (e.g. US Toxic Release Inventory, Australian National Pollution Inventory) and in **emerging countries** (e.g. Indonesia's Program for Pollution Control, Evaluating and Rating).

The relation between global and domestic transparency practices structures the transnational diffusion of right-to-know (Bauhr and Nasiritousi 2012; Florini and Jairaj 2014) (see **Policy diffusion**). International environmental law contains multilateral obligations which advance transparency between states, notably rights to notification and prior informed consent (PIC) concerning cross-border risk-bearing activities. The global regulation of hazardous chemicals, wastes, and genetically modified organisms (GMOs) has featured frequent clashes between exporting and importing countries over the nature and scope of PIC rules (see **Rotterdam Convention**, **Hazardous wastes**

regime, **Biosafety**, and **Stockholm Convention**). While few multi-lateral environmental agreements vest right-to-know entitlements in natural or legal persons, since the 1990s the European Union has created community-wide citizen rights to (environmental) information against both member states and EU administrative bodies.

According to Ludwig Krämer (2012), the most important legal expression of a transnational right-to-know is contained in the information disclosure provisions of the 1998 Aarhus Convention: the Convention on Access to Information, Public Participation in Decision Making and Access to Justice in Environmental Matters (see also **Participation** and **Environmental justice**). Negotiated under the auspices of the UN Economic Commission for Europe (UNECE), the Aarhus Convention creates public information rights across all convention parties, supported by a relatively strong compliance mechanism (see **Compliance and implementation**). They combine passive (request-based) and active disclosure obligations on public authorities: Parties are accorded discretion in enacting these duties, which has led to discrepancies between states. While the 2003 Kiev Protocol to the convention (on pollutant release and transfer registers) has also created indirect obligations on private owners and operators of polluting facilities, there remains a concern that the treaty is compromised by the absence of a right-to-know entitlement against private sector entities generating major environmental impacts (Mason 2014).

Scholarship on transparency has generated mixed findings on policy impacts: it is more likely to work when transparency is embedded in the decision processes of both disclosers and recipients (Fung et al. 2007; Michener 2019). This creates challenging conditions for broad right-to-know obligations—a burden compounded for access to information on transboundary environmental risks and harm. In a global political economy dominated by market liberal imperatives, environmental transparency is weakened by the propensity of private sector disclosers (e.g. transnational corporations) to oppose any expansion of environmental reporting beyond voluntary measures. This has resulted in what Schleifer et al. (2019: 503) call the "dominance of shallow transparency," detached from meaningful accountability for the negative environmental effects of decision-making.

References

Bauhr, Monika and Naghmeh Nasiritousi. 2012. "Resisting Transparency: Corruption, Legitimacy and the Quality of Global Environmental Politics." *Global Environmental Politics* 12(4): 9–29.

Florini, Ann and Bharath Jairaj. 2014. "The National Context for Transparency-based Global Environmental Governance". In *Transparency in Global Environmental Governance*, Eds. Aarti Gupta and Michael Mason, 61–82. Cambridge, MIT Press.

Fung, Archon, Mary Graham, and David Weil. 2007. *Full Disclosure: The Perils and Promises of Transparency*. New York, Cambridge University Press.

Krämer, Ludwig. 2012. "Transnational Access to Environmental Information." *Transnational Environmental Law* 1(1): 95–104.

Mason, Michael. 2014. "So Far but No Further? Transparency in the Aarhus Convention". In *Transparency in Global Environmental Governance*, Eds. Aarti Gupta and Michael Mason, 83–106. Cambridge, MIT Press.

Michener, Gregory. 2019. "Gauging the Impact of Transparency Policies." *Public Administration Review* 79(1): 136–139.

Schleifer, Philip, Matteo Fiorini, and Graeme Auld. 2019. "Transparency in Transnational Governance: The Determinants of Information Disclosure of Voluntary Sustainability Programs." *Regulation & Governance* 13(4): 488–506.

TREATY DESIGN

Ronald Mitchell

University of Oregon, United States

Once states start to negotiate a treaty to address a shared environmental problem, they face numerous choices about treaty design (see also **Treaty negotiations**). These choices include how to describe the problem and what goals to establish; what states and non-state actors to engage; whether to focus on improving knowledge, regulating existing behaviors, or promoting new behaviors; what processes to establish so the treaty can address changes in knowledge, interests, power, and capabilities; what behavioral and financial obligations to impose; and what strategies to use for monitoring and encouraging behavioral and environmental progress (Bodansky 2010). How states design any given treaty reflects both the choices negotiators make among available alternatives and the influence of structural factors that mean certain choices are either practically or politically unavailable.

Much scholarship investigates treaty design as a dependent variable, asking why treaty design varies. Differences in the characteristics of environmental problems, i.e. their "problem structure," often lead states to find certain solutions particularly attractive and dictate that other solutions are not available or not seriously considered (Mitchell 2006). How states design an environmental treaty depends on how, inter alia, scientific knowledge (see **Science**), levels of concern, incentives for action and inaction, and economic and normative power are distributed across states. States will tend to be satisfied with joint research and information exchanges when faced with newly identified environmental problems but demand more ambitious obligations and stricter enforcement when environmental damage is clear, concern is high, and options for action are many (see **Compliance and implementation**). States will tend to incorporate rewards into treaties addressing upstream/downstream problems (*between* states that cause an environmental harm and states that experience it) and sanctions into those addressing **tragedy of the commons** problems (*among* states that both generate and experience a harm). States may make membership open to any state or may limit it to states within a region, states with interests at stake, or states with strong motivations to act (see **Regional governance**). While problem structure makes certain design choices more likely than others, treaty negotiators always retain leeway in the who, what, when, where, and how of treaty design.

Building on this research, much other scholarship investigates treaty design as an independent variable, asking if treaties with certain designs influence the behavior of states, or particular states, more than those with alternative designs (Miles et al. 2002; Bernauer et al. 2013). Binding treaties that contain specific obligations, regularly monitor state behaviors, and hold states to account through review or sanction are claimed to wield greater influence than those lacking such traits. Others claim that treaties wield greater influence if they contain legitimate processes that produce equitable obligations and strong norms and reflect and redress real differences in states' capabilities. And most scholars recognize that the influence of treaties depends considerably on which and how many states join them and that treaty influence varies significantly across states based on their economic and political characteristics.

References

Bernauer, Thomas, Anna Kalbhenn, Vally Koubi, and Gabrielle Spilker. 2013. "Is There a 'Depth Versus Participation' Dilemma in International Cooperation?" *Review of International Organizations* 8(4): 477–497.

Bodansky, Daniel. 2010. *The Art and Craft of International Environmental Law*. Cambridge, MA, Harvard University Press.

Miles, Edward L., Arild Underdal, Steinar Andresen, Jørgen Wettestad, Jon Birger Skjærseth, and Elaine M. Carlin (Eds.). 2002. *Environmental Regime Effectiveness: Confronting Theory with Evidence*. Cambridge, MA, MIT Press.

Mitchell, Ronald B. 2006. "Problem Structure, Institutional Design, and the Relative Effectiveness of International Environmental Agreements." *Global Environmental Politics* 6(3): 72–89.

Young, Oran R. 2011. "Effectiveness of International Environmental Regimes: Existing Knowledge, Cutting-Edge Themes, and Research Strategies." *Proceedings of the National Academy of Sciences* 108(50): 19853–19860.

TREATY NEGOTIATIONS

Daniel Compagnon

Sciences Po Bordeaux, France

In international relations, the dominant conceptualization of global treaty making is based on rational choice models of international cooperation derived from game theory. They analyze the distribution of gains and costs among participating countries (Barrett 2003), and conditions for attaining an optimal negotiation equilibrium maximizing benefits and minimizing costs of participation. Somehow, they merely corroborate intuitive ideas such that the larger the number of parties the lower the chances to reach an ambitious binding agreement (Barret 2003: 355–356). What was also labeled the "law of the least ambitious program" (Underdal 1980; Hovi and Sprintz 2006) highlights the difficulty to deal with global commons when almost all UN member states are involved, but fails to account for more robust and successful global regimes—such as the **ozone regime**. It is the sheer complexity of global issues such as climate change, and the structure of parties' diverging interests that paralyze negotiations rather than the number of parties as such. However, as the 2015 Paris Agreement illustrates, a pledge and review structure might deliver where other approaches have failed (Keohane and Victor 2016) (see **Treaty design**).

Another approach to treaty making follows an empirical, actor-oriented perspective: it addresses issues, negotiation phases, and negotiators' tactics in the formation and governance of international environmental regimes. Prominent in this field, Chasek's phased process fits multilateral negotiations characterized by a very large number of parties, multiple interlinked issues, and various types of actors located either at the core or at the periphery of the process. These include scientists, **nongovernmental organizations**, economic lobbies (see **Business and corporations**), and the media (Chasek 2001). Ahead and after well-publicized UN conferences, a continuous stream of preparatory committees, specialized working groups, and conference of parties (COPs), not to mention a number of ad hoc meetings, constitutes an ongoing process of negotiation. Thus global regimes are altered, sometimes strengthened through additional protocols to the initial framework convention—a pattern followed for the ozone layer, climate change (see **Climate change regime**), and biodiversity (see **Biodiversity regime**)—as member states' positions evolve, **negotiating coalitions** emerge and disintegrate, and new issues and ideas arise.

In environmental treaty making **epistemic communities** play a crucial role in framing problems and solutions. The leadership of skillful **individuals** such as the **United Nations Environment Programme** executive directors, conference chairs, or even executive secretaries (see **Secretariat**) has often salvaged negotiations from doom. Non-state actors have also gained a growing influence since 1992, not only in agenda setting but also in subsequent negotiation phases (Betsill and Corell 2008). State delegations include non-state actors' representatives to enhance national expertise although the latter have no access to closed-doors meetings (Chasek 2001: 198). Access to negotiations and effective engagement remain difficult for the least developed countries that can hardly cope with so many meetings and complex agendas, and which often lack the relevant expertise and resources.

Behind the bitter diplomatic haggling till the last hour dubbed "negotiation by exhaustion" heralded by the media (see **Summit diplomacy**), there is a more discrete, deliberative dimension, rooted in the logic of arguing, aiming at building a consensus, and facilitated by the penetration of the "empowered spaces" by ideas and actors from the "public spaces" (see **Global deliberative democracy**), also including recurrent interactions within networks of government negotiators (Orsini and Compagnon 2013).

This "network diplomacy" is common in the environmental field but also in trade issues and other areas of "low politics." It differs notably from the traditional "club diplomacy" where a handful of professional diplomats typically decide everything. Through social learning such networks sometimes overcome prevailing deadlocks. Many case studies emphasize the importance of procedural flexibility, personal understanding between negotiators meeting regularly over the years, and ad hoc mechanisms to resolve differences in final bargaining phases, including innovative techniques to promote consensus (Davenport et al. 2012). For example, the chair of the final negotiating session of the **Biosafety** Protocol in Montreal in 2000 used colored teddy bears bought in the subway to draw the order of speech for representatives of negotiating blocks. It eased the tension and allowed the last row of discussion to proceed smoothly, creating a shared world vision, within which arguing over the best solutions is legitimate, in a way that effectively influences policymaking at national level.

References

Barrett, Scott. 2003. *Environment and Statecraft: The Strategy of Environmental Treaty-Making*. Oxford, Oxford University Press.

Betsill, Michelle M. and Elisabeth Corell (Eds.). 2008. *NGO Diplomacy: The Influence of Nongovernmental Organizations in International Environmental Negotiations*. Cambridge, MA, MIT Press.

Chasek, Pamela S. 2001. *Earth Negotiation: Analyzing Thirty Years of Environmental Diplomacy*. Tokyo and New York, United Nations University Press.

Davenport, Deborah, Lynn M. Wagner, and Chris Spence. 2012. "Earth Negotiations on a Comfy Couch: Building Negotiator Trust through Innovative Process." In *The Roads from Rio: Lessons Learned from Twenty Years of Multilateral Environmental Negotiations*, Eds. Pamela S. Chasek and Lynn M. Wagner, 39–58. New York, RFF Press.

Hovi, Jon and Detlef F. Sprinz. 2006. "The Limits of the Law of the Least Ambitious Program." *Global Environmental Politics* 6(3): 28–42.

Keohane, Robert O. and David G. Victor. 2016. "Cooperation and Discord in Global Climate Policy." *Nature Climate Change* 6(6): 570–575.

Orsini, Amandine and Daniel Compagnon. 2013. "From Logics to Procedures: Arguing within International Environmental Negotiations." *Critical Policy Studies* 7(3): 273–291.

Underdal, Arild. 1980. *The Politics of International Fisheries Managements: The Case of the Northeast Atlantic*. New York, Columbia University Press.

UN CONVENTION ON THE LAW OF THE SEA

Tim Stephens
University of Sydney, Australia

The United Nations Convention on the Law of the Sea (UNCLOS) was concluded in 1982 and entered into force in 1994. UNCLOS has been described as the "constitution for the oceans" (Koh 1983; see **Ocean protection**) due to its comprehensive coverage of oceans issues, its "package deal" character in which reservations are impermissible, the hurdles placed in the way of amendment, and its nearly universal membership (168 parties).

UNCLOS demarcates coastal state maritime zones (principally the territorial sea, exclusive economic zone, and continental shelf), sets out the rights and duties of coastal and flag states, codifies high sea freedoms including of fishing and navigation, and creates a new regime for sharing the mineral resources of the deep seabed (Rothwell and Stephens 2016). UNCLOS also has a strong environmental focus, providing a unifying framework for the sustainable use of living and nonliving marine resource and the protection of the marine environment from pollution and other impacts (Charney 1994).

The key elements of UNCLOS that advance its objective of promoting "the protection and preservation of the marine environment" (UNCLOS, Preamble) are found in Part XII. Among other things these provisions limit pollution, require monitoring and **assessment** of damaging activities, promote cooperation on a regional and global basis, and encourage the sharing of technical and scientific expertise with developing states. The **conservation** and management of fisheries is also a major focus of the convention (see **Fisheries governance**), and UNCLOS includes special conservation duties for certain species such as the great whales (see **International Whaling Commission**).

One of the strengths of UNCLOS in addressing marine environmental issues is its "umbrella" character; setting out high level obligations that enable the adoption of more specific rules through other treaties. These include the 1995 Fish Stocks Agreement which improves the governance of shared fisheries, and an instrument on biodiversity beyond national jurisdiction which is currently under development (De Santo et al. 2019). Of special importance have been a large collection of International Maritime Organization (IMO) agreements addressing oil pollution, sea dumping, and a range of other pollution issues.

Through its framework approach, UNCLOS has also provided the legal basis for the implementation of contemporary principles of environmental protection including the ecosystem approach, the **precautionary principle**, and ecologically **sustainable development**. Several international institutions established by UNCLOS have also assisted in this task, with the International Tribunal for the Law of the Sea issuing several influential judgments and advisory opinions on sustainable fishing (ITLOS 2015) and the protection of the deep seabed environment from mining (ITLOS 2011).

References

Charney, Jonathan I. 1994. "The Marine Environment and the 1982 United Nations Convention on the Law of the Sea." *International Lawyer* 28(4): 879–902.

De Santo, Elizabeth M., Áslaug Ásgeirsdóttir, Ana Barros-Platiau, Frank Biermann, John Dryzek, L. R. Gonçalves, Rakhyun E. Kim, Elizabeth Mendenhall, Ronald Mitchell, Elizabeth Nyman, Michelle Scobie, Kai Sun, Rachel Tiller, D. G. Webster, and Oran Young. 2019. "Protecting Biodiversity in Areas Beyond National Jurisdiction: An Earth System Governance Perspective." *Earth System Governance* 2: 1–7.

ITLOS. 2011. Seabed Disputes Chamber in Responsibilities and Obligations of States Sponsoring Persons and Entities with Respect to Activities in the Area. Advisory Opinion of February 1, 2011, 10 ITLOS Rep. 7. https://www.itlos.org/fileadmin/itlos/documents/cases/case_no_17/adv_op_010211.pdf

ITLOS. 2015. Request for an Advisory Opinion Submitted by the Sub-Regional Fisheries Commission (SRFC). Advisory Opinion of April 2, 2015. https://www.itlos.org/cases/list-of-cases/case-no-21/.

Koh, Tommy T. B. 1983. "A Constitution for the Oceans." In *The Law of the Sea: United Nations Convention on the Law of the Sea.* New York, St Martin's Press.

Rothwell, Donald R. and Tim Stephens. 2016. *The International Law of the Sea,* 2nd edition. Hart Publishing, Oxford.

UNITED NATIONS ENVIRONMENT PROGRAMME

Steffen Bauer

German Development Institute, Germany

The United Nations Environment Programme (UNEP), or "UN Environment" as it has also been referred to in recent years, is the most visible and lasting institutional achievement of the 1972 United Nations Conference on the Human Environment. It represents the United Nations' "leading global environmental authority that sets the global environmental agenda, that promotes the coherent **implementation** of the environmental dimension of **sustainable development** within the United Nations system and that serves as an authoritative advocate for the global environment" (UNEP 1997).

Yet, the notion of "environment" arrived late on the United Nations' policy agenda; it occupies limited institutional space within the convoluted United Nations system; and, in spite of growing recognition for a global ecological crisis in the **Anthropocene**, it largely remains an issue of low politics in intergovernmental relations (Bauer 2013). Recent reforms aside, this has hardly changed since UNEP was formally established as a minor UN bureaucracy with a small headquarters in the Kenyan capital Nairobi; that is, remote from the United Nations hubs in New York and Geneva. This notwithstanding, UNEP has come to epitomize international environmental governance and represents "the closest thing there is to an overarching global institution for the environment" (DeSombre 2017).

At the same time, the system of international environmental governance, with UNEP as its designated hub, only "developed in an ad hoc and piecemeal manner" (Urho et al. 2019: 87). Consequently, considerable gaps prevail between the expectations that UNEP finds itself confronted with and its limited capability to help solve the world's manifold ecological crises. Its evolution amid an expanding UN system characterized by persistent North–South quarrelling diminished UNEP's political clout from the outset (Ivanova 2012). Moreover, limiting UNEP's scope to international environmental law and sustainable development, thereby neglecting pertinent links to the United Nations' security and human rights agendas, signifies fundamental flaws in the international framing of environmental challenges (Conca 2015).

Contrasting these structural constraints, UNEP has proved an effective agenda setter and negotiation facilitator in international environmental politics (Bauer 2009). As such it has been instrumental in the genesis of numerous multilateral environmental agreements, notably the Framework Convention on Climate Change and the **Desertification Convention**, and it is technically administering many of these treaties as well as corresponding **treaty negotiations** including, inter alia, the Convention on Biological Diversity, the Vienna Convention for the Protection of the Ozone Layer and its Montreal Protocol, and a host of chemicals and waste-related conventions, prominently including the **Basel**, **Minamata**, **Rotterdam**, and **Stockholm** Conventions, as well as treaties pertaining to specific biodiversity and conservation-related issues and regional seas (see also **Secretariats**, **Climate change regime**, **Biodiversity regime**, and **Ozone regime**).

As the **effectiveness** of the respective international regimes varies considerably, so do scholarly attributions regarding UNEP's contribution to their relative success or failure. Taking UNEP's mandate as a yardstick means to acknowledge that it was originally tasked to provide the international community with leadership and guidance on global and regional environmental matters by (1) assessing and monitoring the state of the environment; (2) serving as a norm-building catalyst for international environmental policy and law; and (3) coordinating all of the United Nations' environmental activities, even as pertinent UN agencies trump UNEP either hierarchically or politically (Bauer 2013). While fulfilling the coordination function has never seemed realistic in the first place, UNEP has been successful on the first two counts: it established itself as both the United Nations' environmental consciousness and as a catalyst for environmental multilateralism. By and large this is achieved by raising awareness of the environmental challenges facing the international community, for example through its flagship *Global Environment Outlook* reports, and by the effective promotion of environmental law at international, regional, and national levels (see **Regional governance** and **Scale**).

To a considerable extent, this is also a function of the bureaucratic authority vested in the UNEP secretariat and the leadership thus exerted (see also **Individuals**). It enables UNEP to act as an efficient knowledge broker at the nexus of **science** and environmental policymaking, and as a negotiation facilitator in complex intergovernmental processes. Accordingly, UNEP's influence is most visible along the cognitive and normative dimensions of international environmental governance (Bauer 2009). Ironically, UNEP's evident success in advancing issue-specific multilateral environmental institutions is counteracted by the concomitant proliferation of separate decision-making bodies; as distinct environmental treaties typically take on a life of their own, UNEP's ineptitude in coordinating environmental governance on a systemic level is only compounded further. Moreover, the proliferation of multilateral environmental agreements has intensified the pace, density, and complexity of UNEP's portfolio while at the same time spreading thin its modest resources.

Recognizing these challenges, the United Nations has resolved to strengthen UNEP as a result of the 2012 United Nations Conference on Sustainable Development ("Rio+20"). Among other steps, it has replaced the exclusive former Governing Council by a United Nations Environment Assembly with universal membership and substantially increased the financial contribution from the UN regular budget (Urho et al. 2019). This falls obviously short of transforming UNEP into a full-fledged specialized agency or **World Environment Organization**, the pros and cons of which have been extensively debated by scholars and practitioners (Biermann and Bauer 2005). Yet, while these steps cannot be expected to curb the more fundamental shortcomings of international environmental governance, they help to raise UNEP's political profile and legitimacy.

Ultimately, the reach of UNEP as a central actor of global environmental governance remains confined by its organizational history in the context of the United Nations systemic complexity and the unresolved structural issues this encompasses, notably along the North–South fault line and underlying issues of equity and justice (see **Environmental justice**). The latter especially reflects the prevailing tension between the prerogative of sovereign states to exploit their national resources on the one hand and their responsibility to consider the global impacts of their corresponding socioeconomic activities within the planet's biophysical boundaries on the other hand (see **Sovereignty**).

References

Bauer, Steffen. 2009. "The Secretariat of the United Nations Environment Programme: Tangled Up In Blue." In *Managers of Global Change: The Influence of International Environmental Bureaucracies*, Eds. Frank Biermann and Bernd Siebenhüner, 169–201. Cambridge, MIT Press.

Bauer, Steffen. 2013. "Strengthening the United Nations". In *The Handbook of Global Climate and Environment Policy*, Ed. Robert Falkner, 320–338. Chichester, Wiley-Blackwell.

Biermann, Frank and Steffen Bauer (Eds.). 2005. *A World Environment Organization: Solution or Threat for Effective International Environmental Governance*. Aldershot, Ashgate.

Conca, Ken. 2015. *An Unfinished Foundation: The United Nations and Global Environmental Governance*. Oxford, Oxford University Press.

DeSombre, Elizabeth R. 2017. *Global Environmental Institutions*, 2nd edition. London, Routledge.

Ivanova, Maria. 2012. "Institutional Design and UNEP Reform: Historical Insights on Form, Function and Financing." *International Affairs* 88(3): 565–584.

UNEP, Governing Council. 1997. *Nairobi Declaration of the Heads of Delegation*. Nairobi, UNEP.

Urho, Niko, Maria Ivanova, Anna Dubrova, and Natalia Escobar-Pemberthy. 2019. *International Environmental Governance: Accomplishments and Way Forward*. Copenhagen, Nordic Council.

WETLANDS CONVENTION

Nick Davidson

Nick Davidson Environmental, United Kingdom
Charles Sturt University, Australia

Royal Gardner

Stetson University, United States

The Convention on Wetlands of International Importance especially as Waterfowl Habitat, known as the Ramsar Convention, is a wetland conservation treaty (see **Conservation and preservation**) with 171 contracting Parties (as at January 2020). Concluded in Ramsar, Iran, in February 1971, it entered into force in December 1975.

As an early multilateral environmental agreement, its obligations are general in nature (Bowman 1995). Each Party commits to delivering three primary duties (often referred to as the three Ramsar pillars) (see **Compliance and implementation**): designation and conservation of at least one wetland site as a Wetland of International Importance (called a Ramsar site); the wise use (sustainable use) of all wetlands within its territory; and international cooperation with respect to wetland matters. The Convention endorses ecosystem approaches to protecting the environment with "wise use" defined as "the maintenance of (their) ecological character, achieved through the implementation of ecosystem approaches, within the context of **sustainable development**."

Ramsar parties meet triennially at a Conference of the Parties (COP), the Convention's primary policymaking body (see **Treaty design**). The COP negotiates and adopts resolutions, traditionally on a consensus basis. It can vote on substantive issues but this has never been invoked. While the consensus-based approach ensures the positive support of the greatest number of Parties, it can also result in watered-down resolutions.

The status of adopted resolutions is regarded differently by Parties. Some, such as the United States, view Ramsar resolutions as aspirational and non-binding (Gardner and Connolly 2007). Others consider resolutions adopted by consensus to have legal effect within their domestic regimes. For example, in a case involving the adequacy of an environmental impact **assessment** for a proposed project in a Ramsar site, the Dutch government affirmed that COP Resolutions unanimously adopted are part of the Netherlands' national obligations and are thus legally enforceable (Verschuuren 2008; Gardner and Davidson 2011).

The Ramsar Convention is formally recognized as a UN treaty. However, its **Secretariat**, which facilitates its day-to-day coordination, is based in Switzerland and hosted by the International Union for the Conservation of Nature (IUCN), which was an early proponent for the creation of the convention. During the **treaty negotiations**, when no Party volunteered to host the secretariat due to the financial implications, the IUCN agreed to do so until the Parties, by a two-thirds majority, selected another organization or government. Some Parties have advocated moving the secretariat under the auspices of the **United Nations Environment Programme**, suggesting that this would give Ramsar a greater profile in their countries. Although COP11 in Bucharest in 2012 reached consensus for IUCN to remain as the institutional host of the secretariat, the issue is likely to be revisited.

The convention lacks a formal enforcement mechanism and its **effectiveness** is difficult to quantify. While Ramsar sites are the largest global network of protected areas (over 2,300 sites covering over 253 million hectares), many are under threat from on-site and off-site actions. More generally, wetlands continue to suffer a high rate of loss and increasingly widespread degradation (Darrah et al. 2019; Davidson et al. 2020). Many Parties report implementing less than half the actions to which they have committed under the convention's Strategic Plan. The situation, however, would likely be worse in the absence of the Convention: those Parties that do implement the Convention through national wetland policies or similar instruments report positive outcomes for wetlands (Gardner and Davidson 2011).

References

Bowman, M.J. 1995. "The Ramsar Convention Comes of Age." *Netherlands International Law Review* 42(1): 1–52.

Darrah, Sarah E., Yara Shennan-Farpón, Jonathan Loh, Nick C. Davidson, C. Max Finlayson, Royal C. Gardner, and Matt J. Walpole. 2019. "Improvements to the Wetland Extent Trends (WET) Index as a Tool for Monitoring Natural and Human-made Wetlands." *Ecological Indicators* 99: 294–298.

Davidson, Nick C., Lars Dinesen, Siobhan Fennessy, Max C. Finlayson, Patrick Grillas, Annia Grobicki, Rob J. McInnes, and David A. Stroud. 2020. "Trends in the Ecological Character of the World's Wetlands." *Marine & Freshwater Research* 71(1): 127–138.

Gardner, Royal C. and Kim Diana Connolly. 2007. "The Ramsar Convention on Wetlands: Assessment of International Designations within the United States." *Environmental Law Reporter* 37(2): 10089–10113.

Gardner, Royal C. and Nick Davidson. 2011. "The Ramsar Convention." In *Wetlands – Integrating Multidisciplinary Concepts*, Ed. Ben A. LePage, 189–203. Dordrecht, Springer.

Verschuuren, Jonathan. 2008. "Ramsar Soft Law is Not Soft at All." *Milieu en Recht* 35(1): 28–34.

WORLD BANK

Susan Park

The University of Sydney, Australia

Created in 1944, the International Bank for Reconstruction and Development (IBRD) or "World Bank," is a multilateral financial institution (see also **Sustainable finance**) lending approximately US$20–30 billion annually to its member states. Bank funds come from member state capital that is "callable" or "paid-in," from international capital markets, and income from interest and loan repayments. Loans are provided for projects such as roads, railways, and dams. From the early 1980s the World Bank began to increase its program loans. Known as structural adjustment loans (SALs, now called policy based loans) these aimed to restructure borrowers' economies based on neoliberal economic tenets.

The World Bank has a weighted voting system based on members' capital, and a formula of basic and proportional votes (a "one dollar, one vote" system). All 188 members are represented and voting is consensual but the World Bank has reacted to the "shareholder activism" of the powerful United States which was driven by pressure from civil society in advocating for environmental and social safeguards, gender equality, project quality, transparency (see **Transparency**), accountability, and reducing poverty.

Pressure from environmentalists has been crucial for the World Bank's incorporation of environmental concerns. The debate focused on whether the Bank can become green or whether it has merely greenwashed its operations. The World Bank initially established an environmental unit in 1970 for a mixture of economic arguments in favor of limiting environmental destruction, political support for environmental policies, and intellectual engagement by the then World Bank President Robert McNamara. Yet the "push" for a comprehensive re-evaluation of the Bank's environmental impacts came from mass environmental campaigns in the 1980s such as the campaign over the Narmada Sadar Sarovar dam in India. This led to an increase in the number of environmentalists on staff and the amount of lending for environmental projects, monitoring and evaluation of environmental safeguards, and a mechanism to ensure that people whose local environment was adversely affected by a World Bank-funded project could seek redress. The World Bank also became an implementing agency to the Global Environment Fund.

Scholars argue that the greening resulted from increased oversight by the Bank's member states and targeted action by Bank management that aligned with the culture and incentive structure of Bank staff (Nielson et al. 2006). Haas and Haas (1995) argued that the World Bank analyzed how environmental concerns fit within its aims through a re-evaluation of its beliefs about cause and effect, resulting in a change of the organization's goals to employ new environmental criteria. They distinguished learning from adaptation, arguing that only the **United Nations Environment Programme** and the Bank were capable of the former. This separated the organization's complex learning from tactical responses to pressure to reform. Yet tactical concessions are often seen to be the first step in a process of norm adherence (Park 2010).

Yet Wade (1997) argued that while the Bank had shifted from "environment versus growth" to "**sustainable development**" it had not changed its internal incentive system, thus undermining its environmental rigor (which Goldman 2005 calls "green neoliberalism," see also **Liberal environmentalism**). Environmental activist Bruce Rich (1994) agreed that the Bank greenwashed its operations because its environmental criteria had not been implemented properly and the Bank's loan approval culture prevented sustainable development. Ongoing controversies over the Bank's role in deforestation and large-scale dams, its ban on lending for nuclear power, and its failure to adequately shift toward renewable energy (see also **Energy transition**) challenge the Bank's green image. In comparison, Gutner (2002: 26) found that the World Bank was a greener bank, because it "finances projects with primary environmental goals and attempts to integrate environmental thinking into the broader set of strategic goals it develops." Evidence of this is the Bank's role in the Clean Development Mechanism and in advocating for carbon markets to combat climate change. In 2016 the World Bank implemented a new Environmental and Social Framework (ESF) to shape its lending after four years of intense global consultation.

The ESF came into effect in 2018, but scholars continue to question the Bank's commitment to green lending.

References

Goldman, Michael. 2005. *Imperial Nature: The World Bank and Struggles for Social Justice in the Age of Globalization*. New Haven, CT, Yale University Press.

Gutner, Tamar L. 2002. *Banking on the Environment: Multilateral Development Banks and Their Environmental Performance in Central and Eastern Europe*. Cambridge, MA, MIT Press.

Haas, Peter and Ernst Haas. 1995. "Learning to Learn: Improving International Governance." *Global Governance* 1(3): 255–284.

Nielson, Daniel, Michael Tierney, and Catherine Weaver. 2006. "Bridging the Rationalist-Constructivist Divide: Re-engineering the Culture at the World Bank." *Journal of International Relations and Development* 9(2): 107–139.

Park, Susan. 2010. *World Bank Group Interactions with Environmentalists: Changing International Organisation Identities*. Manchester, Manchester University Press.

Rich, Bruce. 1994. *Mortgaging the Earth: The World Bank, Environmental Impoverishment and the Crisis of Development*. Boston, MA, Beacon Press.

Wade, Robert. 1997. "Greening the Bank: The Struggle over the Environment 1970–1995." In *The World Bank: Its First Half Century*, Eds. Davesh Kapur, John Lewis, and Richard C. Webb, 611–734. Washington, DC, Brookings Institute.

WORLD ENVIRONMENT ORGANIZATION

Frank Biermann

Utrecht University, Netherlands

A "world environment organization" does not exist. Yet proposals to create an international agency on environmental protection have been debated for over forty years (overviews in Biermann and Bauer 2005; Biermann 2014). These proposals use a variety of names for such a new world environment organization, such as "Global Environment Organization," "United Nations Environment Organization," or "United Nations Environmental Protection Organization." What all proposals have in common is the argument for setting up a new specialized intergovernmental organization within the system of the United Nations that would focus on environmental policies.

The first proposal for a world environment organization dates back to US foreign policy strategist George F. Kennan (1970), who argued for an International Environmental Agency encompassing "a small group of advanced nations." Several authors supported this idea at that time. As one outcome of this debate, the United Nations established in 1973 the **United Nations Environment Programme** (UNEP). The creation of a UN environment program was a more modest reform than the strong international environmental organization that some observers had called for then.

Since then, various authors have published proposals arguing for the establishment of a world environment organization to replace, or "upgrade," UNEP (for example, Biermann 2000; Desai 2000; Runge 2001). Virtually all proposals for a world environment organization can be categorized in three ideal type models, which differ regarding the degree of change that is required.

First, the least radical proposals advise upgrading UNEP to a specialized UN agency with full-fledged organizational status. Proponents of this approach have referred to the World Health Organization (WHO) or the International Labour Organization (ILO) as suitable models. The new agency in this model is expected to facilitate norm-building and norm implementation processes (see **Compliance and implementation**). This strength would in particular derive from an enhanced mandate and better capabilities of the agency to build capacities in developing countries, for example by giving the new agency an operational mandate at country level similar to other major international organizations. This differs from UNEP's present "catalytic" mandate that prevents the program from engaging in project implementation. Furthermore, additional legal and political powers could come with the status of a UN special agency. For example, its governing body could approve by qualified majority vote certain regulations that could be binding, under certain conditions, on all members (comparable to the International Maritime Organization), or could adopt drafts of legally binding treaties negotiated under its auspices (comparable to the ILO).

Second, some observers argue for a more fundamental reform to address the substantive and functional overlap between the many international institutions in global environmental governance (see **Institutional interactions**). These advocates of a more centralized governance architecture call for the integration of several existing agencies and programs into one all-encompassing world environment organization. Such an integration of environmental regimes could loosely follow the model of the **World Trade Organization**, which has integrated diverse multilateral trade agreements.

The third and most far-reaching model is that of a hierarchical intergovernmental organization on environmental issues that would be equipped with enforcement powers vis-à-vis states that fail to comply with international agreements, for example along the lines of an "environmental security council." Support for such a powerful agency, however, remains scarce and largely restricted to a few nongovernmental organizations.

More skeptical voices and critics of a new organization have also come forward. Calestous Juma (2000) for example has argued that such proposals divert attention from more pressing problems and fail to acknowledge that centralizing institutional structures is an anachronistic paradigm. Sebastian Oberthür and Thomas Gehring (2005) argued also that cooperation theory would advise against a new agency. Konrad von Moltke (2005) and Adil Najam (2005) proposed as an alternative decentralized institutional clusters to deal with diverse sets of environmental issues rather than entrusting all problems to one central organization.

Politically, the idea of a world environment organization today finds the support of several governments. Notably, at the 2012 UN Conference on Sustainable Development a specialized agency status for UNEP was supported by the member states of the European Union (EU) and of the African Union (AU) as well as a number of other developing countries. Resistance has remained strong, however, from the US, Japan, Russia, and even Brazil, which had earlier been a supporter of a world environment organization but now seemed afraid of an imbalance in favor of the environmental pillar of **sustainable development**. These countries argued that this question requires further debate and analysis (Vijge 2013). As one outcome of these debates, however, the UNEP has been further strengthened and assumed some functions of a world environment organization, notably through the creation of the United Nations Environment Assembly with universal membership.

References

Biermann, Frank. 2000. "The Case for a World Environment Organization." *Environment* 42(9): 22–31.

Biermann Frank. 2014. *Earth System Governance: World Politics in the Anthropocene.* Cambridge, MA, MIT Press.

Biermann, Frank and Steffen Bauer (Eds.). 2005. *A World Environment Organization: Solution or Threat for Effective International Environmental Governance?* Aldershot, Ashgate.

Desai, Bharat. 2000. "Revitalizing International Environmental Institutions: The UN Task Force Report and Beyond." *Indian Journal of International Law* 40(3): 455–504.

Juma, Calestous. 2000. "The Perils of Centralizing Global Environmental Governance." *Environment: Science and Policy for Sustainable Development* 42(9): 44–45.

Kennan, George F. 1970. "To Prevent a World Wasteland: A Proposal." *Foreign Affairs* 48(3): 401–413.

Najam, Adil. 2005. "Neither Necessary, nor Sufficient: Why Organizational Tinkering Will Not Improve Environmental Governance." In *A World Environment Organization: Solution or Threat for Effective International Environmental Governance?*, Eds. Frank Biermann and Steffen Bauer, 235–256. Aldershot, Ashgate.

Oberthür, Sebastian and Thomas Gehring. 2005. "Reforming International Environmental Governance: An Institutional Perspective on Proposals for a World Environment Organization." In *A World Environment Organization: Solution or Threat for International Environmental Governance?*, Eds. Frank Biermann and Steffen Bauer, 205–234. Aldershot, Ashgate.

Runge, C. Ford. 2001. "A Global Environment Organization (GEO) and the World Trading System." *Journal of World Trade* 35(4): 399–426.

Vijge, Marjanneke J. 2013. "The Promise of New Institutionalism: Explaining the Absence of a World or United Nations Environment Organization." *International Environmental Agreements: Politics, Law and Economics* 13(2): 153–176.

von Moltke, Konrad. 2005. "Clustering International Environmental Agreements as an Alternative to a World Environment Organization." In *A World Environment Organization: Solution or Threat for Effective International Environmental Governance?*, Eds. Frank Biermann and Steffen Bauer, 175–204. Aldershot, Ashgate.

WORLD TRADE ORGANIZATION

Fariborz Zelli

Lund University, Sweden

Surrounding the establishment of the World Trade Organization (WTO) in 1994, scholars discussed whether the new organization would contribute to a shift of global environmental governance toward more **market**-based mechanisms (see **Liberal environmentalism**).

The over sixty conventions under the auspices of the WTO indeed include a series of provisions that may conflict with environmental standards, for example with trade restrictions due to unsustainable process and production methods. According to the most favored nation clause, a WTO party has to grant any trade advantage it concedes to any one country to all other parties. The national treatment principle prohibits the discrimination of foreign goods or services from those of "like" domestic goods or services.

The WTO treaties also include clauses that qualify the applicability of these and other non-discrimination principles. The General Agreement on Tariffs and Trade (GATT) grants "general exceptions," including for measures "necessary to protect human, animal or plant life or health" and for the "conservation of exhaustible natural resources" (Article XX). Yet, the abstract phrasing of principles and exceptions leaves considerable room for interpretation—and for legal tensions.

Attempts to address this uncertainty were made at WTO political bodies such as the Committee on Trade and Environment. The committee inter alia covers the relationship to multilateral environmental agreements (MEAs) and the reduction of trade barriers to environmental goods and services. But various efforts, mostly tabled by the EU and Switzerland, to discuss broader exceptions of WTO rules in favor of MEAs were turned down by the US and developing countries who feared eco-protectionist consequences.

Given the inconclusiveness of these debates, the WTO's environmental role has been mainly defined through judicial decisions. The unprecedented WTO **dispute resolution mechanism** has come to cover a series of disputes over domestic environmental laws, from fisheries governance and species protection to natural resources conservation, air pollution, and health standards. While early rulings strictly prioritized free trade principles there is a notable trend toward accommodating environmental norms.

One example: in the 1991 tuna–dolphin dispute, a GATT panel had still interpreted US import bans on Mexican yellowfin tuna—whose fishing methods had violated US standards for dolphin protection—as a breach of the national treatment rule. In the 1998 shrimp–turtle dispute, however, the WTO Dispute Settlement Body widened its understanding: not only the final product, but process and production methods requirements in a product's lifecycle should be taken into account, if such requirements are rooted in multilateral agreements, for example the **biodiversity regime** (Charnovitz 2008; Pauwelyn 2009).

Aside from the Dispute Settlement Body's growing practice of referencing other treaties, MEAs themselves have so far not been directly subject to WTO dispute settlement. This may be surprising, given considerable **institutional interactions**, for example trade restrictions on hazardous waste, endangered species, and ozone-depleting substances, under the **hazardous wastes regime**, the **CITES**, and the Montreal Protocol of the **ozone regime**, respectively. Since these restrictions discriminate against non-members or non-compliers of these MEAs, they may come into conflict with the WTO's most-favored nation principle. Moreover, the biodiversity regime's Cartagena Protocol on **Biosafety** may collide with WTO rules due to its stringent precautionary restrictions and respective requirements for information-sharing prior to trading genetically modified organisms. Another example with legal conflict potential involves the **climate change regime**, which leaves the door open for fiscal measures (subsidies, tariffs, or **taxation**) and regulatory measures (standards, technical regulations, **labeling and certification**) that might discriminate against imported products with greenhouse gas-intensive process and production methods (cf. van Asselt 2014).

Why have these overlaps not entailed a dispute settlement procedure so far? One reply is that MEAs are increasingly referenced in WTO rulings as acceptable specifications. However, some scholars criticize that the Dispute Settlement Body has taken only those external norms into account that suit its own neoliberal worldview (Kulovesi 2011). Others took a closer look behind the scenes of **treaty negotiations**, and early on discovered a certain self-censorship or "chill" effect that avoided more trade-restrictive approaches (Eckersley 2004).

Another reason is that, with the eventual failure of the Doha Round of trade negotiations over agricultural subsidies, the center of gravity in international trade governance has started to shift away from the WTO toward preferential trade agreements and so-called mega-regionals. Examples are the Comprehensive Economic and Trade Agreement (CETA) between Canada and the EU and the Trans-Pacific Partnership (TPP), which include their own sets of environmental provisions (Morin and Jinnah 2018). It is an unresolved question whether the envisaged dispute settlement disciplines under these mega-regionals affect the authority of the WTO Dispute Settlement Body (Schill 2017).

References

Charnovitz, Steve. 2008. "The WTO as an Environmental Agency." In *Institutional Interplay: Biosafety and Trade*, Eds. Oran R. Young, W. Bradnee

Chambers, Joy A. Kim, and Claudia ten Have, 161–191. Tokyo, United Nations University Press.

Eckersley, Robyn. 2004. "The Big Chill: The WTO and Multilateral Environmental Agreements." *Global Environmental Politics* 4(2): 24–50.

Kulovesi, Kati. 2011. *The WTO Dispute Settlement System: Challenges of the Environment, Legitimacy and Fragmentation.* Dordrecht, Kluwer Law International.

Morin, Jean-Frédéric and Sikina Jinnah. 2018. "The Untapped Potential of Preferential Trade Agreements for Climate Governance." *Environmental Politics* 27(3): 541–565.

Pauwelyn, Joost. 2009. *Conflict of Norms in Public International Law: How WTO Law Relates to Other Rules of International Law.* Cambridge, Cambridge University Press.

Schill, Stephan W. 2017. "Authority, Legitimacy, and Fragmentation in the (Envisaged) Dispute Settlement Disciplines in Mega-Regionals." In *Mega-Regional Trade Agreements: CETA, TTIP, and TiSA*, Eds. Stefan Griller, Walter Obwexer, and Erich Vranes, 111–150. Oxford, Oxford University Press.

Van Asselt, Harro. 2014. *The Fragmentation of Global Climate Governance: Consequences and Management of Regime Interactions.* Cheltenham, Edward Elgar.

INDEX

Printed in the United States
By Bookmasters